Shari E. Gladstone
352 West Hills Rd.
Huntington, NY 11743

Nov. 1972.

THE SECRET HISTORY OF AMERICA'S
FIRST CENTRAL INTELLIGENCE AGENCY

OSS

The Secret History of America's First Central Intelligence Agency

R. Harris Smith

University of California Press
Berkeley Los Angeles London 1972

UNIVERSITY OF CALIFORNIA PRESS
BERKELEY AND LOS ANGELES, CALIFORNIA
UNIVERSITY OF CALIFORNIA PRESS, LTD.
LONDON, ENGLAND
COPYRIGHT © 1972, BY
THE REGENTS OF THE UNIVERSITY OF CALIFORNIA
ISBN: 0-520-02023-5
LIBRARY OF CONGRESS CATALOG CARD NUMBER: 73-153553
PRINTED IN THE UNITED STATES OF AMERICA
DESIGNED BY DAVE COMSTOCK

(Pg. 4)—Photoprint by Maurice Constant, 1942, from the Library of Congress collections.

(Pg. 155)—From the Charles W. Thayer Papers, courtesy of Mr. George Thayer.

(Pg. 230)—From Allen Dulles. *The Secret Surrender*, 1965, reprinted by permission of Harper and Row.

(Pg. 249)—From William Peers and Dean Brelis. *Behind the Burma Road*, 1963, reprinted by permission of Little, Brown and Co.

(Pg. 264)—Courtesy of Colonel David Barrett.

(Pp. 271, 299)—From Nicol Smith and Blake Clark, *Into Siam: Underground Kingdom*, 1945, reprinted by permission of The Bobbs-Merrill Co.

(Pp. 339, 343)—Courtesy of Mr. Herbert Bluechel.

(Pg. 355)—Courtesy of Colonel Archimedes Patti.

Contents

Acknowledgments

Since I began
this OSS project in June 1969, I have had the unflagging moral support
of Dr. Paul Seabury, Professor of Political Science at the University of
California at Berkeley. I cannot thank him enough for his cheerful
encouragement. I am also grateful to Dr. Arthur Schlesinger, Jr., who
read the entire manuscript and gave me the great benefit of his comments and criticisms, both as historian and as OSS veteran.

My thanks also to Dr. Eugene Lee, Director of the Institute for
Governmental Studies at Berkeley, who generously allowed me the use
of the Institute's facilities in the course of my writing; to Dr. David
Apter, now of Yale, who helped me obtain an initial travel grant from
the Institute for International Studies at Berkeley; and to my former
graduate advisor, William Sheppard, now chairman of the Public Administration program at California State College, Hayward.

This book could not have been written without the assistance of
some 200 OSS and State Department "alumni" who went to consider-
able trouble to provide me with written and verbal recollections of their
wartime service. My special thanks go to Mrs. Harley Stevens, Nicol
Smith, Peter Tompkins, Dr. H. Stuart Hughes, John Service, Tom
Braden, Colonel Francis Miller, Dr. James Hamilton, and Dr. Walter
Pforzheimer. I also wish to thank Dr. Ernst Lassner and Dr. Kenneth
Glazer for allowing me access to original OSS documentation in the
Preston Goodfellow, Leland Rounds, and Milton Miles Papers, de-
posited at the Hoover Institution, Stanford University.

My dear friends Tom and Nancy High contributed to my work in many ways, but I am especially grateful for the constancy of their friendship.

Grant Barnes, my editor at the University of California Press, deserves a special commendation for faithfully suffering through my crises of confidence during a year and a half of writing.

My father did not live to see the completion of this work, which he and my mother encouraged through many months of gestation. This book is dedicated to them, in belated appreciation of their warmth and understanding.

Preface

In May 1968
I resigned from the Central Intelligence Agency, after a very brief, uneventful, and undistinguished association with the most misunderstood bureaucracy of the American government. Having left Washington for the academic "calm" of the University of California at Berkeley (an equally misunderstood institution), I began this political history of the CIA's organizational forebear, the wartime Office of Strategic Services.

My former employers made it clear at the outset that the classified OSS archives would not be available to me. Quoting Malcolm Muggeridge's observation, "Security, as applied retrospectively to intelligence matters, is a superb device for fitting locks onto empty stables," I accepted my fate and began the laborious research which has produced this very unofficial anatomy of America's first intelligence service.

As an academic journalist seeking to penetrate a time-worn curtain of government secrecy, I often pondered the historic issues recently rehashed in the debate over publication of the "Pentagon Papers." Without delving too deeply into the political dialogue that followed that national sensation, I would suggest one random thought.

Winston Churchill was once asked by an Opposition member of Parliament to differentiate between revelation of a vital state secret and a politically awkward affair. The first, he replied, was a danger to the country, the second a nuisance to the government. His retort begged the question. Who is to decide where nuisance ends and danger begins? In a democracy, the government should not have the unchallenged responsibility for that decision. I am equally reluctant, however, to see that function given exclusively to the American press. While my first impulse is to applaud the position of the *New York Times*, I am left with a nagging concern that instantaneous popular uproar over the disclosure of classified material is not the proper atmosphere in which to forge public policy.

Is there an alternative? For too many years, social scientists have paid scant attention to the broad problem of official secrecy. The majority of American academicians may spend hours denouncing the sinister CIA, yet not a single university in the United States fosters a serious research effort into the organization and activities of the "intelligence community," that massive bureaucratic conglomerate that has played such a major role in our foreign policy.

That vacuum ought to be filled. The academicians should form a partnership with journalists in providing the American citizenry with a reasoned and thoughtful critique of the excesses of clandestine bureaucracy. I offer this book as a first step toward extending intellectual responsibility into a new field of public concern.

R.H.S.
September 1971

OSS

THE SECRET HISTORY OF AMERICA'S
FIRST CENTRAL INTELLIGENCE AGENCY

"It is from numberless diverse acts of courage and belief that human history is shaped. Each time a man stands up for an ideal, or acts to improve the lot of others, or strikes out against injustice, he sends forth a tiny ripple of hope, and crossing each other from a million different centers of energy and daring, those ripples build a current that can sweep down the mightiest walls of oppression and resistance."

—ROBERT F. KENNEDY

1

Donovan's Dreamers

Five months before the Japanese attack on Pearl Harbor precipitated America's entry into the World War, Franklin Roosevelt christened a mysterious addition to his New Deal alphabet bureaucracy. What, asked the Washington rumor-mongers, was this new agency called COI? A "staff of Jewish scribblers," shrilled Herr Goebbels' propaganda machine in Berlin. "Full of politics, ballyhoo, and controversy," chimed in isolationist crusader Charles Lindbergh. At the War Department, uncomprehending generals soon scoffed at a "fly-by-night civilian outfit headed up by a wild man who was trying to horn in on the war." [1]

COI was the Office of the Coordinator of Information and at its helm was William Joseph Donovan, known since his youth as "Wild Bill." A stocky, grey-haired man of 58, Donovan was anything but wild— he was a Hoover Republican, an Irish Catholic, and a millionaire Wall Street lawyer. Yet Roosevelt had chosen him to direct the New Deal's excursion into espionage, sabotage, "black" propaganda, guerrilla warfare, and other "un-American" subversive practices. The President had been impressed by Donovan's impassioned advocacy of American involvement in the European conflict, by his prediction that Britain would not collapse under the pressure of the Luftwaffe, and by his personal audacity and imagination. Donovan had observed the ruthless success of the fascist "fifth column" in Europe and the Balkans, and he longed to create an international secret service for the United States that could prove equal to the Nazi challenge. Roosevelt liked Donovan's organizational vision and was intrigued by his "blend of Wall Street orthodoxy and sophisticated American nationalism." [2]

The President's admiration was not shared by Robert Sherwood, the playwright and FDR speechwriter who headed the COI's propaganda wing. Flanked at his New York headquarters (250 miles from an unsympathetic congress) by a staff of young New Deal enthusiasts, liberal veterans of American journalism, and such literary figures as Thornton Wilder and Stephen Vincent Benét, Sherwood found himself in a continuous struggle with Wall Street attorneys and financial executives in the other branches of Donovan's organization. "It is all right," Sherwood complained, "to have rabid anti-New Dealers in the military establishment . . . but I don't think it appropriate to have them participating in an effort which must be expressive of the President's own philosophy." [3] Beyond political rhetoric, there was also personal conflict between two irreconcilable personalities. New York banker James Warburg, a Roosevelt confidant (and Sherwood assistant), recalled with some exaggeration: "Donovan, accustomed to command, was quick, extremely energetic, and ambitious. Sherwood, a playwright completely inexperienced in working with, under, or over other people, was slow, unpunctual, and moody. In addition, Sherwood resented any authority other than that of the President and was morbidly jealous of any intrusion upon his White House relationship." [4]

The young organization, to which such personal conflicts would later become endemic, could not yet withstand the strain of open hostility at the command level. Six months after America entered the war, the propaganda division was severed from COI and became part of a new Office of War Information. Donovan's organization was then renamed the Office of Strategic Services and given an ambiguous mandate to "plan and operate such special services as may be directed by the United States Joint Chiefs of Staff." [5]

In every respect, OSS was Donovan's child. He nourished the agency in its infancy, and it bore the stamp of his personality. Donovan was a "civilian general"—an eminently successful corporate attorney as well as a World War I hero who held America's three highest military decorations. OSS also existed in a twilight zone of civilian-military identity that displeased the old-line West Pointers, who derided "Donovan's dragoons."

Like most officers who served in his burgeoning organization, Donovan possessed "indefatigable energy and wide-ranging enthusiasm combined with great resourcefulness," to quote his colleague Allen

Dulles.[6] He frequently traveled to lines of combat without concern for his personal safety. "My place is in the field, as well as in Washington," he would often say. "To help my men I must see their problems first-hand." [7] His dynamism and constant movement was the mainstay of an agency that eventually enlisted over thirteen thousand Americans.

His mobility and activism were not the qualities of a conventional administrator. Some said he "ran OSS like a country editor." [8] But the exigencies of war called for unconventional methods, and the absence of a rigid organizational hierarchy enabled an exceptional group of men and women to work with great effectiveness under Donovan's leadership. The agency's psychological staff proudly noted that "OSS undertook and carried out more different types of enterprises calling for more varied skills than any other single organization of its size in the history of our country." [9]

Donovan was an irrepressible optimist. Air Force General "Hap" Arnold remembers him as the "one man who never told me that such and such was not available. He was incapable of a defeatist intelligence answer. . . . He would say 'What do you want? When do you want it? I'll get it for you.' To out-of-the-way places he would send details, or scouts, spies, or small detachments, to secure the information we needed, and would always give us that data in time." [10]

"Woe to the officer," wrote OSS colonel (and later ambassador) David Bruce, "who turned down a project because, on its face, it seemed ridiculous, or at least unusual." [11] Every eccentric schemer with a harebrained plan for secret operations (from phosphorescent foxes to incendiary bats) would find a sympathetic ear in Donovan's office. One aged American businessman devised a scheme for the establishment of clandestine air bases behind the Japanese lines in China. It reached the desk of Adlai Stevenson, then special assistant to the Secretary of the Navy.[a] Stevenson passed it on to Donovan with the comment, "Fearful that your mail may be declining, I enclose another plan for winning the war! You need not tell me how grateful you are." Donovan promptly replied, "Thank you very much for your memorandum. We will work this out together. I ignore nothing—you never can tell." [12]

---

[a] During the 1952 election campaign, Republican Vice-Presidential candidate Richard Nixon declared that Stevenson had disqualified himself for the Presidency by filing a court deposition on behalf of Alger Hiss three years earlier. Donovan, though he backed the Eisenhower ticket, joined 21 prominent attorneys in publicly supporting Stevenson's integrity and deploring Nixon's criticism of the Hiss deposition.

General William "Wild Bill" Donovan, Director of Strategic Services. OSS was a product of his fertile imagination and dynamic leadership.

Inevitably, activism also meant waste. Donovan procured for OSS an unlimited (and largely unvouchered) budget that ran into the hundreds of millions during the four years of the war. Critics later spoke of the funds "squandered by OSS agents who bought or hired planes, automobiles, office equipment, houses, printing plants—anything they needed or thought they did." [13] The mysterious valise of one OSS officer stationed at the American embassy in Vichy France was opened by curious State Department officials who found the case filled with some $200,000 in small bills. Another OSS man was to be assigned to a post on one of the Canary Islands. "But," remembers a Donovan aide, "no commercial steamships called there during wartime. No matter! Buy a ship! One was bought for a million dollars or so. Only after the purchase was made was it realized that it would not be the most secret way to plant an undercover agent to have a special steamship arrive to land him. I never learned what happened to the ship." [14]

Though all wartime agencies operated in disarray, OSS had its own unique brand of administrative confusion. Young officers recruited under the most secret conditions would report for duty to a well-guarded Washington headquarters only to be asked, "Do you have any idea what OSS might have hired you for?" [15]

The general, assistants protectively explained, promoted "the appearance of chaos as a screen to the increasing potency and effectiveness of his organization." [16] But, in fact, Donovan simply refused to be bothered with organizational detail. Such harried administrative officers as Louis Ream (a U.S. Steel executive), Atherton Richards (an Hawaiian pineapple magnate), or James Grafton Rogers (a Yale law professor) "would walk into Donovan's office with dozens of charts; charts for the budget, charts for the administration, charts for the various divisions. . . . Donovan would glance at them, smile at them, approve them with a mild wave of the hand, and then he would have another idea, and he would forget them completely." [17] Standard operating procedures were almost taboo in OSS. Effective action was the sole objective. His own military status notwithstanding, Donovan had little use for West Point formalities. An apocryphal tale that made the rounds at OSS headquarters had it that during the Anzio landing in Italy, Donovan found himself standing on the deck of the command ship beside Major General Mark Clark, the commander of the operation and his superior in rank. According to this story, Donovan put his arm around the gangly General Clark in paternal fashion and asked, "Well, son, what are we going to do next?" It was an appropriate parable for an agency where one out of every four of the 9000 military personnel was a commissioned officer. Rank was bestowed with an ease dictated almost entirely by ad hoc operational requirements; traditional military protocol was superfluous. One captain who led an OSS team behind the Japanese lines in China remembered, "All officers were quite junior, and as long as everybody did his work few of us bothered with military regulations. High brass was unlikely to inspect. There was no saluting, and the men could dress as they pleased. . . . Some men let their hair and beards grow, others favored long walrus mustaches and shaved skulls." [18]

Insubordination became a way of life for OSS officers, but Donovan was unconcerned. He often said, "I'd rather have a young lieutenant with guts enough to disobey an order than a colonel too regimented to think and act for himself." [19] He was frequently called upon to defend the actions of his over-eager subordinates, and it was rarely a simple task. Unaware that a top-secret naval intelligence team had broken the Japanese military code, OSS men in Portugal secretly entered the Japanese embassy and stole a copy of the enemy's codebook. The Japanese discovered the theft and promptly changed their ciphers. Washington was left without a vital source of information, and the Joint Chiefs of Staff were irate.[20] There were other high-level flaps. Donovan's men in Italy smuggled arms to Tito's Communist guerrillas in Yugoslavia without the approval of the British theater commander. And OSS men in Morocco sent Communist agents to Franco's Spain without notifying the American embassy in Madrid. In every case, Donovan supported his officers. He had given his men their freedom of action and he would not allow them to be punished for exercising it with enthusiasm.

OSS officers soon realized that their superiors avoided disciplinary action, even in cases of incompetence or corruption. Operational funds disappeared mysteriously in the hills of Greece, France, and Italy, only to reappear in the bank accounts of a few OSS veterans after the war. Many OSS men also found mistresses, both foreign and domestic, compatible with their clandestine existence. Joining the thieves and Don Juans were the mentally unstable. "We were working with an unusual type of individual," wrote an OSS captain who sent hundreds of agents into occupied France. "Many had natures that fed on danger and excitement. Their appetite for the unconventional and spectacular was far beyond the ordinary. It was not unusual to find a good measure of temperament thrown in." There was often a thin line between unconventionality and instability. Donovan's psychological chief, Dr. Henry Murray of Harvard,[b] noted: "The whole nature of the functions of OSS were particularly inviting to psychopathic characters; it involved sensation, intrigue, the idea of being a mysterious man with secret knowledge." [21]

Safeguards were virtually non-existent. When Donovan finally decided to court-martial two overseas officers (one an incompetent drunkard who was living with his WAC secretary, the other an industrious manager of black market operations in the vicinity of his Neapolitan base), aides protested that court-martial proceedings against *any* officer for *any* reason would be damaging to the secrecy and the morale of the organization.

There was little in the OSS structure to promote respect for formal channels of authority. One civilian liberal who resigned from OSS after objecting, unsuccessfully, to Washington's support of the Italian monarchy, later reflected: "I should have stayed under anyone, however incapable, made whatever promises were necessary about oaths to the House of Savoy, and then used my ingenuity in circumventing both." [22] In Yugoslavia, an OSS lieutenant in Donovan's mission to Tito, a playwright by profession, was told by his colonel to encode a message for radio transmission. "That," replied the lieutenant, "can wait till tomorrow." The colonel reasoned gently, "I'll admit it's not much fun coding, but that's true of lots of things in the army." "Army?" asked the startled lieutenant. "Did you say army? Hell, man, we're not in the army. We're in the OSS." [23] And in China, an OSS captain received an order to report on the attitude of the local populace in his operational area toward the contending Nationalist and Communist forces. He and his teammates suspected that the information was to be passed along to the Chinese government and they had no sympathy for the Chiang Kai-shek regime. Besides, they felt that the internal struggle in China should be just that, a domestic Chinese affair. "Let's put it to a vote," suggested the officer to his fellows. The order "lost" and was disregarded.[24] That was the OSS way.

Donovan himself was sometimes the victim of his own scorn for authority. The young Harvard historian H. Stuart Hughes was serving in an OSS research post in North Africa when Donovan stopped off while on one of his world tours. Convinced that Hughes spoke Italian

[b] Dr. Murray made this remark during testimony as a defense witness in the 1950 trial of Alger Hiss, the former State Department official accused of being a Soviet spy.

admirably, the general ordered him to prepare for a parachute jump into German-occupied Italy. Lacking both language fluency and parachute training, the bewildered Hughes asked his local OSS commander for advice. "Disappear till the general leaves," was the reply. Hughes kept out of sight until Donovan's departure and the assignment was quickly forgotten.[25]

The confusion created by the freedom given OSS officers was abetted by status conflicts within the organization. OSS men who carried out dangerous espionage and sabotage missions behind enemy lines felt an estrangement from their superiors who issued directives from the rear-echelon havens of Washington, London, Algiers, Cairo, New Delhi, and Kunming. Most of the executives at these headquarters were civilians with high military rank but no military training. Field operators scoffed at "bourbon whiskey colonels" with "cellophane commissions" (you could see through them, but they kept the Draft off). This was not simply traditional military resentment of civilian direction. OSS field officers Thomas Braden and Stewart Alsop observed that while "the great majority of the operational men had gone through the Army the hard way, and those who were commissioned had come up through the ranks, a very large proportion of the administrative officers in OSS had received direct commissions in the early days. They had bought uniforms, and put them on, and there they were, soldiers, just like that. Some of these men were excellent executives, and good soldiers, but the operational men often resented their higher rank." [26] Considering the OSS officer's contempt for military hierarchy, tension between desk colonels and field agents was hardly surprising.

It worked both ways. One decidedly conservative OSS executive—the chief of the organization's scientific Research and Development Branch —castigated "many of the personnel I met at a lower level . . . who seemed to be rah-rah youngsters to whom OSS was perhaps an escape from routine military service and a sort of lark." On the other hand, each member of the OSS higher echelons "risked his future status as a banker or trustee or highly placed politician in identifying himself with illegality and unorthodoxy." [27]

Mutual antipathy plagued all aspects of OSS operations. An OSS major working with the Norwegian resistance asked his London headquarters for permission to take and hold a town as a fort from which to waylay the Germans. Relaying a decision of the Supreme Command, OSS headquarters denied the request. But the major tried again. "I am here," he said. "I know what I am doing. I know I can do it; the resistance wants me to do it, and I intend to do it." That made OSS headquarters angry: "You have your orders. Disobedience will be subject to disciplinary action upon your return." [28] Was headquarters bluffing? Probably, but the incident suggests the flavor of "normal" relations with men in the field. Certainly the drive for operational autonomy was no fluke of erratic behavior, nor even a sign of youthful exuberance. A sedate and mature civilian intelligence operator like Allen Dulles, chief of the OSS mission in neutral Switzerland (and postwar Director of the CIA) was equally wary of working too closely with Washington. Writing after the war of his negotiations for the surrender of the German forces in North Italy, Dulles cautiously suggested: "An intelligence officer in the field is supposed to keep his home office informed of what he is doing. That is quite true, but with some reservations, as he may overdo it. If, for example, he tells too much or asks too often for instructions, he is likely to get some he doesn't relish, and what is worse, he may well find headquarters trying to take over the whole conduct of the operation. Only a man on the spot can really pass judgment on the details as contrasted with the policy decisions, which, of course, belong to the boss at headquarters." Dulles added, "It has always amazed me how desk personnel thousands of miles away seem to acquire wisdom and special knowledge about local field conditions which they assume goes deeper than that available to the man on the spot." Almost without exception, Dulles and other OSS operators feared the burden of a high-level decision that might "cramp" their freedom of action.[29]

To the amazement of his executives, General Donovan personally supported the field viewpoint. He made no secret of the fact that his heart was with the officers on the firing line. He proudly assured the Allied commander in Southeast Asia, British Admiral Louis Mountbatten, that "if at any time he wanted something done for which he could not spare two or three thousand men," he should simply "call on OSS and we would send in twenty or thirty men to do the job." [30] And Donovan meant it.

To complete the organizational chaos, political conflicts wracked OSS from its inception. Dedicated conservatives and ardent Communists worked under the same roof with a heterogeneous mass of New Deal Democrats and Willkie Republicans. "Something had to knit together beings so disparate, recruited for tasks so indefinite," recalled OSS London chief David Bruce. "The polarization came from one individual—Donovan." [31]

The general was an experienced politician. He had unsuccessfully campaigned on the Republican ticket for Lieutenant Governor of New York in 1922 and for Governor of that state ten years later. Though his "non-partisan" friendship with Franklin Roosevelt protected OSS in its infancy, Donovan was not averse to taking out additional political insurance. He reasoned correctly that Thomas E. Dewey, the Republican Governor of New York and former District Attorney of New York City, would be the GOP standard bearer for the presidency in 1944; several former assistant D.A.'s from Dewey's office soon appeared in high OSS positions in Europe.[c] And while Allen Dulles was performing some of the finest espionage feats of the war from his OSS Swiss post in 1944, his brother John Foster Dulles was Dewey's chief campaign advisor on foreign affairs. The Republicans, of course, lost the election, and it was rumored in OSS that Donovan's friendship with Roosevelt had cooled considerably by the end of 1944. (The grapevine said that the President had sent Harry Hopkins to discuss Donovan's replacement with one ambitious OSS Deputy Director). After Roosevelt's death, Donovan received even less sympathy from President Truman, who proceeded to dissolve OSS as soon as the war ended.

If Donovan did engage in a mild form of political manipulation, it was only to protect his organization and its operations. In spite of his inherent conservatism, he rarely allowed ideology to guide his wartime actions. In later life he developed an emotional hatred of Communism, but as OSS chief he often insisted that the sole objective of his officers should be the military defeat of the Axis powers. As he told an OSS assistant, "I'd put Stalin on the OSS payroll if I thought it would help us defeat Hitler." [32]

One ex-Communist of an earlier vintage correctly stated: "In the Office of Strategic Services . . . employment of pro-Communists was approved at very high levels provided that they were suited for specific jobs." [33] OSS often welcomed the services of Marxist enthusiasts, so long as they made no attempt to conceal their political affiliations. In a pre-employment investigation, the Security Office did seek to discover secret Communist associations, and in the early stages of the organization's existence some persons were politely expelled because of a suspected allegiance to the Soviet intelligence apparatus. The sister of

[c] In 1950 Governor Dewey vetoed Donovan's proposed candidacy for the U.S. Senate in New York. According to newspaper reports, Dewey "resented such a strong personality as Donovan in his political family, and was definitely afraid that Donovan might overshadow him."

"one of the very highest officials" of the New Deal administration was found placing classified OSS reports in her briefcase one evening. When Donovan personally informed the young woman that her services were no longer needed, she hurled a torrent of abuse at the general's "stinking Fascist organization." [34] But such incidents were rare. In a conscious effort to subordinate all political considerations to the defeat of the enemy, OSS became very tolerant of the political left. The restraint of "security regulations" to prevent infiltration by Axis agents was enough of a hindrance to OSS activism. Further vigilance against America's Russian allies—or their American sympathizers—was asking too much of the rough-and-tumble organization. When confronted after the war with FBI-inspired charges of Communist espionage against the Assistant General Counsel of OSS, Donovan replied that either "you can have an organization that is so secure it does nothing" or "you have to take chances." Said the general, "In that kind of game, if you're afraid of wolves, you have to stay out of the forest." [35]

Donovan found that political leftists were often the most valiant field officers in his espionage and sabotage branches. When the FBI triumphantly presented the general with dossiers of three OSS employees with Communist Party affiliations and demanded their ouster from the organization, Donovan responded, "I know they're Communists; that's why I hired them." The men in question had fought with the Abraham Lincoln Brigade for the Republican Loyalists in the Spanish Civil War of 1936-39. The Brigade was sponsored by the American Communist Party to aid the floundering Spanish Republic when the United States declared its strict neutrality in that battle of left-wing and right-wing ideologies. When some of these Lincoln Brigaders returned from their Spanish battleground after Franco's victory, they were accused of "sedition." Rumor had it that Donovan had taken time out from his corporate practice to provide them with free legal counsel.

Later, when America entered the war, Donovan tapped some of these experts in guerrilla warfare for service behind the lines in Italy, where the resistance forces were led by their fellow veterans of the Spanish Civil War. The agent network established by these American leftists with the aid of their former comrades produced some of the best intelligence in the Mediterranean Theater. When a congressional committee charged that one of these OSS men was "on the honor roll" of the Young Communist League, Donovan had an immediate rejoinder: "I don't know if he's on the Communist honor roll, but for the job he did in Italy, he's on the honor roll of OSS." [36] With Donovan's encouragement, other veterans of the Lincoln Brigade were recruited for OSS work in North Africa, France, Yugoslavia, and China.

A more established faction of the American political left was represented in the OSS Labor Branch, created to work with Socialist trade union groups in the European underground. The Branch was the brainchild of OSS Colonel Heber Blankenhorn, a veteran of Army Intelligence in World War I who had first concocted the idea of aerial propaganda campaigns. In the 1930s, Blankenhorn had championed the cause of organized labor as a staff aide to New York Senator Robert Wagner and later as director of the La Follette Committee's investigation into the anti-union activities of powerful corporations. Blankenhorn convinced Donovan that the European trade unions would constitute the hub of the anti-Nazi resistance and suggested that a special effort be made to develop labor contacts for intelligence and resistance operations.

To help organize a labor unit, Donovan's counter-intelligence chief (and former law clerk), Washington attorney James Murphy, recommended his Chicago legal associate George Bowden, a former I.W.W. organizer who combined a successful tax practice with a prominent membership in the left-wing National Lawyers Guild. Bowden in turn recruited one of his friends in the Chicago bar, a young Jewish attorney named Arthur Goldberg, to become the first chief of the new OSS Labor Branch.[d] At Blankenhorn's suggestion, several key officials of the National Labor Relations Board, a Roosevelt creation designed to prevent anti-union practices in collective bargaining, were brought over to OSS to staff Goldberg's branch. The chief trial examiner of the NLRB became head of OSS labor activities in London. The Board's general counsel, Gerhard Van Arkel, was sent to North Africa as Goldberg's representative and later became a key aide to Allen Dulles in Switzerland and Germany. Throughout the war, these men were an active and vocal force for political liberalism in the conduct of OSS operations.

There were also the progressive writers who found their way into the Morale Operations Branch. MO was considered a rear-echelon insanity by many field officers. The purpose of Morale Operations, according to one of its many female staffers, was to influence "enemy thinking by means of 'black propaganda'" that would appear as though it had

---

[d] Goldberg was President Kennedy's Secretary of Labor, 1961–62; Justice of the Supreme Court, 1962–65; ambassador to the U.N., 1965–68. In 1970, he was the unsuccessful Democratic candidate for Governor of New York.

come "from within the enemy's own ranks." [37] MO therefore distributed forged newspapers and military orders, operated clandestine transmitters that purported to be broadcasting from within enemy territory, and began rumor campaigns. (One MO agent was sent to Greece to spread the rumor of German withdrawals; within weeks another branch of OSS reported this information as an intelligence "scoop.") The most effective MO activity of the war was a "black radio" station based in London and beamed to Berlin. Its staff included a number of Hollywood and Broadway writers (including the talented Abraham Polonsky), liberals and Communists alike, all dedicated to the idealist interpretation of the fight against fascism which Robert Sherwood had once propounded in the COI.[e]

The political left was also well represented among the intellectuals of the OSS Research and Analysis Branch. R&A was the first concerted effort on the part of any world power to apply the talents of its academic community to official analysis of foreign affairs. To study a broad range of political, economic, psychological, geographic, and, of course, military intelligence, Donovan "assembled the best academic and analytical brains that he could beg, borrow, or steal from the universities, laboratories, and museums" of America.[38] The branch resembled a star-studded college faculty. A peek into the R&A offices might reveal a heated discussion between historian Sherman Kent[f] and political scientist Evron Kirkpatrick.[g] A committee meeting of the Economics Division might find Charles Hitch, Emile Despres, Charles Kindelberger, and Richard Ruggles sitting side by side. In other rooms, classicist Norman O. Brown could be writing a report on Greek politics, historian John King Fairbank studying an aspect of Chinese foreign policy, philosopher Herbert Marcuse analyzing German social structure, or anthropologist Cora DuBois pondering the problem of European colonialism in Asia.

[e] Polonsky was accused of Communist sympathies by a congressional committee in 1947. He directed his first film in 1948, then remained "blacklisted" in Hollywood for two decades. Not until 1969 did he overcome the McCarthyite stigma to direct his second movie, "Tell Them Willy Boy Is Here."

[f] Kent was Deputy Director, then Chairman of the CIA's Board of National Estimates, 1950–67.

[g] Kirkpatrick was Deputy Director of State Department Intelligence in 1954. He left State to become Executive Director of the American Political Science Association. In 1955 he also became President of Operations and Policy Research, Inc., a CIA conduit in Washington, D.C.

The political tenor of the branch began at predominant New Deal liberalism and then traveled left on the political spectrum. The results were not always harmonious. The young historian Arthur Schlesinger, Jr., joined government attorney Leonard Meeker [h] and Harvard history instructor Ray Cline [i] in editing the weekly R&A intelligence bulletin in Washington. He later remembered, "I had the job of summarizing and reprinting reports submitted by the regional desks of the Research and Analysis Branch. These were mostly detached and scholarly documents; but the reports from the chief of our Latin American section, in my view, showed a clear Communist slant. In order to document my suspicions, I began to follow Latin American affairs myself and soon was rejecting the party-line reports in favor of my own notes on Latin American developments." But before long, the chief of the Latin American Division, Dr. Maurice Halperin,[j] protested and Schlesinger "was instructed thereafter either to use the reports from the Latin American desk or nothing at all." [39] Other R&A employees had little doubt about Halperin's ideological position. When analysts found the door to the Latin American section locked to outsiders, they joked that Halperin was holding a "cell meeting."

Schlesinger's second assignment in OSS brought him into the company of Marxist economist Paul Sweezy to produce an intelligence summary in London known as the *European Political Report*. Together they presented the concept of a "green revolution" which hypothesized an upsurge of agrarian democracy in southeastern Europe and the Balkans. Sweezy insisted, however, on adding his own unique commentary on political events (of the "Red Army is receiving an enthusiastic welcome in Eastern Europe" variety), which was received with mixed humor and military invective at Eisenhower's headquarters.[40]

[h] Meeker served as State Department Legal Advisor, 1965–69. He was appointed ambassador to Romania in 1969.

[i] Cline was with the CIA in London, 1951–53, then was Agency Station Chief on Taiwan until 1962 when he became CIA Deputy Director for Intelligence. In the Johnson Administration he was Station Chief in Germany, and finally left CIA to become Director of State Department Intelligence in 1969.

[j] In 1953 Halperin was dismissed from a teaching post at Boston University after J. Edgar Hoover told a congressional committee that the professor had been a Communist agent while in OSS. Halperin moved to Mexico in 1958, then to Moscow and Havana, but denied a State Department allegation that he had defected. He is now teaching at a Canadian university.

While Donovan diligently sought left-wing intellectuals and activists for the operational and research branches of OSS, he saw no incongruity in appointing corporate attorneys and business executives as OSS administrators—the Roosevelt haters to whom Robert Sherwood had so vigorously objected. In Washington, the Secret Intelligence Branch that absorbed labor lawyers and Lincoln Brigaders was headed by a vice-president of the International Railways of Central America, the corporate twin of the United Fruit Company. The Morale Operations Branch that employed so many liberal Hollywood writers was directed by the vice-president of an Ohio steel corporation. The Special Operations Branch which maintained liaison with left-wing underground movements throughout the world was successively commanded by two New York corporation lawyers and two Pennsylvania investment bankers. And the OSS commander in Cairo who presided over supply operations to Greek and Yugoslav Communists was the vice-president of a Boston bank. Young attorneys from Donovan's own law firm (address, 2 Wall Street) assumed top administrative posts in Washington, Europe, and the Far East, and others were sent on behind-the-lines missions of diplomatic significance to Thailand and Yugoslavia.

Corporations were more than generous in loaning their executives and resources for OSS service. The J. Walter Thompson Advertising Agency supplied the chief of the OSS Planning Staff, the head of the Morale Operations Branch in London, the executive officer of OSS in Cairo, and a "black propaganda" specialist in Casablanca. The Standard Oil Company provided officers in Spain and Switzerland to watch Axis oil shipments and helped plan the sabotage of Axis-operated petroleum fields in Romania. Paramount Pictures provided foreign currency for espionage operations in Finland and Sweden. The Goldman, Sachs banking firm handled the payment of two million Algerian francs to resistance groups in North Africa. In fact, the corporate spirit permeated the executive offices of Donovan's headquarters. To the general's amusement, a blue-ribbon committee of OSS executives, uneasily chaired by liberal public opinion pollster Elmo Roper, recommended that Donovan's nest of spies and saboteurs should be restructured like a "holding company."

Members of the wealthiest families in America also made their appearance in OSS. Andrew Mellon's son Paul served as administrative officer of the Special Operations Branch in London and later as commander of the Morale Operations Branch in Luxembourg. Paul Mellon's sister, Ailsa (once known as the world's richest woman) was married to her brother's commanding officer, the chief of OSS in London, David Bruce, who was the son of a U.S. senator and a millionaire in his own right. Other Mellons and Mellon in-laws held espionage posts in Madrid, Geneva, and Paris.

J. P. Morgan's sons were both in OSS. Junius Morgan directed the distribution of clandestine operational funds from London while his brother Henry headed the Censorship and Documents Branch which arranged for the cover stories of clandestine agents. A Vanderbilt was executive officer of the Special Operations Branch in Washington. A DuPont directed French espionage projects in Washington. An Archbold (Standard Oil) was an OSS security officer in Calcutta. A Ryan (Equitable Life Insurance) was OSS intelligence reports chief in Italy.

Only the Rockefellers were conspicuously absent from the Donovan ranks. Nelson headed his own agency, the Coordinator of Inter-American Affairs. After an early dispute between their two organizations over responsibility for Latin American propaganda, Rockefeller and Donovan refused to talk to each other for most of the war.[41]

OSS also had a clique of anti-Bolshevik Russian émigrés, some of them descendants of the fallen nobility. Such surnames as Smolianinoff, Lada-Mocarski, Yarrow, and Tolstoy were sprinkled throughout the organization. The wife of Chicago banker Lester Armour (of the meat-packing family), the last OSS commander in London, was a Romanov, a relative of Czar Nicholas. And Russian "Prince" Serge Obolensky headed the OSS Operational Groups which worked with the French Maquis at the time of the Normandy invasion.[k] A former officer of the Imperial Russian Army, Obolensky emigrated to New York for his political health after the revolution, became a hotel baron, married an Astor, and, with his good looks and dashing manner, became the darling of the New York social set. He was a charming individual, intelligent and reasonable—except on the subject of Communism. He called Franco's victory in the Spanish Civil War a "godsend." He wept for the "good, stable, religious, conservative people" of Yugoslavia who were delivered into the "hands of the Reds" by OSS support of Tito. Yet this same ex-Czarist officer found himself working behind the lines with the Communist resistance forces in France. To his discomfiture, he was even honored in a ceremony by the "Bolsheviks" of the Maquis.[42]

Donovan was as quick to defend his corporate officials, blue-blooded members of the establishment, and conservative émigrés as he was to

---

[k] Obolensky was Vice-President of Hilton International, 1945–49. Today, at the age of 82, he still directs a public relations firm in New York.

protect his liberals, Socialists, and Communists. He even believed that his officers—of the political left, right, and center—could accept the doctrine of apolitical pragmatism and work together harmoniously in a common purpose. At times he was right. He chose Dr. James Baxter, the president of Williams College, and Dr. William Langer, the noted Harvard historian, to preside over the intellectual ferment of the R&A Branch; both were registered Republicans. They were also highly competent academicians and the research group functioned effectively under their leadership.[1]

The operational branches did not fare so well in achieving ideological coexistence. Arthur Goldberg of the OSS Labor Branch suggested in a postwar article that there had been considerable ill-feeling between some OSS executives and the more liberal operations officers. According to the future Supreme Court Justice, one of the "mistakes" in OSS was "the selection by General Donovan of men for the higher echelons of the organization who by background and temperament were unsympathetic with Donovan's own conception of the necessity of unstinting cooperation with the resistance movements." [43] Less subtly, Drew Pearson charged that "OSS' top men are nearly all picked from the Red baiters." Donovan, he said, "had succeeded in collecting one of the fanciest groups of dilettante diplomats, Wall Street bankers, and amateur detectives ever seen in Washington," while, at the same time, "the youngsters in uniform recruited by Donovan have done some of the most heroic work of the war." [44]

An OSS officer who served behind the lines in Italy was equally bitter. He railed at the "rotund, happy-go-lucky, devil-may-care young Republican businessmen who sported themselves in the OSS enjoying the thought of sending packages of arms, money, food, etc., by parachute, but who didn't really care if they got there during this or the next moon, while all the time poor devils in the mountains slaved at building fires in the snow, waiting, hoping, night after night, till the whole village, the whole mountain, the whole countryside, knew what was about to happen, and by the time the parachutes *did* drift to earth, some 'bulgar' had betrayed the operation, and the Fascists and the Germans would be waiting on the spot ready to kill and maim the partisans who were doing their best to aid the Allied cause." [45]

Not all of the politically dissatisfied in OSS were supporters of the

[1] In 1950, Langer organized and was first Director of the CIA's Board of National Estimates. He was appointed to the President's Foreign Intelligence Advisory Board in 1961.

left. Alexander Barmine was a former general of the Red Army who fled from the Soviets in 1937 after learning that he was slated for liquidation in one of Stalin's purges.[m] Emigrating to the United States, he was employed by OSS as a translator and advisor on Soviet affairs. In this capacity, he helped Serge Obolensky translate a secretly obtained Russian version of Mao Tse-tung's guerrilla warfare manual. While still employed by OSS in October 1944, he wrote an article for *Reader's Digest* denouncing a venal Communist conspiracy in the United States. One month before the Presidential election, he suggested that the Roosevelt administration, "because of its apparent blindness to the conspiratorial and totalitarian nature of Communism consciously or unconsciously protects in numberless ways the success of the conspiracy. That is why, by orders from Moscow, the Communists are all out for the fourth term" (of FDR). The day after the article appeared, Barmine was discharged from OSS because of "continued absences." A Donovan spokesman denied that the article had been the immediate cause of the discharge, but added that, in any case, OSS employees were not permitted to write "controversial" articles.[46]

Another unhappy conservative was Hilaire du Berrier, a right-wing American journalist interned by the Japanese in China in 1942 for aiding a French resistance group.[n] Du Berrier was finally rescued from a Japanese prison at the end of the war by an OSS team, then recruited by Donovan's officers as a specialist in Indochinese affairs. It was only a matter of months before he left government employ, bitterly complaining that the OSS "left wing, through its directness of purpose and teamwork, managed to squeeze those on the right out of the organization." [47] His experience was shared by another conservative journalist, Ralph de Toledano,[o] who learned in June 1944 that OSS "was tapping me for a parachute mission behind Italian lines—and that a friend in the government who wanted at least a few soldiers on it who were both anti-fascist and anti-Communist had dropped my name in the hat. . . . Having been thoroughly investigated for political reliability, I was assigned for training to a lovely Virginia mansion. My troubles began when I was asked by a fellow trainee what I thought of 'my' congress-

[m] Barmine served as chief of the Russian Branch of the United States Information Agency during the Eisenhower administration.

[n] Du Berrier is now on the staff of the John Birch Society journal, *American Opinion*.

[o] De Toledano is now a contributing editor of William F. Buckley's *National Review*.

man, Representative Vito Marcantonio. I answered that I thought he was a Communist—or might just as well be one. I was questioned further and shortly thereafter OSS dropped me as being 'too anti-Communist.' " [48]

These were the schisms, some real, some imagined, that plagued OSS throughout the war. But the political element should not be exaggerated. Donovan's organization was not entirely torn apart by ideological polarization, for a sizable minority of OSS officers had no strong commitment to either the right or left wings of the organization. These men agreed with Donovan that their primary objective should be victory. They wanted only to "get on with the war" and were unhappy when both their American colleagues and the guerrilla leaders behind enemy lines insisted on injecting politics into military operations. OSS Major William Morgan,[p] a Yale-educated psychologist, recalling his disgruntlement over the constant intrusion of ideology into the French resistance, described his relationship with a Maquis group. "I did not," he said, "care whether they were Socialists or Communists, free-thinkers or atheists. My orders were to lead them against the Germans." [49]

General Donovan possessed the "power to visualize an oak when he saw an acorn," in the words of the OSS Psychological Staff. "For him the day was never sufficient unto itself; it was always teeming with the seeds of a boundless future" and "every completed project bred a host of new ones." As Donovan traversed the globe on frequent world tours, "at every stop, brief as it might be, he would leave a litter of young schemes to be reared and fashioned by his lieutenants and translated into deeds of daring." [50]

Under the general's prodding, OSS grew and expanded—and aroused the resentment of other official bureaucracies. From the moment of the COI's creation, a host of predatory government agencies "forgot their internecine animosities and joined in an attempt to strangle this unwanted newcomer at birth." [51] The grumbling against the new organization became such a deafening roar that President Roosevelt loaned his son James to the COI as a liaison officer to prevent other departments from devouring Donovan's upstarts before they had even set to work.

The Federal Bureau of Investigation looked particularly askance at this newcomer to the clandestine world. J. Edgar Hoover's agents were

[p] Dr. Morgan was Deputy Chief of the CIA Training Staff, 1947–49 and Chief of the CIA's Psychological Assessment Staff, 1949–52.

already entrenched in South America when OSS began to contemplate this FBI preserve with interest. Hoover objected. The dispute became so heated that Roosevelt was forced to intervene. The President awarded Hoover sole responsibility for secret operations south of the border (a decision OSS later disregarded).[q]

This first clash left Hoover with a fear of OSS encroachment that undoubtedly strengthened his natural paranoia about sinister conspiracies. Representatives of the British secret services in the United States were amazed to find that "Hoover keenly resented Donovan's organization from the moment it was established," and his resentment "was inevitably extended towards its British collaborators. . . . It took a long while to convince him that he could not succeed in his determination to exclude the British organization from contact with other U.S. intelligence agencies." [52]

The feud continued. In January 1942 Donovan's officers secretly penetrated the Spanish embassy in Washington and began photographing the code books and other official documents of Franco's pro-Axis government. Hoover learned of this operation and was angered because the COI men were invading his operational territory. The FBI did not bother to register a formal protest. While the COI officers were making one of their nocturnal entries into the embassy in April, two FBI squad cars followed. When Donovan's men were in the building, the cars pulled up outside the embassy and turned on their sirens. The entire neighborhood was awakened and the COI interlopers were sent scurrying. Donovan protested this incredible FBI action to the White House. Instead of reprimanding Hoover, Roosevelt's aides ordered the embassy infiltration project turned over to the Bureau.[53]

As the war went on, OSS relations with the FBI seemed to improve. Two of Hoover's top agents, Baltimore attorney Sidney Rubenstein[r] and 24-year-old Nebraskan J. Evelle Younger,[s] who headed the FBI's

[q] In 1954, Joseph Rendon, an unsuccessful Republican congressional candidate from New Mexico, turned up in Central America to participate in a CIA-fomented coup against the leftist government of Guatemala. He proudly told reporters that he had first warned of Communist infiltration of Guatemala on a 1944 OSS mission to that country. His reports, Rendon added, had been "sabotaged by Democratic Reds and Pinks in Washington."

[r] Rubenstein became security advisor to the U.S. mission to NATO in 1958.

[s] Younger was District Attorney of Los Angeles, 1964–68, and is now Attorney General of California.

National Defense Section, were co-opted by the Counter-Intelligence Branch of OSS for service in the Far East. But Hoover was not appeased. In 1944 he vigorously objected to a proposed exchange of missions between OSS and the Russian NKVD (Moscow's intelligence and secret police organization). The agreement with Moscow, personally negotiated by Donovan, would have meant the first American penetration of the most secret intelligence service of the Soviet Union. Both the American military representative at the Kremlin and Ambassador Averell Harriman hoped "that the relationship thus established would open the door to greater intimacy with other branches of government" in Moscow. Hoover denounced the agreement as "a highly dangerous and most undesirable procedure." Roosevelt was unwilling to challenge Hoover's political power, and the agreement was tabled.[54] *why?*

OSS also had running bouts with the Department of State. The COI had just acquired a few temporary rooms in the State Department Annex in its very early days, when Cordell Hull's assistants first became worried about competition with the new agency. When COI requested access to some State files, Foreign Service officers nervously jibed that Donovan was "a man who could tell you the time if you loaned him your watch." [55] State officials had good cause for anxiety; the helter-skelter but brilliant achievements of Donovan's officers would stand in sharp contrast to the tradition-bound, sluggish actions of the diplomatic service.

To novitiates of the foreign affairs bureaucracy, the contrast came as something of a shock. In 1944, an astute specialist in African affairs left the Research and Analysis Branch of OSS for a new position at the State Department. He was amazed by the change of atmosphere. His OSS environment had been free-wheeling, intellectually stimulating, and politically liberal. In contrast, he found his new Foreign Service colleagues burdened by the restraints of career ambition and the conservatism of a rigid hierarchy. He even encountered instances of racial prejudice that would have seemed anathema to his fellow analysts in OSS. The bewildered professor was Ralph Bunche.[t]

The disappointment Bunche experienced was shared by others who found the State Department hopelessly hamstrung by bureaucratic inertia, a "spirit of smug self-satisfaction," as David Bruce put it.[56] State thus proved an easy prey for OSS dynamism. If for no other reason than the quality of its people, OSS was destined to enter the arena of

[t] Dr. Bunche was Under Secretary-General of the United Nations until his retirement in 1971.

OSS Corporal Arthur Schlesinger, Jr., pictured here as a political intelligence analyst in liberated Paris during the winter of 1944, was one of the many Donovan assistants who gained renown in the post-war years for their intellectual accomplishments and public service.

international diplomacy. Men who had served in top diplomatic posts before the war—such as the American ambassadors to Germany and Italy, the minister to Lithuania, and the deputy governor-general of the Philippines—were quickly tapped by Donovan for top OSS positions. America's first intelligence agency also served as a breeding ground for future statesmen. Since the war, former OSS officers have represented the United States as ambassadors in over twenty countries.[u] The commander of OSS in the European Theater, David Bruce, has served as ambassador to England, France, and Germany and, more recently, as American representative to the Vietnam peace negotiations in Paris. General Donovan was himself named ambassador to Thailand by President Eisenhower. The exclusive "club" of COI and OSS veterans also

[u] Those not mentioned elsewhere in the narrative are Edwin Martin, ambassador to Argentina, 1964–68; Thomas Beale, ambassador to Jamaica, 1965–68; and George Garrett, ambassador to Ireland, 1947–53.

includes Presidential advisors Arthur Schlesinger, Jr., Walt Rostow, Carl Kaysen, Douglass Cater, Clark McGregor,ᵛ former U.N. ambassador Goldberg, former Treasury Secretary C. Douglas Dillon, and CIA Directors Allen Dulles and Richard Helms. Most of these men received their first governmental experience in OSS. ✓

In August 1941, an alarmed State Department signed an uneasy pact with COI assigning some vague responsibility for intelligence collection and overseas propaganda to Donovan's group—a concession accepted by Undersecretary of State Sumner Welles (whose son Ben later appeared in Cairo in OSS uniform). But not all officials at State were happy with the agreement. Assistant Secretary of State Breckinridge Long wrote in his diary in late 1941: "One of the most important things to be controlled is Donovan. His organization is composed of inexperienced people—inexperienced in so far as dealing with high-powered information is concerned. They get all our information and use it ad lib. Sometimes there is a definite flare-back because of lack of judgment in its use." Four months later, in April 1942, he added that Donovan "has been a thorn in the side of a number of the regular agencies of the government for some time—including the Department of State—and more particularly recently in Welles'. He is into everybody's business—knows no bounds of jurisdiction—tries to fill the shoes of each agency charged with responsibility for a war activity. He has almost unlimited money and a regular army at work and agents all over the world." [57]

Special criticism was reserved for Robert Sherwood's COI propaganda division, whose radio broadcasts, according to Long, followed "a policy widely divergent from the official foreign policy and from time to time make trouble for us abroad." [58] The chief of Sherwood's planning board explained that his staff took an independent course only after finding it impossible to receive specific guidelines from the State Department. They decided that "if we could not get anybody to tell us what U.S. government policy was in particular instances, we would have to assume responsibility ourselves for saying what it was. We did so. After a few weeks of this improvisation, the State Department woke up with a start to the realization that one of Donovan's impertinent little offices was making policy for it." [59]

ᵛ McGregor, an officer of OSS guerrilla Detachment 101 in Burma, was elected to Congress from Minnesota in 1960. After an unsuccessful Republican candidacy for the U.S. Senate in 1970, he was appointed Special Assistant to President Nixon for Congressional Relations.

A second dispute involved the OSS use of American diplomatic facilities. The American ambassador to Vichy, Admiral William Leahy, tried to impose restrictions on the espionage operations of OSS agents attached to the American consulates in southern France. "General Donovan accused me of interfering in his work," recalls Leahy. "I told him the diplomatic service was *my* business." [60] In all the neutral countries of Europe—Switzerland, Sweden, Spain, Portugal—the assignment of OSS officers to the American embassies under diplomatic cover met with strong resistance from the professional diplomats. The single appointment to which State did not object was that of a charming editor of *Vogue* as "fashion attaché" at the American embassy in Stockholm. She admirably promoted American clothing design in Sweden while secretly working with the Danish resistance on behalf of OSS. Far less dainty spies and saboteurs reached neutral capitals as "cultural attachés" and were greeted with something less than joy by the American ambassadors.

The State Department next objected to dispensing passports to OSS officers. Mrs. Ruth Shipley, who ran State's passport division as her own personal empire, insisted that Donovan's agents travel abroad with their passports clearly marked "OSS." It took considerable discussion at high levels to convince State that espionage operations were simply incompatible with Mrs. Shipley's whims. Later in the war she struck back by interminably delaying, on "security" grounds, the passports of Japanese-Americans bound for OSS posts in the Far East.[61]

As COI grew into OSS and the organization began to expand, it was inevitable that Donovan's men would fill the diplomatic vacuum created by the State Department's abdication of responsibility. State often jealously fought to preserve petty prerogatives while failing to assume leadership or to provide direction on matters of substance. In Cairo, the American ambassador to the Greek and Yugoslav exile governments refused to represent the United States on an Anglo-American planning committee for political warfare in the Balkans. The diplomat explained that he had received no instructions from Washington. The American view was therefore presented by Turner McBaine, a 32-year-old California attorney in OSS naval uniform with the rank of lieutenant, junior grade, sitting opposite the British ambassador and a British general.[w] That same year in Washington, an OSS colonel queried Assistant Secretary of State Adolf Berle about American policy

[w] McBaine is now a senior partner in a prestigious San Francisco law firm and counsel to the Standard Oil Company of California.

toward Thailand. After a rapid consultation with Cordell Hull, Berle returned with a laconic (and symbolic) response: "We haven't any policy as yet."

Into the breach rushed the OSS. In its initial attempts to gather high-level intelligence, OSS men were forced into activities that smacked of diplomacy. Wartime conditions sometimes prevented regular State personnel from undertaking unusual or hazardous missions and OSS was assigned responsibility. Donovan dispatched his officers on missions to the Dalai Lama of Tibet and the Regent of Thailand. And he sent a beautiful young American war correspondent to rendezvous secretly with the Field Marshal of Finland. Having completed her mission, she stopped briefly at the American embassy in Stockholm to see a Foreign Service officer of long acquaintance. Saying nothing of her OSS affiliation, she subtly asked the diplomat for his opinion of General Donovan's secret service. Replying with great earnestness, the State official confided to her, "I can always smell an OSS officer. We never give them any help."

Another OSS intrusion into the diplomatic process was prompted by the creation of a Foreign Nationalities Branch within the organization. This division was headed by Dewitt Poole, director of the Princeton School for Public Affairs and former State Department Russian expert.ˣ Officially, the purpose of the branch was to observe the legal political activities of a multitude of anti-Axis exile and immigrant groups in the United States, from the semi-official Gaullist delegation in Washington to the handful of refugees who operated a "Free Albanian" press in Boston. "It was Mr. Poole's belief," wrote one of his aides, "that Americans of foreign descent, at a time when freedom had been extinguished in their original homelands, could provide information and services of importance to our military effort and our diplomacy. He believed, in a more subtle and philosophic way, that our foreign policy could draw some measure both of idealism and consistency from these living streams of old-world perceptions, perceptions which had been made the more disinterested and assured by their contact with American life." [62]

One left-wing critic took a decidedly less romantic view of Poole's activities. He charged (somewhat unfairly) that the OSS branch sought to "sustain or restore monarchical, clero-fascistic, reactionary setups" in Europe and "to set off power politics of the most deplorable variety." [63] It was true that Poole's operations had gone far beyond liaison. As the

ˣ Poole served as president of the CIA-funded National Committee for a Free Europe, 1949–51.

number of exile and immigrant groups multiplied, their leaders came
into frequent conflict with one another, and all demanded recognition
of political legitimacy from the American government. Accordingly, the
Foreign Nationalities Branch became involved in political intrigue. At
times this included surveillance of exile leaders by OSS officers, an activity that again incurred the wrath of the FBI. Still other OSS experts
in London surreptitiously opened and resealed the mail pouches that
one government-in-exile had sent to its delegation in Washington. A
comparison of documents sent by pouch with information the exile government was transmitting voluntarily to OSS proved that some details
on resistance activity had been withheld.[64]

Nor did Donovan's officers shrink from playing the role of political
kingmakers, as one postwar chief of state could attest. Syngman Rhee
had unsuccessfully attempted, early in the war, to obtain official recognition of his Korean exile movement. But the State Department was
skeptical, believing that Rhee's Korean Provisional Government was no
more than a "self-constituted club" of expatriates.[65] Rhee turned in
desperation to OSS and received a warm reception from Colonel M.
Preston Goodfellow, a Brooklyn newspaper publisher and former Hearst
executive who was Donovan's Deputy Director for Operations.[y] Through
Goodfellow's intercession, the War Department accorded Rhee limited
recognition as liaison with OSS in recruiting a group of young Koreans
for behind-the-lines service in the Far East.[z] Rhee's standing in official
Washington was thus given a considerable boost. As for the OSS operational plan, most of the agents were selected, trained, and never used.
OSS, nonetheless, had given Rhee his first boost toward postwar political power.[a]

As the end of the war approached, Donovan's men even became
deeply enmeshed in surrender negotiations in Europe. Hitler's generals
"had good reason to fear that they would pay with their lives for any
unauthorized attempt to stop the fighting. This meant that there could
be no parliamentarians crossing enemy lines with white flags, no public

[y] Goodfellow is now president of Overseas Reconstruction, Inc., a
Washington firm with business dealings in Latin America, Southeast Asia,
and the Middle East.

[z] One OSS Korean agent, Diamond Kimm, was hardly a Rhee enthusiast. He was prominent in Communist front activities in Los Angeles
until deported to North Korea in 1965.

[a] In 1946 the War Department sent Goodfellow to Seoul as "economic
and political advisor" to his old friend Syngman Rhee.

parleys, no formalized negotiations." The State Department recognized that a secret organization like OSS was best equipped to undertake "the unusual function of establishing the first contact" with enemy emissaries.[66]

But the professional diplomats were far less convinced of the political sagacity of those OSS men in khaki who parachuted behind enemy lines into occupied territory to contact the anti-Axis resistance forces of Europe and Asia.

"The oppressed peoples must be encouraged to resist and to assist in Axis defeat, and this can be done by inciting them, by assisting them, and by training and organizing them." Sabotage alone would not suffice. "It must be accompanied by efforts to promote revolution." Those words were not written by Stalin. They were found in an October 1941 memorandum to General Donovan from his first Special Operations chief, Robert Solborg, a steel corporation executive and Russian émigré who had once been an officer of the Czar's army.

"The undercover agent must set up his machinery for building up an organization dedicated in the beginning to passive resistance. If his task is successful, passive resistance will lead by natural steps to open violence and even—at the proper time—to armed rebellion." [67] Mao Tse-tung was not the author of these instructions for subversion. They were set forth in December 1943 by another Donovan assistant, J. Freeman Lincoln, a freelance writer who later became an editor of *Fortune* and *Time* magazines.

Even Donovan's executives realized that OSS was confronted with the task of political revolution. There could be no American embassies and no Foreign Service officers in enemy-occupied territory. Yet the competing drives for power in the occupied nations were only intensified by Axis domination and the chaos of war. New social and ideological forces were clamoring for the overthrow of old regimes in Europe, and Asian nationalists were plotting the destruction of colonial rule. It was the "liaison" officers of OSS to whom these revolutionaries often turned in hopeful anticipation.

Robert Welch, founder of the John Birch Society, charged that OSS "frequently threw the weight of American supplies, arms, money, and prestige behind the Communist terrorist organizations of Europe and Asia." [68] There was some truth in this statement. But the full story of OSS relations with the resistance was a complex product of organizational structure, the nature of guerrilla warfare, the ideologies of the men behind the lines, and the competing political interests of America's allies.

OSS had taken its organizational cue from the British, who at the outset of World War II were considered masters of clandestine warfare. The Secret Intelligence Service (known as SIS, MI-6, or "Broadway") had been charged with overseas espionage since the late sixteenth century. An offshoot of SIS, the Special Operations Executive (SOE), was created in 1940 to assist guerrilla movements in the war against Hitler, or, in Churchill's poetic phrase, to "set Europe ablaze."

General Donovan similarly established a Secret Intelligence Branch (SI) and a Special Operations Branch (SO). Like their independent British counterparts, these divisions looked at operational problems from entirely different perspectives. SI was charged with espionage—the secret collection of intelligence information—and SO was given responsibility for sabotage and liaison with underground movements. The operational objectives of these two divisions were not always compatible. The SO principle was to work with resistance groups of any political coloration provided that they were militarily effective against the enemy. The SI branch was interested only in the collection of useful information, not in tactical raids or sabotage. Could an underground group supply valuable intelligence? If so, argued the SI men, OSS must maintain contact with that group. "An intelligence officer," wrote Allen Dulles, summarizing the SI position, "should be free to talk to the devil himself if he could gain any useful knowledge for the conduct or the termination of the war." [69] That was the theory of espionage. But American officers soon discovered that their conversations with particular political devils were often interpreted as implying Washington's recognition and support. OSS faced this same problem in the caves of Mao Tse-tung's headquarters in north China and in the Swiss cafés where American officers met the conservative German militarists who were plotting Hitler's assassination. Since formal organizational divisions in OSS were rarely respected, Special Operations men sometimes collected intelligence and Secret Intelligence officers occasionally fought with the underground. If this was not sufficient to confuse "operational principles" beyond recognition, General Donovan proceeded to create a third branch, the Operational Group Command, in which SI and SO activities were merged. The new Operational Groups were organized by target countries (Italian OG, French OG, and so on) and consisted of 32 men with language qualifications dropped behind the lines in uniform with directives to carry out both espionage and sabotage operations in concert with the resistance.

Regardless of their specific assignments, OSS men who parachuted into enemy territory assumed a very special role in the war. There was nothing particularly romantic about World War II for the American infantry soldier. He saw the death, misery, greed, and brutality that always accompanies armed conflict. But a select group of Donovan's men fought a different war.

Living and working behind the lines with dedicated guerrillas who fought to free their countries from fascist domination, these OSS officers found real meaning in the Roosevelt slogans of the Atlantic Charter. And few American (or British) officers failed to develop a passionate admiration for their partisan friends. The enemy was evil, the resistance was heroic. For lonely Americans hiding on a cold mountain or in a torrid jungle under constant threat of attack, there could be no other truth.

Actor Sterling Hayden was one Donovan officer who served with Tito's guerrillas in Yugoslavia. "We established a tremendously close personal feeling with these people," he later recalled. "We had enormous, I would say unlimited respect for the way they were fighting. . . . We got quite steamed up by it. I myself was steamed up considerably by it. I had never experienced anything quite like that, and it made a tremendous impression on me." [70]

It is not surprising that most OSS field operators were idealists. A majority were under thirty years old and had received their college education during the Depression years. Also, the OSS Psychological Staff, dominated by such young academicians as 30-year-old John Gardner of Mount Holyoke, deliberately sought out potential SO and SI officers who possessed an "ability to get along with other people" and a "freedom from disturbing prejudices." [b] The psychologists similarly shunned the selection of men for overseas service who were burdened by "feelings of national superiority or racial intolerance." [71] This policy proved effective. One admiring war correspondent observed that "race, color, and previous condition of servitude cut no ice whatever" in OSS "so long as one actually wanted to get into the fray and help to win it." [72]

Some of the OSS agents who served in Europe were recent ref-

[b] Dr. Gardner was president of the Carnegie Corporation, 1955–65; Secretary of Health, Education, and Welfare, 1965–68; and is now chairman of the liberal pressure group Common Cause.

ugees from Nazism with a strong social-democratic orientation and "were very articulate in expressing their eagerness to participate in the war against fascism." These men and women came from the ranks of socialist groups such as the Jewish Agency Executive, the International Transport Workers Federation, and the International Federation of Trade Unions. In Asia, many officers had a missionary background and were instilled with a family tradition of evangelical support for social reform. OSS men who fought alongside the anti-Japanese Kachin natives in Burma rarely expressed the anti-oriental racism which is so common today among American soldiers in Vietnam. And OSS was one of the few wartime agencies that effectively integrated American Nisei into its operations in the Far East, this at the time when these loyal Americans were being herded into detention camps on the West Coast.

One Donovan aide noted that the general himself possessed a "basically democratic faith in the unexploited capabilities of the common man." [73] This social idealism pervaded OSS. A sampling of thousands of intelligence analyses produced by the OSS Research Branch reveals certain recurrent terms: democratic, progressive, social reform. These words were more than clichés to the young academicians who used them. They represented the hope, shared by their colleagues behind the lines, for the triumph of universal democracy and the progress of the common men of all nations.

Each officer had his own interpretation of the coming of the democratic millennium. To the Roosevelt liberals in the operational branches, it meant the extension of the New Deal abroad. After all, OSS was a New Deal agency as well as a wartime exigency, and Donovan's organization was "beloved of President Roosevelt." [74] Beverly Bowie, an assistant editor of National Geographic, was the first OSS man to reach Bucharest after the German withdrawal in the fall of 1944. Other American officers arrived to find Bowie already a regular guest at meetings of the Romanian cabinet. "Before they vote on anything," explained the OSS officer with tongue in cheek, "they ask me what I think. I go into a trance and figure out what Franklin D. Roosevelt would do, then give 'em the answer. They pass all my laws unanimously. I never thought running a country was so easy." [75]

Other OSS officers—Republicans, conservatives, and many who simply had no strong political views—were just as devoted to their own brand of social idealism. They also held a basic faith in human progress and the ability of "common men" to improve the world through a common effort. It was an optimism without ideological connotations which eased the pressures of wartime life and clandestine existence.

The resistance forces naturally assumed that these young idealists were official representatives of their nation's foreign policy. "Here, I was America," wrote an OSS colonel who served with the Yugoslav royalist guerrillas. "I had a message, perhaps merely words of courage and encouragement to a long-suffering people." [76] Behind enemy lines, the most casual word that fell from the unguarded lips of the youngest second lieutenant in the American army—he might have been a writer, lawyer, corporation executive, or artist in peacetime—would be considered holy writ by leaders of the resistance. His views had no importance in the eyes of State Department representatives thousands of miles away, but for the fighters of the underground, they were taken as inspired declarations of Washington's policy.

The British certainly recognized that their secret agents would work as unofficial diplomats and London insisted (frequently without success) that officers of the Special Operations Executive who parachuted into enemy territory should execute the political objectives of the Foreign Office. Like their Soviet allies, the British were determined to pursue their own interests as a world power in the course of the battle against the Axis. In Washington, some State Department and OSS executives had similar plans for the establishment of America's postwar imperium, but the rank-and-file of Donovan's secret service had no patience with such grand designs; they believed that Machiavellian power politics were always played at the expense of smaller nations and powerless peoples, and the underdogs of the world were the objects of OSS affection.

A distaste for power politics was as important as ideological anti-Communism in shaping the attitudes of OSS men toward the Russians. Certainly there were conservatives at OSS headquarters who would have preferred a war against the Soviets to a battle against Berlin. But most of Donovan's officers initially hoped for peaceful postwar coexistence with the Kremlin. Twenty years earlier, on an official trip to Russia in 1919, a young Colonel William Donovan had advised the State Department against recognizing an anti-Bolshevik White Russian government. "Workers in Siberia," he had observed, were "yearning for Bolshevism." [77] The Irish Republican was not being sympathetic, only honest and objective. He tried to maintain that objectivity, despite his own conservatism, as director of OSS. His operatives were forbidden to engage in espionage activities within the Soviet Union. (The Russians did not return the courtesy.) When the intelligence pundits at the War Department predicted that Russia would collapse under Nazi attack in 1942, economists of Donovan's Research Branch under the direction of Harvard's Edward Mason and Columbia's Walt Rostow assembled statistics to prove that the Soviet Union could hold out against the Germans.[c] Most OSS men recognized the contribution the Soviet Union could make toward ending the war, and at first hoped that the wartime alliance with Russia might endure. Geroid Robinson, the Columbia historian and chief of the Soviet section of the OSS Research Branch, expressed the thoughts of many of his colleagues when he wrote: "It is more difficult now than it used to be, to unite for the immediate, but not too limited, end of salvage from destruction; but it must be done, if the democrat is to save his democracy, the communist his communism—if anyone is to save anything that has a meaning for him. Yes, it is very hard to unite for Armageddon in this sectarian world. But the thing must be done. There is no other way." [78]

This hope only made greater the disillusionment felt by those OSS officers who were confronted by Soviet belligerence in the last year of the war. In Romania, despite a past working arrangement between OSS and the Soviets in the rescue of Allied fliers, the OSS mission was abruptly ordered to leave the country after Germany's surrender. In Yugoslavia, following Tito's victory, Russian generals who had done little or nothing for the Communist partisans were welcomed with warmth, while OSS men who had struggled alongside the guerrillas for months were expelled from Belgrade. And in Manchuria, OSS teams were virtually imprisoned when they attempted to photograph Soviet dismantling of industrial equipment in violation of Russian treaty commitments. General Donovan responded, months before V-J Day, by ordering his commanders in Cairo and Berlin to turn their attention toward the new Soviet "threat."

OSS had brushed against the edge of a coming Cold War that would later be fought by its successor, the CIA. But at least at the working level of Donovan's organization there had been no venal conspiracy for a new anti-Russian crusade. The OSS lieutenants who disliked Soviet political manipulations had been just as critical of similar tactics by their British allies.

At first, the OSS amateurs had been eager to learn from their ex-

[c] Dr. Rostow was chairman of the State Department Policy Planning Council, 1961–66, and Special Assistant to the President for National Security Affairs, 1966–69.

perienced British cousins in the Secret Intelligence Service and the Special Operations Executive. Even before the creation of COI, Donovan was known to the British as an ardent interventionist. The representative of the combined British secret services in the United States, Sir William Stephenson, had told his superiors in 1940: "There is no doubt that we can achieve infinitely more through Donovan than through any other individual. . . . He is very receptive . . . and can be trusted to represent our needs in the right quarters and in the right way in the U.S.A." [79] After America entered the war, the "closest cooperation with the British was already assumed at the highest level" at Donovan's headquarters.[80] Stephenson gave the general vital information about British operational training methods, clandestine communications, and espionage techniques, and the first OSS operators were trained in secret British schools in Canada. The British felt that OSS, in its formative stages, "could not have survived" without their aid. Donovan knew this as well, and in the later years of the war OSS tried to repay its debt by supplying MI-6 and SOE with technical equipment, foreign currency for use in clandestine operations, and, at times, with extremely valuable intelligence information.

The anglophilia of OSS executives in Washington was shared in the higher echelons of the organization's London office. David Bruce, the OSS commander in the European Theater, later became the popular ambassador to the Court of St. James. And Raymond Guest, a polo-playing socialite who directed OSS maritime operations in France and Scandinavia, was a cousin of Winston Churchill's. The personal relations of such men with the social-club establishment that ran the British secret services brought about relative operational harmony in Western Europe.

But even in London and Washington there were minor irritants. One OSS psychologist found that a British Psychological Assessment Board had been rejecting a high proportion of OSS propagandists, some of them well-known Hollywood screen-writers, New York advertising men, and best-selling authors. The sole reason: the candidates were immigrants of Jewish descent.[81]

Such incidents made it difficult to build a cooperative relationship on the basis of mutual confidence. One officer of the Special Operations Executive, assigned as liaison to Donovan's headquarters, had rented a rat-infested home in the District of Columbia. He complained to a British friend who promised to remedy the situation. One dark night there was a knock on his door. He opened it to find a tall, lanky man with sad eyes. "I am the exterminator," proclaimed the visitor. "For a moment," the SOE man remembered, "I thought that perhaps OSS had at last had enough of me." [82]

In the theaters of war beyond the immediate authority of London and Washington, suspicion between allies was less humorous. When Donovan's representatives went to London in June 1942 to negotiate a worldwide working agreement with SOE, they vehemently insisted that OSS be regarded as an operational partner—not as a junior apprentice, as the British had proposed. The Americans won the argument, but only on paper. SOE reached a peak of obstructive efficiency in preventing OSS operations in Scandinavia and the Balkans on the grounds that these areas were within its exclusive domain. The departure of an OSS mission for the Arab countries was so long delayed by British objections that the impatient American team adopted the motto, "here today, here tomorrow." [83]

Many OSS men began to operate on the general principle that "in intelligence, the British are just as much the enemy as the Germans." [84] They believed that London's secret services were more concerned with expanding England's empire than with defeating the enemy. OSS impatience with Whitehall's political maneuvers was particularly intense in the Far East, where traditional American opposition to colonialism permeated OSS operations. When General Douglas MacArthur refused to permit OSS to operate in the South Pacific, Donovan quickly convinced the British to accept OSS "cooperation" in Southeast Asia. From the standpoint of Allied unity, this was an unfortunate technical arrangement because it established India as a base point for clandestine operations in Burma, Thailand, Malaya, and Indochina. OSS men flew to Calcutta or New Delhi to begin their tours of duty in the Far East only to be "culture-shocked" by ugly manifestations of British imperialism. The OSS representative to the Anglo-American South East Asia Command wrote his wife: "Working with our Cousins has made me cynical about ideals—if we really believe our own propaganda, we would have to declare war on the British, for they have set themselves up as the master-race in India. British rule in India is fascism, there is no dodging that." [85]

At least on the colonial issue, the OSS was in full accord with State Department officers in the Far East, and Donovan's organization became the "faithful secular arm" of the diplomats' "anti-colonialist fundamentalism." [86] Long before the Japanese surrender, OSS planners had suggested that "American cooperation with patriotic, subversive revolutionary groups of southeastern Asia would appreciably increase our offensive power against Japan." [87] When the task of American representation in southern Asia in the immediate postwar period later fell to OSS, Ho Chi Minh and other anticolonial crusaders received their first spiritual impetus from the unauthorized American diplomats of Donovan's band.

In early 1941, before the formation of COI, Ian Fleming, the future creator of "James Bond," then a ranking officer in British Naval Intelligence, suggested to Donovan that he should select as intelligence officers men who possessed the qualities of "absolute discretion, sobriety, devotion to duty, languages, and wide experience." Their age, Fleming added, should be "about 40 to 50." [88] Donovan declined Fleming's advice. Instead, he promised Franklin Roosevelt an international secret service staffed by young officers who were "calculatingly reckless" with "disciplined daring" and "trained for aggressive action." [89] In Rome, Peking, Bangkok, Paris, and Algiers, those were the men of OSS.

2

The Torch of Reaction

On June 25, 1940, the French Republic surrendered to its Nazi invaders. Three weeks later, William Donovan flew to London as an unofficial envoy of President Roosevelt for a first-hand view of the disastrous German victory on the European continent. Returning to Washington later that year, Donovan joined journalist Edgar Ansel Mowrer, Paris correspondent for the Chicago *Daily News*, in writing a series of nationally syndicated, officially inspired newspaper articles dissecting the Wehrmacht onslaught.

"Adolf Hitler's blitz-conquests of Poland, of Norway, of Belgium, Holland, Luxemburg, and France are military masterpieces," they wrote. "In all secrecy and with incredible speed the Nazi leader built up a unique military machine, beside which all other armies in the world were obsolete." But superior military power alone could not account for Germany's lightning victories. Political weakness in the European nations had also contributed to the triumph of the Axis.

The fall of France was a tragic case. The French nation "cracked morally," and "a new set of defeatist leaders sought to purchase the German's mercy, if not his respect, by supine submission to France's conquerors." High-ranking officers of the French Army, wealthy industrialists, and prominent politicians had "ceased to believe in freedom, democracy, or any of the slogans which alone could galvanize the entire country. While not exactly pro-fascist (and certainly not pro-

German) they were hostile to the Third Republic; many had come to believe that an authoritarian regime like that of Italy and Germany was really preferable; it would, they thought, save the position of the privileged classes, and really save France from the disagreeable necessity of defending itself. If there was a war, then let it be against the abominable Bolsheviks. In other words, at least half and perhaps the majority of influential French citizens had come to believe exactly what Hitler wanted them to believe." [1]

Yet these same "men of influence" had come to power in France after "one of the most contemptible surrenders on record." They had given their approval to a degrading armistice agreement that split the country into two zones. Three-fifths of French territory, Paris included, was occupied by Nazi troops. The remainder of France and all of its African colonial empire remained unoccupied, under the rule of a Nazi-tolerated government with its capital at Vichy.

The Vichy regime was personified by its chief of state, the octogenarian hero of World War I, Marshal Henri Philippe Pétain, who evoked nostalgic emotions in the name of Family and Fatherland at a moment of defeat and disgrace. But the real political power fell into the hands of wealthy Admiral Jean Darlan, a cynical military opportunist and an architect of collaboration with the Nazis.

These political reactionaries of Vichy were also violent anglophobes, and their anti-British fanaticism was fanned by Churchill's encouragement of the Free French exile movement of General Charles de Gaulle. In July 1940, after an unfortunate British attack on a Vichy naval fleet in Algerian waters, the Pétain government broke off diplomatic relations with London.

Still neutral in the World War, the United States continued (with Churchill's private encouragement) to maintain formal political contact with Vichy. Roosevelt appointed his old friend, conservative Admiral William Leahy,[a] as ambassador to the Pétain government, with diplomatic instructions to strengthen Vichy's determination to resist further French concessions to the Germans. There was an immediate outcry in the United States against American relations with the Vichy collaborators. In the year before Pearl Harbor, most American liberals (some future OSS officers among them) suspected the State Department of displaying "a sympathy for the Vichy regime that often seemed

[a] Leahy was President Truman's representative on the National Intelligence Authority, the intelligence coordinating board that preceded CIA, 1946–47.

ANTI BRITISH, ANTI Bolshevik

warmer than considerations of diplomatic and strategic expediency could account for." [2]

Part of the secret rationale for Washington's Vichy policy was the intelligence value of a diplomatic presence in France.[3] By the spring of 1941, anti-German officers of the French army's intelligence service were surreptitiously transmitting military and political information to the American military attaché at Vichy, Colonel Robert Schow.[b] Similar gentlemanly espionage was under way in Vichy's unoccupied North African colonies. At Algiers, the State Department was represented by Robert Murphy, a tall, personable, Foreign Service career officer who had attracted the President's eye.[c] An Irish Catholic with markedly conservative views on French politics, Murphy was seen through the somewhat jaundiced eyes of General de Gaulle as "skillful and determined, long familiar with the best society and apparently inclined to believe that France consisted of the people he dined with in town." [4]

In February 1941, Murphy negotiated an economic accord with the Vichy governor ot North Africa, 74-year-old General Maxime Weygand (reportedly the bastard son of "Emperor" Maximilian). The agreement provided that the United States would supply the African colonies with badly needed imports. To insure that these goods stayed out of Nazi hands, the State Department would be allowed to send a special team of diplomatic observers to Algeria, Morocco, and Tunisia.

Washington needed American representatives in Africa for more critical purposes than import control. At the request of nervous War Department officials, who were alarmed by growing German influence in French Africa, Cordell Hull agreed that his "food control officers" should, in reality, perform intelligence duties. Donovan's Coordinator of Information had not yet been created and the task of selecting these agents fell to the military intelligence services. Under the guiding hand

[b] Schow served as Assistant Director of CIA, 1949–51, and chief of Army Intelligence, 1956–58. He then left the Army to join R.C.A.

[c] Murphy was American representative to the Allied military government in occupied Germany, 1945–49; ambassador to Belgium, 1949–51; ambassador to Japan, 1952–53; Under Secretary of State, 1959–60. He retired from State to become president of Corning Glass International, and in 1961 was appointed to the President's Foreign Intelligence Advisory Board, the CIA "watchdog" committee.

of Wallace Phillips, an expatriate businessman who headed the American Chamber of Commerce in London (later Donovan's first espionage advisor), the Army and Navy produced a dozen Americans steeped in French culture and politics to serve as North African "Vice Consuls" under Murphy's direction.

The twelve "disciples," as they were known in Washington, set out for Africa in June 1941. They soon took their positions at Algiers, Tunis, and Casablanca and found themselves uneasily mingling in the gambling casinos with German and Italian officers, spies, double agents, genuine diplomats, informers, and elegantly coiffured prostitutes.

The Gestapo paid little attention to the Vice Consuls. "Since all their thoughts," read a German report, "are centered on their social, sexual, or culinary interests, petty quarrels and jealousies are daily incidents with them. Altogether they represent a perfect picture of the mixture of races and characters in that savage conglomeration called the United States of America, and anyone who observes them can well judge the state of mind and instability that must be prevalent in their country today. . . . Lack of pluck and democratic degeneracy prevails among them, resulting from their too easy life, corrupt morals, and consequent lack of energy. . . . They are totally lacking in method, organization and discipline. . . . We can only congratulate ourselves on the selection of this group of enemy agents who will give us no trouble." [5] But the Nazis had miscalculated. Within weeks, Murphy's amateur spies were flooding Washington with valuable reports on all significant military and political developments in the colonies. Six months later, when the Japanese attack plunged the United States into the war, this intelligence proved essential to America's strategic planning. That same month of December 1941, Donovan's new COI warned Roosevelt of the imminent danger of a German invasion of Morocco by way of Franco's fascist but "neutral" Spain, and suggested an immediate Anglo-American seizure of France's African colonies to preempt a Nazi maneuver.

Roosevelt and Churchill met in Washington at Christmas 1941 to plan their future strategy. North Africa was a major topic of conversation. The two statesmen hoped to find a pro-Allied French leader who could command the allegiance of the conservative French colonial army. They sent a message to General Weygand, ousted from his North African post in November at Nazi insistence: Would the general be willing to return secretly to Algiers to rally the French Army at the moment of an Anglo-American landing? The reply was disappointing; Weygand refused to desert the Pétain regime or support an African uprising.

Even before the overture to Weygand, Donovan had suggested to the President that some prominent French politician be smuggled out of Vichy France to assume the mantle of leadership of an exile movement. American officials had already developed an antipathy to the existing Free French organization of General de Gaulle. He was regarded in Washington as a British creation with dictatorial ambitions and little support among the French people. What was the alternative to Gaullism? A handful of Washington officials had great hopes for a group of Frenchmen, "discovered" by Murphy and his Vice Consuls in Vichy Africa, who declared their fervent opposition to the Germans.

An embryonic underground organization in North Africa included army officers, businessmen, and government officials. All political factions were represented in this kernel of resistance, but at the command level the predominant ideology was extreme conservatism. "People back home," wrote one Vice Consul, "wondered audibly why we didn't find Gaullists or 'liberals' with whom to work. We worked, like everyone else, with what we had, and what we had were people who were French and patriotic to their fingertips but politically the equivalent of any group of stockbrokers in an exclusive Long Island Club." [6]

The Ku Klux Klan would have been a more appropriate analogy. Several leaders of the African underground had been closely associated in past years with a secret French political movement known as the Cagoule. Adherents of a covert paramilitary organization armed by the German and Italian secret services and dedicated to the violent overthrow of republican government in France, the Cagoulards (literally "hooded men") had staged an almost successful coup against the Republic in 1937. The conspiracy reached into the highest levels of French military and banking circles.

One friend of Murphy's with alleged Cagoulard ties was a vegetable oil magnate, Jacques Lemaigre-Dubreuil. A reputation for right-wing political intrigue enabled Lemaigre to transfer his oil business to North Africa with German consent and to remain on close terms with Vichy and Nazi officials of the highest rank. Yet this "two-way collaborationist" quietly assured Murphy of his pro-Allied sympathies.

Allowed by his German colleagues to travel freely between Algiers and France, Lemaigre became indispensable to Murphy's underground plot. The American diplomat convinced Donovan that Lemaigre's dubious political record was "deceptive," that he was actually a "courageous, patriotic Frenchman who hates the Germans and Italians with an intelligent implacability and favors the Allies." [7]

In the spring of 1942, subversive operations in North Africa became the responsibility of the new Coordinator of Information. Two official Donovan representatives joined Murphy's conspiratorial team.

Lieutenant Colonel Robert Solborg was born in Warsaw, the son of a Polish general of the Czar's army who had served on the staff of the Russian governor-general of Poland. During the First World War Solborg was commissioned an officer in the Czarist cavalry. After recovering from a severe wound in 1916, he was assigned to a Russian military purchasing mission in New York.

When the Bolshevik Revolution brought the Soviets to power, Solborg, preferring to avoid a Communist firing squad, acquired American citizenship and enlisted in the American Army. He served briefly as U.S. Military Attaché in Paris, then accepted a position with Armco Steel. When the Second World War broke out in 1939, Solborg was managing director of Armco in Britain and France. Under cover of his business transactions, he traveled to Germany in the spring of 1940 to observe industrial production and later reported his findings to British intelligence. In December 1940, Solborg joined U.S. Army intelligence and spent the next eight months traveling through North Africa, ostensibly as an Armco executive but actually to contact potential French resistance elements on behalf of the War Department.

In October 1941, Donovan asked Solborg to head a Special Operations section of COI. The colonel was first sent to London to study the structure of the British Special Operations Executive (SOE), which had already accumulated a year's experience in working with anti-Axis resistance groups. Returning to Washington, he made a brief attempt to "reconcile" himself to the "haphazard way and stunt-like propensities of Donovan's procedures," then left for Portugal in February 1942 to establish a COI operations center in neutral Lisbon.[8] He was instructed to coordinate his activities with the British and with Murphy in secretly contacting French and Arab underground organizations.

Some months earlier, a second COI officer, Colonel William Eddy, had reached his post at the international zone of Tangier, adjacent to

neutral Spanish Morocco.[d] Born in Syria of missionary parents, Eddy
had been highly decorated for his World War I service as an army
intelligence officer. Turning to the academic world, he headed the
English Department at the American University in Cairo (where he
introduced basketball to the Egyptians), wrote a classic work on
Gulliver's Travels, then returned to the United States to become president of a small New York college. In 1941, he reentered military service
and was appointed U.S. naval attaché at Cairo. Donovan soon convinced
the colonel to leave this post to become the COI's man in Tangier. As
a former intelligence specialist with long experience in the Arab world,
he seemed an ideal choice as Murphy's collaborator in coordinating
subversive operations.

Eddy's first problem was with the British. London's diplomatic
representatives had long since been expelled from Vichy Africa, but
British secret agents (including a beautiful young blonde from His
Majesty's consulate at Tangier who "kept open bed" for notable
Spanish generals) remained active in the region. Unfortunately, the
chief of the British Secret Intelligence Service (MI-6) at Tangier, a
man "who would sell his country, his soul, or his mother for a peseta,"
was violently jealous of the Americans. He allegedly plotted to poison
his own assistant, a British major, for being "too straightforward" with
Donovan's officers.[9]

Eddy learned that other British agents of the Special Operations
Executive, based on Gibraltar, were planning to smuggle supplies on a
Portuguese ship to an underground group in Morocco. In February 1942,
Eddy went to "the Rock" and persuaded the SOE chief, a London
banker, to abandon his own plan in favor of the COI's projects.

Two American schemes emerged at this time. The first was a plot
to replace the pro-Vichy Arab Prime Minister at Tunis with an official
more favorable to the Allies. It was suggested that some members of
the old man's family might be bribed into staging a palace revolt. In
March, Donovan made fifty thousand dollars available for the plot,
but Murphy abruptly vetoed the idea. He knew that the French had
"jealously guarded their empire from any outsiders who might be disposed to meddle with the native populations"; and he had assured
Lemaigre's group that "we considered relations between France and

[d] Eddy was ambassador to Saudi Arabia, 1944–46, and head of State
Department Intelligence, 1946–47. Until his death in 1962, he was a Middle East consultant to the Arabian-American Oil Company and an official
of the CIA-funded American Friends of the Middle East.

the African peoples in French Africa to be purely an affair between them." Murphy was "shocked" by the COI plot. "Nothing," he concluded, "would have enraged our French colleagues more than this kind of monkey business, or been more ruinous to our chances of obtaining the support of French military forces." [10] In the coming months, a score of COI and OSS plans to "meddle with the native populations" (who outnumbered the French in North Africa by twelve to one) would be dealt a similar death blow by cautious diplomats.

Murphy favored a second project, put forward by Lemaigre, to bring about a revolution in the French colonial army and establish a pro-Allied provisional government in North Africa, secretly supported by American arms and money. Eddy and the underground leaders had drawn up a schedule of extensive armament requirements, and in March 1942 the colonel sent them on to Washington. Donovan was not impressed; he found the French requests for arms shipments "enormous and quite out of proportion to the projected operations." [11]

Eddy and Murphy pleaded that the French underground was the only source of opposition to the Axis in Vichy Africa. "We will not find such leaders elsewhere," Eddy cabled Donovan, "and we dare not lose them now. . . . They are taking all the risk; they will receive, distribute, and use the supplies, every step being taken with the threat of execution as traitors if they are uncovered. The least we can do is to help supply them on their own terms, which are generous and gallant." [12]

In April Eddy sent a new request for a half million dollars in operational funds and massive arms shipments, including thousands of motorcycles, planes, howitzers, tanks, and mines—enough to equip an entire army of liberation. The Lemaigre group had convinced the Americans of the urgency of the situation. French reports predicted a German invasion at any moment and Eddy dispatched a priority message to COI headquarters: "If Murphy and I cannot be trusted with a few million francs in an emergency then I should be called back and someone who can be trusted sent. . . . We have days before us, not weeks," he warned anxiously. "We are desperately hoping and waiting." [13]

In Washington, Donovan's aides shared Eddy's anxiety. "The war may be won or lost by our response to Colonel Eddy," wrote one COI planner, "and certainly the day of victory will be indefinitely advanced or retarded." [14] But the Joint Chiefs of Staff felt differently. The generals questioned the reliability of the Lemaigre group and suspected that materiel shipped to the French underground might end up in the hands of the Germans. On April 20 the Joint Chiefs decided against furnishing arms to the African conspirators, advising instead that funds should be "judiciously" expended in building up a guerrilla resistance group. This was a severe blow to the COI, but Donovan urged Eddy not to be discouraged. "If we are right," he wired the colonel with characteristic buoyancy, "it will work out right." [15]

That same month, events in France seemed to lend credence to Eddy's warning that the Germans might soon seize power in Africa. At Vichy, the notorious French demagogue Pierre Laval, a socialist-turned-fascist whose collaborationist views had been too extreme for even the Pétain government to stomach, was suddenly thrust into the political limelight. With Nazi support, Laval became Premier of the Vichy regime, replacing Admiral Darlan, who was shifted to the command of the French armed forces. Laval immediately introduced drastic measures against French Jews in the unoccupied zone, began sending French conscript labor to Germany, and called openly for a Nazi victory. The liberal outcry in America against continued diplomatic recognition of this regime now became a furor.

The State Department held fast. Ambassador Leahy was recalled to Washington to emphasize American displeasure with Laval, but diplomatic relations were not severed. A skeleton staff was still maintained in the American embassy at Vichy. The State Department could not tell the outraged American liberals that some of these remaining "diplomats" were, in reality, intelligence officers performing useful services for the Allies.

Not that the State Department emissaries were all that helpful in the conduct of COI espionage. Despite Donovan's vehement objections, Ambassador Leahy had prevented COI officers from sending "spy messages" under the "cloak of diplomatic immunity"; he believed that such communications would be a "serious reflection on our foreign service." [16] The ambassador had also been jittery about contacts with the burgeoning French resistance. Donovan's men were relieved when Leahy at last departed for Washington.

Thomas Cassady, a Chicago banker and personal friend of Navy Secretary Frank Knox, had first come to Vichy in January 1942 as a naval intelligence officer, transferring to the newly created OSS in June. Cassady was already in close communication with pro-Allied French intelligence officers when in early August (with no thanks to the State Department) he was joined by 32-year-old OSS Colonel Nicol

Smith. A graduate of Choate and Stanford, the wealthy and witty Smith had devoted his life to writing and lecturing about his travels to the most exotic parts of the world. Donovan had first asked that Smith be appointed a "cultural ataché" as a cover for his intelligence duties; the State Department informed OSS that all had been arranged. But in asking the Vichy embassy in Washington for its consent to this diplomatic appointment, a State Department official had virtually told the French outright that Smith would use his position as a screen for espionage! [17]

Colonel Smith reached France fearful that his cover had been "blown." "I feel," he wrote shortly after his arrival, "that I have been transported to Graustark or some other fabled kingdom. Vichy is mad. That is the Vichy one sees but there is another that lies just below the surface. On all sides are members of the German Gestapo. You find them at bars. They are seated next to you at the opera. . . . You expect to find them in your bed and perhaps you would not be far wrong. . . . Nearly every servant at the hotel is in the pay of either the Germans or the French. . . . I have received anonymous letters to have this or that place blown up. All sorts of traps have been prepared. Foreign ladies of a type never to have noticed me in the past, in fact of a type to have avoided me, now find me irresistible. I have met an enormous number of people and am asked out constantly to dine and to lunch. I drink two bottles of Vichy water a day to neutralize the effects of this generosity."

Smith found considerable pro-Allied sentiment in the unoccupied zone. Younger officials of the Foreign Ministry were happy to pass intelligence to the Americans. Resistance groups had organized and were "ready for the word to be given to commence active sabotage or whatever is asked of them." Many Frenchmen objected (though not too loudly) when Jewish émigrés were "rounded up and sent back into occupied territory," stuffed together "in boxcars under the most disgraceful conditions." Yet Smith also discovered a determined and sizable pro-fascist minority in the Vichy zone, "men who are not aristocrats but little capitalists and openly tell you that they prefer Germany to Russia. When you ask them why, they reply, 'The Russians are monsters and if they win, anarchy will prevail.' " [18]

The Vichy embassy in Washington proved another important source of intelligence. When one OSS officer suggested purloining the French military codes from the embassy safe in the spring of 1942, he was told that such measures were unnecessary. Excluding the Vichy ambassador and his aides, virtually the entire embassy staff—diplomats, secretaries, even janitors—were passing information to American and British intelligence agents. OSS had its own contacts at the embassy. One French military attaché provided such invaluable information that Donovan later requested a special Presidential dispensation allowing him to remain in the United States for the duration of the war.[19]

The most impressive body of French military intelligence was flowing into Washington from Murphy's Vice Consuls in Africa. Donovan told Cordell Hull in May 1942 that the war effort would suffer if these officers were not kept at their posts as intelligence observers. The War Department agreed. But the Joint Chiefs remained skeptical of the value of Murphy's resistance contacts and continued to oppose arms shipments to the Lemaigre group. The discouraged French soon returned to Murphy the operational funds advanced by Donovan and presented the Americans with an ultimatum: All plans for a coup would be abandoned if an American guarantee of military assistance were not received by May 20.

Eddy believed such assurances to the French to be all the more vital because the British remained perfectly willing to go their own way and begin arms shipments to Algeria. Between the British initiative and the French ultimatum, Eddy became disheartened and fell back on the old COI contingency plan—direct dealings with the Arabs. "With the hope of the French fading," he wrote Washington, "I propose to approach Moorish leaders in Spanish Morocco regarding future sabotage of the Axis." [20]

Then, quite suddenly, the French plan was revived. On May 22, after the expiration of the Lemaigre deadline, Murphy was delighted to see the French underground leaders again request COI funds. Given this respite, Eddy decided to go to Washington to personally support the underground's request for American equipment.

Why the French change of heart? Murphy explained in a mysterious note to Donovan's headquarters, "With a bit of luck and daring, I have developed a lead to the one remaining 'white hope' among French generals capable of getting France into the war again on our side and inviting us to occupy North Africa. Since the Weygand fiasco, my friends here are extremely chary in telling us things, and I had to give my officer's word that I would not pronounce the general's name to anybody except General Marshall. They are afraid that we would give him the same 'build up' we gave Weygand and thus blow him up promptly. Suffice it to say that he is in France and a very able rope climber for his age. 'Nuff said.' " [21]

The unnamed general was Henri Giraud, a 60-year-old military hero who had escaped from an "impregnable" German prison where he had been confined since the armistice (reportedly by climbing down a wire-filled rope smuggled to him in a bottle of jam). After successfully evading the Gestapo, Giraud had reached unoccupied France on April 27. The collaborationist Laval did his utmost to induce the general to return to captivity and placate the Germans, but without success. Instead, Giraud remained in Vichy territory under the wing of his friend, Marshal Pétain.

When he learned of Giraud's escape, Murphy's confidant, Lemaigre-Dubreuil, visited the general at Lyon in southern France on May 19 and found him already laying plans for an uprising against the Germans in metropolitan France. Lemaigre could not convince Giraud to abandon this idea in favor of a North African rebellion.

At this point, Colonel Solborg, Donovan's representative in Portugal, began to play an active part in the political intrigue. Solborg had grown impatient in his Lisbon office while Eddy and Murphy vainly pleaded for American arms. What the African underground needed, he concluded, was a prominent French figure to act as its leader. Solborg also had his eye on Giraud.

Without specifically informing Washington of his plans, Solborg secured Donovan's carte blanche approval to deal with the French "on a high plane." His first step was a trip to London to confer with de Gaulle and other exile figures. He was unimpressed by the Free French leader, but reported to Donovan that de Gaulle was "enthusiastic" about Giraud. According to the colonel's incredible report, the haughty French general had named Giraud as the one man whom he could accept as his superior; Solborg hastily decided that Giraud was the wave of the future.

The colonel's next move was impetuous. Since his arrival at Lisbon in February, he had not yet traveled to North Africa, and for good reason—the State Department had forbidden him to make the short journey, believing that his intelligence connection was known to the Germans and fearing that he might compromise Murphy's underground contacts. Without informing Donovan, but with the approval of Army intelligence in Washington, Solborg disregarded his COI orders and in early June crossed over from Lisbon to Tangier. Finding Colonel Eddy absent (he had already left for Washington), Solborg went on to Casablanca. There, at Murphy's behest, he met with Lemaigre.

The vegetable oil magnate proposed a plan "to set up temporary government in North Africa, money end to be cared for by lend lease." The Allies would arrange for some "provocatory action" by the Axis, giving the French an excuse to ask the United States "to send soldiers in order to protect the country." Lemaigre was confident that the French military forces in Africa, "in the mood they are now in, will be happy to carry out instructions" from the rebels.[22]

Solborg replied that no agreement would be possible "unless a leader could be produced" by the French "able to inspire our government and whose position is sufficiently important to ask our armed aid when the right time arrives." [23] Lemaigre claimed to be able to produce Giraud as figurehead of the African conspiracy and offered to travel to France at once to sound out the general. Solborg agreed to go to Algiers to await Lemaigre's return, and the Frenchman left for Vichy. After paying a courtesy call on Laval to maintain his public standing as a good collaborator, Lemaigre went on to Lyon to confer secretly with Giraud. The general still insisted on an uprising in metropolitan France, but he agreed to consider both plans. Giraud now began to dream of simultaneous revolts in France and Africa which would establish him as grand leader of a united French resistance.

While Lemaigre was in France, Solborg received an unexpected cable in Algiers. Donovan had just learned of the colonel's trip to North Africa, and on June 15 he wired Solborg, "It was agreed between us (you gave your promise) that no activities were to be carried on in North Africa. You are directed to stop immediately whatever you may be doing, go to Lisbon and await orders." [24] Solborg was "greatly depressed" and left immediately for Portugal. He then flew to Washington to report in person to Donovan.

On his arrival, Solborg found that the OSS chief was infuriated over his North African journey and would not even see him. He began to bombard Donovan with memoranda in the hope of salvaging his project. "No promises were made, nor hopes held out to the French in North Africa," insisted Solborg. "The general with whom I have been negotiating represents today the highest authority, overshadowing that of Weygand, de Gaulle, and everybody else. He is a fighting general and a true and patriotic Frenchman. . . . We must not let the big man down, for there is nobody else on whom we could depend." [25]

On one of the few occasions of the war, Donovan remained completely intransigent. He believed that the very future of OSS depended on its success in North Africa and he was unwilling to tolerate Solborg's insubordination. He dropped the colonel from the ranks of OSS and refused to pursue the matter further.[e]

By the time Solborg arrived in Washington to receive his chilly greeting at OSS headquarters, Colonel Eddy had already left the capital, after presenting an impressive progress report to the Joint Chiefs of Staff on June 10. He told the generals about Murphy's efficient intelligence network but laid greater emphasis on American contacts with the pro-Allied underground.

Relieved of his OSS Lisbon post by General Donovan, the still-proud Col. Robert Solborg (center), descendant of czarist generals, received a French military decoration in Casablanca after the Allied North African landings.

Eddy estimated that he and Murphy controlled a resistance force of ten thousand Arab irregulars in Morocco under special direction of two OSS men who had reached Tangier in May. These Arab experts, old college friends from Harvard days, were Carleton Coon, an anthro-

[e] Solborg remained in Lisbon for the duration of the war as U.S. military attaché. He held the same post in Brussels, 1945–48, then returned to Armco Steel as president of its European subsidiary until his retirement in 1959. He now represents a Canadian investment company in Paris.

pologist who had done an exhaustive study of the rebellious Riff tribes of
Morocco, and Boston insurance executive Gordon Browne, once resident
in Casablanca as a leather and wool exporter. Eddy neglected to mention that Coon and Browne had found their efforts blocked at every
turn. The entrenched Arab oligarchy played a wily political game and
was not prepared to risk its position of power on behalf of the Allies.
Worse yet, the State Department had ordered OSS to avoid all contact
with insurgent Arab groups; Murphy's French underground leaders were
"very touchy" and feared that the Americans "might try to turn the
Moors against them." [26]

OSS thus faced a wall of opposition when it proposed that the renowned Riff leader Abd-el-Krim be brought back from French-imposed
exile on Reunion Island to lead a revolt of 50,000 Moors in Spanish
Morocco if Franco should prove hostile to an Allied landing. The project
met a rapid demise. The War Department feared that a "Christian-
Moslem war" might result. Someone also recalled that Abd-el-Krim had
first been taken prisoner in 1926 by a French colonial colonel named
Henri Giraud. And Murphy was still reluctant to "play politics" with
the Arabs. One Vice Consul wrote: "We had no intention of making
trouble for the French. Whatever our private opinions, as Americans,
about imperialism, we were in North Africa as guests and really as
allies of the French people in all but name. We were not there to preach
democracy or independence." [27]

Colonel Eddy therefore stressed that the heart of the African
resistance was European, that the underground had the "finest kind of
leadership, in a separatist movement led by French patriots, some of
whom are Royalists." [28] The colonel warned that pro-Allied French officials were being replaced at an alarming rate by Laval's henchmen.
The whole movement, he said, was disintegrating because of lack of
Allied support. He proposed that arms be immediately smuggled to
Morocco under cover of a "seaweed salvage company." These weapons,
he stressed, would be useful in the event of an Allied landing.

Only when he returned to Tangier on July 11 did Eddy realize
the accuracy of his warning. In late June, the Vichy police in Morocco,
spurred on by the German Armistice Commission, had arrested 300
supporters of the underground. The purge had damaged a major portion
of the resistance movement beyond repair and strengthened the position
of the pro-Vichy French fascists.

Another disappointment followed. Murphy had received no word
from Solborg since the colonel had left Algiers for Lisbon. The French

were again becoming discouraged. Eddy and Murphy offered to provide the Lemaigre group with additional funds and with some small arms shipments from Gibraltar, but this was considerably less than the assistance of which Solborg had spoken. Neither Murphy nor Eddy knew that the unfortunate colonel had been ousted from his OSS position.

In an attempt to salvage the details of the Solborg-Lemaigre plan, Eddy went to London in late July. His original intent was to secure British aid for the venture. But while in the British capital, he came upon Colonel Edward Buxton, a New England textile manufacturer, prominent Republican stalwart, and Assistant Director of OSS. Buxton arranged a dinner party at which Eddy was to meet with Generals James Doolittle, George Patton, and George Strong, newly appointed chief of Army intelligence (and a bitter rival of Donovan). If Eddy could convince this group of hard-nosed military men of the value of his plan, he would then have a direct line to the War Department.

Dressed in Marine uniform, with five rows of World War I ribbons, and walking with a "noticeable limp from old wounds," Eddy's appearance provoked Patton's ribald remark, "The son of a bitch's been shot at enough, hasn't he?" [29] Even General Strong was impressed by Eddy's seemingly factual, detailed account of the French underground—its strength, organization, leadership, and potential. And all three took particular note of Eddy's conclusion: "If we sent an expeditionary force to North Africa, there would be only token resistance." [30]

The colonel returned to North Africa with the happy news that the OSS plans had been well received by the Army brass. Eddy flew back to London at the beginning of August with specific estimates of the pro-Allied French forces. Lemaigre left for France for further talks with Giraud. And Murphy himself was suddenly called back to Washington.

Murphy and Eddy were then told of a top secret decision by Anglo-American strategic planners. An invasion of North Africa would be launched before the end of the year under the command of General Dwight D. Eisenhower. Suddenly the OSS-Giraud conspiracy had become the backbone of the first major American offensive of the war.

In planning the invasion, political problems posed themselves immediately. Roosevelt secured Churchill's agreement that the landings, code-named TORCH, should be a predominantly American operation (with the United States handling the diplomatic aspects). The Presi-

dent and his advisors believed that anglophobic French commanders in
North Africa would offer less resistance to a landing led by American
troops with British forces remaining in the background.

At the secret service level, a similar agreement had been reached
in June 1942 as part of a comprehensive operational accord with the
British SOE, negotiated in London by OSS Colonels Preston Good-
fellow (the Brooklyn publisher who befriended Syngman Rhee) and
Garland Williams, an official of the New York Narcotics Commission.
In the first of several wartime delineations of "spheres of influence" for
clandestine activity, OSS took primary responsibility for subversion in
North Africa (as well as China, Korea, the South Pacific, and Finland).
The British, in turn, assumed temporary predominance in India, West
Africa, the Balkans, and the Middle East. Western Europe was con-
sidered joint territory.[31]

The question of Gaullist participation in the invasion was more
difficult to resolve. Earlier in the year, both Solborg and Eddy had
agreed to accept a Free French officer as liaison to the OSS mission
at Tangier. "In this way we should give satisfaction to the Free French,"
wrote Solborg, "thus pleasing de Gaulle, and at the same time completely control their activities in North Africa." This "slight concession"
would preempt independent Gaullist maneuvers, which "from a political
point of view might be undesirable." [32]

Solborg's departure from OSS spelled an end to this proposal. Instead, Washington was bombarded with reports from North Africa
warning that de Gaulle's forces (now known as the "Fighting French")
should be entirely excluded from TORCH, lest they force the Vichy
troops into open opposition to the landings. Eddy felt that the "highest,
military, diplomatic, and political influences should be brought to bear"
to prevent the Gaullists from joining the landing force. And Murphy,
prodded by Lemaigre, hinted that de Gaulle might be "capable of
treachery" if he were even informed of the plan.[33]

Washington took these suggestions seriously. For over a year, anti-
Gaullist sentiment had been building in the State Department and at
the White House. If OSS headquarters took a more objective view, it
was only because a determined faction of Gaullist admirers lingered
within the Donovan organization. The more vocal pro-Gaullists in COI
had not, unfortunately, survived the transition to OSS. Most of the
Free French enthusiasts in Robert Sherwood's propaganda branch
left OSS for the new Office of War Information. The first chief of the
COI Pictorial Records Division, former *Time* Paris correspondent Rich-

ard de Rochemont,[f] resigned from Donovan's agency to head "France Forever," the official group of Gaullist supporters in the United States. He later declined a position with the Secret Intelligence Branch of OSS because, he said, "I felt their French policy was not going to be fruitful." [34]

The remaining pro-Gaullists in OSS in the summer of 1942 were clearly in the minority. For the greater number of OSS officials, first contacts with de Gaulle's envoys had been disappointing. Donovan spoke to the President of the "deplorable condition of the whole Free French movement in this country," and OSS reports accurately characterized the Gaullist delegation in Washington as wracked by internal dissension, intrigue, and petty bickering. The delegation secretary even admitted to Allen Dulles (then head of the OSS office in New York) that the Gaullists were having difficulty in drawing many distinguished French exiles to their cause. "De Gaullism," declared one exiled French general to an OSS official, "is simply the expression of one man's ambition." [35]

Intelligence from France was often contradictory. Some OSS reports indicated that de Gaulle had considerable support among the French people. But other sources described the Gaullist movement as "infested with German spies," and the Fighting French leader was himself depicted as being "devoid of all aptitude as a statesman and a personality." [36] That impression was scarcely dispelled by the French general's ultra-nationalism and personal pretentiousness. The first London chief of OSS, William Phillips (a veteran diplomat who had served as American ambassador to Belgium, Canada, and Mussolini's Italy) remembered his first meeting with de Gaulle.

"I was struck," wrote Phillips, "by his appearance, and his coolness; he was way above average height, with a strikingly high and narrow head. He greeted me perfunctorily without the ghost of a smile. In his expressionless eyes I thought I saw myself reflected as a 'mere civilian,' while he was the foremost French leader. . . . Without preliminaries he mentioned the 'misunderstanding' which our continued diplomatic representation in Vichy was causing among the French people. In forcible French he said it was leading the French people to believe that America was condoning the German occupation of France. . . . I learned then and later that de Gaulle was never without complaints. But his principal grievance that day against Great Britain and the

[f] De Rochemont was producer of the "March of Time," 1943–52, and vice-president of the J. Walter Thompson Company, 1953–55.

United States was their failure to recognize his political as well as his
military leadership, in view of 'the fact,' as he called it, that ninety per
cent of the French people accepted him in both capacities. I realized
when I left him that he was a difficult man to deal with." [37]

The very fact that de Gaulle, in spite of his personal idiosyn-
cracies, had to be considered so seriously in Allied planning was evidence
of his growing strength as a symbol of the French resistance. During the
summer of 1942, the once obscure French general gained the allegiance
of the new civilian, politically motivated underground movements that
had grown up in the unoccupied zone of France.

Even the anti-Gaullist State Department accepted this fact and
made arrangements for consultation and cooperation between the American military authorities in London and the Fighting French. But de
Gaulle was disappointed when no further official recognition was forthcoming. He bitterly complained to a State Department representative
that Washington's entire Vichy policy was "badly inspired" by Admiral
Leahy and General Donovan, who were "well intentioned but mistaken." [38]

Whatever Donovan's personal feelings about de Gaulle, he made
no attempt to prevent some of his key subordinates from establishing
close working relations with the Fighting French. The first OSS Secret
Intelligence chief in London, Whitney Shepardson,[g] was considered "a
friend" by André Dewavrin, who headed de Gaulle's secret service.
Shepardson, a Rhodes scholar, graduate of Harvard Law School, executive of the Council on Foreign Relations, and an experienced international businessman, had been deeply involved in world affairs since
his attendance at the Versailles Peace Conference of 1919. He was a
"large, strong man, prudent and reflective" who often admitted to Dewavrin that the State Department erred in refusing to recognize de
Gaulle as the "uncontestable chief" of a unified French resistance.[39]

The Gaullists found an even more dedicated champion in W. Arthur Roseborough, a 42-year-old lawyer who headed the Western Europe
desk of the OSS Secret Intelligence Branch in Washington. Roseborough was also a Rhodes scholar, a former legal secretary to Frank
Kellogg at the World Court; for over a decade he had worked as an
attorney in the Paris office of Sullivan and Cromwell, the Dulles brothers'
law firm. He "spoke French admirably," recalled Dewavrin. "He had

[g] Shepardson was director of the Carnegie Corporation's British Do-
minions and Colonies Fund, 1946–53, and president of the CIA-funded
Free Europe Committee, 1953–56.

lived in Paris for many years and adored our country. His greatest desire was to return there as soon as the 'boche' had been chased away. . . . He understood us perfectly and quickly realized that our ideas on the organization and potential of the resistance were exact. He also understood the force that General de Gaulle represented vis-à-vis France and he showed particular disappointment in seeing the United States engage in a policy which could only bring hopeless divisions and difficulties. Not only did he understand our chief, but he said so, perhaps even with too much fervor and conviction. . . . I found in him a loyal and brilliant friend." [40]

The Gaullist officers in London frequently introduced Roseborough and Shepardson to agents recently returned from occupied France. In June 1942, the Americans also met one of the top leaders of the French resistance movement, Emmanuel d'Astier de la Vigerie, secretly exfiltrated to London by the SOE. D'Astier, the product of a distinguished French noble family, was leftist in his politics and committed to Gaullism. At the urging of Roseborough and other friendly OSS men he was flown to Washington in an attempt to convince American officials that the underground in the Vichy unoccupied zone was united in its recognition of de Gaulle's leadership. Though he encountered some interest at OSS headquarters, D'Astier discovered, to his disappointment, that State Department officers considered him "a sort of little highland chieftain who had been seduced by an adventure and by a symbol." [41]

D'Astier's visit led to a special London conference in early September 1942 between OSS representatives and other delegates of resistance groups who had been smuggled out of France for the purpose. These underground leaders of southern France were united in their denunciation of the Vichy regime and anyone connected with it. They declared that the French people would never support Pétain, Laval, or even Giraud (whom they described as a "pure Fascist"). They told the Americans that resistance groups of both political left and right "accepted de Gaulle as their leader" and "would work unitedly in their resistance efforts under his direction."

The OSS negotiators concluded that the Gaullist movement was, unquestionably, "the most powerful in France." Roseborough went one step further. He told Donovan after the September conference that de Gaulle, more than any other man, had become "*the* symbol of French resistance," that there was "a very serious risk that the leaders of the best organized resistance groups would look upon any movement led by Giraud, or other generals who have 'ridden along' with Vichy, as merely representing the Vichy ideology under a somewhat different cloak—an attempt to save the regime and maintain its elements in power." [42] Roseborough recommended that OSS should begin to actively support and supply the Gaullists, while seeking to reconcile the Fighting French with Giraud's following. His suggestion was supported by the OSS Planning Staff (headed by Kenneth Hinks, former European director of the J. Walter Thompson Advertising Agency). But the idea was tabled. Churchill and Roosevelt had already agreed that the Gaullists should not be included in the landing force. Responding to Admiral Leahy's allegations of lax security within the Fighting French organization, Roosevelt even insisted that de Gaulle should not be informed of the TORCH plans until after the landings had already begun.

Throughout the war, the Gaullists suffered from this reputation for inefficient security measures. ("You put three Frenchmen and a bottle of whiskey in the same room," wrote one OSS operative. "Then all you have to do is sit back and take mental notes until the bottle is finished. With the emptying of the bottle their supply of information will be as clean as their bottles.") [43] One particular incident marred the pre-TORCH plans of OSS for cooperation with the Fighting French. Since the earlier proposal of Colonel Solborg to attach a Gaullist officer to the OSS team at Tangier, de Gaulle's aides had frequently requested the dispatch of one of their men to North Africa. The arrangements were finally made, with OSS assistance, and the Gaullist officer left London in a British plane. But the aircraft crashed or was shot down over Spain, the Frenchman was killed, and his papers, which contained highly classified information, were seized by the Spanish police (and undoubtedly made available to the Germans). The episode led to severe criticism of the security of the Gaullist secret service.[44] And the plans of Shepardson and Roseborough met a quiet death, drowned in frantic arrangements for the coming invasion.

Preparations for TORCH were in full swing. Colonel Eddy went to Washington to present a preliminary plan for OSS subversive action on D-Day, and Donovan set aside two million dollars for these secret maneuvers. ("Donovan did not seem to be short of money!" quipped Admiral Leahy.) [45] Most of Eddy's suggestions were approved by the Joint Chiefs on September 11 with the proviso that control of all secret activities should be vested in the Supreme Commander, General Eisenhower.

Eddy and Donovan discovered, however, that Eisenhower's staff planners showed no sympathy for unorthodox clandestine operations. OSS had proposed that members of the Nazi military staff in North Africa (many of them Gestapo officers) be assassinated when the landings began. The assignment for this cold-blooded task had already been accepted by the father of a French boy shot by the Germans in Paris. Eisenhower's aides did not take the suggestion seriously and it was "squashed at a higher level." (Eddy was forced to fall back on a contingency plan; a British-educated black African, who quoted Shakespeare in clipped, elegant English, agreed to drop Mickey Finns into the drinks of local German officials.)[46]

Eddy had also arranged to smuggle out of Morocco two experienced hydrographers (one the captain of a tugboat company, the other chief pilot of Port Lyautey) who were familiar with the North African coastline. These men could accompany the landing force and guide it safely to the selected landing points. The hydrographers were met, upon their arrival in London, by angry British intelligence men, who accused Eddy of "unauthorized body-snatching." Eisenhower demanded to know why OSS had taken this action without his approval. A short investigation revealed that the project had been eagerly approved by General Patton, who had neglected to inform Eisenhower's staff. It was a foreboding sign of the lack of coordination that would soon engulf the entire TORCH operation.[47]

Leaving Eddy to plot subversion in Tangier, Murphy had come to Washington in late August for conferences with Roosevelt and the Joint Chiefs of Staff. The diplomat first appeared at OSS headquarters and Donovan assigned one of his assistants, 35-year-old Edmond Taylor, a journalist of Missouri French ancestry, to assist Murphy in preparing his operational plan for the President.[h] Paris correspondent for the Chicago *Tribune* before the war, and the author of an authoritative study of Nazi psychological warfare in France, Taylor was already an experienced in-fighter, having spent years in bitter ideological disputes with his newspaper's renowned isolationist publisher. He had originally joined the Sherwood branch of COI, but he remained with OSS when the propaganda group departed.

Murphy's plans for an uprising of the North African underground under Giraud's command "fired my imagination," Taylor recalled. The

[h] Taylor was a staff writer for the *Reporter* until the demise of that journal in 1968. He is now a freelance writer living in France.

liberal journalist would have preferred that the Gaullists "be more closely associated with the scheme," but he remained silent, "knowing from bitter experience the almost hysterical anti-Gaullism prevalent in the State Department and the White House." [48] His silence would soon be broken.

At his meeting with the President, Murphy told Roosevelt that the French administration, army, and police would cooperate with the landing forces in Algeria and Morocco—if there were no Gaullist or British participation, if the Giraud-Lemaigre group were recognized as the provisional government of North Africa, and if the administration of the colonies were left entirely in French hands. Roosevelt accepted these conditions as a reasonable exchange for the peaceful "deliverance" of North Africa to the Allies.[49]

In mid-September Murphy left Washington for London, traveling incognito and carrying a draft directive from the President appointing him Eisenhower's political advisor. Murphy was also placed in charge of all OSS activities. Eddy was to be titular OSS chief and a member of Eisenhower's staff at Gibraltar, but would actually take his instructions from Murphy in Algiers by secret radio.

Murphy returned to North Africa in October and set the underground activity in motion.[50] The Vice Consuls prepared voluminous reports on harbors and beaches and other aspects of the landing operations, and kept the German and Italian military staffs at Casablanca and Algiers under close surveillance. The French underground was now informed that an invasion was imminent, although they were not yet told the specific date for D-Day.

As Lemaigre and his associates made preparations to bring Giraud from his residence in France to Algiers, an unexpected figure appeared on the scene. Representatives of Admiral Jean Darlan—the renowned exponent of Vichy collaboration with the Nazis—hinted to Murphy that their man might be willing to shift his allegiance to the Allies. These advances could not be taken lightly. Darlan was commander of all Vichy armed forces and had special influence with the French Navy, which was expected to present the principal opposition to the landing forces. In Algiers and London, the name of Darlan was conjured with as a drastic alternative to Giraud.

The Americans began to question the viability of Giraud's "leadership" after a secret conference held in Algeria at the end of October. Responding to the requests of Giraud's military representatives for a strategic meeting, a group of American staff officers headed by Eisenhower's deputy, General Mark Clark, was transported by submerged submarine to the Algerian coast.[i] The team waded ashore by nightfall in small boats to be met on the beach by Murphy and Vice Consul Ridgeway Knight,[j] a former executive of Cartier's, born and educated in Paris. Clark and his men then met with French officers at a nearby villa to discuss plans for the landings.

At this conspiratorial assembly, Giraud's representatives first set forth new conditions for his participation—he was to be given supreme command of TORCH and a simultaneous military uprising was to take place in Vichy France with the support of Allied troops. Clark ruled out a second landing immediately, but hedged on the command question, leaving this for Eisenhower to settle personally with Giraud. Like Murphy, Clark was under orders not to divulge the date of the landings to the French. But on the very day of the conference, October 23, the first slow convoys of TORCH troops set out for Algiers and Casablanca. Not until November 5 were the French at last informed that D-Day had been set for November 8, only three days hence. The flabbergasted French asked for a postponement. Eisenhower wired his refusal.

The underground tried to make the best of things. Giraud was secretly taken out of France by submarine and transferred to a flying boat. He did not reach Gibraltar until the late afternoon of November 7, only hours before the landing. The weary general was greeted by Eisenhower and OSS Major Leon Dostert.[k] A Frenchman by birth, Dostert had come to the United States for academic studies and remained as a French instructor at Georgetown University. He had applied for American citizenship after the fall of France and was recruited by OSS as an assistant to Arthur Roseborough on the French SI desk. Unlike Roseborough, Dostert was a vocal critic of the Gaullists, a fact known to State Department officials, who seconded Dostert to Eisenhower's staff as an interpreter for Giraud.

But Dostert's presence did not ease Eisenhower's dealings with the stubborn Giraud. The French general might have been flown to Algiers

[i] In 1955, Clark headed an Intelligence Task Force of the Hoover Commission charged with reviewing the organization and operations of CIA. Clark's group recommended that more military officers be brought into the Agency.

[j] Knight served as ambassador to Syria, 1961–65, and ambassador to Belgium, 1965–69; he is presently ambassador to Portugal.

[k] Dostert was director of the Interpreters Division of the United Nations, 1946–47, and later chairman of the Department of Linguistics at Occidental College.

in time to see the Allied forces disembark, but instead he chose to resume his demands for supreme command of TORCH and an immediate Allied invasion of France. Six hours of argument were to no avail. Giraud would not cooperate.

Meanwhile, the TORCH fleet appeared off the coasts of Morocco and Algeria. "We come among you," began an Allied broadcast taped by Roosevelt in Washington, "to repulse the cruel invaders who would remove forever your rights of self-government, your rights to religious freedom, and your rights to live your own lives in peace and security." [51]

The OSS-directed underground moved into action. In Morocco, the pro-Allied French Army commander arrested the Vichy governor. In Algiers, despite the failure of OSS to supply cases of Sten guns, revolvers, and plastic explosive, as Murphy had promised, several hundred young supporters of the underground (many of them pro-Gaullist) seized the key positions in the city and awaited the arrival of American troops.

But the GI's were late. On both the Moroccan and Algerian coasts, the British Navy landed their American passengers at the wrong spots and the soldiers did not reach their destination until hours later. Before the troops could arrive, the pro-Allied general in Morocco was arrested by Vichy police. So were the young French patriots in Algiers. The plans for a peaceful landing collapsed as American forces encountered active opposition from the French. Men were dying on the landing crafts, on the beaches, and in the streets.

In the midst of this disaster, who should appear in Algiers but the Vichy collaborator Admiral Darlan. Informed of Darlan's presence, Murphy was faced with a dilemma—Americans and Frenchmen were slaughtering each other and Giraud was not even on the scene. When Giraud, after a change of heart, finally arrived in Algiers, 36 hours late, Murphy discovered that he could not command the support of the pro-Vichy commanders who had already overwhelmed the insurgents. In desperation, the diplomat turned to Darlan, who still spoke with the "legal authority" of the Pétain regime.

The admiral stalled while the senseless massacre continued and Nazi troops poured into Tunisia in the east to resist an Allied advance. After further contretemps (and secret encouragement from Pétain) Darlan agreed on the afternoon of November 8 to authorize a cease-fire in Algiers. Theatening and cajoling Darlan, General Mark Clark finally persuaded him to issue a similar order to halt the fighting in the re-

mainder of French Africa on November 10. Darlan agreed to act only
after hearing the news from Europe—the Nazis had violated their
armistice agreement and invaded the unoccupied Vichy zone of metropolitan France.

In return for Darlan's cooperation, Murphy and Clark agreed that
he should assume political authority in North Africa as a "representative" of Pétain (who publicly repudiated his fellow collaborator). The
Americans also gave assurances that the anti-Vichy French officers who
had aided Murphy during the landings would be branded as traitors and
deprived of their commands. Through all this, Giraud stood by, vacillat-
ing, refusing to assault Darlan's authority. His silence was rewarded
with a nominal post as commander of the French forces in North
Africa.

As the most reactionary French generals flocked to Darlan, the in-
delicate General Clark assembled Allied reporters in Algiers on November 12 and announced that the "yellow-bellied sons of bitches" had
come to terms. Fighting ceased in Morocco and Algeria. In Tunisia,
French resistance came too late. The Germans had already taken the
colony and it would be six months and thousands of lives later before
Eisenhower could recapture it. In three days of senseless fighting, 1400
Americans and 700 Frenchmen had died. One Vice Consul suggested
that the French troops had "fought as soldiers, in a tradition of great
discipline, and were delighted to have lost." [52]

The last week of November, Admiral Jean François Darlan was
officially installed as French High Commissioner of North Africa. This
American "deal with Darlan" unleashed a new wave of liberal criticism
in the United States. Under public pressure, Roosevelt declared that the
political policy of Murphy, Clark, and Eisenhower in North Africa was
"only a temporary expedient, justified solely by the stress of battle." No
"permanent arrangement," insisted the President, would be made with
the pudgy little admiral.[53]

Yet as the New Year approached, American acquiescence in Darlan's continued rule became increasingly embarrassing. Allied correspondents in Algiers reported in devastating detail the true conditions
of life under the Darlan regime—Jews still persecuted under anti-semitic
Vichy decrees that remained in force, concentration camps still filled
with political prisoners, fascist political groups still allowed to flourish.
No attempt had been made to expunge reactionary elements from the
government bureaucracy. The Vichy-appointed generals of Darlan's

"Imperial Council" who had openly resisted the TORCH landings freely declared their intention to recreate an authoritarian Pétain regime-in-miniature at Algiers.[54]

These conditions met with meager objection from either the American military authorities or Roosevelt's "personal representative," Robert Murphy. Nor did the formal OSS organization offer vocal criticism of American policy. When Colonel Eddy was named official OSS commander in the North African Theater in late November, he noted that "the general future for our sort of work is obscure." [55] Eddy knew that an independent OSS organization could only function through the good will of Robert Murphy, and he obligingly co-opted many of Murphy's Vice Consuls as his OSS aides. Some of these men bemoaned the effects of the Darlan accord in alienating the anti-Vichy underground with which they had worked for the past year.[56] But there was little fervor in their protests.

More heated criticism came from a small group of American officials in Algiers attached to the Anglo-American Psychological Warfare Branch (PWB) of Eisenhower's headquarters. Included in this group was OSS officer Edmond Taylor, the Chicago journalist who had assisted Murphy four months before in drafting his operational memo for the President. Donovan had sent Taylor to London in late September to represent him on the interallied subcommittee charged with planning the political warfare aspects of the invasion. This group was later enlarged to form the PWB, a team of 60 British and American propaganda specialists who reached Gibraltar in time "to see the vanguard of the invasion armada steam through the straits in the November dusk." Two days after the Clark-Darlan agreement, the PWB descended on Algiers under the formal command of a professional American Army colonel who had the "foredoomed mission" of keeping his liberal journalists "inside the bounds of official orthodoxy." [57] Taylor, with simulated OSS colonel's rank, was officially chief of the intelligence section of PWB. Unofficially, he was looked upon by his PWB colleagues from the Office of War Information as an *eminence grise* of the anti-Darlan movement within the American bureaucracy.

The PWB was rapidly transformed into a haven for American critics of the Darlan compromise. "The moral havoc wrought by the accord," Taylor recalls, "was extreme, and though I could not share the indignation of those who felt the most betrayed by it, I found their sense of betrayal all too understandable." [58] PWB officers openly proclaimed their sympathy for Gaullism; some wore the Cross of Lorraine in their lapels. And Taylor and his officers sought out the Frenchmen of the anti-Vichy underground to assure them that not all American officials had abandoned them for the sake of political expediency.

The Lemaigre clique of the pre-TORCH underground had, of course, been disappointed by the turn of events, but they remained in the background as "advisors" to the unhappy General Giraud, hoping for a change in the political wind. A more disaffected segment of anti-Vichy French rallied around a "colorful and attractive, if anachronistic figure, half crusader, half condottiere," [59] the peculiar Henri d'Astier de la Vigerie. A 42-year-old officer of French intelligence at Algiers, Henri was the brother of Emmanuel d'Astier, the Gaullist resistance leader who had toured Washington earlier that year. Unlike his Socialist brother, Henri was a monarchist and allegedly a former supporter (like Lemaigre) of the prewar Cagoule conspiracy. He was somehow able to reconcile these political passions of the right with a sympathy for de Gaulle and the Fighting French.

D'Astier was named chief of the Algiers police under the Darlan administration, but at the same time he remained leader of a politically alienated underground. His following was difficult to label. It included a minority of dedicated, liberal supporters of de Gaulle, most of them young, some with Communist sympathies. But a more important faction of the disenchanted were monarchists dedicated to the Comte de Paris, the Bourbon Pretender to the French "throne."

These unhappy Frenchmen found a sympathetic ear at the Psychological Warfare Branch. The PWB had taken up offices at the Hotel de Cornouailles in the center of Algiers and its activities went far beyond official duties of propaganda and censorship. PWB headquarters became a rallying point for d'Astier's unhappy Gaullists of all political hues. "Though it was no part of my official duties," writes Taylor, "I decided to appoint myself a sort of unofficial liaison officer to this group, to listen sympathetically to their grievances, and to do what little I could to obtain redress for them." [60]

Taylor's first opportunity came on December 6, when twenty-two young Gaullists were ordered arrested by Darlan's police for painting "Vive Roosevelt, à bas Darlan" and similar slogans on the walls of Algiers. Four of these fugitives fled to PWB headquarters to appeal for American protection. Taylor's solution, effected "arbitrarily and illegally," was to have the young men taken into the custody of American military police. They were thus saved from "a long, harsh term of imprisonment in a penitentiary controlled by unreconstructed Vichyite officials." [61]

A similar technique was employed by PWB when the French administration refused to take action against outright fascist sympathizers, some of them German agents, who walked the streets of Algiers unmolested. The PWB officers ordered American military police to intern the more blatant fascist politicians and pro-Nazi journalists. When the MPs failed to act, Taylor's men carried out their own arrests, without warrants, in the best "Chicago gangster style" (to quote a Gaullist admirer).[62] Eisenhower's Allied Force Headquarters was perturbed by these arrests; one PWB officer was declared personna non grata in Algiers by his own military command. Eisenhower later remarked that the PWB had given him more trouble than all the Germans in Africa.[63]

In mid-December two young Gaullists came to PWB headquarters with information that Henri d'Astier was involved in a conspiracy to replace Darlan with the royalist Comte de Paris as head of a new French provisional government. Taylor's informants believed that d'Astier might even promote an armed coup d'état to achieve his aims. They noted that the Comte de Paris had already arrived secretly in the city. Taylor warned Murphy, but the diplomat seemed unconcerned.

On December 24, 1942, Admiral Darlan was shot and fatally wounded in his office by a 20-year-old royalist, Fernand Bonnier de la Chapelle. Condemned to death by a hastily summoned court-martial, the assassin was rushed before a firing squad on the morning of December 26. All appeals for clemency had been denied by the new High Commissioner for North Africa—General Henri Giraud, elected soon after the assassination by Darlan's "Imperial Council" (with the heavy-handed backing of Washington).[64]

A wave of suspicion swept Algeria in the week that followed. Some Washington officials were convinced that the Gaullists had plotted the assassination. Chapelle was linked to d'Astier, and it was remembered that a third d'Astier brother, a Gaullist general, had come to Algiers only days before, carrying the sum of $35,000, allegedly to help organize the Fighting French movement in North Africa. Chapelle was also revealed to be a member of the pro-Gaullist Corps Franc d'Afrique, a new commando unit formed under the direction of OSS Arab specialist and Harvard anthropologist Carleton Coon. Colonel Eddy hastily dispatched Coon to the Tunisian front before he too could be accused of collusion in the murder. The Vichy and Nazi press soon announced that the affair had been planned by British intelligence agents; Churchill urged Eisenhower to blame the assassination on German spies.

But the really tragic aftermath of the Darlan murder was an unexpected resurgence of Vichy repression. Giraud placed one of the most reactionary generals of the pre-TORCH regime in charge of the investigation of Darlan's death, and this man used his position to persecute the leaders of the Algiers Gaullist underground.

On the evening of December 29, an American officer of the PWB rushed to the Hotel de Cornouailles to announce heatedly, "They've arrested all our friends!" Squads of Vichy police had seized top Gaullist leaders at their homes, handcuffed them, and whisked them out of the city at gunpoint. The incredible charge: an alleged conspiracy to assassinate Giraud and Murphy.

The prisoners, Taylor learned, were being taken to a concentration camp 150 miles to the south of Algiers, later to be transferred to a penal colony in the Sahara desert. American officers feared they might never reach their final destination, that they would be tried by a summary court-martial and quickly executed. The PWB men protested through "every bureaucratic channel, political and military, formal and informal, in a vain attempt to make AFHQ realize the catastrophic effect on world opinion if we tolerated this vindictive Vichy counteroffensive against the underground allies who had risked their lives in our common cause a few weeks earlier." [65]

In desperation, Taylor again used his "nonexistent authority" to telephone the commander of the American military police at a checkpoint through which the prisoner convoy had to pass. He demanded that the group be intercepted on its way south and detained on the pretext that a group of pro-Allied sympathizers had been kidnapped by "German agents" dressed as French police. The MP's responded and set up an improvised roadblock of army trucks. But it was too late. All but the last carful of prisoners in the convoy had already passed the outpost.

The last vehicle was detained, however, and the French guards were watched by American soldiers armed with submachine guns while the Gaullist prisoners phoned PWB headquarters. "Don't worry," Taylor assured his friends. "Murphy will not allow the United States to be mixed up in this matter." [66] The American authorities, said Taylor, would secure their freedom.

Hours went by. In Algiers, Taylor finally reached Murphy at Allied headquarters and explained the situation. Surely the President's rep-

resentative would not permit these men, his faithful aides before the
landings, to be arrested on the pretext that they had designs on his life?
To Taylor's amazement, Murphy replied that he was sorry, but he could
not interfere in an internal French matter.

In the days that followed, Taylor pleaded with other American
officials to intervene on behalf of the prisoners, but the response was
always negative. As Taylor put it: "The more diplomatic of my interlocutors sometimes expressed a mild, humanitarian concern, counter-
balanced by a reluctance to interfere in 'a purely French domestic affair,' but others made no effort to conceal their spite. Those Gaullist
troublemakers and conspirators, it seemed, were no better than enemy
agents. They were against United States policy in North Africa, therefore they were sabotaging the Allied war effort. Whatever was being
done to them, it served them right. Darlan had been our son-of-a-bitch,
and Giraud was now, and whoever was against an officially approved
son-of-a-bitch must ipso facto be against us." [67]

The Hotel de Cornouailles, PWB headquarters, then became a
sectarian sanctuary for the politically dispossessed of "liberated" North
Africa. Gaullists being hunted by the police hid in the closets of American officers. Some were even smuggled onto British ships leaving for
London (there to join the Fighting French). Taylor and his men
frantically collected weapons from the homes of Gaullist underground
leaders. The arms had first come from Murphy and the OSS for use
during the TORCH landings. But under a Giraud decree their possession by French civilians was technically illegal; the owners risked heavy
prison sentences.

One of the refugees who fled to the hotel was Henri d'Astier. The
Algiers police chief had learned that his own police agents were looking for him with orders to shoot on sight. Taylor calmed the hysterical
royalist-Gaullist and then provided him with a PWB jeep to take him
to the cathedral for mass (he was devoutly Catholic, the nephew of a
Cardinal), "just to make sure there was no mishap on the way." Two
weeks later, d'Astier was finally arrested and charged with complicity
in the murder of Darlan.[68]

Taylor had meanwhile contracted pneumonia and was confined
to a sickbed. His room was nonetheless frequented by "French and
American fellow conspirators who came to report the latest inhumanity,
the latest injustice, the latest absurdity committed in poor Giraud's
name, or to seek a redress that I was less than ever able to obtain." [69]
Sympathetic British officers arrived to complete a perfunctory investiga-

tion and then to clear Taylor of charges that he had been harboring suspects wanted by the French police.

On the evening of December 31, 1942, New Year's Eve, all the Gaullists in Algiers (all who were not in prison) congregated at PWB Headquarters with their American and British friends. "The evening was a merry one. At midnight all the guns in Algiers went off, the machine guns fired a round and multicolored rockets burst from the nearby slopes. The white town was lit up by converging tracer bullets of the anti-aircraft units and all the sirens of the ships in the port simultaneously broke the silence of the night." [70] At the Hotel de Cournouailles, the deafening noise of war machines was drowned out as American and British officers joined French patriots in singing a chorus of the "Marseillaise."

Several thousand miles away in Washington, another New Year's celebration was under way at the White House. For entertainment, the President had chosen a new film which would soon break all box office records in the United States. Millions of Americans would be captivated by this romance starring Humphrey Bogart and Ingrid Bergman, which was also, ironically, an unabashed condemnation of Vichy France and a glorification of the Gaullist resistance. For Franklin Roosevelt, the movie held a deeper significance. It was titled *Casablanca*.[71]

Scamporino for a parachute mission into Italy. Tompkins spoke Italian fluently and was thoroughly familiar with the political atmosphere of the country, where his family had lived as expatriates before the war. In 1939, fresh from studies at Harvard, Columbia, and the Sorbonne, he had been a foreign correspondent in Rome for the New York *Herald Tribune.*

Though his parents had been on intimate terms with most of the royal entourage of Victor Emmanuel, Tompkins' own sympathies lay with the democratic left of the anti-fascist movement. He was also willing to work with the Communists in fighting fascism. In Tunisia, he met an Italian Communist exile who agreed to infiltrate Naples and provide the Allies with military intelligence through his party's underground network. But the British SOE vetoed the plan. Through the months of July and August 1943, SOE consistently delayed Tompkins' own infiltration into Italy as well. "The British," he concluded, "were loath to let an American agent into what they considered their own sphere of influence." [6]

As OSS officers nervously awaited the Salerno landing, Badoglio's representatives finally agreed to Italy's desertion of her Axis partner. On September 8, Eisenhower announced that the Italian government had signed an armistice. The following day, Anglo-American forces commanded by General Mark Clark landed at Salerno. They encountered heavy opposition from German units who rushed toward the beachhead. Neither Badoglio nor the King said a word to the Italian Army about opposing the Wehrmacht.

When an OSS team commanded by Russian émigré Colonel Serge Obolensky parachuted to the island of Sardinia on September 13 to bring Badoglio's surrender message to the commander of the Italian garrison, they found 270,000 Italian troops standing by idly as 19,000 German soldiers withdrew. Obolensky "could not blame" the Italians. "They had been fighting alongside the Germans every step of the way. Now they were suddenly expected to turn against them. Little wonder that the morale of the entire Italian army was affected as the news spread like wildfire." [7]

Other Allied observers were less understanding as they saw German units on the mainland moving south to oppose the Allied landings with little opposition from confused Italian troops who had been given no orders to resist. The King and the royal family, trailed by the Italian High Command, fled Rome for the safety of the Allied lines, leaving the Holy City defenseless. The King withheld any statement about opposition to the Germans until days later, when he was safely ensconced far to the south at the eastern port of Brindisi. Scattered army units in Rome, left without leadership or directives, joined ill-equipped leftist partisans in battling crack German paratroops. As the King and Badoglio made good their escape, the revitalized underground—members of six anti-fascist political parties—formed a Committee of National Liberation (CLN) and issued a general call for insurrection. Their cause was doomed. A day later, Rome and all of northern and central Italy surrendered to the Germans.

At Salerno, Clark's forces had barely established a beachhead when two OSS groups joined the assault. At the last moment, Peter Tompkins was attached to a special OSS naval team that accompanied the landing forces in a high-speed British motorboat. The commander of this "MacGregor" unit, 28-year-old Republican Party publicity director John Shaheen,[g] had joined New York journalist Marcello Girosi [h] in hatching a wild OSS plot to reach the Italian Naval Command and convince the admirals to turn their fleet over to the Allies. No one bothered to inform Shaheen that the main body of the Italian navy, by previous secret agreement, had already sailed from Genoa to surrender to the British at Malta.[8]

The OSS men under Downes's command had also waded ashore at Salerno and were hurriedly assigned to gather combat intelligence at the front for Darby's Rangers. Downes established his special detachment headquarters in an Amalfi hotel that had once served as a monastery and began filling a flood of requests for information about opposing German units.

Two weeks later, General Donovan appeared in Amalfi to inspect the 90-man detachment. He joined Downes on a short jaunt to the Isle of Capri, just across the bay from beleaguered Naples, which was still in German hands. On the way, Downes learned of Donovan's plans for OSS reorganization. Colonel Eddy had taken ill and would be replaced by a new commander in Algiers, a West Point colonel who would have overall control of Italian operations. Another colonel, Ellery Huntington, Jr., a Wall Street attorney (and All-American Yale quarterback in 1913), was to become commander of the OSS detachment at Mark Clark's headquarters. Downes would remain in Italy as chief of

[g] Shaheen is now president of several international oil companies and a large contributor to Republican Party campaign coffers.

[h] Since the 1950s, Girosi has been the producer of Italian and American movies starring Sophia Loren.

counter-intelligence only. Finally, the general added, all future Italian operations were to be governed by an order written at the "highest political level." OSS would only be permitted to work with or recruit Italians who pledged their loyalty to the King.

Downes was irate. He told Donovan point-blank that he would not serve under Huntington, "a good-natured incompetent, but a man politically important in New York." [9] (Huntington had reportedly been a key fund-raiser for Donovan's gubernatorial campaign in 1932). Nor could he accept the political directive. "How," he asked the general, "could we betray all the Italian democrats, almost to a man rabidly anti-House of Savoy, by insisting that they swear allegiance to the ridiculous little king who had saddled them with fascism and thumped for Mussolini until military defeat was inevitable?" [10]

The conversation was interrupted by their arrival at Capri. The "MacGregor" team was already there, plotting a new daredevil operation to rescue an Italian scientist and admiral from behind the German lines. The whole island was peaceful, isolated from the nearby war. "Elegant ladies in sun suits and big hats strolled about followed by their little dogs and gigolos. The smart hotels were open and at cafe tables the indolent conversation of the idle rich was to be heard." [11] Caught up in this unreal atmosphere, Donovan announced that his first interest was to visit the villa of Mona Williams, a prominent New York socialite and wife of a multi-millionaire utilities magnate (who had made the second largest contribution to Donovan's 1932 campaign).[12] The general had promised to protect her spacious resort home from being "ruined by a lot of British enlisted personnel." He assigned the task to Downes, who replied curtly, "I don't want to fight a war protecting Mrs. Williams' pleasure dome." [13]

That evening, back at Amalfi, Donovan called Downes to his room and told him frankly, but without rancor, that he would be relieved of his OSS position after the fall of Naples. He offered Downes any other OSS post that he might choose—outside of Italy. Donovan then returned to Capri and reassigned the task of requisitioning the Williams villa to 34-year-old Henry Ringling North of the MacGregor team.[i] The Yale-educated brother of the Ringling Circus heir had just completed a far more significant assignment, liberating political prisoners from fascist jails.

---

[i] Ironically, North's roommate and close friend at Yale was the son of Charles Bedeaux, the French-American "speed-up king" arrested for treason at the insistence of OSS men in Algiers.

Donovan also found Peter Tompkins on Capri. Leaving his Mac-Gregor colleagues to their commando operations, the young journalist offered to help guide the general through the labyrinth of Italian politics. They should begin, Tompkins suggested, with the one man who, for twenty years, had represented the spirit of the Italian anti-fascist resistance—the aged historian and philosopher, Benedetto Croce.

Only a week before, Croce had been rescued from his villa behind the German lines in Sorrento and brought to Capri by a small team of British SOE officers.[14] Their commander, tall, slim, boyish-looking Major Malcolm Munthe, the son of a well-known Swedish novelist, had directed the SOE office in Stockholm since 1940. His chief aide was SOE Captain Max Salvadori, an Italian-born professor and refugee from fascism who had worked for the British MI-6 since 1939 as coordinator of Italian exile activities in the United States.[j] Like many of their OSS colleagues, Munthe and Salvadori had little respect for the Italian King.

Because of the flight of Victor Emmanuel and his generals to safety, millions of Italians troops were disarmed, dispersed and dishonored by the numerically inferior Germans. A Nazi commando team had also taken advantage of the chaos to rescue Mussolini from imprisonment. The Italian dictator was installed at the head of a puppet fascist republic in the north.

Despite these fruits of royal cowardice, the Allies recognized the King's government as a legitimate regime. The anti-fascist resistance thought otherwise. Its sentiments found eloquent expression in the words of the 78-year-old Croce, a Neapolitan intellectual of worldwide renown. For years he had lived defiantly under a fascist regime he despised, openly criticizing the Duce's despotism.

Croce was a political conservative who had no use for socialism and admired the institution of monarchy, Victor Emmanuel notwithstanding. His symbolic leadership of the resistance in its infancy was not an ideological but a moral one. Throughout Italy, Croce was acclaimed as the man who had dared stand up to fascism.

On September 22, amid the sound of explosions across the bay in Naples, Tompkins brought Donovan to meet the short, stocky Croce at his villa on Capri. They were also joined by Colonel John Whitaker, a former Chicago *Daily News* correspondent in Rome, ousted from Italy in 1941 because his dispatches had displeased Mussolini. Whitaker was Edmond Taylor's successor as OSS representative to the Psychological

[j] Salvadori is now Professor of History at Smith College.

Warfare Branch. He made no secret of his own distaste for the King. "The royal family," he had publicly declared, was "as bankrupt politically as Mussolini." [15]

Croce agreed. For his cowardice, said the old man, Victor Emmanuel was forever discredited among the Italian people. The Allies, Croce told Donovan, should now form a new Italian volunteer corps that would fight directly under Anglo-American command and pledge its allegiance to the Italian nation—but not to the King. To command such a legion, Croce proposed retired General Giuseppe Pavone, a World War I hero, "a patriot and a liberal." [16]

Donovan and Tompkins thanked Croce for his suggestions and took a PT boat back to Fifth Army headquarters at Salerno. There the general gave his enthusiastic backing to Croce's plan, adding that the volunteer corps might be supplied and directed by OSS. Tompkins, meanwhile, went looking for the OSS Fifth Army detachment to deliver some newly acquired intelligence from occupied Naples. He finally located the headquarters in an old stone farmhouse where Downes' nemesis, Colonel Ellery Huntington, had already taken command. The 50-year-old colonel, Tompkins remembers, was "very pleasant," but "spoke not a word of Italian and understood less of intelligence." [17]

Huntington's aides introduced Tompkins to another visitor, Raimondo Craveri, Croce's son-in-law and an official of a powerful, politically leftist Italian bank. Craveri had just come through the German lines from Rome, where he had worked with the Committee of National Liberation (CLN) as a leader of the newly formed Action Party. The Actionists, young descendants of a pre-war intellectual anti-fascist movement, described themselves as "liberal-socialists." In coming months, the Action Party would supply the underground—and the OSS —with dynamic resistance leadership.

Tompkins and Craveri returned to Capri on September 30 to find the Allies about to enter Naples behind the retreating Germans. The city was without water, light, gas, phone service, or railway facilities. All had been sabotaged by the Germans after the Neapolitan anti-fascists staged the first successful underground uprising in Europe.

Downes remained at the helm of his OSS group as it entered Naples, to begin his last days in Italy. He and Tompkins requisitioned a large four-story palazzo on a narrow back street, unceremoniously ousting a notorious fascist industrialist who threatened retribution from his "important" American friends. (He was a Bank of America director). This building became OSS headquarters in Naples, as well as a refuge for Pavone, Croce, Craveri, and "any other visiting anti-fascists who needed bed and board." [18]

Immediate preparations were begun for the Pavone corps, now formally called the Gruppi Combattenti Italiani. The obese, bearded Italian General Pavone and his staff moved into a spacious office building and soon recruited hundreds of young men eager to fight the Nazis, but not under the command of the royalist generals who had deserted them.

At Fifth Army headquarters, located in the King's Palace at Caserta, several miles from Naples, Colonel Huntington was actively promoting the Pavone corps. In spite of London's enthusiasm for Badoglio and the King, the volunteer group also received vigorous support from SOE Major Munthe. He hailed Pavone as an "uncompromising, full-blooded individualist" and "an ideal military leader." [19] Munthe's aide, Max Salvadori, was piqued because General Donovan seemed "disposed to help Pavone as long as he accepts American help exclusively. Let him have it that way, if it gives him satisfaction," wrote Salvadori. "The important thing is that Pavone should be able to get things done." [20]

The Pavone corps was making progress when Croce sent his son-in-law, Raimondo Craveri, to Brindisi on Italy's eastern coast to discuss the project with Badoglio. On October 4, Craveri and Alberto Tarchiani,[k] a veteran anti-fascist editor, presented the marshal with a copy of Donovan's memorandum endorsing the volunteer corps. They noted that the OSS chief was "a man of considerable political influence in the United States, personally friendly with Roosevelt." [21]

Donovan's name meant nothing to Badoglio (they had met only briefly in 1935 while Donovan toured the Italian front in Ethiopia) and he discounted the general's importance. The highest Allied military representatives had already encouraged the King's Prime Minister to form his own corps of regular army soldiers, loyal to the monarchy. Nonetheless, Badoglio was impressed by Tarchiani's argument that the Pavone corps would preempt domination of the resistance by the "usual Communist elements." He promised his support.

Badoglio soon had second thoughts. At British instigation, the size of the corps was first trimmed to 500 men, then broken up into small teams for commando operations. Finally, after the Badoglio government had formed its own Royal Army combat group under command of a

k Tarchiani was Italy's first postwar ambassador to the United States.

pro-monarchist general, the British-dominated Allied Control Commission ordered Pavone's brigade disbanded on November 9. OSS was left with a barracks full of willing young recruits prepared to give their lives for Italy, but not for its King.

As the Germans unexpectedly held off the Allies at entrenched positions far to the south of Rome, the U.S. Fifth Army was screaming for behind-the-lines intelligence. Why not use Pavone's unemployed partisans as espionage agents? Again there were political complications. Badoglio's officers convinced the Allied command that the only genuine underground in German territory was composed of former royalist officers in contact with the Italian Army's military intelligence service, the SIM. Desperately in need of Italian agents, Mark Clark was willing to forget that the SIM had developed its professional expertise through two decades of fascist repression and dictatorship.

Wrote Tompkins, "I had little faith in the professionals, not only because of their record in the war against us, but because I suspected, and with good reason, that they would invent large portions of their intelligence." [22] But other OSS men were less reticent about working with the SIM. One of these was Downes' good friend, André Bourgoin, the French officer who had been so helpful in Morocco. He had followed Downes to Italy as a regular member of the OSS staff, and, as a career officer of French intelligence, he felt a natural inclination to work with his counterparts in the Italian Army rather than the amateur anti-fascist partisans. An intense rivalry grew up between Bourgoin and Tompkins, who accused his French colleague of recruiting "ex-fascists, petty professional informers, and outright double agents." [23]

When Allied headquarters supported Bourgoin's position, Tompkins and his friend Craveri hit upon a plan. They formed a secret espionage corps to formalize OSS aid to anti-fascists of the Committees of National Liberation. This new group, the Organizazione della Resistenza Italiani (ORI), absorbed many of Pavone's volunteers and recruited new agents by aiding the desertion of a group of radio operators from Royal Italian submarines lying idle in the harbor of Naples. The Craveri group remained a secret—from the Germans, from the Badoglio Government, from Colonel Huntington, and from the Corvo section at Algiers.

Tompkins agreed to maintain and supply Craveri's agents and to infiltrate them into the north to work with the partisans in collecting and transmitting military intelligence. In return, Craveri would have the

use of these men for his own political purposes, to stimulate the anti-
fascist (and anti-Badoglio) resistance. In time, the secret ORI became
the communications hub of the entire northern underground.

Tompkins and Craveri were particularly careful to camouflage the
ORI from the British. Major Munthe's SOE group was friendly enough
to the anti-fascists, but more exalted emissaries of Whitehall seemed
fanatically devoted to the royal government. A political impasse resulted after OSS Swiss chief Allen Dulles (who personally supported the
Badoglio-monarchy forces) transmitted to Naples a manifesto issued
by the CLN underground in Rome.[24] The document denounced the
Badoglio government and the King and called for a new constitutional
regime. Spurred by the stand of their Roman comrades, the southern
anti-fascists refused to join Badoglio's cabinet until the King abdicated.

Croce then proposed the idea of a regency. The King and his son,
Prince Humbert, would both abdicate in favor of Humbert's six-year-
old son. Badoglio would act as the boy's regent while Count Carlo
Sforza, a pre-fascist foreign minister greatly respected in Washington,
would become Prime Minister. After meeting with Croce and Sforza,
Badoglio seemed receptive. But again, Victor Emmanuel refused.

The political deadlock signalled a break in Anglo-American unity.
Roosevelt thought the regency a fine solution. He sent General Donovan to inform Badoglio (who suddenly recognized the OSS chief as an
"old friend") that Italy could only be considered a full ally when true
democratic government had been established. The six parties of the
anti-fascist CLN (the Communists included) would have to be brought
into the cabinet, said Roosevelt, even if that meant the King's exit.[25]
Churchill, on the other hand, still cleaved to the monarchy and insisted that any political reforms be held in check until the Allies freed
Rome. But by mid-November it was obvious that the Allied drive for the
Holy City had bogged down.

The schism between British and American policy was intense at the
secret service level. The British lodged a formal complaint that Colonel
Huntington's OSS detachment had become "embroiled in Italian
politics" by their support of anti-monarchist forces. Shortly thereafter,
Huntington was replaced as OSS commander, Fifth Army, by Colonel
John Haskell, one of Donovan's finest executives, a West Point graduate and vice-president of the New York Stock Exchange.[1] Haskell's

[1] Haskell was chief of the Marshall Plan mission to Sweden, 1948–49;
U.S. defense advisor to NATO, 1955–60; and Paris representative of Bankers Trust Company, 1960–68.

brother Joe had just become head of the SO Branch in London. Their father was a man of prominence—Donovan's commander in World War I, director of American relief programs in Russia in the 1920s, and, at that moment, Democratic candidate for Lieutenant Governor of New York.

The younger Haskell was placed in a quandary by the competing claims of SIM and anti-fascist agents. The colonel tried to view the situation from an objective and purely military standpoint. As professional army officers, the royalists made better intelligence observers, reasoned Haskell, whereas the ORI volunteers seemed to produce superior radio operators. Yet joint intelligence missions were impossible, since the royalist and anti-monarchist agents refused to work together. OSS was even forced to establish separate training camps for the two groups. Haskell was just beginning to make some sense of this confused situation when Donovan tapped him in December to head the prospective OSS mission to Moscow (later cancelled at J. Edgar Hoover's insistence). He was replaced at the small but comfortable OSS villa west of Caserta by still another bewildered colonel.

The British SOE had its own problems. In November Major Munthe's superior at Algiers decided that British liaison with the northern resistance should be conducted only through SIM channels. Munthe and Salvadori protested, but to no avail. On Christmas Eve 1943, Munthe was instructed to have no further dealings with the anti-fascist underground in Rome. "We are liquidated," said Munthe in despair.[26]

The British authorities next refused to allow the southern anti-fascist parties to hold a conclave in Naples in December. Croce and Sforza complained directly to Washington and only then were they permitted to plan for a congress far from Naples in the east coast port of Bari, where the proceedings would be kept under strict surveillance by the royalist military police.

The only hopeful sign was in the military situation. In late December, Churchill conceived a military thrust to break the impasse in which the Allies were stalled far to the south of Rome. The new plan called for an amphibious landing at Anzio to the rear of the German lines and only thirty miles south of the Italian capital.

Plans for the invasion were under way when General Donovan returned to Naples, just back from a meeting with Russian intelligence officials in Moscow. The general wanted an OSS officer infiltrated into Rome in advance of the landing. He selected Peter Tompkins for this task. The young officer was delighted by this opportunity to free himself from bitter conflict with André Bourgoin, then conducting agent infiltrations from the island of Corsica.

Donovan's instructions to Tompkins were explicit: he was to prevent the Badogliani and CNL underground factions from beginning a civil war at the moment of liberation, and to coordinate the sabotage and intelligence operations of the resistance in support of the Allied landing. After obtaining the names of underground contacts in Rome from his friends in the Action and Communist Parties at Naples, Tompkins flew to Corsica on January 20. From there he was infiltrated by boat to the mainland 100 kilometers north of Rome. As the OSS man stepped ashore, a Socialist delegate of the Rome CLN climbed into the same rubber dinghy on his way south to Bari, where he would present the views of the resistance at the coming anti-fascist congress.

Tompkins made his way to Rome. Reaching the city only a day before the scheduled landing at Anzio, he found the underground torn by political differences. The CLN, headed by a pre-fascist Prime Minister, Ivanoe Bonomi, directed a primarily leftist agent network, while a royalist colonel had, with official SIM sanction, formed his

Anxiously awaiting his secret mission to Nazi-occupied Rome in January 1944, days before the Anzio invasion, Peter Tompkins stood beside General Donovan's plane on the island of French Corsica.

own intelligence organization. Days before Tompkins' arrival, this Badogliano officer and most of his aides had been suddenly captured in a German raid. Severely weakened by this blow, the royalists still refused to work in concert with the CLN against the Nazis.

Tompkins was also shocked to discover that one of Bourgoin's Italian agents in Rome, a thirteen-year veteran of the SIM who went by the code name "Coniglio," had been passing himself off as the personal political representative of the Allied command. Although Coniglio had given some support to the CLN parties, he reserved special favoritism (and OSS operational funds) for a cabal of industrialists whose principal concern was saving their economic interests in the north from destruction.

Having made this unhappy survey of the Roman situation, Tompkins learned that the British and American armies had landed at Anzio on the morning of January 22. But the Allied commanders remained stalled at the beachhead just long enough to allow the Germans to bring up reinforcements. The liberation of Rome was again postponed and Tompkins received an anguished message from John Croze, a French-American officer who commanded the OSS group at Anzio, pleading for intelligence about enemy troop movements toward the beachhead.

It was impossible for Tompkins to operate an effective espionage network and still maintain complete political neutrality. The SIM-Badogliani intelligence had proved worthless and sometimes dangerously misleading. The most effective spy system in Rome was directed by the Socialist Party underground, whose leaders readily agreed to channel information to Tompkins and his young Socialist assistant, Baron Franco Malfatti,[m] for transmission to the military command at Anzio. Tompkins hoped to keep this arrangement secret. He did not wish to be accused of political favoritism at a time when the CLN and Badogliani were in open conflict in the south.

On January 28, 1944, a week after the landings, the congress of the Committees for National Liberation met at an old theater in Bari. Representatives of the Rome CLN, exfiltrated to the south by OSS, presented a resolution calling for the creation of an anti-fascist government with all constitutional powers to rival the Badoglio royalist regime. Benedetto Croce proposed a compromise—that "moral" pressure be exerted on the King to force his abdication. The proposal was adopted. An executive junta of the Congress addressed a letter to the

[m] Malfatti is now Italian ambassador to France.

King asking his renunciation of the throne. Again, Victor Emmanuel rebuffed their demand.

The royalist forces were not without their supporters in OSS. Like Bourgoin, "Prince" Serge Obolensky, in charge of the OSS Italian Operational Groups at Brindisi, preferred to work with the SIM. When he left for London in April, he passed along his royalist contacts to his successor, Russell Livermore, a prominent New York attorney, former Republican legislator, and close friend of Donovan's.

The OSS command in Italy had also passed to a Badoglio admirer, Colonel Clifton C. Carter, the son of a West Point professor, and a professional officer with important political conections (his brother Marshall [n] was a personal aide to the Chairman of the Joint Chiefs of Staff). Carter and his second-in-command, Major J. H. Angleton, an expatriate businessman who owned a subsidiary of the National Cash Register Company in Milan, held frequent meetings with Badoglio. The Marshal made repeated requests for stronger American support of his government. Playing on Carter's conservatism, he made veiled threats of an alliance with Russia, quickly adding his personal belief that such a diplomatic move would not be "beneficial to the Europe of the after-war." Badoglio then tried to play off the Americans against their Allies. Why, he asked Carter, had the United States "thrown the Mediterranean to the British"? It was time for Washington to "begin to assert its power" and independence from London.[27]

Badoglio knew of OSS difficulties with His Majesty's officers. The British military command had attempted to set up British and American "spheres of influence" for secret operations in North Italy. The OSS zones, according to this plan, would receive one-third of the supplies dropped to the northern resistance, while the SOE areas would be given the other two-thirds. Colonel Carter vigorously objected and the argument was carried all the way back to Allied headquarters in Algiers, where the British proposal was finally defeated.

Carter also had difficulties in his own organization. Many officers of his SI Branch were critical of the SIM organization. They believed that "some of these former enemies, who ostensibly had changed their allegiances were actually engaged in betraying our OSS personnel to the enemy." One OSS agent sent north to Venice in early 1944 had been immediately captured by the Germans. OSS headquarters later

[n] Marshall Carter was Deputy Director of CIA, 1962–65. From 1965 to 1969 he was Director of America's code-breaking bureaucracy, the National Security Agency.

learned that his Nazi captors "showed him a dossier they had. It contained his photograph—the same photograph that had been taken at SIM headquarters in Brindisi before he left there; it also contained detailed reports on his training in Brindisi and listed names and places indicating that the enemy had counter-espionage agents working in responsible positions right at SIM headquarters." [28]

Particularly vocal criticism of the SIM came from the Abraham Lincoln Brigaders of the Secret Intelligence Branch. Downes's original team of leftists had been reinforced, after his departure, by two 29-year-old lieutenants, Milton Wolff and Irving Fajans, who had also fought for the Spanish Loyalists.° These Lincoln Brigaders worked with Communist and Socialist agents on a basis of mutual trust; their espionage work was often the most effective in the Theater.[29] But they found an enemy in Colonel Carter. When the young officers insisted on supplementing their intelligence work with futile attempts to convert fellow OSS men to their ideological view, Carter, in a moment of anger, threatened to have them shot.

On February 7, six OSS officers who had also been working with Craveri and the CLN agents paid a visit on Benedetto Croce in Naples. They asked the old philosopher what the Allies could do to best aid the Italian resistance. Croce abruptly replied, "Advise the king to abdicate." He went on to denounce Victor Emmanuel as a "superannuated representative of fascism." Asked if Prince Humbert, the King's son, might be acceptable as a substitute, Croce implied that this would be a reasonable solution.[30]

The OSS men may have dropped a hint in the right official nook, for a week later Allied representatives welcomed a political plan of the CLN's executive junta suggesting that Victor Emmanuel abdicate in favor of Humbert. But the King, with Churchill's active support, continued to resist. Washington was still pressing for a change in London's stubborn royalist policy when a diplomatic bombshell rocked Allied headquarters.

On March 13, the Soviet Union, without consulting London or Washington, granted full diplomatic recognition to Badoglio's royalist government. It was a great victory for the King and a tremendous blow to the anti-fascist parties. The executive junta was left floundering as the Italian Communists loyally supported Moscow's position. On March 28, Palmiro Togliatti, the veteran leader of the Italian Com-

° In 1953, Wolff and Fajans declined to tell a Senate committee if they had belonged to the Communist Party while serving in OSS.

Peter Tompkins (left) in the cellar of his Rome hideout. This is where he stored weapons and ammunition and the secret radio he used to transmit intelligence from his Socialist espionage network to Allied headquarters.

munists, returned from exile in Moscow to regain command of his party. He soon announced that the Communists had put aside their republican principles in the interest of the war effort and were now willing to join the royalist cabinet. The CLN coalition had cracked.

The unholy alliance of Communists and Badogliani complicated Peter Tompkins' clandestine existence in Rome. For the past two months he had been sending superb military intelligence, acquired from his Socialist friends, to the Allies, still stalled at Anzio. But he was having serious difficulties with Bourgoin's SIM agent, Coniglio, who continued his political manipulations with millions of lire in OSS operational funds and began cultivating ties to the Badogliani. Tompkins had been willing to transmit the SIM officer's intelligence on his own radio, but he refused to send a report asserting that the CLN resistance in north Italy was "inferior in numbers, organization, and technical proficiency" to the royalists. In desperation, the Badogliani accused Tompkins of political favoritism.[31]

The royalists tried to outflank the OSS man by making overtures to the Communist underground in Rome, offering money and SIM assistance. Tompkins was concerned that the Communist defection in the south might ease the way for a similar alliance behind the lines. He hurriedly arranged a meeting with the chief of the Communist resistance in Rome. Would the Communists continue to work together with OSS in an "ethical rapport" against the enemy? The leftist leader was not unfriendly but he had his own pressing question: Why did the British and Americans seem intent on treating the northern anti-fascist partisans as enemies? Tompkins had no adequate reply. If Togliatti was at fault for his collaboration with the royalists, the Allied command was equally guilty for its distrust of the resistance.

Several days later, Tompkins had his first serious misfortune. His radio operator was arrested by fascist police and his transmitter seized. Unable to send further intelligence, Tompkins spent the months of April and May fleeing from the fascists. These were also months of tragedy for the CLN underground. Nine Communist leaders were arrested. The Socialist resistance was also hard-pressed as two of its highest officials were taken into fascist custody. Tompkins suspected treachery. "Someone high up in the underground had been selling left-wing party members down the river." [32] One possibility was Coniglio, who had become a full-fledged booster of the royalists and was plotting with the Badogliani to prevent a CLN takeover on the day of liberation.

The royalists felt their moment was at hand. In the south, the Communist defection had forced the CLN executive junta into a compromise agreement. The King assented to his retirement from public affairs (but not abdication) after the liberation of Rome. Royal authority would then be conferred on his son Humbert as "Lieutenant General of the Realm." Despite considerable criticism from the Actionists and Socialists, it was agreed that Badoglio would remain Prime Minister for a time in a new CLN cabinet. On April 24, a Badoglio-CLN government took the oath of allegiance to the monarchy. Under Allied (and Communist) pressure, the CLN ministers were also forced to agree to postpone any talk of social reform. Badoglio told Colonel Carter the new government was functioning "as smoothly as an orchestra." [33]

This regrettable political compromise preceded a military break-through. On May 12, the Allies mounted a new drive to capture Rome from their Anzio foothold. Tompkins was meanwhile concerned that the Roman Badogliani, disregarding the new coalition at Brindisi, might do anything to prevent the CLN underground from seizing power. The monarchists were desperate enough to betray anti-fascist leaders to the Gestapo.

As the British and American armies approached the city during the first days of June, the Allied command seemed to have one objective in common with the Badogliani. With GIs only ten miles from Rome, the Allied radio warned the CLN partisans to await explicit instructions before beginning an uprising. Tompkins correctly surmised that the caveat was designed to prevent a left-wing insurrection before the Allies could occupy the city. But his Socialist underground teams still had the task of capturing hundreds of German and fascist agents who would be left in Rome as the Nazis departed. "And if those dumb mugs at the base do not let me carry it out the way it should be done," he wrote in his diary, "I may have to do it without their knowledge." 34

On the afternoon of June 3, Tompkins learned that the Germans were about to pull out of Rome as the Allies approached. The young officer hurriedly wrote out "official orders" to the city's Italian commander on an OSS letterhead, embellished with the seal of a specially prepared OSS rubber stamp, and impressively signed by "OSS officer in charge, Rome area." He ordered the Italian Army and police to prevent sabotage by the retreating Germans and to arrest and intern German and fascist deserters. The Italians, surprisingly, agreed to implement the "orders." By the evening of June 4, Rome was delivered intact to Allied soldiers.

The liberation of Rome seemed to presage a new political beginning for Italy. The King was not allowed to return to the capital. Victor Emmanuel appointed his son Humbert Lieutenant General of the Realm and then quietly retired from the political scene. The CLN ministers, strengthened by support of their Roman colleagues, forced Badoglio to resign as well. He was replaced by Ivanoe Bonomi, chairman of the Rome CLN, a conservative who had been Premier of Italy before the fascist rise to power. This respected elder statesman seemed the ideal man to unite the leaders of the anti-fascist movement.

But political harmony was only momentary. The British found a new monarchist ally in Prince Humbert. Whitehall then began to court the anti-fascist conservatives in an effort to play off the right and left wings of the CLN. Britannia had its way; the formerly united Committee of National Liberation splintered as the political parties resumed their traditional parliamentary bickering.

For OSS, the Allied entry into the Holy City meant another reorganization, this time personally supervised by Donovan. (Fresh from
Normandy, the general was on hand for a private audience with the
Pope, who had given similar honors to Gestapo officers the previous
month.) Colonel Carter stayed on for a time as OSS chief in Rome,
enthroned in a delightful villa which Mussolini had built for his mistress. But only an OSS research unit and the Counter-Intelligence
Branch, X-2, maintained their base of operations in the city. When
Peter Tompkins returned to Washington, his lists of suspected enemy
agents were inherited by the X-2 chief, James Angleton, the son of
Colonel Carter's executive officer and a thin, Yale-educated amateur
poet with an amazing capacity for Byzantine intrigue.[p]

The locus of OSS activity remained at Caserta headquarters near
Naples, which absorbed the Mediterranean Theater staff that had been
working at Algiers. The OSS Theater commander was Colonel Edward
Glavin, a graduate of West Point and Oxford. It was rumored at headquarters that Glavin's was a "political" appointment. At the outset of
the war, he had been on the staff of General Hugh Drum, who according to the grapevine was to become Secretary of War in the event
New York Governor Thomas E. Dewey defeated Roosevelt in that
year's presidential elections. Glavin's OSS position, according to this
theory, was one guarantee of the political future of Donovan's organization. Another was the appointment of Colonel Thomas Early as
Glavin's executive officer—his cousin was a member of Roosevelt's staff
and one of the President's oldest friends. Unfortunately, neither Glavin
nor Early were very competent administrators. The Theater staff was
held together through the ability of Glavin's adjutant, Norman New-
house, the son of immigrant Russian Jews and editor of a Long Island
newspaper.

Aware of these command problems at Caserta, Donovan took pains
to place able executives in charge of the operational branches. Special
Operations came under the purview of Philadelphia banker William
Davis, Jr., who had done a remarkable job of working with conflicting
French secret service factions in North Africa. "Black" propaganda was
directed by a former Berlin manager of the United Press, Frederick
Oechsner.

The Secret Intelligence Branch required special care. The SI
Branch chief in London, Princeton political scientist William Maddox,

[p] According to Soviet double agent Kim Philby, Angleton was chief of
the CIA's Office of Special Operations in 1949.

was brought to Caserta to replace a Bank of America official as overseer of espionage operations in the Theater. Dr. Milton Katz, a Harvard law professor, left his post as counsel to the War Production Board in Washington to become Maddox's deputy.[q]

A special SI division was created for central European operations. An advertising executive of the General Foods Corporation, Howard Chapin, was given responsibility for sending intelligence agents to Czechoslovakia, Hungary, Austria, and Germany. Chapin's assistant, Ohio attorney Gilmore Flues, took command of the Hungarian section and was charged with avoiding any repetition of an earlier operation that had ended in disaster for OSS.[r]

Hungary had declared war on the United States and joined the Germans in fighting the Soviets in 1941. But a group of politicians in the Hungarian cabinet lost faith in the promise of Axis victory and approached the British to discuss a Badoglio-style surrender. The first contact was made in January 1943 through a Hungarian Socialist exile who was working for SOE in Istanbul. Further overtures were made to OSS chief Allen Dulles in Switzerland by the Hungarian minister at Berne. Ensuing diplomatic discussions were stymied when the Hungarians, apprehensive about an invasion by their neighboring Russian enemies, insisted that American and British troops march to Budapest before a surrender was announced. The Allies refused and insisted on unconditional capitulation. In February 1944, the Hungarians seemed close enough to agreement to warrant the dispatch of a military mission to Budapest. A three-man OSS team was formed under the command of Colonel Florimond Duke, a stocky former advertising director of *Time* magazine, who headed the Balkan SI desk in Washington. His assistants were both young liberals recruited by Arthur Goldberg's Labor Branch—Captain Guy Nunn,[s] a Stanford-educated freelance writer, and Major Alfred Suarez, a radio expert and Loyalist veteran of the Spanish Civil War. The group left Brindisi on March 15, 1944, en route to Budapest with a personal message from Roosevelt to the Hungarian government.

But the Hungarian peace feelers to the Allies had also become

[q] Katz directed the Marshall Plan organization in Europe, 1950–51. He is now a Professor of International Law at Harvard.

[r] Flues was Assistant Secretary of the Treasury during the Eisenhower administration.

[s] Nunn later became Assistant Director of the International Affairs Department of the United Auto Workers union.

known in Berlin. (Some Donovan aides believed that OSS leftists had "leaked" the Duke team's mission to the Russians, who then indirectly informed the Nazis in order to prevent a western "deal" with the right-wing Hungarian government.) While the OSS team prepared for its drop, Hitler decided to send the Wehrmacht against his wavering Axis partner. Duke and his men entered the country in the midst of a surprise German invasion, and before they could meet with the Hungarian Premier, the Nazis took control. The subjugated Hungarians obligingly handed Duke's team over to the Germans.[35]

Hoping to prevent a recurrence of the Hungarian disaster, Donovan's officers concentrated their talents and resources on the East Europe and Balkan ventures of OSS Italy; Italian operations suffered accordingly. Disagreements with the British, who were reluctant to arm the Italian resistance forces, were rife. SO commander William Davis, who had worked closely with the SOE in North Africa, discovered to his consternation that both the American and British secret services "went their own way" in Italy. There were frequent disputes over "what guerrilla groups should be supported and what equipment they should have." When Davis received a new assignment in China, he was "not all that sorry to leave." [36]

Donovan was also personally concerned about the open hostility between his executives and the Italian-American officers who handled the day-to-day details of operations in northern Italy. Washington officials complained of "Mafia types" working in Glavin's command. One OSS man who trained Italian-American officers in the Operational Group Command remembered them as "tough little boys from New York and Chicago, with a few live hoods mixed in. . . . Their one desire was to get over to the old country and start throwing knives." [37] A very few OSS men had indeed been recruited directly from the ranks of Murder, Inc., and the Philadelphia "Purple Gang."

Washington's principal thorn in the Mediterranean Theater was the fiercely independent Italian SI section at Brindisi, commanded by Earl Brennan's first recruits, Max Corvo and Vincent Scamporino. The Special Operations men grumbled that SI refused to provide them with intelligence that might help in planning sabotage missions. There were also unsubstantiated allegations of mismanagement. When John O'Gara, executive vice-president of Macy's in New York, was appointed OSS Inspector General in late 1944, he was assigned the priority task of investigating Earl Brennan's branch. O'Gara even sent an accountant to Italy to check financial records. No irregularities could be found.

Corvo's group was occasionally charged with pursuing its own political policy. One OSS "special agent," Serafino Romualdi, admitted that he had done just that.[t] He was an Italian Socialist exile who emigrated to the United States when the fascists seized power and joined the staff of David Dubinsky's International Ladies' Garment Workers Union in New York. In 1942, Romualdi was sent to South America by Nelson Rockefeller's Coordinator of Inter-American Affairs to organize a congress of anti-fascist exiles in Uruguay. Upon his return to Washington, Assistant Secretary of State Adolf Berle recommended Romualdi to OSS as an advisor on Italian labor problems.

Sent to Italy in July 1944 with the assimilated rank of OSS major, Romualdi "hit it off right away" with Scamporino and Corvo. Headquartered in the apartment of his brother-in-law, Giuseppe Lupis,[u] an Italian Socialist leader, Romualdi, with or without the approval of his OSS superiors, began political manipulations "to strengthen the Socialist forces at the expense of the Communists. We were preparing for the day—which many of us regarded as inevitable—when the Communists would have to be opposed." [38]

Romualdi provided Socialist politicos with scarce food and vitamins, then tried to persuade them to avoid any alliance with the Communists. He also channeled funds from the Italian-American Labor Council to Socialist union men who were willing to split from the Communist-dominated general labor federation. In October 1944, Scamporino sent Romualdi to the Franco-Swiss border, allegedly to deliver two planeloads of arms and ammunition to the French resistance. His real mission, "planned outside normal channels," was to smuggle the noted Socialist author Ignazio Silone into Italy from his exile in Switzerland (where he had been in contact with Allen Dulles' staff). Romualdi believed that Silone, a well-known anti-fascist (and anti-Communist) intellectual, would provide inspiring leadership for the socialist right wing.

Romualdi went on to other delicate missions (including a mysterious tête-à-tête with Prince Humbert) as the OSS Italians conspired and plotted.[39] But they were not alone; all of liberated Italy reeked of political conspiracy. The leaders of the anti-fascist parties "argued end-

---

[t] Romualdi was later Latin American representative of the CIA-funded Free Trade Union Committee of the American Federation of Labor.

[u] Lupis was Italian Undersecretary for Foreign Affairs, 1962–63, and Minister of Merchant Marine, 1968–69. He became Minister of Tourism in 1970.

lessly, they spun ideological webs, they jockeyed for position, as Rome began to exude the close, heavy, atmosphere of old-fashioned parliamentarianism." "The Bonomi government was going stale," observed Harvard historian H. Stuart Hughes, who headed the OSS Research Branch at Rome. "It was whirling in a void where its words and actions mattered very little. Reality lay elsewhere. . . . All eyes turned toward the North." [40]

At Milan, far behind the German lines, the underground was actively working against the enemy under the direction of the Committee for National Liberation of Upper Italy (CLNAI). Dominated by the Communist and Action Parties, the CLNAI attempted to unite and coordinate the various politically oriented guerrilla bands. But these military legions were also beset by bitter ideological squabbling, which intensified as Italy became a secondary Theater of War.

The Germans retreated to new hard-line defenses in the Italian north which the Allies, hurriedly shifting troop units to the Normandy front, were unable to breach. Partisan warfare was a viable alternative to frontal assault, but SOE and OSS officers sent to establish liaison with the resistance were hampered by anti-partisan prejudice at Allied headquarters.

The OSS men who parachuted into the north at the beginning of August 1944, days before Florence was liberated with the aid of the city's underground, were besieged by questions from suspicious partisan leaders. Why was the Anglo-American command so niggardly in assisting the guerrillas? Did the pro-monarchist Allies hope to squelch a general insurrection by the 100,000 leftist partisans who had joined the northern resistance?

The Americans could only explain that the resources of the Allied secret service organizations in Italy were severely taxed by emergency operations in Eastern Europe. There was some truth in this. In late August the Czech resistance rose in open rebellion. On September 25, a large OSS group was dispatched from Bari to the lower Tatra mountains, far to the east of Prague, to make contact with the guerrillas.[v] Hounded by Nazi units determined to crush the uprising, and unable to reach the resistance forces, the OSS men remained in hiding while their supplies dwindled. On the verge of starvation, they awaited an OSS

[v] This was the last OSS mission in Czechoslovakia until May 1945, when a team under the command of OSS Lieutenant Eugene Fodor entered Prague after liberation. Fodor is now publisher of the famous travel guide series that bears his name.

supply drop on Christmas Day, 1944. Before the shipment arrived, a
Slovakian informer betrayed them to the Germans. Only two American
officers escaped to the Russian lines.[41]

In Bucharest on August 23, the Romanian King Michael staged a
coup against the fascist general who had led the country into a partnership with Berlin. As Russian tanks rolled toward the city, the King
tardily declared war on Germany. A week later, the special OSS mission
"Bughouse," commanded by Russell Dorr, a former Donovan law partner, flew to Bucharest to capture German records and survey damage to
the Ploesti oil refineries.[w] Working under cover of an air rescue mission, Frederick Burkhardt,[x] a 32-year-old philosophy professor at the
University of Wisconsin, joined 29-year-old Philip Coombs,[y] an economics instructor at Williams College, in locating forty mailbags full
of German military documents left undestroyed at Luftwaffe headquarters. They also discovered the records of the Nazi espionage apparatus for southeast Europe. This voluminous archive was rapidly
shipped back to Italy before Soviet NKVD men could claim the documents for themselves. OSS analysts at Caserta were kept occupied for
weeks sorting this intelligence "scoop." [42]

That same month, in distant London, General Stanislav Kopanski,
chief of staff of the Polish forces in exile, rushed to OSS headquarters at
Grosvenor Square for an urgent meeting with Colonel Theodore Palmer,
assistant business manager of the *New York Times* and deputy SI
chief in the European Theater. Kopanski announced that the Polish resistance had launched an insurrection against the Germans in Warsaw.
He begged Palmer for massive OSS supply shipments to save the rebels
from slaughter at the hands of their numerically superior enemy. Soviet
troops not far from the Polish capital refused to lift a hand to aid the
insurgents, who comprised the anti-Communist segment of the underground. Palmer promised OSS assistance. From early August until the

[w] Dorr was chief of the Marshall Plan mission to Turkey in 1948, and
resident representative of the International Bank for Reconstruction and
Development in Iran in 1957–58. He became Washington representative
of the Chase Manhattan Bank in 1959.

[x] Dr. Burkhardt was President of Bennington College, 1947–57. He
has been president of the American Council of Learned Societies since
1957.

[y] Dr. Coombs was Assistant Secretary of State for Educational and
Cultural Affairs during the Kennedy administration. He is now Research
Director of the International Institute for Educational Planning in Paris.

failure of the rebellion in October, all available OSS and SOE supply shipments from both Italy and London were diverted to Poland in a fruitless effort to aid the Warsaw revolt.[43]

The Italian partisans could not be expected to sympathize with the supply problems that beset the British and Americans. They were engaged in active guerrilla warfare against the Germans and their very survival depended on air drops from the south. Nor were the Communists the only critics of Allied parsimony. Action Party leader Ferruccio Parri was the most prominent spokesman for the CLNAI underground. A tall, slight, pale man with an huge shock of white hair, he was an idealistic, emotional veteran of the anti-fascist cause who had been in and out of Mussolini's jails since 1927. Donald Downes described him as "the perfect symbol of the resistance to police-ism, state-ism, and brutality." [44]

For the past year, Parri had been meeting at the Swiss border with Allied agents whom he called "Arturo" (Allen Dulles of OSS) and "Rossi" (John McCaffery of the SOE, who used the cover of "assistant press attaché" at the British Legation in Berne). Parri frequently complained to his secret service interlocutors of a dearth of Allied assistance to the partisans, but McCaffery rebuffed the Italian's protests with the warning, "You have friends. Don't try to lose them." [45]

Relations between the northern partisans and the Allied command had seriously deteriorated by the time OSS received permission to establish more direct liaison with the CLNAI. Operational control of the projected mission was given to Colonel William Suhling, a southern businessman with interests in the tobacco industry who had transferred to OSS from the Medical Administrative Corps. He was commander of Company D, a northern OSS advance base near Siena just south of the German lines.

General Donovan met with Colonels Glavin and Suhling and Major Corvo of the Italian SI section to discuss the liaison team that was to be dispatched to the north. To head the mission, Donovan selected a husky 40-year-old Harvard-educated attorney for the Securities and Exchange Commission, Major William Holohan. Since the Major spoke no Italian, he was given an Italian-American team-mate, Lieutenant Aldo Icardi, to act as interpreter. A 23-year-old graduate of the University of Pittsburgh, Icardi had been chosen for the mission by Corvo and Scamporino, his superiors at Bari. At the last moment, the Holohan team was also joined by three other Italian-

Americans from the OSS Operational Groups who were preparing to jump in the same area near Milan to work with partisan bands. The two teams were merged in the interests of efficiency.

On September 26, Holohan, carrying $16,000 in operational funds, led his group in a parachute jump to a mountainous area some fifty miles northwest of Milan, not far from the Swiss border. They were first met by an agent of the ORI intelligence network (created a year before by Raimondo Craveri and Peter Tompkins). A meeting was then arranged with Ferruccio Parri.

Holohan told the CLNAI leader he had been instructed to move his OSS team into Milan as soon as the Germans evacuated the city, then to act as liaison between the partisans and Allied headquarters at the time of liberation. Parri welcomed the Americans, hoping their arrival might signify an improvement on recent dealings with their SOE counterparts.

Contrary to OSS predictions, however, the Germans did not evacuate Milan and the Allied drive was again halted by strong German defenses. As American troops were transferred to the French front and British soldiers to Greece (where His Majesty's forces sought to quell a rebellion by leftist guerrillas), the Allied command decided to bed down for the winter. While military operations ground to a halt, each plane-load of clothes and supplies became a life-or-death matter for partisans suffering from attack by the enemy and assault from the elements.

The burden of these supply missions fell to OSS, and American liaison men working with the guerrilla groups were given the unenviable responsibility for distributing this materiel. The Holohan team became one of those missions forced to decide which partisan groups should get priority in supply drops and monetary aid.

While laying plans for supply sorties in November, Holohan received a complaint from the most renowned commander of the Communist Garibaldini partisans, Moscow-trained Vincenzo Moscatelli. In a meeting with Moscatelli on December 2, Holohan assured the guerrilla leader that his mission intended to supply all partisan forces indiscriminately, with regard only for their ability to harass the enemy. But Moscatelli was skeptical of American promises. As if to justify his suspicions, that very day two planes dropped a shipment of 44 automatic weapons, all of which ended up in the hands of partisans loyal to the conservative Christian Democratic Party.

Four days later, Major Holohan disappeared under mysterious circumstances while his team was moving its base to avoid capture in a German dragnet. Lieutenant Icardi radioed OSS Headquarters at Siena that the major had been killed in an enemy ambush. In a widely publicized postwar legal squabble, a different version emerged.[46] An Italian court found Icardi and his OSS sergeant (a young New York factory worker of Sicilian descent) guilty in absentia of Holohan's murder. The court alleged that Icardi absconded with his superior's operational funds and then, after poisoning and shooting Holohan, dumped his body into a lake. As the case proceeded through an extradition hearing, a congressional investigation, and then a perjury trial, Holohan was pictured as a devout Catholic who had opposed granting financial and materiel support to the Communists. Either out of fear of partisan retribution or of leftist sympathies, Icardi, it was charged, had murdered the major in order to supply the Garibaldini without interference.

In his defense, Icardi challenged the alleged political motive. He claimed he had steadfastly supported the OSS policy of "working with pro-Communist and anti-Communist partisans, whichever could at a given time deliver a more effective blow at the Germans." Neutrality was not a simple policy, the lieutenant recalled. There were "accusations of arms burying, arms selling, and arms bartering." The left-wing partisans accused the Americans of favoring right-wing guerrillas, and vice versa. "Our mission," he said, "was in the middle . . . harassed

Wehrmacht troops retreated along a north Italian highway in April 1945 as Lt. Aldo Icardi (center), dressed incognito in civilian clothes and wide-brimmed hat, plotted guerrilla strategy with Italian partisan leaders.

and burdened with the responsibility of using both forces to fight our common enemy, but never able to make a decision or a move that was not criticized by someone." [47]

Icardi's words rang true to the men who served behind the lines in Italy. Political problems were intense, especially for the British. Resistance leaders usually blamed the lack of assistance on London's devious foreign policy and its servants at the British Theater Command. A few vocally anti-CLNAI officers of SOE reinforced partisan suspicions, to the lament of more sympathetic British agents. One SOE man attached to the Garibaldini constantly sent requests for supplies to his headquarters. But in spite of his frequent messages, "couched in language which became ruder as time went on," the supply planes never came. "The more ardent Communists among them liked to believe that their politics were responsible for this apparently deliberate withholding of arms, and short of a plane-load of Bren guns falling at their feet, or better still on their thick skulls, the theory was difficult to kill no matter how strongly we might protest that so long as they were willing to fight they might be anarchists for all we or our employers cared." [48]

The partisans expected more of the OSS men and their disappointment was simply that much greater when plane-loads of American materiel failed to arrive. A few OSS officers, like the Lincoln Brigaders who survived Colonel Carter's venom to continue their espionage operations, remained on good terms with leftist guerrillas. Other Americans were less fortunate. A 26-year-old OSS major of German descent who dropped into northwestern Italy reported that the Garibaldini leaders were "20 per cent for liberation and 80 per cent for Russia. We soon found that they were burying the German arms they had captured, to save them for use after the war was over and the Americans had pulled out of Italy. What the Italians did after the war was their own business," he added, "but we were dropping weapons to the partisans for the purpose of saving American lives. I wanted our weapons used for this." In return for his protests, the major discovered that the local Communist political commissar was plotting to have him murdered. He barely escaped. But in spite of all his mishaps, the major, like most OSS officers, retained an unswerving admiration for the rank-and-file of the resistance. The great majority of Communist guerrillas, he believed, were "fine and brave" and eager to work with him in fighting the Nazis.[49]

As Mark Clark prepared his final offensive against the Germans, Allied headquarters began to take a greater interest in the thousands of partisans active in the Po valley of northern Italy, the industrial heartland of the country. To aid the resistance, Allen Dulles had stationed two officers in Lugano at the Swiss-Italian frontier. For the past year, Donald Jones, an ex-newspaperman, had maintained liaison with the partisans, who liked and respected him. In the fall of 1944, by special agreement between Dulles and Max Corvo, Jones was joined by Captain Emilio Daddario, 26, a Connecticut attorney from the Italian SI section at Brindisi.[z]

In November 1944, Jones and Daddario arranged for a CLNAI delegation to be transported to southern Italy for talks with the Allied command. A small group headed by Ferruccio Parri was flown to Naples via liberated France only to receive an unenthusiastic welcome from suspicious British commanders. They found no warmer reception in Rome, where a new right-of-center Bonomi cabinet had been formed without the participation of the Socialist or Action parties.

Nonetheless, the British and American military men agreed to a secret accord, signed in the Italian capital on December 8, 1944. The Allies promised financial aid and shipments of arms and supplies to the guerrillas. In return, the CLNAI agreed to obey all Allied directives, to concentrate upon safeguarding northern industrial plants from the Germans, and to stage a rapid disarmament after liberation.

Allen Dulles met the CLNAI emissaries upon their return to Switzerland and found them "considerably heartened by the show of Allied faith and support." [50] Despite Dulles' warning that the Germans had increased surveillance of the Swiss border, Parri began his trek back to Milan. The 54-year-old resistance leader hiked across a high mountain pass, crossed a lake in a small boat, and then caught a train to the city.

Parri had hardly settled in his flat when he was arrested on December 31 and carted off to Gestapo headquarters in Milan. After an ill-fated partisan attempt to free him, he was moved to a more secure prison in Verona. The CLNAI sent Mrs. Wally Castelbarco, the daughter of Arturo Toscanini, to ask Dulles to negotiate with the Germans for Parri's release. For the moment, this proved impossible.

Dulles, however, was in contact with the Nazis. Without Musso-

[z] Daddario was elected a Democratic congressman from Connecticut in 1958. In 1970 he was the unsuccessful Democratic candidate for Governor of Connecticut.

lini's knowledge, the Germans had offered various peace "deals" to the OSS man through Catholic Church and Italian industrialist channels. Dulles received these overtures with relative indifference. He knew that the peace feelers emanated from the Gestapo hierarchy. And he saw the SS men "through the eyes of our friends in the Italian resistance, who feared them and hated them and had frequently suffered at their hands." [51]

Dulles was scarcely more enthusiastic when another peace feeler reached his office during the last week of February 1945, relayed by a short, balding industrialist, Baron Luigi Parilli.[a] A Knight of Malta, Papal Chamberlain, and the son of an Italian admiral, Parilli seemed to know all the right people in important places, including German headquarters. One Gestapo officer who participated in the peace negotiations remembers, "Baron Parilli had been determined for some time to move heaven and earth if need be to save Upper Italy from destruction and to prevent the retreating German forces from applying a policy of 'scorched earth' which would have meant the ruin of Italy's industrial installations there. As an Italian, Parilli was a patriot, but in this case his patriotism was reinforced by his personal interests. Chiefly thanks to his enormously rich father-in-law, the Milan industrialist Posch, Baron Parilli was also a captain of industry with a big stake in the fate of industry in the North Italian plain." [52]

Dulles was prepared to disregard Parilli's approach as the fruitless effort of another desperate Italian industrialist. But when the Baron proved that he represented the top SS commander in north Italy, General Karl Wolff, Dulles presented the Nazis with a demand to test their sincerity—the release of Ferruccio Parri.

Suspecting that Dulles was grooming Parri as "the future strong man of Italy," the Germans granted his demand.[53] On March 8, an SS captain from Milan arrived in Switzerland, accompanied by Parri and another partisan leader, both just released from internment. Parri was hastily installed as a "patient" in an expensive Zurich medical clinic. When Dulles entered his room, the emotional Parri "broke into tears and threw his arms around me." [54] Without a word to the Italian about the German peace feelers, Dulles then rushed off to meet with General Wolff and his aides, who had secretly joined Baron Parilli in a trip to Zurich that same day.

[a] In 1948 Parilli was reportedly involved in a CIA operation to prevent a leftist victory in the Italian general elections. It was also rumored that he had concocted a plan to transport ex-Nazis from Germany to Paraguay.

The Nazi general offered the unconditional surrender of his own troops and promised an effort to convince Wehrmacht commanders to capitulate as well. Caserta and Washington were immediately apprised of the meeting. The following day, Dulles received an unexpected message from Allied headquarters in Italy. Two senior staff officers of the Theater Command were on their way to Switzerland with a contingent of OSS staff personnel to begin the second stage of the surrender talks, now code-named SUNRISE. On March 13, American General Lyman Lemnitzer and British General Terence Airey reached Lyon in southern France to await a meeting with Wolff. They were accompanied by David Crockett, the capable manager of OSS operational funds at Caserta (and former executive director of a Boston short-wave station, secretly financed by the British MI-6 before Pearl Harbor).[b]

That same week, two representatives of the CLNAI arrived in Berne for a stategy meeting requested weeks earlier by OSS and SOE. Dulles had no intention of informing the partisans of his dealings with the Germans. He removed the two resistance leaders from the scene by sending them to France for a discussion with Lemnitzer and Airey, who were themselves idled by the lull in the negotiations.

The generals made it clear to the Italian emissaries that they were concerned about the threat of a revolution in northern Italy after the liberation, similar to the leftist revolt in Greece. The Theater command knew that an "official Soviet Army mission" (actually a handful of Russian officers who walked over the Yugoslav border) was working with the Communist Garibaldini, who comprised almost a majority of the armed resistance.[55] SOE liaison officers (but not their OSS counterparts) had already been ordered to "discourage any indiscriminate expansion" of the partisan bands and to exercise caution in arming the guerrillas.[56]

The CLNAI envoys could only assure the generals that despite the strength of the Garibaldini, the Greek debacle would not be repeated in north Italy. The Italians then joined Parri in another flight to Naples for further "consultations," while Airey and Lemnitzer crossed into Switzerland to meet with General Wolff. On March 19, at the Swiss border town of Ascona, the surrender negotiations proceeded (despite some bungling interference by Colonel Glavin). Wolff then returned to his Italian headquarters to sound out the Wehrmacht commanders.

For the next month, the negotiations were stalled, by obstruction

[b] Crockett is now deputy to the director of the Massachusetts General Hospital in Boston.

from Wolff's superiors in Berlin and by objections from the wary
Soviet government. On April 20 Dulles received orders from Washington to break off all contact with the Germans. Churchill and Roosevelt
were not willing to risk a major confrontation with Moscow over
questionable German peace feelers.

Dulles was still sorely disappointed with Washington's order when
Wolff and a top Wehrmacht officer appeared unexpectedly at the Swiss
border on April 23. They were both prepared to sign the surrender of
all German forces in north Italy. Still bound by orders from Washington, Dulles kept the Nazis waiting while he asked for new instructions.

Northern Italy was already in a "turbulent state" as partisans
throughout the Po valley began "rising for the kill." [57] Four days after
the beginning of the Allied spring offensive, Mark Clark publicly urged
the partisans to be patient. The time for insurrection, he said, had not
yet arrived. But the underground would not remain quiescent. On April
10, Communist headquarters in Milan issued final plans for an imminent
uprising. The Garibaldini were warned that a "combination of firmness,
tact, and skill must be employed" in dealing with the OSS and SOE
liaison missions. "We must be prepared to face the fact that the Allies
may decide, for one reason or another, to withhold their support" of the
open rebellion.[58]

If the leftist partisans had known of Dulles' SUNRISE negotiations with the Nazis, they might well have questioned the Allies'
motives in these talks. At a special meeting of the CLNAI on April 19,
Parri, who had just returned from Naples, told his resistance comrades
that the Allies seemed less interested in the partisan contribution to
liberation than in the danger of a left-wing revolution. It seemed that
the primary objective of the Theater command was to prevent the
Germans from sabotaging northern power plants and economic interests
of Italian industrialists. (Had the suspicious Marxists of the resistance
been adept at research, they might have discovered that most of these
power installations were owned by a multinational corporation called
"Italian Superpower." One director of that company was a Chicago
banker whose son, New York banker James Russell Forgan, was a close
friend of Allen Dulles and had just replaced David Bruce as commander
of OSS in the European theater.)

At that same meeting of the CLNAI, the resistance delegates
issued a proclamation calling on the German and fascist forces to "surrender or perish." Then the revolt began. On the evening of April 19,

partisans seized command of the city of Bologna from the Germans and handed it over to the advancing Allied troops. A Communist mayor was elected as Mark Clark's army raced northward.

On April 24, while Dulles awaited further word from Washington, the first American units crossed the Po River. This military advance served as a spontaneous signal for partisan uprisings in all the northern industrial cities. Bloody battles raged in Turin and Genoa until the guerrillas forced the German garrisons to surrender.

Confusion reigned in Milan. A general strike was in progress and armed partisans prepared to attack the Germans. In Switzerland, meanwhile, Dulles, who had heard nothing from Washington, agreed that General Wolff should return to his Italian headquarters "to keep order and avert ruthless violence and destruction in North Italy." [59] Wolff crossed the border on April 25. He stopped at an SS command post in a requisitioned villa thirty miles north of Milan and contacted the Gestapo commander in the city, Colonel Rauff. Wolff learned that the center of Milan was still held by the SS; partisans controlled the outlying districts. Germans and Italian patriots faced each other with their guns at the ready, but no shots had yet been fired. Wolff ordered Rauff to keep his men out of an open battle with the Italians.

The SS general had just settled in his villa when he discovered that he was himself surrounded by Italian partisans who had moved up in force to seal off the Swiss border. Wolff feared that they might, at any moment, storm the villa and kill its German residents. A rescue mission organized by Rauff and the Cardinal of Milan (a sometime fascist stalwart who had once said that Mussolini's Ethiopian aggression was consonant with Christian ideals) failed to penetrate the partisan roadblocks. Wolff managed, however, to send word of his predicament to Dulles in Switzerland. The Nazi general then settled down in his villa for the night, hoping to survive until dawn.

Dulles received Wolff's message. Concerned that the partisans might capture Wolff and "take their joyful moment of vengeance" (thus jeopardizing the surrender plans), Dulles felt it imperative to save the Gestapo general.[60] That unenviable task was imparted to Donald Jones and Emilio Daddario, the OSS men at the Swiss border. They had just begun to form a rescue party on the afternoon of April 26 when they learned that Mussolini, after an abortive armistice discussion with the CLNAI, had fled north to Lake Como, and was hiding not far from Wolff's villa. The local prefect was trying to persuade the dictator to surrender to the OSS. He sent Jones a message to sound out the possibilities. The inquiry was relayed to Dulles, who promptly rejected it. The OSS master spy refused to bring the fascist dictator into a neutral country, where he might be given temporary political asylum. Jones was instructed to "keep clear" of the Duce.

On the evening of April 26, Jones crossed the frontier into Italy at the head of a hastily recruited party of Swiss intelligence officers, SS troops, and Italian guerrillas. The convoy soon came under partisan attack. Jones leaped out of his car, hoping the guerrillas would recognize him. Luckily the team leader knew him as an American friend and ordered a cease-fire. The remainder of the journey was troubled by no more than sporadic sniper fire and the explosion of an occasional hand grenade. The rescue team finally reached Lake Como, snatched Wolff from his beleaguered villa, and returned to Lugano before dusk on the morning of April 27.

Jones's OSS partner Emilio Daddario then set out on his own trip to Milan, where an uneasy peace still existed between German and partisan units. He also stopped at the SS villa at Lake Como and came upon the fascist Marshal Rudolfo Graziani, who had deserted Mussolini's party as the Duce fled toward the Swiss border. Graziani offered to surrender, so Daddario took him in tow and continued south to Milan.

General Wolff, in the meantime, had decided to make a second attempt to reach his headquarters at Bolzano, 125 miles northeast of Milan. He took a circuitous route through Switzerland toward the Austrian border, then south into an Italian region where the partisans were still weak. Dulles felt it essential that the German should reach Bolzano to arrange an orderly surrender, because SUNRISE had been resurrected. Washington had reversed its previous order. The German envoys were now to be flown to Caserta to sign the surrender instrument. They left by plane on the morning of April 28.

That afternoon, Mussolini and his mistress, captured earlier near the Swiss border by local partisans, were put in the custody of a squad of Communists led by Colonel Walter Audisio. In past months, this partisan colonel had been part of a Garibaldini brigade, armed and trained by a 13-man OSS Operational Group. Most of the Garibaldini had given "complete support and cooperation" to the OSS team. But not Audisio. The Americans saw him as an ambitious man with "fascist tendencies." [61] Now he became Mussolini's executioner. The Duce was shot at the gates of a villa and his body transported south to Milan.

Still later that day, Captain Daddario and his prisoner, Graziani, drove into Milan in a partisan automobile. He requisitioned the Hotel

Milano as OSS Headquarters, then drove to Gestapo headquarters, still surrounded by armed partisans in the center of the city. While Daddario was conferring with Colonel Rauff, the Gestapo chief, another OSS officer arrived. It was the late Major Holohan's aide (and alleged murderer) Lieutenant Aldo Icardi, who had been operating an intelligence network in the north since Holohan's disappearance.

The situation was touchy. The German command post was ringed by hostile guerrillas. Many of the partisan commanders pressed the CLNAI to authorize an attack. The resistance leaders were cautious, but they were incensed by Rauff's insistence that he would surrender only to the Allies. A battle might break out at any moment. And it was uncertain when the first British and American troops would enter the city.

Daddario and Icardi began their "delicate diplomacy," ferrying between Nazis and belligerent guerrillas, hoping to keep both groups in check. That evening, as the OSS men retired to their hotel, and while the uneasy peace remained in effect, the bodies of Mussolini and his mistress were unloaded from a truck. They were hung head downward from the roof of a gas station in the center of Milan. On the morning of April 29, thousands of Italians filed by in a festive atmosphere to see their ex-dictator degraded.

Daddario and Icardi were soon visited by Socialist partisans who had decided to inflict a similar retribution on Marshal Graziani. A delegation of six guerrillas, armed to the teeth, demanded that the Americans hand over the fascist marshal. When Daddario refused, the partisans started up the stairs to the locked room on the fifth floor of the hotel where Graziani had been deposited.

Daddario and Icardi raced ahead and posted themselves in front of Graziani's door. Neither officer was armed. Daddario declared that the partisans would first have to eliminate him to capture Graziani. The Socialists backed down and departed, "amid a flood of oaths and blasphemies about the American coddling the filthy fascists." [62]

A day later, Allied troops moved into the city and the Gestapo troops surrendered. Later that week, on May 2, SUNRISE went into effect. The Nazis not already captured by partisan or Allied units surrendered peacefully. To his critics in Berlin, General Wolff explained that his actions had prevented a "Communist uprising" that would have established a "Soviet republic in northern Italy." [63]

Having inadvertently saved a Gestapo general and a fascist marshal and effected a surrender that prevented much bloodshed (but also robbed the partisans of their moment of glory), OSS officers then flocked to Bolzano, the headquarters of the SS and the Wehrmacht, to celebrate the peace. Gero V. S. Gaevernitz, Dulles' German advisor and an instrumental figure in the surrender negotiations, was there, exchanging champagne toasts with Wolff and his men. So was Theodore Ryan, chief of the SI reports section at Caserta, the son of a multi-millionaire, a graduate of Yale Law School, and a prominent Connecticut Republican.ᶜ Ryan took charge of the vast art treasures of Florence, which Wolff had moved to safety during earlier months of fighting.

Incensed partisans in the Bolzano area were barely restrained by OSS Sergeant Salvadore Fabrega, a Spaniard who fought for the Loyalists, joined the French Foreign Legion after Franco's victory, then emigrated to the United States. He had been first to reach Gestapo headquarters, and with the aid of six escaped French prisoners of war, he had the unhappy task of preventing the Italians from butchering the Germans.[64]

He was soon relieved by a joint British-American intelligence team, who had come from Caserta to "debrief" the German command. The mission was headed by Russell Livermore, the New York Republican attorney who commanded the OSS Operational Groups. Another team member was John McCulloch, an Oxford-educated writer, editor of a Latin American journal for the Foreign Policy Association, and head of the German section of SI in Italy.

McCulloch remembers, "The town of Bolzano at that time was fairly neatly divided into a German-speaking section and an Italian-speaking section. . . . As our little caravan passed through the Italian district, we were showered with flowers and offers of wine. When we crossed into the German-speaking half, we were met by three German generals, who had been standing on a street corner in a cold drizzle for the last couple hours. . . .

"Since the Germans were still in uniform (and were to be for another week) various questions of protocol arose. One was the matter of saluting. If a German soldier saluted us, should we return the salute? We caucused on this matter, and decided that we would, provided that the salute was a conventional one, and not the hand-raised-to-the-heavens 'Heil Hitler' type. . . .

"During this pre–V-E Day week we had no problems with the Germans. Our difficulties, though they turned out to be minor ones,

ᶜ Ryan served as Republican Minority Leader and president pro tem of the Connecticut State Senate, 1953–57.

came from another source. . . . One evening, I found a great com-
motion in the square. A number of trucks had suddenly appeared with
Italian partisans. . . . They were about to batter down the doors of
the German officers' building, and a man who appeared to be in
charge gave me to understand that they proposed to lynch a certain
German lieutenant who—they assured me—had been guilty of various
crimes.

"Summoning up my best Italian, I told the partisan leader that, although the Germans were still technically in charge of the town, authority had actually passed to the British and the Americans and that
we couldn't permit an out-and-out bloodbath. I sent one of our GI's,
who happened to be in the neighborhood, back to our headquarters to
summon help—moral if not physical—and arranged that an American
tank, also there by chance, should circle the square with the Stars and
Stripes prominently displayed. Within a few minutes an American
officer arrived who was of Italian descent and had worked closely with
the Italian partisans. He was able to persuade them that no good
could come of an Italian-German confrontation and that justice would,
in the end, be served. . . .

"After all this, V-E Day itself was something of an anticlimax. We
celebrated it with champagne, which we had taken from the Germans,
who had taken it from the French. In the midst of our party a German
major arrived, sat down casually at the piano and started playing
Strauss waltzes. This was interrupted when an upper-level British officer
gruffly declared that this was 'a bad show,' 'not at all the thing to do,'
etc. I had to explain to the German major that, while we liked his
music, this was neither the time nor the place for it." [65] For the Nazis,
the festivities ended on May 12, when Allied troops finally arrived to
transport SS General Wolff and his entire staff to a prisoner internment camp.[d]

In the days after liberation, OSS might have showed more gratitude to the partisans. Since Peter Tompkins had first formed his ORI
intelligence network two years before, OSS had given legal contracts to
Italian agents who went behind the lines to collect intelligence. These
promised $200 per month in salary and a $5000 life insurance policy.
When the agents came to collect their accumulated salaries after V-E
Day, OSS agreed to pay, but only at the legal exchange rate. The black

[d] Despite testimony on his behalf from Dulles' German advisor, Gero
Gaevernitz, Wolff was tried by a German court for war crimes in 1964
and sentenced to fifteen years imprisonment.

market rate of dollars-to-lire which prevailed for virtually all other transactions was three to four times higher. One agent formally protested.
The payments, he said, should be more in accordance with financial
realities. He received a reply from a bright young Republican attorney
in the OSS General Counsel's Office, informing him that payment at
black market rates would be in "contravention of the law"—an odd
concern for an espionage organization.

Partisan agents did receive, however, a handsome parchment document with an impressive red seal, signed personally by General Donovan. It read: "This statement renders testimony by our sincere gratitude
to . . . for his disinterested aid to this office and to the United States
Army in the battle for the liberation of Italy." [66] Unfortunately, a handful of the documents fell into the hands of ex-fascists who used them to
prove their past "allegiance" to the Allies.

Some OSS men could not help but wonder—had SUNRISE been
a misnomer?

5

Of Communists
and Kings

In the spring
of 1944, diplomat Harold Macmillan was relieved to see responsibility
for British and American clandestine operations in the Balkans passed
from Middle East headquarters at Cairo to the Allied command in
Italy. Cairo was "suspect" by the Americans, he noted. The city was
"somehow connected in their minds with Imperialism, Kipling, and all
that." [1]

OSS relations with the British secret services in the Egyptian capital
had been troubled by mutual mistrust since 1942, when the first Donovan envoy to the Middle East—a former advertising director of the
United Fruit Company—received an icy reception from British officials.
"Our people in Cairo," confessed an SOE officer, "frankly wished to
keep any similar American organization out of the theater altogether,
or if this was not practicable, to keep it under strict control. . . . This
attitude was unfortunate because it naturally made the Americans suspicious and eager to conceal their plans from us." [2]

Even before OSS began to staff a regular Middle Eastern headquarters, the British had discovered that the Egyptian climate seemed
to encourage petty stratagems. "Nobody who did not experience it,"
wrote a British colonel, "can possibly imagine the atmosphere of
jealousy, suspicion, and intrigue which embittered the relations between
the various secret and semi-secret departments in Cairo. . . . I knew of
a lieutenant colonel in SOE who had asked the signals authorities
whether they could install a device on his telephone whereby what his

her officers said to him could be recorded and presumably used evidence against them. It was not quite Hobbes's war of every man against every man. But certainly every secret organization seemed to be set against every other secret organization." [3] Americans who arrived on the scene in 1943 learned that the SOE detachment had already suffered through the replacement of three directors in as many years. The entire British secret bureaucracy was torn by bitter factionalism; fervent champions of competing Balkan resistance groups were united only in their equal distaste for emissaries of the Foreign Office.

OSS experienced similar growing pains in Cairo. First to be purged was the detachment's executive officer, Greek-American importer Ulius Amoss.[a] He had achieved some notoriety by his "import" of an ex-convict from the United States for purposes of expert assassination. Amoss was eventually relieved of his post in the summer of 1943 for "financial mismanagement." "He knew nothing," declared one OSS executive, "and messed up everything he touched." [4] Weeks after Amoss's recall, Donovan replaced the West Point colonel then commanding OSS Cairo with Choate-Harvard Colonel John Toulmin, a vice-president of the First National Bank of Boston.

Installed in an ornate villa that "looked like a bastard version of the Taj Mahal," [5] Toulmin set to work immediately to guard his OSS operational sphere against British inroads. Through no fault of the colonel and his aggressive aides, OSS had already been relegated to a secondary position in the Middle East itself. In late 1942, Donovan had organized an "Expedition 90" to work in the Arab countries. The mission was planned by Colonel Harold Hoskins, an executive of a New York textile firm with business experience in the Mideast.[b] Born in Beirut of missionary parents, a cousin of William Eddy, and a distant relative of the Dulles brothers, his opinion carried considerable weight at OSS headquarters. Hoskins felt that "the British had done nothing for the Middle East and were, therefore, completely discredited throughout the Arab world. The colonel believed, however, that the Arabs respected the Americans because they had no imperialistic designs and because their interests were purely cultural. . . . He recommended that

---

[a] In 1946, Amoss founded an international private intelligence organization that later became tied to Senate Joseph McCarthy; see Chapter Eleven.

[b] Hoskins was director of the State Department's Foreign Service Institute, 1955–61.

he should be sent to the Middle East by OSS to start an underground organization for enlisting the good will of the Arab side." [6]

The British took sharp issue with this plan. "It appeared to us," wrote an SOE official, "that almost by definition, his objective could not be achieved except by denigrating the efforts of the British. This hardly seemed to be furthering our common efforts. . . . All this we pointed out to the colonel and his OSS sponsors, but we gathered that none of our objections carried much weight. . . . At this stage the argument was taken over from us by our embassy and the State Department, and I believe grew a good deal fiercer and hotter." [7] Whitehall emerged triumphant from the dispute. "Expedition 90" was scaled down to a "preliminary survey mission"; then the entire plan was tabled.

Toulmin involuntarily accepted British operational predominance in the Middle East. But London's victory left room for some notable achievements by an unusual assortment of American officers. OSS intelligence was collected from the Arab world by Dr. Stephen Penrose, Jr.,[c] of the Near East College Association and his 27-year-old assistant, Cal Tech history instructor Kermit Roosevelt (a grandson of the "Rough Rider" President).[d] One of Penrose's field agents was German-educated Rabbi Nelson Glueck, a distinguished archaeologist who had first discovered the site of King Solomon's mines.[e] Using archaeological explorations of the American School for Oriental Research at Jerusalem as a cover, Glueck created an espionage network among the Arabs of Transjordan.[8] An entirely separate Allied intelligence effort was conducted by the Jewish Agency Executive, whose Mideast agents performed some of the most suicidal Balkan missions of the war for OSS and SOE while cherishing their ultimate dream of a Zionist state in Palestine.

In Eastern Europe, Toulmin's command found new responsibilities, which it shared with a semi-autonomous base in neutral Turkey. The colonel had discovered his Istanbul outpost to be disastrously infiltrated

[c] Penrose was President of the American University of Beirut from 1948 until his death in 1954.

[d] Roosevelt engineered the CIA coup against Mossadegh in Iran in 1953, left the CIA to become vice-president for governmental relations of Gulf Oil, 1958–64, and is now a partner in a Washington public relations firms that represents, among other international clients, the government of Iran.

[e] Glueck was President of the Hebrew Union College in Cincinnati from 1947 until his death in 1971.

by Axis agents and pro-German officers of "Eminyet," the Turkish Security Service.[9] The British also complained to Washington that Donovan's Istanbul operatives had failed to inform London of Bulgarian peace feelers. Toulmin finally decided to replace the Turkish base chief, a Chicago banker, with 35-year-old Frank Wisner, an imaginative Wall Street lawyer with a Mississippi twang.[f] Under its new commander, the Istanbul outpost established an effective espionage organization that reached into the German-occupied countries of southeastern Europe. Following in the steps of the "Bughouse Mission" to Soviet-liberated Romania, Wisner moved to Bucharest in September 1944 to head the OSS detachment in that city (until its expulsion by the Russians the following year).[10]

All this activity was only peripheral to the principal objective of the OSS Cairo staff—operations in the Balkans. Again the British had a head start in this strategically important region. There had been only a handful of OSS representatives in Cairo in September 1942 when SOE men first parachuted into the Greek mountains. British officers found the resistance hopelessly divided between the conservative, republican EDES group under the command of rotund, bearded Napoleon Zervas, and the EAM–ELAS force, dominated by the Greek Communist Party. While Churchill and his Foreign Office assistants in London were determined to save the postwar throne of the exiled Greek King George, SOE men encountered little royalist sentiment among either of these competing guerrilla armies. The only concern of the first SOE commander in Greece, a professional army brigadier, was to mold the republican and leftist partisans into a united fighting force against the Germans.[11] His political neutrality, however, came under increasingly sharp attack from both ends of the political spectrum. The leftist EAM–ELAS became uncooperative as the guerrillas began to suspect the British of secretly plotting against them. Then the right-wing exile government and the Greek King in Cairo complained to Churchill that SOE was violating Foreign Office directives by aiding the leftists (who refused to accept the return of the King after the war). Churchill obligingly replaced the SOE brigadier with his 26-year-old second-in-command, a baron's son whose political conservatism was more in line with London's thinking. The Prime Minister also made it

---

[f] Wisner was chief of the CIA's Office of Policy Coordination, 1948–52; CIA Deputy Director for Plans, 1953–58. He went to London for a time as CIA station chief, resigned from the agency in 1962 after suffering a nervous breakdown, and committed suicide in 1965.

clear that British actions in Greece were to be directed toward one goal
—the return of the monarchy. This SOE housecleaning had just occurred when the first OSS men appeared behind the lines in Greece.

As the British began to openly favor the more conservative EDES
guerrillas, the leftists turned to OSS for support. "We hoped," wrote
the chief of the Communist-dominated EAM–ELAS bands, "that the
arrival of the Americans might do something to change the situation
and that they would inform the service which had sent them of the
true state of affairs. Moreover, from our first talks, we saw that they
spoke frankly and made no secret of the fact that America was not interested in political objectives but only in finishing the war quickly,
and they showed that they took a stand directly opposed to that of the
British." [12] The apparent sympathy of these American officers for the
leftist partisans was not lost on the new SOE commander. He accused
these first OSS arrivals of "crusading for EAM–ELAS against the
British." Worse yet, in British eyes, Americans of Greek descent were
arriving in the hills of Hellas in OSS uniforms. London believed these
Greek-Americans would become "an innocent channel" for Communist
propaganda.[13]

More candid British officers admitted that many American operatives who held no brief for the Greek Communists were, nonetheless,
hostile to their SOE colleagues. One Greek-American officer attached
to a British team remained carefully aloof from the leftist partisans.
But, to the equal dismay of his SOE teammates, the OSS man was "a
rank Anglophobe. His hatred of England and anything British completely warped his outlook and he was impossible to get on with on that
account. He regarded almost every officer of the British Army over the
rank of captain as the degenerate son of a lord or duke." [14] —

A few OSS officers did manage to get along with their British allies.
The Greek desk of SI Branch at Cairo was headed by Dr. Rodney
Young,[g] a Princeton archaeologist who had spent several years at the
American School of Classical Studies in Athens. He and his 28-year-old
successor, Oxford-educated political scientist Stephen Bailey,[h] worked
in relative harmony with their opposite numbers in MI-6.

OSS men of the Special Operations Branch were not as fortunate.
George Vournas, a Washington attorney who headed an influential
Greek-American fraternal organization in the United States, came to
Cairo in 1943 to work on OSS resistance operations. He recalls the

[g] Young is now curator of the University of Pennsylvania Museum.
[h] Bailey is President of Syracuse University.

spirit of the times: "Speaking for myself and my fellow officers in the Middle East, we had no favorites a priori. We were in favor of the group that fought the enemy and thereby advanced the hope of victory. As the fight progressed you would find fellow officers to be for ELAS or EDES depending on their performance." But the British, Vournas believed, "were not interested in Greek liberation or even effective prosecution of the war, but in naked imperial interest. . . . The plethora of British bureaus and agents (whose numbers were such that they were literally stepping on the toes of each other) played Greek cabinet ministers (whose very subsistence depended on the salaries advanced by the British) one against another; one Greek general or admiral against another. . . . It happened that the EAM was the most numerous and effective organization. Had it been the EDES under Napoleon Zervas instead, that, too, would have been undermined instead of being showered with gold sovereigns, unless it faithfully toed the British line." [15]

The conflict between guerrilla groups escalated into civil war after Athens was liberated from the Germans in December 1944. When the exile government, somewhat liberalized under Prime Minister George Papandreou, returned to the capital under the protection of British troops, the EAM–ELAS partisans broke into open rebellion. The British Army took a respite of several months from the war against Hitler to suppress the revolt. In the midst of this battle, the OSS officers who remained in the country, including a young Greek-American attorney, Thomas Karamessines,[1] tried to maintain a position of neutrality, despite the overtures of the ELAS commander, who loved to quote Abraham Lincoln and Upton Sinclair in fractured English. A truce between the leftists and the government was finally arranged, with the aid of an OSS doctor. He had set up a hospital behind the lines during the German occupation to treat ELAS wounded and the leftists trusted him. He alone was able to shuttle freely between the ELAS and British lines, eventually convincing the guerrillas to release several thousand hostages as the prelude to a cease-fire.[16]

The Greek revolt led to an important alteration in the operational directive of OSS Cairo. In early 1945, Colonel Toulmin returned to the United States and was replaced by Colonel Harry Aldrich, a professional Army officer who had been stationed in China in the 1930s, observing Japanese aggression in the Far East. Aldrich and his deputy,

[1] Karamessines has been CIA Deputy Director for Plans since 1967.

young Wall Street attorney Lawrence Houston,[j] were summoned by General Donovan to a special briefing session some months after the debacle in Athens. Donovan, according to Allen Dulles, provided Aldrich and Houston with "oral instructions" that "the main target for intelligence operations should now become discovering what the Soviets were doing in the Balkans rather than German operations in the Middle East. The German threat was receding. The Soviet danger was already looming." Donovan "realized this," said Dulles, "but, for obvious reasons, he could not put such instructions in an official dispatch." [17]

Donovan's new directive was, in part, an outgrowth of the events in Greece. But more important, the general was concerned with Russian influence to the north of Athens, in another important area of the Balkans.

Shortly after the German invasion and subjugation of Yugoslavia in April 1941, the Allied propaganda services began to manufacture a legend, a heroic tale of a bearded and bespectacled colonel named Draza Mihailovic.[18] Chief of staff of a Yugoslav Army unit at the time of his country's capitulation, he had refused to surrender. Taking to the hills in the wake of the Nazi victory, he formed a guerrilla army to fight the invaders. Calling themselves Chetniks after a similar anti-Bulgar guerrilla group of the First World War, Mihailovic's troops pledged their loyalty and devotion to King Peter, the teenaged monarch who fled Yugoslavia during the invasion to establish a government-in-exile at London.

The British established first radio contact with the Yugoslav guerrillas in September 1941, and soon after King Peter gave his official blessing to the Chetniks. Mihailovic was promoted to the rank of general and appointed War Minister of the exile government. The British Broadcasting Company began to herald the Chetniks as the first organized underground of occupied Europe, urging all patriotic Yugoslavs to join this irregular army. The American and Soviet press echoed London, and Mihailovic became a universal symbol of the anti-Nazi resistance. Eager to establish more direct contact with the Chetniks, the SOE infiltrated one of its officers into Yugoslavia by submarine in October. "Everything in human power," Churchill told his generals, should be done to aid the guerrillas.[19]

[j] Houston is now General Counsel of CIA.

At COI headquarters in Washington, these events were viewed with special interest. General Donovan was already well versed in Yugoslav affairs. He had gone to Belgrade as a special envoy of Roosevelt in early 1941 to urge Yugoslav political and military leaders to resist the Axis. His presence in that capital city only days before a successful coup against a pro-German regime, led to charges by American isolationists that Donovan had engineered the revolt on behalf of the White House.[20] Within weeks of the palace revolution, Yugoslavia was overrun by the Wehrmacht and Donovan helped found the American Friends of Yugoslavia, a bipartisan committee resolved to "support and strengthen the Yugoslav will to resist." [21]

In the spring of 1942, Donovan sent one of his aides to Cairo to confer with the commanding general of the exiled Yugoslav armed forces. The OSS emissary agreed to supply the Yugoslav Air Force with four American bombers to be used in transporting 5000 pistols and 2000 submachine guns by parachute drop to the Chetniks. The agreement also provided for the dispatch of OSS liaison officers to Mihailovic. All seemed well, on paper. But the Yugoslav general who signed the accord became involved in political difficulties with his exile government and was quickly deprived of his command. The carefully negotiated operational pact followed him into oblivion.

Three months later, on an official visit to America, King Peter received renewed assurances of assistance from Roosevelt. The King recalled, "I saw General Bill Donovan as the President had advised and discussed aid to Mihailovic with him. He assured me that such aid would be forthcoming as soon as there were enough long-range bombers in the Middle East to permit." Donovan described the Chetniks "as a prime force of resistance in Europe and said that Americans would be honored to give it all aid." Peter was delighted that the OSS chief "had already given orders for the instructions dropped with food and arms parcels to be printed in Serbian." [22] Only later did the King learn that the packages never reached Chetnik territory. Though wrapped in the tricolor of the Yugoslav flag and bearing a greeting in Serbian from Roosevelt to Mihailovic's valiant warriors, much of the food was used in the winter of 1942 to supply the civilian populace of Malta.

The Chetniks received only one small arms shipment from SOE that entire year. This British parsimony was not, however, caused by a bureaucratic snarl. For while the American and British public heard daily tributes to Mihailovic's successes against the enemy, secret reports from William Hudson, the first SOE officer sent to Chetnik territory, were causing a stir in London. The tall, powerfully built mining engineer was not a newcomer to Yugoslavia; he had worked for a British company in Serbia for some years before the war and had served MI-6 in Belgrade prior to the invasion. Nor could he be accused of left-wing sympathies. (Three years later, as commander of an SOE mission to the non-Communist Polish resistance, Hudson was jailed by the Soviets.)

Because of his well-deserved reputation as a trained and politically moderate intelligence officer, Hudson's observations of a second resistance force in Yugoslavia were read with interest at Whitehall. Known as Partisans, the soldiers of this new guerrilla army wore red stars on their caps and were led by handsome, Soviet-trained Communist Josip Broz—called Tito by his followers. Hudson's dispatches told of open warfare between the Partisans and Chetniks. The SOE man insisted on a unity conference between the leaders of the two contending resistance forces, but two meetings between Mihailovic and Tito ended only in bitter vituperation. Fighting broke out anew, with each side blaming the other for truce violations. Hudson then left the Chetnik camp and joined a Partisan group. He was impressed by the military prowess of the Partisans, and had already grown impatient with Mihailovic's reluctance to take vigorous military action against the enemy for fear of provoking German mass reprisals.

That the conflict was indeed serious was poignantly brought home to London when the second SOE officer sent into the country in 1942 was found murdered, allegedly by bandits. The British suspected that he had been caught in the cross-fire of intrigue between Partisan and Chetnik bands.[23]

Searching for an understanding of this political schism, London was puzzled by Mihailovic's own ideological position. He was commonly regarded as a conservative, yet before the war some of Yugoslavia's more rightist military officers had called him a Socialist. One pro-Chetnik enthusiast suggested that "those who knew his personal library in Belgrade say that it contained many standard leftist works, and this at a time when the possession of such works was a state crime." [24] Some said the Chetnik chief was a Russophile, and his frequent attempts to establish close relations with the Soviets during the war seemed to support that rumor. And although there were many political reactionaries in his retinue, Mihailovic's supporters also came to include adherents of the left. Even King Peter, as a student at Cambridge, chose to join the University Socialist Club, where he was looked on as "a freak." [25]

Complicating any political analysis was the traditional ethnic rivalry between the Serbs and Croats of Yugoslavia, which, in London's view, lay at the root of the Partisan-Chetnik conflict. The Croats had long resented the domination of the Yugoslav governmental machinery by the Serbs. Their grievances were abetted by religious differences, the Croats adhering to Catholicism and the Serbs to the Orthodox Church. Ethnic dissension pervaded Yugoslav politics. A precarious and deteriorating balance was struck between the Serbs and Croats in the exile government. More importantly, Mihailovic was a Serb and Tito a Croat, and although many Serbs originally joined the Partisans, the Croat influence came to predominate.

OSS received its own lesson in ethnic rivalry. American-Yugoslavs of Serb ancestry had become fervent champions of the Chetnik cause, while those of Croat origin rallied to support of the Partisan movement. The spokesman for the American Croats was Ivan Subasic, the prewar governor of Croatia. He had escaped from Yugoslavia at the time of the invasion and chose exile in the United States (unlike most displaced Yugoslav politicians, who followed the King to London). Subasic first came to the attention of OSS in September 1942 when he

General Mihailovic (right), idolized as a Chetnik hero, denounced as a German collaborator, spent a moment of relaxed frivolity at his Serbian headquarters with Capt. Nicholas Lallich, chief of an OSS air rescue mission sent to Yugoslavia in the summer of 1944.

helped arrange a State Department–sponsored "unity conference" to curb the Serb-Croat dissension among Yugoslav-Americans. Donovan's officers continued to maintain close contact with the Croat leader. Two years later he would be called upon to play a more direct role in Yugoslavia's unfolding political drama.

The Nazis were of course happy to promote the Serb-Croat conflict, and they did so by appointing two puppet political leaders in occupied Yugoslavia. A collaborationist Serb general was installed in Belgrade, while the Croat Ante Pavelic became the quisling leader of an "Independent Croatia." In his zeal to please his Axis friends, Pavelic established a pro-Nazi militia called the Ustashi, which began to massacre the Serb minority in Croatia. Charges soon began to fly. Tito, claimed the Chetniks, was supporting the Ustashi in their murderous acts against the Serbs. Mihailovic, the Partisans retorted, was actively working with Serb collaborators, Nazis, and Italian Fascists of the occupation army.

To the extent that subordinate commanders of both Chetnik and Partisan groups felt their survival required temporary accommodations with the enemy, there was indeed collaboration.[26] But in the minds of the British, the charges against the Chetniks were of greater import. London's attitude was clearly affected by Hudson's military reports of Chetnik inactivity and Partisan aggressiveness. There also began, in July 1942, a massive propaganda campaign against Mihailovic in both Britain and the United States, accusing him of open collaboration with the enemy. The first accusations were broadcast by a clandestine station called "Radio Free Yugoslavia." The transmitter was actually located in the Soviet Union and the programs were prepared by Partisan representatives in Russia. The charges were picked up by the Western press, which began to make increased mention of Tito's forces and to downplay the former Chetnik heroes.

In early 1943, a British diplomatic official in Switzerland offered to introduce OSS representative Allen Dulles to a young Montenegrin "theology student" who was actually an agent of Tito's Partisans. Though he later met with Tito's agents, Dulles "was very anti-Communist and felt the Allies must stick to Mihailovic and not fall into a trap prepared by Communist propagandists." [27]

London took a different tack. A new group of SOE officers had already been sent to Yugoslavia. Their reports not only confirmed Hudson's original observations of Chetnik inertia, but also noted that some Mihailovic lieutenants were on remarkably friendly terms with

Italian occupation troops. Whether such collaboration was actually dictated by the requirements of guerrilla survival, the information was not well received in London. Nor was the SOE dispatch of March 1943 which reported that Mihailovic, while severely criticizing the British for lack of aid, had defended Chetnik dealings with the Italians as his "sole adequate source of benefit and assurance." [28] Foreign Minister Anthony Eden informed King Peter's government in May that future British aid to Mihailovic would cease unless the Chetniks ended all collaboration with the enemy.

Plans were in progress at this time for the coming invasion of Italy. The Allies hoped to create a military diversion through widespread guerrilla sabotage in the Balkans to force the Germans to deploy their units away from the Italian peninsula. When London concluded that the Chetniks could not perform this function, SOE, with Churchill's personal approval, sent several of its officers to make the first formal contacts with the Partisans.

An aging Canadian major parachuted to Partisan headquarters in Croatia. His extreme religious piety became strangely entwined with an emotional attachment to the Communist guerrillas and he soon concluded, "The spirit that permeated the life of the Partisan was essentially and fundamentally religious zeal." This "faith and trust in the Almighty" had "effected unity and was leading the people on to final victory, when truth would be revealed in love and freedom." [29]

Luckily for Tito, other SOE officers were more worldly than the Canadian major. As a demonstration of the Prime Minister's personal interest in the Yugoslav situation, SOE Captain William Deakin was sent to Tito's Bosnian headquarters in late May. An Oxford historian who had assisted Churchill in researching his biography of Marlborough, Deakin had been recalled from an assignment with the SOE liaison mission in the United States to receive his Yugoslav mission. Within weeks of his arrival in Partisan territory, Deakin's "brilliant messages" to London had "left no doubt as to the military value of Tito's movement." [30] Churchill then personally decided to send an official SOE mission to Partisan headquarters.

By the summer of 1943, Roosevelt had also resolved to send American observers to both Partisan and Chetnik bands. But OSS found that decision difficult to implement because Cairo SOE went to great lengths to prevent OSS infiltration into the Balkans. Plans to land OSS men on the Yugoslav coast were consistently blocked by the British Navy, which at SOE instigation "requisitioned" every small vessel that OSS requested. ("Can't the British Empire," demanded one irate OSS official at Allied headquarters, "afford to release two small fishing boats to the United States?") It finally required General Donovan's personal intervention in London to clear the way for OSS Yugoslav missions.

Then new problems arose on the home front. Officer recruitment for Yugoslav operations was being expedited through the New York OSS office by Francis Kalnay, a Hungarian-born writer who had compiled a well-known handbook for immigrants before the war. Kalnay's efforts, however, were blocked by Pittsburgh investment banker Joseph Scribner, then assistant chief of the Special Operations Branch in Washington. Scribner and other OSS executives suspected Kalnay's Yugoslavs of "Communistic tendencies" and questioned the OSS man's own political motives.[k]

Many Yugoslavs were hired and trained by OSS and then abruptly dismissed because of suspected political sympathies for Tito. The most interesting of these unfortunate recruits was Stephen Dedijer, the brother of one of Tito's closest aides.[l] He had come to the United States in the late 1930s on secret instructions from Moscow to edit a Croat-language Communist newspaper. After his recruitment and dismissal from OSS, he joined an American paratrooper unit. He was considered such an outstanding soldier that he became a personal bodyguard to an American general, whom he often amused by parachuting from a plane shouting "Long Live Stalin!" in place of the more traditional "Geronimo!"

By the end of the summer, the difficulties in Washington were overcome. Yugoslav recruiting proceeded under the watchful eyes of André Smoliannoff, an executive of the DuPont stock brokerage, and Dr. Grenville Holden, a Harvard-trained economist from Sylvania Electric. Donovan was soon ready to send his men into the Yugoslav hinterland. The general's plans were to affect the lives of two OSS officers who had just made a chance acquaintance at a British parachute training camp in Palestine.

A California oil geologist (and former Olympic star while at Stanford), Linn Farish had enlisted in the Canadian Army before Amer-

---

[k] Kalnay later became a noted writer of children's stories. His ideological ghost returned to haunt CIA employees during the McCarthy era; see Chapter Eleven.

[l] Dedijer served for a time as chairman of the Yugoslav Atomic Energy Commission until he broke with Tito and left the country. He now teaches at a Swedish University.

ica's entry into the war, serving with the Royal Engineers in Persia, then
transferring to a British commando group. While undergoing paratroop
training, Farish was recruited by OSS and commissioned a major. His
friend, Colonel Albert Seitz, was an engineer by profession.[m] He had
spent some time at West Point and had also served in the Royal
Canadian Mounted Police. Both men were tall, husky, well-trained
soldiers. They met at a "jump training" camp near Haifa, then received
parallel orders to report to Cairo for assignment. Farish learned that he
had been selected to serve as OSS representative with the SOE mission
to Tito. Seitz, paradoxically, was to head the OSS team to Mihailovic's
camp. At the outset, neither officer had much knowledge of the Tito-
Mihailovic conflict. Seitz recalls that they "discussed the reported friction . . . and the matter did not appear insurmountable." [31]

Both Farish and Seitz would have the important task of determining whether the two competing resistance groups were deserving of
American aid. But as they prepared for their respective parachute missions in September 1943, a third OSS officer in Cairo had already
reached his own decision. After reading laudatory British intelligence reports on the Partisan movement, Major Louis Huot was determined to
assist Tito's guerrillas. Raised in an atmosphere of Minnesota populism,
he had come to Europe during the prewar decade to observe first-hand
the alarming growth of European fascism. As a reporter for the Paris
edition of the Chicago *Tribune* and later as European manager of an
American press service, Huot developed a well-deserved reputation as a
daring liberal journalist. Serving as an OSS communications specialist
in North Africa, Huot met with Tito's representatives who had made
their way to OSS Headquarters in Algiers. Together they formulated a
plan for maritime supply of the Communist guerrillas. Establishing a
base at Bari, Italy (which had been occupied by the Allies just days
before, during the Salerno invasion), Huot, with the encouragement of
the SO Branch chief at Cairo, Harvard anthropologist and TORCH
veteran Carleton Coon, organized a fleet of small ships to ferry
clothes and ammunition to the Yugoslav mainland.

As Huot's preparations were under way, the official SOE mission to
the Partisans, including Major Farish as OSS observer, had reached
Tito's headquarters. During the following months, much of the development of British policy in Yugoslavia would center on the com-

[m] Seitz worked on CIA Balkan operations, 1946–52, and appeared in
Loas in 1957 as chief of a U.S. "training assistance group."

mander of this mission, 32-year-old British Brigadier Fitzroy MacLean.[n]
After service during the 1930s as a diplomatic attaché with secret intelligence duties in Paris and Moscow, MacLean had worked on
clandestine operations in the Middle East. Elected to a Conservative
Party seat in Parliament, the lanky officer had secured the political confidence of the Prime Minister. Churchill personally selected him for the
Yugoslav assignment.

MacLean's years in Stalinist Moscow had left him "deeply and
lastingly conscious of the expansionist tendencies of international Communism and of its intimate connection with Soviet foreign policy." He
knew that the Partisans were under Communist leadership and surmised that "their ultimate aim would undoubtedly be to establish in
Yugoslavia a Communist regime closely linked to Moscow." The SOE
commander was also aware that some Foreign Office diplomats were
violently opposed to any manifestation of Balkan Communism. This
troubled him. "Although, as a Conservative," recalled MacLean, "I had
no liking for Communists or Communism, I had not fancied the idea
of having to intrigue politically against men with whom I was cooper-
ating militarily." Before his departure, MacLean posed this dilemma to
Churchill. The Prime Minister reassured him. The major SOE task
in Yugoslavia, said Churchill, would be "to help find out who was killing the most Germans and suggest means by which we could help
them to kill more. Politics must be a secondary consideration." [32] After
his arrival by parachute in the Yugoslav countryside, MacLean, immediately impressed with the military capabilities of the Partisans, began to transmit the reports that would lead to a major change in
British policy.

OSS Major Huot had not bothered with such bureaucratic tasks.
Completing the arrangements for his secret fleet, he personally
accompanied one of the first maritime voyages to the Yugoslav coast in
October for the express purpose of meeting with Tito. "One day," recalls Tito's official biographer, "a rather strange man appeared on
Partisan territory. He was an officer of the United States Army, a major,
who said that his name was Huot. He asked to see Tito, but inquired
all the time whether there were any British officers in the vicinity. At
that very moment, a British officer came along. The American immediately asked the town major to hide him in another room so that

[n] MacLean was Conservative Parliamentary Under-Secretary of State
and Financial Secretary of the British War Office, 1954–57.

the Englishman should not see him. The town major did as he was asked, but was at a complete loss to understand what the American officer was after. The facts were simple, however. Major Louis Huot had not obtained permission from the Allied Command to come to Yugoslavia. He had come on his own initiative to assist the Partisans." [33]

Huot made his way to Partisan headquarters and soon found himself in Tito's presence. The American officer was immediately struck by the charismatic figure who stood before him. "Compact, broad-shouldered, deep-chested and flat-bellied, there was strength—plain physical stamina—implicit in every line of him, and there were pride and assurance in the carriage of his rectangular head." Tito held out his hand. "Welcome," he said in English.

Ushered into a makeshift office built of unpainted cedar wood, Huot had a long conversation with the veteran Yugoslav Communist. "We have the warmest affection for the United States," Tito assured the major, "and are happy to be indebted to you and your countrymen for the help you have given us. You have now seen enough of our country to realize how great is our need of supplies." As he spoke, the guerrilla chief made a deep impression on the OSS officer. "Here was no simple warrior," wrote Huot, "no primitive leader of fighting men. He might be that, but he was much more besides. Thinker, statesman, artist. . . . He appeared to be all these, and soldier as well; and there was a light in his face that glowed and flickered and subsided as he talked, but never went away—a light that comes only from long service in the tyranny of dreams. . . . Whatever this man might be and no matter what he signified, here was a force to reckon with, a leader men would follow through the very gates of hell." [34]

"We are fighting for democracy," Tito declared. And though Huot observed the use of the Russian political commissar system in the Partisan army, the OSS officer firmly believed that Tito "was planning no Communist revolution for his country. He was working out the pattern of a new and democratic popular front movement which would embrace all the elements in his community capable of resisting the invader." [35]

Huot left Yugoslavia in the company of Linn Farish, who, after a month with the MacLean mission, had come to share the enthusiasm of his British colleagues for the Partisans. Returning to Italy, Farish immediately embarked on a journey to Washington to present a personal report of his experiences. Huot, meanwhile, proceeded with his operational plans. The OSS man, notes Tito's biographer, "sent us over four hundred tons of uniforms, medical supplies, ammunition and other items, which could not be found in Yugoslavia. . . . This amounted to more than the total aid we had hitherto received from the Allies. We were planning on further quantities of supplies when one day this energetic American disappeared from Bari. He had been posted elsewhere." [36]

The Partisans were unaware that they owed Huot's sudden disappearance to the British. The major and his OSS team had begun their smuggling operation without prior approval from Allied headquarters in Italy. The British theater commander became upset when he learned that OSS had launched an operation having deep political implications without his knowledge or consent, and Brigadier MacLean, for his own reasons, fanned the general's anger. According to Louis Adamic,° a Yugoslav-American writer with close ties to the OSS liberal faction at Cairo, Huot's departure was also hastened by a high OSS official at Middle East headquarters "whose anti-Communism, operating untrammeled in the absence of an American policy, made him—in spite of his inherent American anti-Britishism—a ready tool of British policy." [37] The upshot was that Huot was sent to London, while his teammates were placed under house arrest on a charge of insubordination. They were held only a short time, when at General Donovan's insistence the charges were dropped. Donovan had his own ideas about the Yugoslav political conflict. But he felt that his officers should not be punished for their zeal. "If you court-martial them," he declared, "you'd also have to court-martial me, because I gave them the freedom of action to do what they did."

The strangest aspect of the whole affair was that the British should have first raised objections to Huot's operations in support of the Partisans. At that very time, Brigadier MacLean was urging Churchill to throw Whitehall's official support to Tito. The brigadier was brought out of Yugoslavia in November 1943 and taken to Cairo to meet with Foreign Minister Anthony Eden, then on his way to the Big Three Conference at Teheran. He gave Eden a report for the Prime Minister which described the Partisan movement as "very definitely under Communist leadership and firmly oriented towards Moscow." MacLean hastily added, however, "that as a resistance movement it was highly effective and that its effectiveness could be considerably increased by

° Adamic was mysteriously murdered at his home in New Jersey in 1951. One theory held that the killers were Chetnik fanatics, another suggested they were Stalinist MVD agents.

Allied help; but that, whether we gave such assistance or not, Tito and
his followers would exercise decisive influence in Yugoslavia after the
liberation." [38]

Roosevelt, also on his way to Teheran, had already received Linn
Farish's report in Washington. Like MacLean, Farish had words of
praise for the Partisans as a military force. Admitting that the Communists played a leading role in the guerrilla movement, Farish believed nonetheless that they had "not been able to indoctrinate it along
strictly Party lines." He noted that "the average Partisan is very sympathetic to the USA and the Allied cause. . . . As an American, the
observer was at times embarrassed by the enthusiastic reception which
he received and the implicit faith of the people that the United States
would come to their aid." The OSS officer left no doubt as to his own
sentiments. "If ever," he wrote, "a movement had the background of
indomitable will and courage with which to build great things, it is to
be found in Yugoslavia." [39]

While reading this glowing account of Tito's army, Roosevelt was,
unlike Churchill, giving equally serious consideration to a conflicting
source of information on the Yugoslav situation—the OSS mission to
Mihailovic. In August 1943, 32-year-old OSS Lieutenant Walter Mansfield parachuted to Mihailovic's Serbian headquarters.[p] Just as Deakin
and MacLean had been personal representatives of Churchill, Mansfield was General Donovan's personal envoy. After graduation from
Harvard, he had worked as an attorney in Donovan's law firm. The
lieutenant shared Donovan's political views (like the general, he was a
confirmed Republican) and the OSS chief had great respect for the
young officer's opinions.

No sooner had Mansfield reached Mihailovic's camp than the
Chetnik general besieged him with requests for increased American
support. Mansfield transmitted Mihailovic's pleas for aid to OSS Cairo
but "privately I felt that the issue must be settled on a much higher
plane. I felt it would be a sorry situation if Allied missions on both sides
found themselves using Allied equipment to destroy each other rather
than the Germans." Mansfield hoped for a compromise agreement under
which "Tito would stay in Bosnia and to the north, and Mihailovic in
Serbia, his stronghold." [40] This plan would later form the basis for
General Donovan's recommendations to the President.

In September, after Mansfield was joined by Colonel Seitz, Farish's

[p] Mansfield is now a federal court judge in New York City.

comrade from Palestine "jump training," Mihailovic, sensing an imminent betrayal by Whitehall, turned to the two OSS officers "in his
anger, and pleaded for more American teams to come in and see for
themselves what his guerrillas were doing." The Chetniks, Seitz later
reflected, "were never quite sure what was in the mind of the British;
they felt that British politicians would not hesitate to throw the Balkans
to the Communists if by so doing the British would be reasonably certain they could retain their hold on Greece and the eastern Mediterranean. With the Americans, the Serbs believed there was no purpose
except to win the war by fighting the Axis; no political or territorial
aspirations, and that we meant what we said without qualification."

The SOE mission suspected that by making overtures to the OSS
men, Mihailovic hoped to play off the Americans against the British.
To prevent such a ploy, the British brigadier who commanded the SOE
mission at Chetnik headquarters attempted to muzzle his American
colleagues. "I was there," Seitz remembers, "simply to give an Allied
illusion to the Yugoslavs. The mission was British and the whole show
would remain a British show. I would be permitted to see or talk to

*Women cried and the ground was strewn with flowers as a Chetnik major
(left foreground) introduced (left to right) OSS Col. Albert Seitz, SOE
Col. William Hudson, and OSS Lt. Walter Mansfield, to the jubilant
inhabitants of a Yugoslav village. The Allied officers were on an intelligence-
gathering tour of occupied Serbia in December 1943.*

Mihailovic only at the discretion of the brigadier. Walter would not be permitted near the headquarters. . . . I was even forbidden to address Mihailovic in French. Further, any message destined for my people would be subject to the brigadier's censorship." Seitz protested the SOE restrictions to Cairo. OSS headquarters supported the colonel's right to independent and uncensored communications. He simply ignored the other British dictates.

Despite his difficulties with the British and his obvious sympathy for the Chetniks, Seitz continually protested that "any talk of postwar politics before the Germans were driven out seemed sacrilege." [41] He was dedicated to fighting the Nazis and believed that his reports should be aimed primarily at military intelligence. On November 6 (only weeks before the Teheran Conference) Seitz and Mansfield therefore began an extensive inspection tour of the Chetnik forces throughout Serbia in order to obtain a comprehensive picture of Mihailovic's strength. They held long conferences with each guerrilla commander to discuss his past and proposed operations and the size and effectiveness of his group. Their conclusions would later have an important impact on American policy. But lacking their own radio transmitter, they were unable to communicate with OSS Cairo while in the hinterland. And after several weeks they found themselves completely cut off from Mihailovic's camp by German units, and were unable to relay their final observations to Donovan. Meanwhile, the Teheran conference was approaching.

General Donovan met with the President in Cairo shortly before the Big Three Conference. On the basis of first reports from Farish and Seitz, Donovan had concluded that both the Partisans and the Chetniks were of strategic value to the Allies. He therefore proposed a unity plan to Roosevelt. The President accepted the idea, which he first suggested to King Peter at a meeting in Cairo. Yugoslavia, under Donovan's arrangement, would be divided into two separate operational zones. Tito would control the western sector and Mihailovic the eastern region. Both guerrilla armies would be responsible to the Allied command in Italy. Donovan also proposed that if either guerrilla leader refused to abide by the terms of the agreement, he should be threatened with Allied boycott. With his usual enthusiasm, the OSS chief offered to parachute into Yugoslavia to personally attempt the "reconciliation" of Tito and Mihailovic.[42]

The proposal was forgotten at Teheran. Churchill went into the conference determined on a declaration of full Allied support for Tito. Roosevelt was unwilling to dispute the issue with his British and Russian colleagues. The President obligingly presented Stalin with a copy of Major Farish's pro-Tito report and then endorsed the official Conference decision that the Partisans "should be supported by supplies and equipment to the greatest extent possible." [43]

Did Roosevelt believe that he was abandoning Mihailovic by accepting the Teheran statement? Both the King and the British Foreign Office suspected the President of insincerity. The truth of the matter probably lies in the very real uncertainty of American policy in the face of British determination. On December 8, the House of Commons was officially informed that His Majesty's Government was "supporting the Partisan forces and giving them more support than General Mihailovic." [44] The following day, the State Department responded with the ambiguous statement that the United States would support both Partisans and Chetniks "from the point of view of their military effectiveness, without, during the fighting, entering into discussions of political differences which may have arisen among them." [45]

Even at Whitehall there was uncertainty about Churchill's new policy. Returning to Cairo from Teheran, the Prime Minister told King Peter that "Tito would be his man" and "there would be no more aid to Mihailovic whatsoever; all was to go to Tito." [46] Churchill also promised the young monarch, however, that he could return to Yugoslavia within six months to reclaim his throne. This may have been Churchill's design. But the Partisans made no secret of their opposition to the return of the monarchy and their position drew support from representatives of Churchill's own Foreign Office, who predicted that "the Partisans would eventually rule Yugoslavia and that the monarchy had little future." [47]

Though British officialdom was divided in its attitude toward the King, Whitehall seemed united in its support of Tito after Teheran. SOE began massive aid shipments to the Partisans: in the months of December and January alone, Tito received twenty times as many tons of supplies as had been sent to Mihailovic since 1942. MacLean returned to Partisan headquarters to direct the new effort, bringing with him a letter of greeting from Churchill. To dramatize his personal interest, the Prime Minister also sent his son Randolph to join the SOE mission at the beginning of 1944.

In Washington, Roosevelt turned to Donovan for a response to this British initiative, but the general was still awaiting the report of

Seitz and Mansfield. The OSS men had at last found their way to Mihailovic's headquarters in December and Seitz set out immediately for the Adriatic coast. But he ran into German units and again became stranded inland, this time with a Partisan group in Montenegro. There he was joined by a team of SOE officers who had just left Albania and were also waiting to be evacuated. As the weeks passed, recalls one of the Englishmen, Seitz "fretted even more than the rest of us; for he was convinced that the 'boys in Washington' were gnawing their nails in their anxiety to have his report in time for what he continually referred to as the 'Spring Offensive.' " [48]

The colonel's restlessness was intensified by Partisan hostility toward him and his British colleagues (who had been working with proroyalist guerrillas in Albania). Wrote one SOE man, "They abused us to our faces as 'collaborators,' 'fascists,' and 'reactionaries'; invited us to concerts where anti-British and anti-American songs were sung and insulting speeches made about our countries; watched our movements and put a guard on our house—officially to protect us but really to keep a check on our visitors." [49] Seitz incited a minor riot when he excitedly drew his pistol on a Partisan "guard"; the altercation luckily ended without violence.

A brief respite from Partisan hostility came with the arrival of the Communist military genius Peko Dapcevic at the guerrilla camp.[q] Seitz, though a dedicated American proponent of the Chetniks, saw General Dapcevic as a "magnificent tactician and a courageous fighter" who "would rank among the first in the Balkans as a fighter against the Germans. . . . The more I saw of Dapcevic the better I liked him. He spoke the language of a soldier." And "while an intensive loyalty to Tito was apparent, the thing that made him tick was a mingled patriotism for his country and genuine love of fighting." [50]

As Seitz remained stranded in the pleasant company of Dapcevic, Mansfield had better fortune. He arrived in Cairo by PT boat in February, the first American officer to return from Serbian territory. His favorable view of the Chetniks was, of course, warmly received by Mihailovic supporters in London and Cairo. King Peter even referred to Mansfield's report in a pleading letter to King George of England. A month later, Seitz at last succeeded in leaving Yugoslavia by plane after reaching "a state bordering on anxiety neurosis about his report." [51] He met Mansfield in Cairo and the two OSS officers were flown to Wash-

[q] Dapcevic was Chief of Staff of the Yugoslav Army until he fell out of favor with Tito in the 1950s.

ington in April to personally present their observations to General Donovan.

The Chetniks, Seitz and Mansfield insisted, were carrying on effective military operations of great strategic value to the Allied war effort. Discounting allegations of Chetnik collaboration, they argued that Mihailovic had justifiably refused to accept British directives for "inconsequential harassment" of the Germans. If given Allied assistance, concluded the OSS men, "Mihailovic could put into the field an army trained and hardened for war, of over 300,000 fit for combat." [52] And with that assessment of the Chetnik cause, they were both given their freedom from further Yugoslav intrigue. Seitz was sent into France to work with the Maquis; Mansfield joined the OSS contingent in China.

The Chetniks had thus gained new respectability in Washington. Donovan decided to send a larger mission to Serbia, principally for intelligence duties. The men were selected, assembled in Italy, and briefed in preparation for their departure. At the last moment, the operation was cancelled—at the insistence of London. The stage was now set for Allied conflict. With typical understatement, one British diplomat warned, "There is definite danger that General Donovan's organization will not necessarily pursue the same policy as SOE." [53]

Support of Tito was not really at issue. OSS was already bulging with admirers of the Communist guerrilla leader. In Washington, the Balkan section of R&A Branch under the direction of a young Harvard historian, Robert Wolff, produced unabashed pro-Partisan reports.[54] A group of equally enthusiastic operational officers had been formed in Italy around the nucleus of Major Huot's ill-fated team—this time with Washington's approval. Leader of the SO unit was Major Hans Tofte, 33, a Danish-born businessman who had once worked for the East Asia Company in China.[r] Recruited by the British as a leader of the Danish underground, he had gone on to OSS service and American citizenship. Assisting Tofte was 32-year-old Lieutenant Robert Thompson, a Philadelphia newspaper reporter, born of missionary parents in Jerusalem.

Junior officer of the team was the tall and handsome Sterling Hayden, then an emotional 28-year-old lieutenant who had entered OSS through a friendship with Donovan's son. As an ex-merchant seaman

[r] Tofte was a ranking CIA officer in Japan, Korea, Argentina, and Colombia until his dismissal from the agency in 1966 in a widely publicized security fiasco.

(who had achieved overnight motion picture fame) Hayden was put
in charge of a new operational base at the small port of Monopoli,
thirty miles south of Bari. With the aid of 400 Partisans, and using a
fleet of fourteen schooners (supplied by the Wrigley's Chewing Gum
executive who commanded the OSS Maritime Unit at Cairo), Hayden's
group ran supplies through the German Adriatic blockade to the Par-
tisan-held offshore island of Vis. Then Hayden's "relentlessly dedicated
group of visionaries . . . cudgeled a conservative British command into
releasing stockpiles of captured Italian equipment" for Tito's forces.[55]

In short order, Hayden developed a "tremendously close personal
feeling" and "unlimited respect" for the Partisan troops who had
"fought in spite of reprisals, had fought through bitter winters high in
the mountains, with little clothing, next to no food, and only the arms
they could scrape from the backs of their foes." [56] The young actor
(who later had a brief flirtation with the American Communist Party)
remembered "in the interior of Yugoslavia when the crews of planes
would leave their shoes, anything they could spare, with the Partisans,
they were that impressed and I don't think a GI impresses too easily as
a rule." For most OSS officers, these sympathies were not at all ideological: "We knew they were Communist-led, we knew they had commissars, but there was very little discussion of that. . . . Once in a
while when we were back in Italy we would sit around and a few at Bari
headquarters would talk a little bit about what was going on, but we
never got very much involved in it. . . . There were no involved or detailed political discussions at all." [57]

There were, inevitably, a few OSS and SOE officers who also
sympathized with Partisan political doctrine. In Cairo, the intelligence
officer of the SOE Yugoslav section had been secretary of the University Communist Club at Cambridge. OSS Captain George Wuchinich received the Distinguished Service Cross for his nine months
of service with Tito's forces. He had fought with the Abraham Lincoln
Brigade in the Spanish Civil War; on a later OSS assignment to China,
he eagerly sought contact with the Chinese Communists. But these
were the exceptions. Most OSS officers who worked with Tito's
guerrillas were not political ideologues. They saw Tito's troops only as
courageous and dedicated fighters against a common enemy. Other
Americans, like Seitz and Mansfield, had taken a similar view of the
Chetniks. An OSS colonel would later observe, "Scarcely an officer who
had anything to do with the Chetniks or Partisans had not taken sides
violently." [58] That was an inevitable result of service behind the lines.

As OSS cooperated with the British in supplying Tito's burgeoning forces by sea and air, the SO and SI Branches sent dozens of American officers to Partisan territory to work with the guerrillas. The increased OSS effort also required a close working relationship with Tito's representatives in Italy. One young Partisan girl became secretary to an OSS major who headed the Yugoslav section of SI Branch at Bari headquarters. She had access to classified information, but there was nothing sinister in that—the intelligence had originally been obtained from her fellow Partisans. The young woman's OSS career, however, came to an abrupt end. A Yugoslav-American OSS man demanded her dismissal when she attempted to persuade him to desert the American Army and to join Tito's forces as a "political commissar." [59]

As the number of Partisans working in southern Italy with OSS and SOE detachments increased, so did the frequency of Chetnik allegations of mistreatment. When two Chetniks who worked for OSS at Bari mysteriously disappeared, it was rumored that they had been kidnapped and murdered by Tito's agents. Two other Chetniks, personal representatives of Mihailovic, claimed that they had been robbed by British officers in Italy. (The British replied that they had only deprived Mihailovic's envoys of "one hundred uncensored letters as well as golden sovereigns, jewels, and watches which were identified as being the proceeds of a burglary on the safe of the Royal Jugoslav Government in Cairo.") [60] Political disputes among Bari Yugoslavs became so heated that OSS officers who had spent some time with the Chetniks were warned not to be seen in the streets of the town unless armed against Partisan sympathizers.

In this confused and emotionally charged atmosphere, Washington was desperate for "objective information" about Tito and his apparently close ties to the Soviets. A Russian military mission reached Partisan headquarters in February 1944 and a few small Soviet supply drops were made shortly after. But Partisan enthusiasm seemed out of proportion to the extent of Moscow's niggardly aid. An admittedly anti-Partisan SOE man observed an American supply drop to Tito's guerrillas from Italian planes that had become available to OSS after the surrender of the Badoglio government. "The drops were badly needed," he recalled, "for they contained food, clothing, and medical stores. . . . These supplies came from the Americans, but the political commissar used all his ingenuity to persuade his men and the peasants that they came from Russia. He went to the trouble of explaining that the initials, U.S., which were clearly stamped on the packages, stood for 'Unione Sovietica'; had not the planes been Italian? Then of course the labeling would be in Italian." [61]

To investigate the entire Yugoslav situation and its political ramifications, OSS sent a "businessman's intellectual," Colonel Richard Weil, Jr., to Tito's headquarters as chief of SI operations in Partisan territory.[s] The 37-year-old officer, a descendant of the distinguished New York Jewish family which had long owned Macy's department store, loved to quote Aristotle and debate issues of metaphysics. At Yale he had written poetry for the literary magazine and, upon graduation, was grief-stricken when parental pressure forced him to abandon his dreams of a literary career and join the family business. In his new OSS position, Weil turned his frustrated talents as a writer to analyses of Tito's personality and politics. His reports showed amazing foresight. In spite of Tito's "known affiliation with Russian Communism," wrote Weil, "most of the population seem to regard him first as a patriot and the liberator of his country and secondarily as a Communist. . . . For whatever it may be worth, my own guess is that if he is convinced that there is a clearcut choice between the two, on any issue, his country will come first." [62] Predicting inevitable Partisan political success in postwar Yugoslavia, the colonel added a personal endorsement of Tito's request for broader political relations with the United States. When he left Tito in March, Weil carried with him a letter of greeting from the Communist marshal to President Roosevelt. The official note declared, "For the fulfillment of their strivings the people of Yugoslavia expect the aid of your great democratic country, of the people of the U.S.A., and of yourself." [63]

While OSS courted Tito's friendship, the real bone of contention between American and British policy—the future of Mihailovic—was still unresolved in the spring of 1944. In late February, the question was brought to a head when the British Commander at Cairo ordered *all* Allied officers attached to the Chetniks, including thirty SOE men, to leave Serbian territory.

Only one American, Lieutenant George Muselin, remained at Mihailovic's headquarters. A hulking former University of Pittsburgh

[s] Weil became president of Macy's, New York, in 1949. He resigned from the company in 1952 to direct an overseas quarterly sponsored by the Ford Foundation. Until his death in 1958, he was also president of the National Association for Mental Health.

football star born of immigrant Yugoslav parents, Muselin had joined the Chetniks in October of the previous year. OSS might well have accepted his evacuation without serious argument had not Lieutenant Mansfield appeared in Cairo in February with his laudatory report on Tito's enemies. As a result of this fresh information, Muselin was ordered to remain with Mihailovic when the British officers departed. The OSS command felt that the lieutenant should continue to collect any on-the-spot intelligence which the Chetniks might provide, even if Mihailovic were to be given no future Allied assistance. Registering a strong objection to this OSS position, the British ambassador at Cairo warned his State Department colleagues against "our being played off one against the other, even on the level of the OSS and SOE." [64]

An immediate policy confrontation was delayed by difficulties which the British encountered in safely transporting their own officers out of German-infested Serbia. Though the initial order for withdrawal came in February, the last SOE man was not evacuated until June. Lieutenant Muselin took the opportunity of the delay to stall his own departure. But he too was eventually flown out, at the personal insistence of Churchill. The Prime Minister left no doubt that Mihailovic's unconditional exit from the political scene was essential to his foreign policy in Yugoslavia.

Regarding the Muselin incident as evidence of American political bias for the Chetniks, Whitehall felt that "under OSS inspiration," the State Department "inclines to Mihailovic and cannot follow the P.M.'s pro-Tito policy." [65] This was certainly an exaggeration of the simple OSS fear of placing all its intelligence eggs in one resistance basket. It was true, however, that Donovan and his Washington aides hoped, in spite of British objections, to reestablish an OSS presence in Serbia.

The opportunity presented itself in July. Washington learned that over 100 Allied airmen had been rescued by the Chetniks and were awaiting evacuation. And Mihailovic specifically requested that American rather than British officers undertake the rescue operation. Here was an unquestionable "humanitarian" justification for OSS personnel to return to Chetnik territory. A rescue team of three officers was hurriedly assembled and dispatched by direct order of President Roosevelt on July 26. At its head was the same Lieutenant Muselin who had left the Chetniks seven weeks earlier. But the group was given explicit instructions. It was not to function either as a liaison mission or as an intelligence team. Its sole task would be the evacuation of airmen. (Such rescue units were already operating in cooperation with the Partisans, who had aided hundreds of downed Allied fliers.)[66]

While the Muselin operation was under way in late August, one of the rescue planes that flew into Chetnik territory brought a new group of three OSS officers to Serbia. This team's orders were to work as an intelligence mission—the very proposal that the British had blocked six months before. Commander of the group was Lieutenant Colonel Robert McDowell, an OSS desk officer from Cairo who had once taught Balkan history at the University of Michigan. McDowell made no secret of his violently pro-Chetnik (and anti-Partisan) prejudices when his group arrived at this most sensitive moment in the Yugoslav civil war.

At the beginning of September, Mihailovic at last called for a "general mobilization" of the Yugoslav populace against the Germans. But it was already the beginning of the end for the Chetnik general. That same month, the Partisans launched their long-expected invasion of Serbia, directed as much against the Chetniks as the Germans. Then a verbal coup de grace was delivered by King Peter in a September speech from London. Under the prodding of Churchill, the King called upon the Yugoslav people to unite and join the National Liberation Army under Tito's leadership. Without naming Mihailovic, Peter condemned "that misuse of the name of the King and the authority of the Crown by which an attempt has been made to justify collaboration with the enemy, and to provoke discord among our fighting people in the very gravest days of their history." [67]

McDowell's mission inevitably became embroiled in the conflict. In mid-September, the German command at Belgrade established contact with McDowell at Mihailovic's headquarters for the purpose of discussing a surrender. Two meetings took place between McDowell and a Nazi representative, who declared that the Germans in Yugoslavia wished to surrender to the Americans and Chetniks rather than to the Russians and Partisans. These discussions were duly reported to Allied headquarters, which quickly ordered that the contact with the Germans be broken off. With the Red Army massed at the Yugoslav border, it would have been a diplomatic disaster for the United States to accept what would clearly have been, in Soviet eyes, the "separate surrender" Moscow so feared.

When the Partisans learned of the McDowell negotiations, they were infuriated, charging that the OSS Colonel had joined Mihailovic in treasonous collaboration. Tito's aides condemned McDowell for "or-

ganizing and taking part in Chetnik operations against the Partisans."
They "continued to demand McDowell's withdrawal on the ground
that he was giving the Chetniks political prestige they didn't deserve." [68]
In October, Tito took up the issue personally with Brigadier MacLean.
He warned that the McDowell team's presence "was certain to react
unfavorably on Partisan relations with the United States and Great
Britain." Tito claimed McDowell was encouraging Mihailovic with
promises of future American support. "Mention of Mihailovic," observed MacLean, "makes Tito and his followers see even redder than
usual and they are completely baffled as to why there could be any adequate reason for the American government maintaining a mission with
Mihailovic." [69]

McDowell and his men had in fact been ordered to leave Serbia
in September, again as a result of Churchill's personal intervention. But
they were unable to withdraw because of the increased tempo of fighting in the area and turbulent weather conditions which prevented
American planes from landing. The team was finally flown out of Yugoslavia on November 15, but not before one of the officers was arrested
and whisked off to Bulgaria by advancing Russian troops.

On the same day as McDowell's departure, the British suggested
that OSS evacuate Mihailovic to the United States, where he would
be placed in "honorable forced residence." The Foreign Office believed
the Chetnik leader "would be much happier living in the United States
than elsewhere as there are so many Serbs who were residing in America." [70] Both Washington and Mihailovic rejected this solution to
Whitehall's "Chetnik Problem" and, on December 11 the last member
of the OSS rescue unit left Chetnik territory. It was the final OSS contact with Draza Mihailovic. For the next year, the general and his loyal
Chetnik followers, pursued all over the Yugoslav countryside by Partisan forces, remained convinced that "sooner or later, America [would]
help them in their struggle." [71] Months after V-E Day, Mihailovic was
finally captured and brought to trial as a war criminal. The man once
hailed as the hero of the European resistance was found guilty of treason by Tito's courts. He was executed in 1946.

As Mihailovic's star began to fall, OSS strengthened its resolve to
remain on friendly terms with Tito and his Partisans. Shortly after the
Teheran Conference, the British commander at Cairo asked General
Donovan to send a larger group of OSS officers to join Linn Farish,
who had remained with the SOE mission to Tito. OSS "declined this

invitation." Donovan did not "care to send American officers to serve
as juniors with a British political mission," and he proposed instead the
dispatch of an independent American team.[72] Cordell Hull gave his
approval in May. Some months later, Colonel Ellery Huntington, the
Wall Street attorney who had replaced Donald Downes as chief of OSS
in Italy, was chosen to head the new mission. The State Department
felt that someone with diplomatic experience should also accompany
the group. On a trip to London, Brigadier MacLean had a chance
meeting in a hotel bar with Charles Thayer, an old State Department
friend from MacLean's Moscow days, then serving with the European
Advisory Commission.[t] A West Point graduate with eight years of
diplomatic service in Germany and Russia (where he introduced polo
to the Red Army), the 34-year-old Thayer shared MacLean's jaundiced
view of the Soviets. The brigadier was therefore delighted to suggest
Thayer's appointment as political advisor to the OSS group. This arrangement was acceptable to Washington, Thayer was commissioned
a Lieutenant Colonel, and the "Independent U.S. Military Mission to
Marshal Tito" (the initial adjective stressed at Donovan's insistence)
parachuted into Partisan territory south of Belgrade in August.

The future of King Peter was then the burning political issue.
Churchill still cherished the hope of a reconciliation between Tito and
Peter once the Chetniks were removed from active contention as a
postwar political force. Though the Partisans continued to express hostility toward the monarchy, the Prime Minister believed a political
union could yet be achieved through the efforts of some mutually acceptable intermediary. In May 1944, OSS supplied Whitehall with its
missing link—the former Governor of Croatia, Ivan Subasic. Donovan's
people had remained in close contact with the Croat exile throughout
the war and now strongly advised him to accept the British proposal
to serve as deus ex machina. Subasic readily assented. Both the British
and Americans then pressed Subasic upon the King as his political
salvation. In a May letter, Roosevelt commended Subasic's "wise counsel" to Peter.[73] This was followed by a visit from General Donovan,
who was "very keen" that the King make Subasic his Prime Minister.[74]

Churchill was a bit less politic than the Americans. Without a
word to the King, he had Subasic flown to London "in the first aircraft
available" and on May 24 announced to Parliament that Peter would

[t] Thayer served as the first director of the Voice of America, 1948–49.
He resigned from the State Department in 1953 after a public attack on
his loyalty by Senator Joseph McCarthy.

dismiss his Prime Minister and form a new cabinet under Subasic. The statement was made without Peter's consent; the King was "flabbergasted and deeply affronted." [75] But under pressure from both Roosevelt and Churchill, the adolescent monarch relented. On June 1, he appointed the Croat leader to head a new cabinet in which Mihailovic's name was conspicuously absent.

The next step in Churchill's plan was to arrange a meeting between Tito and Subasic (with the King waiting on the sidelines). Tito left his island headquarters in the Adriatic—he had been evacuated from the mainland when the Germans overran his camp—and reached Italy on June 4. Subasic came a week later with King Peter, who remained at Malta while the talks were in progress. The British believed that Tito was then in a "chastened mood." American diplomats agreed that the Partisan marshal was now "much more under British influence and control." [76]

It was a poor judgment. The talks led to the signing of an initial accord that represented an almost unconditional acceptance of Partisan demands. Yet the British still felt reasonably optimistic about the future. The British Theater Commander in Italy invited Tito to visit Allied headquarters at Caserta. Since Tito refused to see the King, he would not accept the invitation until Peter had left Italy. The Communist marshal finally came to Naples in August. In a surprise move, Churchill flew to Italy to meet with him personally, still hoping to make Tito "his man." Not to be outdone by the British, General Donovan entertained the Partisan leader at the Capri villa of a New York millionaire (the same mansion which Donald Downes had refused to "requisition" a year earlier). Donovan's diplomatic gesture seemed to destroy London's theory of an OSS conspiracy against the Partisans.

On his departure from Italy, Tito prepared his own surprise for the Allies. He mysteriously disappeared from his headquarters, to the complete puzzlement (and irritation) of his SOE friends. At this inauspicious moment, the new OSS mission under Huntington and Thayer reached Yugoslavia. Stafford Reid, one of Robert Murphy's original Vice-Consuls from the TORCH operation, was Huntington's aide. The team executive officer was Marine Captain William Cary, a 34-year-old government tax lawyer with degrees from Harvard and Yale.[u] Rounding out the team was the music critic of a Cincinnati

---

[u] Cary, a Professor of Law at Columbia, served as Chairman of the U.S. Securities and Exchange Commission during the Kennedy administration.

newspaper, a liberal New York playwright, and several Yugoslav-Americans.

The aging Colonel Huntington soon left the mission, and Thayer, already the mission's chief intelligence analyst, assumed command. The witty, pipe-smoking officer entered the country with one major political prejudice—a strong anti-Soviet bias, acquired during years of diplomatic service in Stalin's Moscow. As for the Partisans, he kept an open mind. While watching a victory parade of Tito's guerrillas, Thayer reflected, "At that moment I envied the men who had watched them develop over the years. But perhaps it was just as well I hadn't. Close association with them had produced in many the emotional attachment which sometimes leads to strange political judgments. In Yugoslavia, you needed all the detachment you could find." [77]

The OSS colonel's main worry was the Partisan-Soviet relationship. In his reports to Robert Joyce,[v] a Yale-educated foreign service officer who had left a Havana diplomatic post to head the SI Balkan section at Bari, Thayer noted that the Russians looked down on the Yugoslavs as "poor, ignorant peasants . . . uneducated, politically backward, and utterly uncultured." After a warm reception from the chief of the Soviet Military Mission, Thayer cynically wondered whether the Russian general hadn't "read his mail from Moscow, or whether, by his demonstrative collaboration with the Americans, he wasn't showing his little Yugoslav brothers that they were still a second-rate, uncultured small nation not fit to associate on equal terms with the big boys like Russia and America." [78]

There were disturbing signs of increasing Partisan commitment to the Russians in spite of Soviet haughtiness. MacLean told Thayer that Tito had probably "disappeared" to attend a conference with Soviet generals in Romania. Tito, the brigadier believed, would attempt to persuade the Russians not to send troops into Yugoslavia. But the real truth was soon revealed. Tito had actually flown to Moscow for a first meeting with Stalin, his political comrade. Their discussion was followed by an announcement from the Soviet command at Bucharest that Tito had authorized the Red Army to cross the Yugoslav border. The Russians entered the country on September 29.

Shortly before the Soviet move, MacLean had recommended that London continue its policy of "giving assistance and friendly advice

[v] As a member of the State Department's Policy Planning Staff in 1949, Joyce was State's liaison with CIA on an ill-fated guerrilla invasion of Albania, betrayed to the Russians by double agent Kim Philby.

Celebrating the liberation of Belgrade in October 1944, OSS Col. Charles Thayer (center), West Point graduate and State Department veteran, was cheerful in the company of Marshal Tito (left) and Soviet General Kisiliev (right), commander of the Russian mission to the Yugoslav Partisans.

and encouraging as much as possible Tito's ambition to be chief of a strong and powerful democratic state rather than a puppet of the Soviet Union or any other power." [79] The brigadier believed that neither the King nor Subasic would be of any political importance after the war. If the Allies, argued MacLean, should attempt to force the King on the Yugoslav marshal, they would "push Tito into the arms of the Russian bear. He may not be too anxious for that suffocating embrace. But (if he is cold-shouldered by the U.S. and Great Britain) he will have no alternative." [80] In later years, this view would seem amazingly prescient. But in the winter of 1944 MacLean's policy appeared nothing less than a monumental disaster.

Thayer accepted MacLean's views on the inevitability of a Partisan victory, but seemed less cheerful about the political results. "Tito, the Communist," he wrote, "was here to stay, whether we liked it or not. We'd better get used to it unless we were prepared to take on the Red Army along with the Wehrmacht." Nothing "short of military measures," he told Washington, would "alter the present course of events in Yugoslavia." [81]

The Americans and British had good cause for pessimism. One week before the Red Army entered Yugoslavia, Tito's Chief of Staff, Arso Jovanovic, issued an order forbidding the movement of OSS and SOE officers beyond the headquarters area. This meant that Allied officers would not be allowed to advance freely into the Yugoslav interior as it was liberated by the Partisans and Russians. OSS believed the order represented Tito's desire to "curtail and control American and British representation in the country now that he believes the civil war is all but in the bag and now that British and American supplies are no longer needed." [82] General Donovan reacted swiftly by cancelling supply drops to the Partisans and halting American flights for the evacuation of Partisan wounded (thousands of whom had already been flown to safety on Allied planes). But Partisan confidence had been immeasurably bolstered by the liberation of Belgrade on October 20, an action supported by Soviet troops. The American retaliation served only to further embitter the Yugoslav Communists.

One day after the Germans were driven from the capital, MacLean and Thayer witnessed a wild display of gunfire from the rejoicing Partisan troops. They asked Peko Dapcevic (the Partisan general who had so impressed Colonel Seitz earlier in the year) why the soldiers were wasting valuable ammunition in this way. Dapcevic candidly replied, "They know that now they're linked up with the Russians, they'll have all the supplies they need. It won't have to come from you any more." Wrote Thayer, "We didn't forget Peko's crack. It was no surprise and we both had warned our people that once Tito hooked up with the Red Army, things were going to be different. Just the same, the switch was a bit abrupt." [83]

OSS men in outlying areas of the country were, at the same time, being harassed by Partisan commissars who hoped to discredit the Americans in the eyes of the guerrilla rank-and-file. A few officers were prepared for the challenge. OSS Captain John Blatnik, a 33-year-old Minnesotan of Yugoslav descent, spent eight months with the Partisans behind the lines.[w] In December 1944, the guerrilla commissar in Blatnik's operational area attempted to bait the captain in front of his

[w] Blatnik is now a United States congressman from Minnesota.

Partisan friends by bitterly condemning the appointment of former U.S. Steel President Edward Stettinius as Secretary of State. Blatnik, who had been elected to the Minnesota senate before the war on the Democratic Farmer-Labor ticket, delighted the Partisans and out-flanked the commissar with the retort, "I agree it was a terrible choice. But you don't know the half of it. Let me tell you how Stettinius fought us union men when we tried to organize the steel plants." The Partisans were enthralled with Blatnik's tale of how the steel workers had won their union rights. It was the last time the commissar had any political arguments with the OSS captain.[84]

The hostility of the Partisan commissars to their former American comrades-in-arms was not reflected in the attitude of their leader. Thayer had many conversations with Tito and only rarely did the marshal choose to be argumentative. On one occasion, the OSS colonel complained of the "lack of cooperation and hospitality experienced by American field officers." Tito replied bluntly that "the majority of Americans were opposed to his regime but what were they going to do about it." He also criticized the "meager supplies furnished him by the Allies." Thayer countered that Roosevelt and the American press had shown nothing but friendliness for the Partisans. He noted that OSS and SOE had equipped almost half of the Partisan formations and later gave Tito complete lists of equipment furnished by the Allies, information which "impressed and surprised" the Communist leader.[85] (Tito's lieutenants frequently complained, "we did not receive the help we had requested, or when something was sent to us it was only in small quantities."[86] OSS and SOE supplied the Partisans with 76,000 tons of materiel, 95 per cent of the total supplies received from abroad.)

Tito was usually far more amiable than his subordinates, despite tensions between the Yugoslavs and Americans in early 1945. In Rome, Tito's envoys held fruitless discussions with Allied officers over Anglo-American refugee aid to the Yugoslav civilian populace. The talks, Thayer recalls, "dragged on for months. . . . Every time the subject of the negotiations came up between us, Tito would readily agree that the Allied demands were acceptable to him, but the next day his representatives in Rome would reject them." The exasperated Thayer finally sent a cable to Italy: "Urgently suggest you send Allied negotiators to Belgrade to deal with the horse's mouth instead of wasting time at the other end."[87] When the negotiators finally arrived in the Yugoslav capital to speak with Tito personally, the issue was resolved within half an hour.

On another occasion, Thayer was informed that the U.S. Air Force had mistakenly bombed the wrong area of Bosnia, killing some Partisan troops, including one of Tito's best generals. "It was bad news for me," remembered Thayer, "as I'd recently been having a rough time trying to work out several agreements with Tito, and I knew the incident wouldn't make him any easier to deal with." The OSS colonel rushed to the marshal's residence to apologize on behalf of the American air commander. "I've already had a message from the general saying how sorry he is about the mistake," said Thayer gingerly, expecting the worst. Tito replied wistfully, "I'm sure he is. Tell him I understand. In times like these, what can you expect?" [88]

While Thayer found Tito mildly cooperative, both Churchill and General Donovan were becoming increasingly disturbed by the trend of political events. They now realized that Subasic would never emerge as a political personality strong enough to counterbalance the Partisan hero. New meetings between the two men at the end of 1944 resulted only in the confirmation of Tito's position as the country's supreme political authority. A provisional government was to be established which would clearly be controlled by the Partisan political council, with only token representation for the King. "It was the best that could be hoped for," MacLean told Thayer with Panglossian assurance. But the OSS colonel deduced that Subasic had simply been overwhelmed by the "extent of Tito's following and of their determination to break away from the past." [89]

The new accord was subject to the King's approval and MacLean flew to London with the document. Subasic did not accompany him. Instead the Croat "Prime Minister" flew unexpectedly to Moscow, in the belief that the trip would ease the position of Tito, "who is clearly suspect by the extremists in his own party." [90] There was no longer any doubt that Subasic was being eclipsed by Tito's dynamism or that Moscow was becoming primus inter pares of the Allied powers in Yugoslavia.

Soviet primacy also meant that King Peter would inevitably be relegated to the same depths of political obscurity as Mihailovic. Although Churchill genuinely hoped to preserve the Yugoslav monarchy, other British officials were less dedicated. Harold Macmillan of the Foreign Office wrote that Churchill "has a most remarkable fondness for Kings. But really it would be a terrible error to sabotage the very hopeful development because of King Peter. I do not believe there is any chance of this poor boy regaining his throne whatever we may do, and it is far more important to avoid civil war in Yugoslavia and strengthen British

A monarch without a country, teen-aged King Peter II, accompanied by his OSS confidant, Russian émigré Bernard Yarrow, proudly posed in London's Windsor Park beside a plane presented to him as a gift from President Roosevelt.

influence there." Macmillan later put it even more succinctly—"Winston *must* abandon the King." [91]

Like Mihailovic before him, Peter turned to the United States in desperation. Bernard Yarrow,[x] a Russian émigré and assistant to New York District Attorney Thomas E. Dewey before his recruitment into OSS in 1942, had been sent to London by Donovan as OSS liaison with the exile governments of Czechoslovakia, Poland, and Yugoslavia. Yarrow kept in close touch with both Subasic and the King, whom he recalls as "young, immature, harassed by his political advisors" and having "little influence on the march of events that finally culminated in Tito's overall takeover." In Peter's frequent talks with Yarrow, he at-

[x] Yarrow joined the Dulles brothers' law firm, Sullivan and Cromwell, after the war and became senior vice-president of the CIA-funded Radio Free Europe in 1952.

tempted to demonstrate his friendliness by relaying to OSS the full details of his personal conversations with Churchill. The King asked, however, that OSS keep the reports confidential. "Churchill may be annoyed," added Yarrow, "if he suspects that [the] King is talking." [92] But the intelligence was of little consequence. Tito was unquestionably the master of Yugoslavia and, unlike Churchill, he had no fondness for kings.

Churchill continued to pressure Peter to sign the second Subasic accord. The King at first refused, but it made little difference. The monarchy was already doomed when the Big Three Conference at Yalta endorsed the substance of the Tito-Subasic agreement. By the end of 1945, Tito had shifted Subasic from Prime Minister to Foreign Minister and then to house arrest. "Elections" held in November formalized the power of the Communist government. The monarchy was quietly forgotten. Events in Yugoslavia, Churchill told Peter, had disappointed his fondest hopes.

Having lost their bets on Mihailovic, Subasic, and Peter, the British and Americans then appeared to lose their final wager on Tito's continued friendship. A violent dispute between Tito and the Anglo-Americans over the occupation of Italian Trieste threatened to break into armed conflict. As the Americans stood firm, Thayer found that Tito was "growing less and less accessible, and I was told I could take my business to his chief of cabinet." [93] Many of Tito's subordinates were, by this point, openly hostile to the Americans, particularly the marshal's Chief of Staff, Arso Jovanovic, a former royalist officer who felt a defensive need to prove himself a militant Communist.[y] Thayer saw Jovanovic as a "sour, sullen sort of fellow, the exact opposite of the affable Tito. . . . By the time we got to Belgrade he made himself practically inaccessible and let it be known that anything the Americans wanted could be put in writing." [94] It was Jovanovic who issued the order forbidding OSS and SOE men to leave the headquarters area. He also blocked the transmission of Partisan combat intelligence to the Americans. In May 1945 Jovanovic delivered the final blow, abruptly requesting that the British and American Military Missions leave Yugoslavia as soon as possible. This was seen as a Yugoslav retaliation for the Allied position on Trieste. Thayer had by this time left his

[y] When the Tito-Stalin dispute broke out in 1948, Jovanovic chose to side with Moscow and was forced to flee the country. At the Romanian border, he impetuously drew his gun on a confused Yugoslav border guard and was killed.

post to join OSS in Vienna and had been replaced by 29-year-old Lieutenant Colonel Franklin Lindsay, a veteran of behind-the-lines service
in southern Austria.[z] Lindsay pointed out to Jovanovic the benefits of
political recognition and supplies which the Allied missions had
brought to Yugoslavia. The Partisan replied angrily that his forces
would have won without Allied support and then "went into a rage"
over U.S. policy on Trieste.[95] OSS sadly ordered its Belgrade mission
to withdraw from the country.

Even as the British and Americans prepared to depart, lamenting
what seemed a disastrous diplomatic error, there were signs of an unexpected future. In a speech of May 1945, Tito declared, "We demand
that everyone shall be master of his own house. We do not want to
pay other people's bills. We do not want to be used as a bribe in international bargaining. We do not want to get involved in a policy of
spheres of influence." Tito meant his warning for the British. But in
June, the Russian ambassador irately informed the Yugoslav Foreign
Ministry that if Tito "should once again permit such an attack on the
Soviet Union we shall be forced to reply with open criticism in the
press and disavow him." [96]

Two years later, a handful of British and American citizens would
chuckle to themselves as they learned of Yugoslavia's excommunication
from the Stalinist international faith. The more reflective of the OSS
and SOE veterans would also ponder the senselessness of the bitter
civil war they had witnessed.

Shortly before his relief as commander of the OSS mission to Tito
(and his tragic death in a plane crash), Major Linn Farish had already
begun to wonder. In his final OSS report of July 1944, he wrote: "I personally do not feel that I can go on with the work in Yugoslavia unless
I can sincerely feel that every possible honest effort is being made to
put an end to the civil strife. It is not nice to see arms dropped by one
group of our airmen to be turned against men who have rescued and
protected their brothers-in-arms. It is not a pleasant sight to see our
wounded lying side by side with the men who had rescued and cared
for them—and to realize that the bullet holes in the rescuers could have
resulted from American ammunition, fired from American rifles,

[z] Lindsay was deputy chief of the CIA Office of Policy Coordination,
1949–51. He joined the Ford Foundation in 1953, served on several Presidential commissions, and, since 1962, has been president of the Itek Corporation. After the 1968 election, President-elect Nixon asked Lindsay to
head a secret task force on CIA reorganization.

dropped from American aircraft flown by American pilots. At one time I worried because America was not getting the proper recognition for her participation in supply operations. Now I wonder—do we want it? The issues in Yugoslavia are ones which will have to be faced in many parts of the world. The Yugoslavians with their wild, turbulent, strong-willed nature have abandoned reason and resorted to force. Is this the shape of things to come? Are we all of us sacrificing to end this war only to have dozens of little wars spring up which may well merge into one gigantic conflict involving all mankind?" [97]

⑥

"Contre Nous De La Tyrannie"

"Ah, those first OSS arrivals in London! How well I remember them," reminisced the British wit Malcolm Muggeridge, "arriving like jeune filles en fleur straight from a finishing school, all fresh and innocent, to start work in our frowsty old intelligence brothel. All too soon they were ravished and corrupted, becoming indistinguishable from seasoned pros who had been in the game for a quarter century or more." [1]

The first herculean task of these OSS newcomers was to find their way through the labyrinthine "intelligence brothel" known as the British Secret Service. But how to convince His Majesty's officers to lead the way? General Donovan believed the first requirement was an OSS commander who possessed those qualities most appreciated by the class-conscious elite who guarded Whitehall's official secrets. In his selection of David Kirkpatrick Este Bruce, he could have come no closer to the ideal.[a] The 44-year-old multi-millionaire was a handsome, cultured representative of the American upper class.

Bruce touched all the social and political bases. His father had been a prominent United States Senator. His wife, the daughter of Andrew Mellon, the steel magnate and Republican Secretary of the Trea-

[a] Bruce's distinguished career has included service as chief of the Marshall Plan mission to France, 1948–49; U.S. ambassador to France, 1949–52; ambassador to Germany, 1957–59; ambassador to Britain, 1961–69; and American delegate to the Vietnam Peace Conference in Paris, 1970–71.

sury, was called the world's richest woman. Bruce was himself an active Democrat who had served in the legislatures of both Maryland and Virginia. He had also practiced law in Baltimore, spent two years at a State Department post in Rome, served on the boards of directors of over twenty corporations, and had even written a history of the American presidency.

Bruce had known Donovan before the war as "an adversary to be feared" in "frequent encounters on the squash courts." [2] In the summer of 1941, Bruce was representing the American Red Cross in London when Donovan asked him to return to Washington to head the espionage section of COI. A year later, he was back in England as London chief of OSS.

At his headquarters in Grosvenor Square, Bruce was surrounded by other American gentlemen who were equally well received in London's exclusive social clubs. The OSS executive officer was a New York investment banker. Bruce's first Research and Analysis chief was a vice-president of the Chase National Bank. Many of the bluebloods Donovan had assembled in Washington found their way to a safe post and a Saville Row–tailored military uniform in England.

These men had been sent to London to work with their British opposite numbers, an often trying responsibility. "Almost immediately on my arrival in London," remembers OSS veteran Lyman Kirkpatrick, Jr.,[b] "I found myself plunged into a series of lunches that would last from 1 P.M. through a good part of the afternoon, and dinners that lasted well past midnight. Our European friends were formidable consumers of alcoholic beverages, with apparently little effect, and I always wondered whether they also put in the same long office hours that we did." The entire routine was quite a "strain on the liver." [3]

Beyond digestive pitfalls, OSS liaison officers had to learn to tread diplomatically as they were drawn into the sensitive organizational squabbles of their British counterparts. The Americans were first forced to take sides in the old rivalry between the British Security Service (MI-5), which was responsible for counter-intelligence in Britain and the Commonwealth, and the Secret Intelligence Service (MI-6), which engaged in both espionage and counter-intelligence on foreign soil.[4]

Liaison with MI-5 was quickly preempted by J. Edgar Hoover and

[b] Kirkpatrick served as Assistant Director, Inspector General, and Executive Director of CIA until his retirement from the government in 1965. He is now a professor of political science at Brown University.

his FBI legal attaché at the American embassy in London. Since OSS and the Secret Intelligence Service both mistrusted their respective competitors in the counter-intelligence field, the Hoover alliance with MI-5 provided a first poignant reason for close cooperation between Donovan's officers and MI-6.

Working with the counter-intelligence section of MI-6 to penetrate the German espionage network in Europe was an OSS team headed by Norman Holmes Pearson, a distinguished Yale professor of English. He was assisted by Robert Blum,[c] a Yale instructor in international relations, and liberal Chicago attorney Hubert Will.[d] One of their British opposite numbers, the enigmatic Soviet double-agent "Kim" Philby, delighted in taking potshots at Pearson's amateur sleuths.[5]

Counter-intelligence was only a sidelight for MI-6. Its principal function was foreign espionage and here the British found eager American students in Donovan's Secret Intelligence Branch. David Bruce's SI chief was Dr. William Maddox, a learned professor of political science who had taught international affairs at Harvard and Princeton.[e] With the assistance of Russell D'Oench, the grandson of the founder of the Grace Shipping Lines, Maddox developed a close working arrangement with MI-6. The British transmitted reams of intelligence information to Maddox's staff.

General Donovan was not satisfied. He felt liaison was not enough —SI Branch would have to develop its own espionage networks of secret agents in Europe. Maddox objected. "Nothing," he wrote Washington, "should be done that would jeopardize the fruitful relationship" with MI-6.[6] And the British left no doubt that they would not welcome American autonomy in spy operations on the continent. But Washington remained adamant through the spring of 1943, pressing Bruce and Maddox to be more aggressive in demanding an espionage partnership with the British.

Donovan's Special Operations Branch had already won the "partnership" argument, at least on paper. Their British counterparts in the

[c] As chief of a CIA-connected Special Technical and Economic Mission to Indochina in 1950–51, Blum openly opposed American support for French colonialism in Vietnam, Laos, and Cambodia. From 1953 until 1962, he was president of the Asia Foundation.

[d] Will is now a federal district court judge in Chicago.

[e] Dr. Maddox was Director of the State Department's Foreign Service Institute, 1947–49. After a distinguished career in the Foreign Service, he became President of the Pratt Institute in 1967.

Special Operations Executive, who directed and assisted resistance networks in occupied Europe, agreed to a new operational pact with OSS
in January 1943. Colonel Ellery Huntington (later the OSS commander
in Italy and Yugoslavia) joined the SOE chief, London banker Charles
Hambro, in adopting a plan for full cooperation between the Americans and British in supporting the European anti-Nazi underground.

A spirit of cooperation could not be created overnight, however.
SOE had been operating behind the lines for two years and had already
created an enormous organizational machinery when the first half dozen
American SO officers came to London at the beginning of 1943. A trio
of young Donovan recruits—Paul van der Stricht, Franklin Canfield,
and John Bross—were accepted by the British as clandestine apprentices
at SOE headquarters.[f] All three were articulate attorneys in their early
thirties with experience in leading New York law firms. Until they
and other new American arrivals could master the techniques of special
operations and until OSS could convince the British that American tech-
nology and manpower would prove valuable in aiding the European
resistance movements, the Huntington-Hambro agreement would remain only a prophesy of future partnership.

The OSS novices found these subtleties of Anglo-American liaison
confusing enough. MI-6 and SOE had yet to be persuaded to treat the
Americans as genuine equals in clandestine warfare. But there the task
of liaison had only begun. Most occupied nations of Europe were represented in London by exile governments which maintained their own
secret service organizations to collect intelligence and work with underground groups in their homelands. Beside dealing with the British, OSS
also had to keep in constant contact with the Norwegian, Belgian,
Dutch, Czech, and Polish spy chiefs.

From the standpoint of future military operations, the most im-
portant exile secret service in London was General de Gaulle's Bureau
Central de Renseignements et d'Action (BCRA), headed by a "cool,
steely eyed, and efficient" professional army officer, 32-year-old André
Dewavrin.[7] A former military professor at St. Cyr, the French West
Point, Dewavrin went by the nom-de-guerre of Colonel "Passy."

Passy and most of his lieutenants were political conservatives and
fervent anti-Communists. In the emotional atmosphere of French exile

---

[f] Van der Stricht is now vice-chairman of Warner-Lambert Pharma-
ceutical Co. Canfield spent many of the postwar years on the legal staff
of the Standard Oil Company in London. Bross was a special assistant to
the Director of CIA until his retirement in 1971.

politics, Passy was often accused of past membership in the Cagoule, the pro-fascist conspiracy to which Jacques Lemaigre-Dubrueil, the vegetable oil magnate and confidant of General Giraud, had once owed allegiance. Passy's BCRA was also depicted by some critics as a Gestapo-in-miniature which kidnapped and even murdered Frenchmen in London who refused to swear allegiance to de Gaulle.[g] These pernicious rumors were taken seriously in Washington; General Donovan personally asked de Gaulle's propaganda chief for a written rebuttal to charges against the BCRA.[8]

The OSS men in London gave no credence to allegations of misconduct by Passy's service. The Americans *were* irritated, however, by the Gaullist insistence on the inseparability of politics and secret operations. Unlike the other foreign intelligence services in London, the BCRA was at a diplomatic disadvantage—de Gaulle's Fighting French movement was not recognized as a government in exile. Passy's agents thus felt compelled to add political agitation to their espionage, sabotage, and resistance activities. To the dismay of most American officers, the BCRA was determined not only to win the war and liberate France, but also to unite the French nation under the leadership of Charles de Gaulle.

Neither OSS nor the British secret services could escape a three-year history of stormy Allied relations with the Fighting French and their arrogant leader. On more than one occasion since his lonely flight to London in June 1940, de Gaulle had been at loggerheads with his reluctant British protectors. He had also railed against Washington's Vichy policy and had fumed at the Americans for their support of Darlan and Giraud.

Despite de Gaulle's temperament, the British MI-6 had somehow managed to remain on friendly terms with Passy's BCRA; the Americans of the OSS Secret Intelligence Branch followed suit. "Passy and his outfit were energetic, expanding, and anxious to establish U.S. relationships," SI chief William Maddox remembers. "We were all impressed with what Passy and his people were doing and with the massive raw intelligence he turned over to us from his field agents." Looking toward "la jour de gloire" when Allied forces would breach the defenses of Hitler's Fortress Europe, Maddox also reasoned that the Gaullists

[g] In 1947, on the demand of his leftist enemies in the French government, Dewavrin was arrested and imprisoned on a charge of misappropriating funds of the French intelligence service.

"would probably set up or control the first new government" in France after the liberation. Working with Passy was thus a simple matter of "pragmatic realism." [9]

The hopeful signs of harmony between the BCRA and Maddox's espionage staff were unnerving to some British intelligence officials who had carefully begun courting the Gaullists long before the Americans appeared in London. First to take offense was the Assistant Chief of MI-6, Sir Claude Marjoribank Dansey, affectionately known to Passy and de Gaulle as "Uncle Claude." This "crusty old spirit," a close friend of Churchill's, a veteran soldier and intelligence expert, had a reputation for both "unnecessary combativeness" and severe criticism of all things American.[10] He was outraged when his French friends began a new romance with the OSS upstarts. In retaliation, he organized MI-6 opposition to the Anglo-American espionage partnership General Donovan so avidly desired.

Whatever their personal attitudes toward Gaullism, the young officers of Donovan's Special Operations Branch hoped to avoid similar difficulties over French policy with their British counterparts in SOE. Of the first SO Branch arrivals, Belgian-born attorney Paul van der Stricht was outspoken in his defense of the Fighting French, while his fellow officer Franklin Canfield, a legal associate of Allen Dulles and one of the original Murphy Vice-Consuls in North Africa, was more willing to work with non-Gaullist exile groups. But these individual opinions on French politics were of secondary importance to Donovan's basic objective—"infiltrating" the well-developed SOE establishment.

By opting for the closest possible cooperation with the British, the OSS men inadvertently inherited SOE's problems with Passy and the BCRA. For two years, the Gaullists had lodged bitter complaints about the French Section of SOE, commanded by Maurice Buckmaster, a former manager of Ford Motors in France. For both political and security reasons, the Buckmaster unit had been instructed to organize resistance networks entirely independent of the BCRA's own efforts. The British group sent some 400 non-Gaullist agents into France during the war; their activities remained a constant source of friction between Passy and the British.[11]

OSS and SOE could not entirely ignore the BCRA, if for no other reason than the emergence of resistance networks in France that would accept only de Gaulle as their chief. Despite the fierce independence of the various underground leaders, progress had been made toward unifying the resistance through the efforts of Jean Moulin, a courageous civil servant who had been named de Gaulle's personal representative in occupied France. After the German occupation of the Vichy zone in November 1942, three major resistance groups had agreed to merge their military reserves into a united Armée Secrète under the command of a short, aging Gaullist army officer, General Charles Delestraint.[12]

In February 1943 Moulin and Delestraint were secretly brought to London to begin a series of high-level conferences with British military strategists, SOE planners, and finally, representatives of OSS. The French emissaries had come to engage Allied support for the resistance and to secure Anglo-American cooperation with the underground well in advance of an invasion of the continent. But Moulin and Delestraint also wanted to discuss politics. They were disturbed by Washington's effort to bolster the prestige of General Giraud in Algiers. They told their OSS interlocutors that Giraud had no significant following in France, and that the resistance, despite internal disagreements, was united in its acclamation of de Gaulle as the symbol of Free France.[13] Their words were translated into positive action in May when several French underground groups joined clandestine trade union federations and political parties to form a political front, the National Resistance Council, which proclaimed its allegiance to General de Gaulle.

While the resistance moved toward unity under the Gaullist banner, the BCRA accused OSS of scheming to weaken and divide the underground forces, all for the benefit of Giraud.[14] The alleged plot was traced to Allen Dulles, the OSS chief in neutral Switzerland.[h] Early in 1943, Dulles had made contact with a young French journalist, Guillain de Benouville, a Catholic conservative once active in right-wing, pro-monarchist political circles.[i] De Benouville declared himself a Gaullist, but the BCRA was suspicious. In 1941, he had joined an apolitical underground group known as Carte, which had been sustained by the Buckmaster section of SOE, and later by OSS officers at the American embassy in Vichy. De Benouville had become the Carte courier to Switzerland, making frequent trips to Geneva to meet with British agents.

After the TORCH landings and the German occupation of Vichy,

[h] Many "definitive" French histories also name Dulles as an OSS conspirator at Vichy in a 1941 attempt to boost a general of Pétain's Armistice Army as leader of the underground in place of de Gaulle. Dulles did not even arrive in Europe until a year later.

[i] In 1967, de Benouville was President of the French Press Association and a prominent corporate director.

de Benouville had switched his allegiance to the Gaullist resistance organization Combat, an association of professional men, intellectuals, and military career officers (later to number philosopher Albert Camus among its activists). Because of his past experience, de Benouville was chosen as Combat emissary to the Swiss capital, where he met with Dulles and his advisor on French affairs, attorney Max Shoop, the Paris representative of the Dulles brothers' law firm before the war. Through de Benouville, OSS offered large sums of money to the underground in exchange for military intelligence, providing that this arrangement was approved by the Gaullists in London.

The BCRA did not approve. Nor did Jean Moulin, then in the midst of an argument with the resistance chiefs over London's bid for greater control of underground activities. Moulin and Passy insisted that the resistance had no right to accept funds from the Americans. In defense of his negotiations, de Benouville noted that the London Gaullists had just cut the resistance budget at a time when increased expenditure, not economy, was called for. The Nazis had begun a compulsory labor program to transport young Frenchmen to Germany for service to the Third Reich. To escape the German dragnet, thousands of young men fled to the mountains and forests where they formed military units and made contact with the resistance. These groups borrowed a term from Corsican banditry and became known as the Maquis (literally "men of the underbrush"). De Benouville insisted that the Maquis could only be organized and armed with OSS money. Unconvinced, Moulin continued to demand that the contact with the Americans be broken off. The resistance, in turn, accused the London Gaullists of "bad faith." The argument continued in "a nasty climate of constant and futile argument, frayed nerves, and hair-trigger tempers," with only the Gestapo reaping the benefits.[15]

Why were the London Gaullists so adamant in their opposition to the OSS proposal? Passy believed that the American offer was nothing more than a Washington plot to aid the cause of General Giraud. Dulles denied having any such intention. "Our American friends," wrote de Benouville, "had, in effect, declared with some vehemence that the only thing that interested them was that we should fight the war. They repeated again and again that it made not the slightest difference to them whether we were partisans of one French general or the other. Since we declared that General de Gaulle was our chief and our federator, our American friends unhesitatingly accepted our point of view as a basis for a working agreement with us." [16]

Word reached the BCRA, however, that the U.S. military attaché in Berne had arranged a meeting on May 8 between emissaries of Combat and agents of Giraud's military intelligence service, the DSR/SM.ʲ The alleged purpose of the rendezvous was to convince the resistance leaders to work with Giraud's secret service instead of the BCRA. When word of this meeting reached Passy, he was understandably irate.

Passy had long regarded the professional, "Vichy-tainted" intelligence officers of the DSR/SM with ill-concealed hostility. Since TORCH, the Gaullist and Giraudist secret services had worked in open competition on behalf of their rival political chiefs.[17] Passy saw all activities of the DSR/SM as an extension of Giraud's influence. Now the Americans, he believed, were conspiring to extend that influence into the ranks of the Gaullist resistance.

All these suspicions of plots and counter-plots were abruptly forgotten, or temporarily set aside, as hopeful and tragic events unfolded in Africa and France. On May 30, after prolonged negotiations, General de Gaulle finally accepted the political marriage which Churchill and Roosevelt had conceived at the Casablanca Conference. The general and his political entourage left London for Algiers to join Giraud in forming a theoretically united French Committee of National Liberation.[18]

Concurrently, a disaster occurred in southern France. The Gestapo, having tightened their stranglehold on the harried underground, at last moved to decapitate the resistance leadership. On June 9, General Delestraint, commander of the Armée Secrète, was seized by the Germans; eleven days later, Jean Moulin was arrested. Both men were to die at the hands of the Nazis.

Ironically, this severe blow to the resistance was struck at the precise moment that the underground forces first began to seriously figure in the thinking of Allied strategists. At the TRIDENT Conference in Washington at the end of May 1943, the Combined Chiefs of Staff made their first commitment to launch an Allied invasion of occupied France.[19]

The decision to proceed with the cross-channel invasion, code-named OVERLORD and tentatively scheduled for May 1, 1944, was reaffirmed by Churchill and Roosevelt at their August meeting in Quebec. The strategic undertaking sparked a reassessment of relations between the British and American secret services.

For months, OSS Headquarters in Washington had incessantly

ʲ "Direction de Service de Renseignements et de Sécurité Militaire."

urged David Bruce and SI chief William Maddox to demand an equal voice in the continental intelligence operations launched by the British MI-6. Finally, on May 29, after a long series of meetings between Bruce and Stewart Menzies, the professional Army officer and well-connected aristocrat who headed MI-6 (known cryptically by the initial "C"), the British offered OSS an equal partnership in European espionage in anticipation of an Allied landing in France. Donovan was elated; America would soon have a spy system in the Old World.

Soon after the Bruce-Menzies accord, "Uncle Claude" Dansey, the scourge of OSS intelligence officers, reluctantly presented Maddox with a proposed operational plan, code-named SUSSEX. It called for Anglo-American collaboration in the dispatch of fifty two-man intelligence teams throughout northern France in advance of the OVER-LORD landings. The French agents would parachute 40 to 60 miles inland from the English channel, blanketing an area that stretched from Brittany to the Belgian border, collecting military information of immediate importance to the Allied command.

OSS was delighted with this concrete operational blueprint and the espionage partnership it represented. But Dansey was not yet ready to surrender. Weeks after SUSSEX was first proposed, it had become "increasingly and painfully clear" that some British intelligence officials were still exerting "power and influence" to prevent the establishment of an "equal, independent and coordinate" American espionage service. While many MI-6 officers were friendly to OSS,[k] a "few men" like Dansey "naturally but shortsightedly" sought to maintain the "omnipotence" of their intelligence network in Europe. For these MI-6 diehards, OSS would always remain a "distinctly junior partner." [20]

In its bureaucratic struggle with the British, OSS received no succor from the general who headed U.S. Army intelligence in London. He was slow to lend his own imprimatur to the SUSSEX plan and considered Donovan's organization an "irregular trespass on his own orthodox prerogatives." At a confrontation in the office of General Jake Devers, the American Theater commander in London, the Army intelligence man left no doubt that he did not "trust General Donovan or his ideas." Donovan replied in a low voice, without any inflection of emotion: "Unless the general apologizes at once, I

[k] Ironically, the most cooperative was Wilfred Dunderdale, a veteran MI-6 operative in Paris and chief of the British intelligence section that maintained liaison with Giraud's espionage service.

shall have to tear him to pieces physically and throw his remains through these windows into Grosvenor Square." [21] The Army intelligence man made a handsome apology and shortly afterward gave his stamp of approval to SUSSEX.

Problems with the British were not so easily resolved. Believing that Maddox and his staff had become too involved in the complexities of MI-6 liaison, Washington assembled a special team to direct American participation in SUSSEX. The group flew to London in mid-September under the command of Colonel Francis Pickens Miller, a leading Southern liberal and internationalist. Born in Kentucky, reared and educated in Virginia, Miller had many years of overseas experience—as an American officer in France during World War I, as a Rhodes scholar at Oxford, as chairman of the World Student Christian Federation in Geneva. Like David Bruce, Miller was an active Democrat, a member of the Virginia House of Delegates.[1] In 1941 the soft-spoken Virginian, a fervent advocate of American intervention in the European war, joined the COI as chairman of Robert Sherwood's propaganda planning board, switching to the SI Branch in Washington after Pearl Harbor and the creation of OSS.

Miller had recruited his own staff. Donald Coster, an official of the J. Walter Thompson advertising agency and a veteran of OSS operations in Casablanca, was the team executive officer.[m] The actual planning of espionage operations was in the hands of Dr. Justin McCortney O'Brien, a conservative Irish-American who taught French at Columbia University and strongly sympathized with Gaullism. He was assisted by a fellow Harvard alumnus, Chicago attorney Ray Brittenham.[n]

Miller's group set to work to build a genuine partnership with the British, encouraged by the progress already made at SOE headquarters, where new executive leadership had promoted a cooperative spirit. In September the London banker who commanded SOE was replaced by General Colin Gubbins, a much-decorated regular Army officer. Donovan felt his own SO contingent in London needed the

[1] Miller was the unsuccessful Democratic candidate for Governor of Virginia in 1949 and for U.S. Senator in 1952.

[m] Coster headed the advertising department of the New York *Herald Tribune* Paris edition, 1951–53. After three years in CIA, he became deputy director of U.S. foreign aid programs in South Vietnam, 1959–62 and director of the Agency for International Development in Algiers in 1963.

[n] Brittenham is now Senior vice-president and general counsel of the International Telephone and Telegraph Co.

firm hand and "political pull" of a career Army man with Pentagon connections, and in October he found the ideal candidate in Colonel Joseph Haskell (whose brother John was then commanding OSS Italy). A general's son, a West Pointer, and a former Army intelligence officer, the 35-year-old Haskell had spent months on the Army's planning staff for the OVERLORD invasion. He had "inside" connections at the European theater command, and through his efforts OSS gained respectability in American military circles in London.°

The British were impressed as well. Through Haskell's military connections, OSS acquired the use of two strategic bomber squadrons for agent drops and supply sorties to the resistance. Recognizing this first step toward a genuine American contribution to European special operations, SOE at last offered Donovan's SO Branch a formal merger. A joint unit was formed under the command of Haskell and a British brigadier, who reported directly to the Anglo-American Theater Headquarters.[22]

Direct OSS participation in French operations had already begun. In June the first American officer had dropped into France, though under SOE auspices, to organize a sabotage network. The first full-fledged OSS member of an inter-Allied mission, 30-year-old Peter Ortiz, a Marine captain and veteran of the Foreign Legion, spent Christmas of 1943 at a Maquis camp in southeastern France.[23]

By insisting that all American Special Operations officers be screened and trained at British installations, SOE postponed the influx of OSS men into occupied France that might have begun that fall. Unperturbed by the delay, Haskell's staff was already looking ahead to the resistance operations that would accompany the invasion of the continent; General Donovan placed highest priority on a remarkable international secret service plan code-named JEDBURGH.

The Jed teams, as they were called in OVERLORD vernacular, were to be composed of one OSS or SOE officer, one officer of French nationality, and one British or American enlisted man as radio operator. The Jeds were to parachute in uniform to resistance groups throughout France during the weeks following the Allied landings. They would act as liaison with the underground, arm and train the Maquis, boost "patriotic morale," and coordinate resistance activity with Allied military strategy.[24]

° Haskell was vice-president of the National Distillers and Chemical Corporation, 1957–63, and now heads a management consultant firm in New York.

The Jed plan called for 50 American officers fluent in French; the task of scouring southern Army camps for this vanguard of the liberation was assigned to Wall Street attorney George Sharp, who headed the West Europe desk of the Special Operations Branch in Washington. A leading partner of Allen Dulles' law firm and son of the American ambassador to France during World War I, Sharp was equal to the responsibility. Assisted by Franklin Canfield, one of the SO pioneers in London (also a Dulles legal associate), Sharp filled his quota by November.

A more hazardous process strewn with political pitfalls was the recruitment of Frenchmen for both special operations and espionage missions. Many of the French émigrés interviewed by OSS were recent arrivals with long-nurtured political antagonisms. Some were anglophobes who refused to volunteer for hazardous duty unless assured that they would be "handled" only by American officers.

The recruitment of French agents for SUSSEX espionage was especially complicated. The leading lights of the SI French desk in Washington—Alfred DuPont, an architect unaffiliated with his family's huge chemical concern, and Geoffrey Atkinson, a professor of Romance Languages at Amherst—had failed to locate an adequate supply of prospective spies in the United States. French refugees in America, long absent from the homeland, had no knowledge of the latest colloquialisms, were unaware of the changes in daily life under German domination, and had become too "soft" for lonely, dangerous espionage assignments. The BCRA also objected that many of these émigrés were "tainted by Vichyism" (often a euphemism for opposition to de Gaulle).[25]

OSS soon abandoned the SUSSEX search and decided that the greater number of the 100 agents would have to be provided by the BCRA from military reserves in North Africa. Passy was willing to help, but the decision was no longer his; the locus of French politics had shifted to Algiers and Passy had to present the case for SUSSEX to the politically divided French Committee of National Liberation. The BCRA chief made his proposal in August. Two months passed before any action was taken; the de Gaulle-Giraud tangle again snarled OSS operational planning.

The manifest competition for political power between the two French generals brought their respective secret services into direct confrontation. The BCRA, established in Algiers under the direction of an ex-police official, Commandant André Pelabon, categorically refused to work with the Giraudist intelligence group, the DSR/SM, whose leaders had embarked on a desperate maneuver to ally with the dissident elements of the French resistance.

Since the arrest of Jean Moulin and General Delestraint, the Armée Secrète had been reconstituted into a powerful partisan underground that claimed the allegiance of thousands. But the vigorous Communist military underground, the Francs Tireurs et Partisans (FTP) remained aloof from the Gaullist military cadres. The Giraudists saw in this an opportunity for a temporary coalition.

For months, the Communist-dominated underground on the island of French Corsica, off the Italian coast, had been plotting an uprising against the German and Italian garrisons with the encouragement of Giraudist agents. In July a huge arms shipment had been dispatched to the Corsican resistance, a joint venture of the DSR/SM, SOE, and the OSS Special Operations Branch at Algiers, then commanded by a Giraudist proponent, Robert Pflieger, an American businessman with interests in the Congo and a love for big-game hunting.[p]

When word reached Corsica that the Italians had surrendered, a spontaneous popular uprising broke out against the Germans; the Communist underground appealed to Algiers for support. Giraud responded by sending French troops to the island. De Gaulle was infuriated. He had not been consulted about the operation. After a tempestuous meeting of the Committee of National Liberation, Giraud flew to Corsica to take personal direction of the campaign. On October 4, the island was free.[26]

It was a short-lived triumph for Giraud. Alarmed by the readiness of the DSR/SM to unite with his Communist critics, de Gaulle directed a member of his military staff, General Cochet, to bring the Giraudist secret service under control of the BCRA. Headquartered at the entrance to the Casbah in Algiers, the irascible Cochet began an ill-fated attempt at "coordination" of the two services in an atmosphere of bitter mutual recrimination.

OSS Headquarters in London, meanwhile, was still awaiting the BCRA's recruitment of French agents for SUSSEX. At the end of October, General Cochet flew to London to assure OSS and MI-6 that he was willing to help. The first thirty recruits, he said, would soon arrive in Britain.

November arrived, but the agents did not. Early that month in

---

[p] At the time of his death in 1955, Pflieger was president of the American Chamber of Commerce in Brussels.

Algiers, the Committee of National Liberation had been enlarged to include representatives of the resistance. When the new Committee roster was published, Giraud's name was conspicuously absent. Believing that he had gained the upper hand, de Gaulle made another attempt to bring the last refuge of Giraudism, the DSR/SM, under his control. General Cochet was relieved, and de Gaulle placed his propaganda chief Jacques Soustelle, an ambitious anthropologist with an expertise on the Mexican Aztecs, in charge of a new intelligence directorate.[q] Assisted by Passy as his technical assistant, Soustelle's objective was to bring the DSR/SM to heel by the beginning of December. Giraud and his intelligence aides resisted. On the advice of his Algiers lieutenants, General Donovan impulsively stepped into the breach in support of the Giraudists, thus "affording the Gaullists a heaven-sent opportunity for smearing their adversaries as 'tools of a foreign power.'"[27]

The battle of the secret services went on, and no SUSSEX agents had reached London. Then in December a few French recruits arrived. They had been selected by Donovan's man in Casablanca, David King, one of the original Murphy Vice Consuls during the TORCH operation. King was a man of wide experience who had fought in the French Foreign Legion, sold burlap in India, interpreted for a diplomatic mission in Ethiopia, and made a small fortune in the business world. But as a spy recruiter he was an abject failure; his agents could not meet the rigorous requirements of SUSSEX.

Disgusted by the long delay, Colonel Miller, the liberal Virginian who directed the OSS facet of SUSSEX, sent one of his officers to Algiers in late December to help accelerate recruitment. The recipient of this unhappy assignment was Robert Lambert, a French-born owner of a textile import firm in New York. In Algiers, Lambert first called on André Pelabon, commander of the BCRA in North Africa. The Frenchman promptly treated Miller's emissary to a diatribe against OSS Algiers, whose officers, he said, continued to promote the dying Giraudist cause.[28]

Lambert then learned that since the purge of Arthur Roseborough and other pro-Gaullist OSS dissenters in North Africa, the SI Branch at Algiers had been directed by 29-year-old New York attorney Henry

[q] Soustelle was Governor-General of Algeria, 1955–56. He fled into exile in 1962 after being implicated in a right-wing plot by diehard opponents of Algerian independence to overthrow the government of his old friend de Gaulle.

Hyde, a vigorous opponent of Gaullism. Hyde's father, the inheritor of an insurance company fortune, had been a fervent Francophile and notorious host of society extravaganzas at the turn of the century. Embarrassed by a government investigation of his business holdings, the elder Hyde had moved to France, where his son Henry was born. The young man, completely bilingual, had studied at Cambridge University and received a law degree from Harvard. Married to the daughter of a French baron and conservative senator, Hyde's views on French politics were often jokingly described by his American colleagues as bordering on monarchism. He lost no opportunity to support the DSR/SM against the Gaullist organization of Pelabon, Passy, and Soustelle.

Finding Pelabon less than eager to aid an American organization that included such anti-Gaullists as Hyde, Lambert turned next to the MI-6 representative in Algiers, but the British officer explained apologetically that he was on icy terms with both French factions and had not even met anyone at OSS headquarters. Lambert was astounded. No one in Algiers seemed to realize the urgency of the situation. OVERLORD was only five months away.

At the Cairo Conference in December 1943, the Combined Chiefs of Staff committed themselves irrevocably to OVERLORD, and appointed General Dwight D. Eisenhower commander of SHAEF (Supreme Headquarters, Allied Expeditionary Force), the Anglo-American bureaucracy that would direct the cross-channel invasion of France. Eisenhower flew to London in mid-January with a poignant warning for his new staff. "I don't mind if one officer refers to another as that son of a bitch," he declared, "but the instant I hear of any American officer referring to a brother officer as that British son of a bitch, out he goes." [29]

OSS men did their best to promote Allied cooperation. Emerging victorious from a polite disagreement with MI-6 and British Field Marshal Montgomery over their right to independent agent communications, the officers of Colonel Miller's SUSSEX team then found that "the British were marvelous" and "opened all doors to us." [30] To insure full coordination, a tripartite SUSSEX committee was formed in January, chaired by Commander Kenneth Cohen of British intelligence. Colonel Miller represented OSS while Colonel Passy's most brilliant espionage agent, former film producer Gilbert Renault-Roulier (nom de guerre, Rémy), spoke for the French. [31] The very fact of equal Gaullist representation was a major victory for the long-ignored BCRA.

Renault-Roulier soon left for Algiers to assist the beleaguered Lieutenant Lambert in speeding SUSSEX preparations. Together, Roulier and Lambert struggled through the channels of French military hierarchy until, in a personal meeting with de Gaulle, they secured the right to recruit agents directly from the ranks of the French Army in Africa. By March 87 Frenchmen destined for espionage assignments had left for England.

A month later, on April 9, the first OSS-directed SUSSEX agents parachuted into France, equipped with automatic pistols, concealed hacksaws for emergency escapes, and "L" pills (suicide tablets). The daring Frenchmen began sending their vital intelligence messages to London weeks before the Allied invasion was to begin.[32]

Special operations were also progressing, or so it seemed. The first OSS supply sortie to the French resistance was flown on January 4. Unfortunately, that achievement provoked diplomatic debate. Because of a sudden decision by Churchill to boost SOE assistance to the underground, the American supply program was dwarfed by the British effort. De Gaulle made a snide comment about the paucity of Washington's aid and Cordell Hull immediately took offense. Eisenhower decided it was time to protect resistance operations from the ravages of international diplomacy.

On March 23, Eisenhower's headquarters assumed control of all secret service activity connected with the OVERLORD landings. The joint special operations unit formed by OSS and SOE was divorced entirely from its parent organizations and eventually renamed Special Force Headquarters, reporting directly to SHAEF. A similar Anglo-American unit, the Special Projects Operations Center, was formed in Algiers under the joint command of OSS Colonel William Davis, Jr., a Philadelphia banker, and SOE Colonel John Anstey, a director of the Imperial Tobacco Company, to coordinate resistance activities in southern France, where a secondary Allied landing was to take place. The objectives of all this organizational tumult were to harness the French underground to the regular military command and, hopefully, to eliminate political considerations from Allied dealings with the resistance.

Although, as the BCRA had often insisted, politics and special operations would prove inseparable, some OSS men made a brave attempt at limiting themselves to military jargon. Example: "The Maquis invariably asked for more [arms] than they needed—anticipating future recruits and responding to the natural wish to build up a reserve—and we had to prune their requests to a size within our capacity to deliver and which, at the same time, would maintain their effectiveness." [33] Political translation: Many Allied officers, especially the British, feared that well-armed and competing resistance forces might use the occasion of the Allied landings to "indulge themselves in a first-rate civil war." Resistance forces already claimed 100 to 350 thousand adherents, a potentially violent element in a liberated France that might well be plagued by "fundamental political and social disequilibrium." [34]

Heightened French political invective did little to calm the fears of SHAEF planners. In Algiers, the center of the "external resistance," the OSS and SOE men of the Special Projects Operations Center, laboring in a group of well-guarded huts and tents outside the city, were accosted by a multitude of French factions, all "interested in building up private little armies, looking forward to the day when they would go back to France." [35]

The "internal resistance" was, in theory, more unified. In March, de Gaulle announced the creation of the Forces Françaises de l'Interieur (FFI), a "united" military underground that would include the Armée Secrète and Maquis units of Gaullist, Giraudist, and Communist persuasion. Yet OSS and SOE knew that resistance unity, despite de Gaulle's pronouncements, was still a political dream.

The Giraudists continued to plot and intrigue in a hopeless effort to stem the Gaullist tide. Since Giraud's elimination from the Committee of National Liberation in November, the general, who retained joint command with de Gaulle of the French armed forces, had been forsaken by his American backers—with one exception.

Henry Hyde's Secret Intelligence Branch of OSS Algiers had become the rallying point for a small group of French dissidents who could never accept the fact of Gaullist supremacy. The senior schemer of this faction was none other than Jacques Lemaigre-Dubrueil, the reactionary oil magnate who had played such an important role in TORCH. The intellectual light of the dissidents was the famed French writer and pioneer aviator, Antoine de Saint-Exupéry,[r] an old and close friend of General Donovan's, who had consistently condemned Gaullism as "a fascism without a doctrine." [36] Finally, the cabal found an agent extraordinaire in Paul Dungler, the self-proclaimed leader of the non-Gaullist resistance in the Franco-German border province of Alsace-Lorraine.

[r] Saint-Exupéry was killed in a plane crash later that year, possibly a victim of political assassination.

Hyde pact of Post to put reactionary General Giraud in charge of French troops [handwritten annotation]

Dungler had long maintained close contact with Marshal Pétain and his collaborationist entourage at Vichy. In the summer of 1943, the old soldier had sent Dungler to Algiers with an offer of reconciliation for Giraud and de Gaulle, an incredible proposal indignantly rejected by both generals. Dungler then languished in Algiers until January 1944, when Hyde's SI Branch and Giraud's still-independent intelligence service, the DSR/SM, agreed to send him on a special mission to France without the knowledge of the Gaullists. Soustelle and Passy learned of the plan, however, and, suspecting that Dungler's assignment was to negotiate with Pétain for Giraud's return to France "at the head of French troops," they immediately secured a directive from de Gaulle ordering Dungler's arrest.[37] He took refuge in Lemaigre-Dubrueil's villa until OSS men secreted him to an American airfield. In mid-January, he was parachuted to an area near Vichy with wireless transmitters and codes.
Dulles [handwritten annotation]

Then the "plot" became more confused. Dungler was instructed by OSS to make contact in Nice with anti-Hitler officers of the Abwehr, the German military intelligence service (and professional rivals of Heinrich Himmler's Gestapo). With the apparent knowledge of Allen Dulles, the OSS chief in Switzerland, Marshal Pétain's aides concocted a fantastic scheme. The anti-Hitler Opposition in Berlin had long plotted the Fuehrer's assassination; dissident German officers in France proposed to use the occasion of the dictator's prospective demise to negotiate a peace treaty with Giraud and the Americans in North Africa. Dungler was to provide the radio communication for this unlikely coup.[38]

Everything went wrong. After Dungler's departure, Gaullist officers had taken control of the radio facilities of the DSR/SM in Algiers; Dungler was unable to make contact with his superiors. Then in late February, Heinrich Himmler learned of the Abwehr contact with Vichy and OSS. The Gestapo chief, always eager to damage the position of his intelligence rivals in the German bureaucracy, had Dungler arrested and his Abwehr contacts recalled to Germany.

This ignominious end to the Dungler mission was followed by the final defeat of Giraud and his secret services in North Africa. At the beginning of April, the general was relieved of his military command and placed on the army's reserve list." [s] Some top officials of the DSR/

[s] Giraud, after recovering from a wound inflicted by a Moslem assassin, returned to France months after the liberation of Paris. He was given an obscure administrative post and died in 1949.

SM were also retired, while others—particularly the French counter-espionage experts who were highly regarded in British intelligence circles —were co-opted by Soustelle's Gaullist organization for future operations.

The French Communists, despite their own curious record of political alliances, condemned de Gaulle's warm acceptance of right-wing Giraudist officers and condemned the whole Gaullist movement as "a pack of cryptofascists whose real aim was to rivet the rule of the elite back onto a resuscitated capitalist republic." [39] In France itself, the Communist-led guerrillas, the FTP, refused to incorporate themselves into de Gaulle's FFI partisan army, except in a purely formal sense. Since the capture of Jean Moulin by the Germans, the Communists had also taken control of the National Resistance Council and its military action committee, thus forming a shadow government in potential opposition to de Gaulle's newly proclaimed Provisional French Government at Algiers.

OSS had already run afoul of the Communists. For months Arthur Goldberg's Labor Branch had been sending funds to the clandestine French Confederation of Labor. This underground union group included a socialist majority and a Communist minority, which began a campaign to seize control of the organization. Goldberg's money had been going to the Socialist leadership; the Communists insisted that the funds be divided between the two political factions. When OSS refused, the funding operation was publicly exposed in the Communist underground press, making Goldberg's activities known to the Gestapo.

In the bitter aftermath of this incident, many OSS men in London were delighted when de Gaulle sent one of his young generals, Joseph Pierre Koenig, as military emissary to SHAEF. Koenig's objective was to be recognized by the Allies as official commander of the FFI and voice of the resistance in Allied war councils. In that post, he could help check the potential Communist domination of the underground. Koenig set up headquarters in London, using BCRA personnel for his staff, and petitioned SHAEF to appoint him commander of the French resistance. Because of diehard opposition to de Gaulle at the White House, the appointment was delayed. Not until May 30 was Koenig named chief of the FFI and then the appointment was only nominal. The Gaullists wanted more—full control of OSS and SOE resistance operations in France. David Bruce and SOE commander Colin Gubbins met with Koenig to discuss the French request for a new tripartite staff that would absorb the BCRA and Special Force Headquarters under

Koenig's command. But the British and many OSS men were cool to the idea. Political reorganizations should have been made months before; OVERLORD was about to begin.[40]

The pressure of invasion preparations had begun to show on the faces of tired OSS planners. Personality conflicts were rife. William Maddox, chief of the SI Branch, had already been transferred to Italy after he and SUSSEX director Francis Miller began a bitter jurisdictional battle which Colonel Bruce had attempted, in vain, to mediate. Maddox's stopgap replacement was Alan Scaife, a Pittsburgh industrialist and a cousin of David Bruce's wife. Then in early May the SI post was taken by John Haskell, the stock exchange executive originally slated to head Donovan's ill-fated mission to Russia, and the brother of Joe Haskell, who commanded the Special Operations Branch. A little brotherly cooperation, Donovan believed, might be just the necessary ingredient to insure OSS effectiveness during the European invasion.

But the OSS chief was still worried, and at the end of May he came to London to personally inspect the progress of Bruce's detachment. After a cursory examination of the various branch offices, the general called a staff meeting and announced: "Gentlemen, I find that here in London you have been doing too much planning. Plans are no good on the day of battle. I ask you to throw your plans out of the window." [41]

While a few irate officers took Donovan's words as a personal affront (Colonel Miller requested a transfer out of OSS), many OSS men seemed to take the general's words to heart. Planning went "out of the window" and confusion again reigned.

Nothing was more confusing than the still unresolved question of the French role in resistance operations. Eisenhower refused to relinquish control of Special Force Headquarters to Koenig, though the French general was treated diplomatically by OSS and SOE. On the eve of OVERLORD, David Bruce and General Gubbins of SOE called on Koenig and Passy and asked whether the French had any objection to the BBC's transmission of coded messages for a general resistance uprising. This was no more than a polite gesture, for the decision had already been taken and the orders issued.[42]

It was not always possible to be polite. During the first days of June, Colonel Renault-Roulier, the BCRA representative on the SUSSEX coordinating committee, came to the office of his OSS counterpart, Colonel Miller, to say that General de Gaulle "wished to know where the landing would take place." Roulier, recalls Miller, "went to my map on the wall, pointed to the Normandy Coast, and asked if that was the area. Our orders were strict, and I was mum, but he had been of such tremendous help that it hurt me not to tell. He was equally distressed when I withdrew into my shell." [43]

The French were not the only ones to be kept in the dark. One day Major Arthur Goldberg stumbled into a London office where "something big" was obviously being discussed. "Are you bigoted?" the officer in charge demanded of him. "No!" replied the liberal attorney, somewhat flustered. He was asked to leave immediately.[44] Only later did he learn that BIGOT was the code-word for those officers entitled to know that the British and Americans would invade the beaches of Normandy during the first week of June 1944.

In the early morning hours of June 6, thousands of British and American ships set out across the English Channel to begin the great military crusade that would wrest Europe from the hands of the Nazis. On board one of these vessels, the U.S. cruiser *Tuscaloosa*, were General Donovan and Colonel Bruce.

Donovan's participation in OVERLORD had, for security reasons, been expressly forbidden by Secretary of the Navy Forrestal. The irrepressible "Wild Bill" had appealed the order to an old friend, the admiral commanding American naval forces in Europe. "You and I are old and expendable," argued the OSS chief. "What better end for us than to die in Normandy with enemy bullets in our bellies?" The startled admiral was unsympathetic. Nevertheless, by other devious means, Donovan reached France together with the invasion armada.[45]

"When we finally got ashore in Normandy," David Bruce remembers, "I had maladroitly, in taking evasive action when fired upon by enemy aircraft, fallen on the General and gashed him badly in the throat with my steel helmet. It must have cut close to the jugular vein, for he bled profusely. At this time he wore, and it was the only occasion when I knew him to do so, the ribbon of the Medal of Honor, in those days everywhere recognizable. We sauntered inland to an American aircraft battery, the furthermost position occupied by our people in that sector. Beyond was a huge open field, enclosed at the far end by a tight hedge. In the field, three presumably French peasants appeared to be digging up roots or vegetables. Donovan approached the Battery Captain and said he was going forward to question his three French agents who were expecting him. The captain, looking at his bloody throat and the Congressional Medal, warned him this was dangerous, but let him proceed.

"As we progressed," Bruce continues, "our alleged agents disappeared, Donovan and I came to a halt in the lee of a hedgerow that was being subjected to intermittent German machine-gun fire. Flattened out, the general turned to me and said: 'David, we mustn't be captured, we know too much.' 'Yes, Sir,' I answered mechanically. 'Have you your pill?' he demanded. I confessed I was not carrying the instantaneous death pellet concocted by our scientific adviser. . . . 'Never mind,' replied the resourceful general, 'I have two of them.' Thereupon, still lying prone, he disgorged the contents of all his pockets. There were a number of hotel keys, a passport, currency of several nationalities, photographs of grandchildren, travel orders, newspaper clippings, and heaven knows what else, but no pills. 'Never mind,' said Donovan, 'we can do without them, but if we get out of here you must send a message to Gibbs, the Hall Porter at Claridges in London, telling him on no account to allow the servants in the hotel to touch some dangerous medicines in my bathroom.'

This humanitarian disposition having been made," concludes Bruce, "Donovan whispered to me: 'I must shoot first.' 'Yes, Sir,' I responded, 'but can we do much against machine-guns with our pistols?' 'Oh, you don't understand,' he said. 'I mean if we are about to be captured I'll shoot you first. After all, I am your Commanding Officer.' " [46]

The general would undoubtedly have made good on his promise, but both men survived D-Day. Donovan flew off to Rome, and Bruce, soon joined by his staff, established a temporary headquarters at the western border of the Allied beachhead, waiting for Eisenhower's forces to break out of Normandy in a two-pronged drive toward Brittany in the west and Paris in the east.

Bruce supervised a complex OSS machinery that included 100 French SUSSEX agents roaming through northern France to report on German troop movements and an equal number of Jedburghs and other special operations officers working with the resistance throughout the country to harass the hard-pressed Wehrmacht forces.

Many of these behind-the-lines operatives were inspiring models of dedication and courage. Jacques Voyer, a veteran Gaullist espionage agent at the age of 21, had parachuted to Chartres for OSS in early April and sent London a steady stream of intelligence on German movements and bombing targets. Four days after D-Day, Voyer was driving a motorcycle past a German convoy when he stopped to note the strength of the troop unit. Halted by two Nazi officers, he knocked both men down and took flight. Before he could escape, he was shot in the shoulder and the ankle, then knocked unconscious with the butt of a rifle. Dragged to prison, he endured eight days of torture but could not be broken. On June 27, he was executed. Buried in a lonely field, he wore an iron Cross of Lorraine, pinned to his coat by members of the resistance.[47]

Such heroism contrasted with inanity at higher (and safer) levels of Bruce's organization. Attached to each American Army in Normandy were separate field detachments representing the various operational branches of OSS. Unfortunately, the work of the various units was "not very well coordinated, and often the personnel didn't know each other, or even about the work of the others," a muddled situation which "didn't help the image of the OSS with the military."[48] Army intelligence officers delighted in telling the tale of the OSS counter-intelligence officer, a Radcliffe history instructor in calmer times, who burst irately into the presence of Chicago journalist Kenneth Downs, commander of field detachments for the Secret Intelligence Branch.[t] "One of *your* espionage officers," wailed the historian, "has arrested one of *my* double agents!"

Then there was the aging OSS colonel, an executive of General Electric, who was briefing an OSS agent on his mission. Pulling down a large wall map of France dotted with mysterious symbols and markers, the colonel not only mispronounced the name of the "drop zone," but spent some ten minutes searching for the location of the town before an aide whispered that it was several hundred miles to the north.

Another London briefing was given to British-born Jedburgh officer Bernard Knox, a Cambridge graduate in classical literature, who jumped into Brittany assured by his OSS superiors that the area would be "free of German troops."[u] The professor commented acidly: "There was, as always, something wrong with the briefing; we landed right in the middle of the German Second Parachute Division [and] had a very hectic time running away from them."[49]

The French suffered similar pangs of confusion, and on one occasion the resistance paid the horrible consequences. The Vercors region

[t] Downs is now a partner of ex-CIA official Kermit Roosevelt in a Washington public relations firm.

[u] Dr. Knox is now Director of the Center for Hellenic Studies in Washington, D.C.

of southeastern France was an Alpine natural fortress—400 square miles of isolated, heavily wooded mountains and plateaus—which had been a pocket of Maquis resistance since the fall of 1943. Some 3500 Maquis loyalists, joined by OSS and SOE liaison officers, had assembled there awaiting D-Day and the call to action.[50]

After OVERLORD, the Vercors Maquis began extended forays against the Germans, believing mistakenly that the BCRA had accepted their strategic plan for the arrival of an Allied airborne force armed with heavy weapons to support the resistance. In London, the proposal had in fact been ignored, lost in the administrative shuffle between the BCRA and the new FFI staff of General Koenig.

The Germans, meanwhile, resolved to destroy the Vercors Maquis. The first enemy attack on June 13 was surprisingly rebuffed by a confident resistance. Yet the expected airborne division did not arrive. Instead, in late June, OSS dropped an Operational Group of 15 men to the plateau to urge the resistance forces to avoid pitched battle and "incline them toward more useful guerrilla tactics." [51] But it was too late to alter the Vercors strategy.

When the paratroopers failed to appear, the Maquis pleaded with OSS for the dispatch of mortars and other heavy weapons for defense against the attacking Germans. On June 25, OSS began a series of daylight supply sorties to the resistance throughout France. One-fifth of the small arms—but no heavy weapons—arrived in the Vercors.

On July 14, Bastille Day, the still-buoyant Maquis publicly proclaimed a Free Republic of the Vercors. That same day an OSS supply drop brought hundreds of rifles and automatic weapons, but still no mortars or airborne troops. The Germans sent planes over the drop zone, bombing and strafing the men on the ground who were trying to gather the supplies. The attack was the prelude to a concerted assault by 22,000 German soldiers. An advance force of SS troops began massacring Maquis and civilians alike. A counterattack led by OSS officers failed to hold them off. Resistance pleas for assistance to London and Algiers went unanswered. "We shall not forget the bitterness of having been abandoned alone and without support in time of battle," wired the FFI commander.[52]

On July 23, the Germans broke through the French defenses. While the OSS liaison officers organized the escape of some Maquis units, the Nazis turned the Vercors into a field of martyrdom. Men, women, and children were murdered indiscriminately, their bodies hanged and suspended from meat hooks in butcher shops. Hospitals were burned, villages wiped off the map. The Vercors dream ended in an orgy of death.

Did the Allies learn anything from the Vercors disaster? If there was any tragic "moral," it was the need to minimize bureaucratic wrangling in London. The point seemed lost on the secret services. In spite of Eisenhower's initial refusal, General Koenig continued to insist that he be granted control over OSS and SOE operations in France—a justifiable demand but an issue that should have been resolved months before the invasion. Having acquired a sudden appreciation of the military value of the resistance, Ike finally acceded to Koenig's request. In late June, while the fight in Normandy went on, an unwieldy structure dubbed EMFFI (Etat-Major des Forces Françaises de l'Intérieur) was created to integrate Koenig's BCRA staff and the Anglo-American Special Force Headquarters. The tardy amalgamation was chaotic. Some OSS men gave Koenig "complete and unquestioning support"; other American officers questioned the efficacy of this "political move" so late in the war.[53] As for the French, veteran Gaullists and "reformed" Giraudists were thrown together in a headquarters "nauseatingly full of intrigue." [54]

American officers working with the resistance in Franch knew nothing of these organizational pains. Already contemptuous of the "desk men" in London, the Jeds and other special operations officers were incensed when radio messages went unanswered or their Maquis friends waited impatiently for supply sorties which never came. From the moment they had parachuted into the French night, these OSS men had begun life in the special world of the Maquis, a world radically different from the neat, austere planning offices of the British capital.

The OSS arrivals would be met by a Maquis reception committee, often composed of "ill-clothed country boys" who had waited long hours in the cold night to greet a "parachutiste Américain." The welcome was warm and emotional. The newcomers would sometimes be dashed off at breakneck speed in an antique Citroën to a lavish dinner of contraband food and abundant quantities of wine, accompanied by innumerable toasts to "l'Amérique, la France, and l'Angleterre," to Roosevelt, de Gaulle, and Churchill.[55]

The OSS men became "kings of their particular castles. They were men of position and power in their neighborhoods, had money to spend and lived well from sources so hidden that even scavenging Nazis could not locate the supply." Money stolen from collaborationist banks was abundant, as were "pleasant social contacts." [56]

Wall Street attorney and OSS Major Reeve Schley, Jr., was surrounded by admiring French children in the town of Herisson, which he and team mate John Alsop "liberated" during their wanderings behind the German lines in the summer of 1944.

American officers traveling with the Maquis to "liberate" small towns and villages came to expect a riotous reception as conquering heroes. Champagne flowed freely. Weeping women competed for the privilege of kissing the OSS liberators. Children came up to offer gifts of candy and flowers. Jedburgh Michael Burke,[v] a handsome 26-year-old football star from the University of Pennsylvania, was accosted by an eighty-year-old Frenchman, who with tears in his eyes sobbed "To think that General Eisenhower thought enough of our little village to send an American officer here to help us." [57]

And in the secret camps of the Maquis, there were also celebrations —feasting, drinking, toasting, and patriotic songs. Thrust into this happy milieu in late July were OSS officers Reeve Schley, Jr., 36, a very near-sighted Wall Street lawyer with a love for thoroughbred horses, and

[v] Burke was general manager of the Ringling Brothers Circus, 1954–56; president of the CBS network in Europe, 1958–62; and is now president of the New York Yankees baseball club.

John Alsop, 29, the articulate, pipe-smoking brother of journalist Joseph Alsop.[w] Both men were Yale graduates from wealthy families. Neither spoke fluent French, and neither was musically inclined.

At one Maquis celebration, the Frenchmen roared the "Marseillaise," SOE officers sang "God Save the King," then everyone looked expectantly at Schley and Alsop. To their great embarrassment, they could not sing the "Star Spangled Banner"—they simply didn't know the words. Improvisation was called for, but Schley and Alsop could produce only one song known to both of them. Their British translators announced to the French that it was a specially composed anthem of international goodwill. Singing with gusto to the tune of "Hark, the Herald Angels Sing," the OSS men gave a moving rendition of a ballad currently popular in the bars of London: "Uncle George and Aunty Mabel/Fainted at the breakfast table. . . ." Their success was instant. French peasants, FFI and Communist FTP alike, saluted and stood quivering to attention. More weeping women, more flowers. The amateur diplomats of OSS had scored another triumph.[58]

If there was abundant benevolence among allies behind the lines, there was also ideological conflict, sometimes intensely bitter. John Alsop's brother, Stewart,[x] who had left an editor's job in New York to join the British Army and then OSS, jumped into southern France on a JEDBURGH mission, accompanied by a Gaullist career army officer, a graduate of the French military academy, St. Cyr. Their original assignment was to join a Communist FTP guerrilla unit, a mission perfectly acceptable to the 30-year-old Alsop, an outspoken New Dealer. But they vehemently anti-Communist Frenchman refused; he insisted that they work, instead, with the Gaullist FFI partisans. Alsop, who had been led to believe the Maquis was politically unified, received his first lesson in resistance politics, the hard way.

A few OSS men reached France with firm political prejudices of their own. New York socialite Serge Obolensky, the Russian émigré and former Czarist "prince," was placed in command of a uniformed OSS Operational Group in central France that was, ironically, assigned to aid a Communist Maquis group. At a victory celebration following the liberation of the town of Chateauroux, Obolensky made a speech

---

[w] Alsop was the unsuccessful Republican candidate for Governor of Connecticut in 1962. He is now Republican National Committeeman from that state.

[x] Stewart Alsop, a well-known author and columnist, is now a senior editor of *Newsweek*.

from a balcony, placed a bouquet of roses on the grave of a resistance hero, then joined the FTP commander in reviewing a parade of the local partisans. To Obolensky's discomfiture, the guerrilla leaders were all "Reds" who gave the Bolshevik clenched-fist salute. The OSS colonel left France firmly convinced that "the Maquis varied greatly: the conservatives were well-informed, very responsible, and good soldiers; others, most of these in leftist groups, were trigger-happy, cocky, and foolish. So there were really two lines in the French underground, one serious and disciplined, but inclined to lack initiative; the other reckless, dangerous, and veering over to the complete dominance of the Reds." [59]

Without indulging in the political invective, some American officers reached similar conclusions. The FTP Communists were frequently charged with lack of discipline or excessive zeal. William Grell, a Belgian-born officer who had managed one of Serge Obolensky's hotels in New York, parachuted to Limoges in southwestern France, an area of FTP strength, to coordinate OSS resistance activities. Teamed with OSS Lieutenant William Macomber, Jr., a 24-year-old pre-law graduate of Yale, Grell began a trek through the German lines toward American-held territory.[y] On the way, he was challenged by FTP sentries. "These people worried us nearly as much as the Germans," he later wrote. "They were all youngsters, itching for a chance to blaze away with their Stens, and their enthusiasm, plus the notoriously light trigger pull of the Sten, made us nervous." [60]

Not all OSS observers attributed special qualities of impulsiveness to the FTP. Reports from France indicated that Gaullists as well as Communists provoked tactically useless skirmishes with the Germans, engaged in acts of sabotage unsanctioned by London, and went "on a spree of shaving the heads of female collaborators, some of them pretty prostitutes whose only crime had been sleeping with Germans." [61]

Yet the Communists had one special strike against them—a reputation as revolutionaries bent on seizing power by violent means. Much of this notoriety was acquired in southern France at the time of the Allied landings on the Riviera. The southern landings, code-named DRAGOON, had originally been planned as a diversionary attack that

---

[y] Macomber left a CIA post in 1953 to join the State Department as special assistant to John Foster Dulles. He was U.S. ambassador to Jordan, 1961–64, and assistant administrator of the Agency for International Development, 1964–67; he is now Deputy Under Secretary of State.

would occur simultaneously with the Normandy invasion. For logistical reasons DRAGOON, to be launched by French and American forces from North Africa, was postponed. Finally, on August 15, as Allied forces in the north approached Paris, American troops landed on the famed beaches of the Côte d'Azur near Nice.

Overall direction of OSS operations for the DRAGOON landings had been given to Edward Gamble, Jr., a capable Virginian, the manager of a New York brokerage house dealing in government bonds. Espionage operations remained in the hands of SI chief Henry Hyde, who had abandoned Giraudist intrigue to create a very effective intelligence network in southern France. As in London, dealings with the resistance were managed by a joint headquarters staffed with British, French, and American officers.

The OSS operatives sent to southern France from Algiers were often involved in touchy political situations, although not the outright civil war predicted by some officers on Eisenhower's staff. The resistance in the region was, undeniably, directed by Communists, some of them fiery advocates of Marxist dogma who considered the OSS parachutists the vanguard of Gaullist reaction.[62]

SHAEF was particularly concerned about the political intentions of Maquis units formed by Spanish Republican exiles, many of them Communists who had fled to France after the fascist victory in the Spanish Civil War. OSS decided to send a liaison mission to sound out this unpredictable Spanish Maquis. The team was to be headed by Colonel Peter Dewey, a talented young journalist and writer whose father was a conservative Republican congressman. But Dewey (later to lead an important OSS mission to Indochina) was transferred to another behind-the-lines project and his command devolved upon a clever 25-year-old Spanish émigré, Ricardo Sicre, a veteran of Donald Downes' Moroccan team who was able to deal effectively (and calmly) with his leftist countrymen.[z] The much-feared revolution of the Spanish Republican Maquis never occurred.

OSS officers also worked with French Communist guerrillas who had been trained by the Spanish Republicans. Captain Geoffrey M. T. Jones, 25, a Princeton alumnus from a wealthy eastern family, joined one of these groups, a unit of 150 FTP Communists "out in the middle

[z] Sicre is reportedly one of the wealthiest men in Spain today. He is also vice-president of the World Commerce Corporation, a firm founded after the war by General Donovan and William Stephenson of British intelligence.

of nowhere on this mountain." [a] Jones remembers: "Early in my stay, one morning they had a formation to honor me. They all drew themselves up and sang the 'Internationale' and then they sang the 'Marseillaise.' They were really carried away with the idea of being Communists. They called each other 'Comrade' and had a political commissar for each one of their three battalions. . . . Later when I took about twenty of them into a small action, and the guns started going off, I looked around and I only had two left! Not that I blame them. . . . They really didn't get much military training. . . . They seemed to think it was more romantic just to live up there on the mountaintop and call each other 'Comrade.' " [63]

Like other American officers, Jones watched the FTP launch premature uprisings in an attempt to take control of local governments before the Gaullists could do so. Both factions went to bitter extremes. But Jones could not blame the power struggle on his Maquis friends. "Our outfit," he said, "was made up of a wonderful group of people for whom, I guess, I was the catalyst. These were the Frenchmen who honestly produced results for their country. These were the kind of people that are worth respecting and the hell with the ones who were busy denouncing each other in order to get political power." [64]

London did not see it that way. SHAEF feared a massive leftist rebellion by thousands of FTP adherents. And the BCRA fanned Allied fears with reports that "a Communist coup d'etat is to be expected." [65] Army Intelligence was equally alarmed. Only in the academic quarters of the OSS Research Branch did calm prevail. The executive officer of the London research unit, British-born Allan Evans,[b] discussed the French furor with fellow Harvard historian Crane Brinton,[c] an expert on the French Revolution of the eighteenth century. Would the Reign of Terror be repeated in Marxist trappings? Brinton thought not. On a three-month research tour of liberated France, he found little evidence of "genuine large-scale organized social violence." Nor did he believe the French Communists had "any intention of trying to seize power" by revolutionary means. The Communists with whom Brinton spoke "seemed very mild indeed, not at all bloodthirsty revolutionists," and "cooing doves compared with their forbears of 1792–94 about whom

[a] Jones left the CIA in 1948 to begin a successful career as a public relations executive.

[b] Dr. Evans was head of State Department Intelligence, 1947–59.

[c] Brinton's book *The Anatomy of a Revolution* was reportedly used by CIA officers in the early 1950s as a blueprint for coups d'etat.

I may be credited with pretty intimate knowledge." The professor concluded, "A Communist Dictatorship? I should lay 100 to 1 against it." [66]

General de Gaulle would not accept those odds. He knew the Paris resistance forces were led by Communists and he believed that the fate of the French capital would determine the politics of postwar France. De Gaulle had therefore instructed his military delegate in the occupied capital, the young General Jacques Chaban-Delmas, to prevent the outbreak of an insurrection that would, inevitably, be directed by his leftist rivals.[d]

But the Paris underground could not be restrained. On the morning of Saturday, August 19, sporadic fighting broke out all over the city as the resistance systematically seized control of government buildings. The next day, Sunday, a truce agreement was accepted by the Germans and de Gaulle's emissaries, who saw a last chance to "save" Paris for their leader. The Communists—and many loyal but militant Gaullists—denounced the agreement and vowed that the fight would go on. The cease-fire ended abruptly.

That same Sunday, far to the west in Normandy, General de Gaulle, who had just learned of the uprising, met with Eisenhower in a fruitless attempt to convince the Allied commander to abandon his strategy of bypassing Paris, thus avoiding a costly battle with the city's 20,000 German occupiers.

De Gaulle could not accept the military rationale for delaying the liberation of the capital, and he suspected a last desperate attempt by Washington to prevent the political triumph of his French Provisional Government. BCRA intelligence indicated that Allen Dulles' OSS office in Switzerland had approved a "scheme that inclined to silence or set aside de Gaulle" by placing the reins of French government in the hands of a senior statesman of the prewar Third Republic.[67] Was Eisenhower, de Gaulle wondered, stalling the liberation of Paris to give Washington's plan time to crystallize?

On Monday, August 21, barricades appeared in the streets of the world's most beautiful city; Nazi tanks were sent to demolish them. The Communist commander of the Paris resistance sent a radio message to London, asking for a massive arms drop to the city's insurrectionists. The Gaullists, defeated in their attempt to prolong the cease-fire, cabled a different request. They pleaded for Allied troops to move into Paris immediately.

General George Patton's troops were headquartered at Chartres,

[d] Chaban-Delmas is now Prime Minister of France.

some 50 miles southwest of Paris, but a rumor reached the city that "the Americans" were even closer—at the village of Rambouillet, just 30 miles from the capital. Unfortunately, "the Americans" consisted only of David Bruce and his OSS staff, who had travelled far ahead of Patton's forces to collect useful intelligence along the road to the city. At a local hotel in the village, Bruce had joined forces with a motley force of local FFI partisans and their unofficial "capitaine," the adventurous war correspondent Ernest Hemingway.

The writer was no stranger to OSS. He had been a frequent companion of raucous Jedburghs in the pubs of London, and his own son John had parachuted to southern France weeks earlier on an OSS mission to the resistance. "We were enchanted to see him," wrote Bruce, who gave Hemingway a hand-written order appointing him OSS chief of his constantly growing group of resistance fighters.[68] Hemingway collected an arsenal to defend the village against possible attack by the Germans (who were only miles away) and began to gather intelligence that might prove useful in an Allied drive toward the capital.

Colonel Bruce, for one, could not understand why the liberation had not already begun. "It is maddening," he wrote in his diary, "to be

On the road to Paris: At the village of Rambouillet, Col. David Bruce (left), OSS commander in the European Theater, joined war correspondent Ernest Hemingway (center) and his band of French partisans, awaiting the final Allied drive to liberate the French capital.

only thirty miles from Paris, to interrogate every hour some Frenchman who has just come from there and who reports that even a very small task force could easily move in, and to know that our Army is being forced to wait and for what reason? Yesterday, the resistance people, hearing we were in Versailles and were moving on to Paris, rose prematurely and are said to have suffered considerable losses." [69]

At Bruce's OSS headquarters in London on the following day, August 22, preparations were under way for the large-scale arms drop requested by the resistance. At the last moment, General Koenig, asserting his authority over OSS operations, postponed the sortie by 24 hours. He too hoped the Allies might yet reach Paris before tons of arms and ammunition were dropped to the city's Communist underground.[70]

General von Choltitz, the fat, bald, monocled commander of the city's Wehrmacht garrison was, ironically, just as eager for the arrival of Allied troops—the excuse he needed to disregard his Fuehrer's orders to lay waste to the historic city. Von Choltitz secretly encouraged the dispatch to the American lines of a French delegation which would urge the Allies to make haste. The chief emissary was treasurer of the Gaullist resistance of Paris, Alexandre de Saint Phalle, a conservative banker with important American connections. (The former European director of a Wall Street brokerage firm, St. Phalle was married to the daughter of a U.S. Supreme Court Justice; his nephew Thibaut was serving as an OSS intelligence officer in China.) Before the St. Phalle group could reach Patton's headquarters, Eisenhower had already reversed himself and made the fateful decision. The only French military unit in northern France, the Second Armored Division of General Jacques Leclerc, was ordered to proceed immediately to liberate the French capital.

The tempo of street fighting in Paris increased on Wednesday, August 23, while the resistance faced a growing shortage of arms. Yet in London, Koenig had permanently cancelled the planned OSS arms drop; he had just learned that French troops were about to enter the capital.

Where was Leclerc's division? "Like the Scarlet Pimpernel," Bruce recorded, "it is said to have been seen here, there, and everywhere." That afternoon, Leclerc finally arrived at Rambouillet in a three-star jeep. "He is tall, spare, handsome, stern-visaged, and a striking figure," Bruce observed. Hemingway and the OSS colonel were presented to the French general. Leclerc greeted them rudely with a remark Hemingway translated as "Buzz off, you unspeakables!" [71]

Leclerc's 16,000 troops began the last lap of their trek to Paris in a heavy rain on the morning of Thursday August 24. Bruce, Hemingway, and their FFI "army" went along. As the convoy proceeded along the road to the capital, "the streets were lined with people. All houses were gay with flags," Bruce remembers, "and the population almost hysterical with joy. Our progress was extremely slow, and there were many long halts as road blocks were cleared, or small points of enemy resistance eliminated. During these stops we were mobbed by the bystanders. . . . When they knew we were Americans, that seemed to increase their enthusiasm." [72] Bruce's party was besieged with gifts of wine, fruit, and flowers; the populace went hoarse shouting "Vive la France." OSS officer Benjamin Welles, son of the former Undersecretary of State, was with another part of the caravan. "A physical wave of human emotion picked us up and carried us into the heart of Paris," he recalled. "It was like groping through a dream." [73]

Only three of Leclerc's tanks made it into Paris that evening. The division, encountering German opposition, was delayed at the outskirts of the city. Though heavy street fighting continued, the Parisians went wild with joy on the eve of their liberation. The "Marseillaise" echoed from Montmartre to the Left Bank cafes which hosted partisan machine-gun emplacements. Every church bell in Paris pealed to announce the Allied arrival.

Friday, August 25, was the great day. Leclerc's column, accompanied by an American infantry division, roared into the city, flushing out pockets of German resistance with the aid of the victorious resistance. Bruce and Hemingway were with the advance units as they fought their way through an artillery battle to the Arc de Triomphe. From the roof of that magnificent edifice, the Americans commanded a spectacular view of burning tanks and trucks, and sniper fire throughout the city.

Finding the Champs Elysées completely bare of traffic, Bruce and Hemingway, accompanied by a railroad engineer in BCRA uniform and two truckloads of FFI partisans, decided to perform their own symbolic act of liberation. While Generals Leclerc and de Gaulle received the German surrender in a railway station, and while the valorous Communist resistance buried its dead and nursed its wounded, the OSS colonel and the dashing writer made their way through thousands of cheering men and women to the most exclusive hotel in Paris, the Ritz. The building was completely undamaged and entirely deserted, except for the manager, who welcomed the distinguished American visitors at the door and asked Hemingway if there was anything the Ritz could

offer him. The writer looked at his buoyant, shabbily dressed FFI proletariat already roaming through the lobby of the upper-class hostelry.
"How about seventy-three dry martinis?", he asked.[74] The OSS had
come to Paris.

While the battle for France continued and the invasion of the
Third Reich loomed ahead, David Bruce established his headquarters
at the Hotel Gallia, and OSS staff officers from Britain flocked to their
new sinecure in the French capital. London remained the base, however, for operations in northern Europe, another area of traditional
British political influence.

OSS had made its first Scandinavian inroads, two years earlier, in
Finland. Since the Russian invasion of their country in November
1939, the Finns had considered their conflict with the neighboring
Soviets as a separate war, unrelated to the larger European conflagra-
tion. After the German attack on Russia in July 1941, Finland became
a "co-belligerent" (but not a full-fledged ally) of Berlin in battling the
Red Army. In December, under pressure from Moscow, Churchill reluctantly declared war on Finland. The United States, however, remained at peace with the Finns. An American legation continued to
function at Helsinki.[75]

Early 1942 saw the Nazis using Finnish territory as a base of
operations against Russia. The Finns became increasingly dependent
on the Nazis for supplies, and more and more fearful of a full-scale
German occupation. High officials of the Helsinki government were
therefore reluctant to offend the Germans by an overt display of friendship for the United States. American diplomats found it difficult to
pursue meaningful discussions with Finnish leaders, who were under
Gestapo surveillance. The nation's military and political strongman,
Marshal Karl Mannerheim, a conservative soldier of the Darlan and
Badoglio stripe, became completely inaccessible to the American minister.

At this point, OSS recruited Therese Bonney, an attractive and
vivacious American habitué of Paris society, for a very special mission.
As a freelance war correspondent, she had established a close personal
friendship with Mannerheim during her sympathetic coverage of the
Russo-Finnish war. In June 1942, she agreed to return to Finland for
OSS to contact her old friend. Her instructions were to persuade the
Finns to abandon Hitler.

When Therese Bonney arrived in London under cover of a jour-

nalistic assignment from *Colliers,* the British MI-6 attempted to stall
her mission as long as possible. Only after a protest to the British ambassador in Washington was she allowed to board a flight for Stockholm. There she came up against a more formidable antagonist—the
Gestapo. Miss Bonney, who had once been arrested by the German SS
in occupied France, was kept under constant surveillance by the Nazis.
Finally, with the protection of Finnish Army officers, she reached Helsinki and managed to arrange a clandestine rendezvous with Mannerheim. Although she failed to persuade the marshal to break with the
Nazis (Finland did not declare war on Germany until 1944), she returned to Washington with vital information about Finland's military
posture and the extent of Nazi influence in Helsinki government circles.

This intelligence was of considerable value to Stanton Griffis,
Donovan's second "special agent" to Finland.[e] Griffis was Chairman of
the Board of Madison Square Garden, owner of Brentano's book chain,
and a top executive of Paramount Pictures. Paramount held large quantities of foreign funds in many European capitals, and OSS was ready
to put this money to good use. Donovan asked Griffis to tour Scandinavia and the Iberian peninsula to make arrangements. Leaving a
bevy of Swedish beauties in Stockholm with promises of movie contracts, he flew to Helsinki in December 1942 to arrange an intelligence
network that would relay information from the Russian front back to
the American embassy in Sweden.[76]

Unlike Therese Bonney, who carried out her mission on her own
resources, Griffis was assisted by OSS staffers in Stockholm who had
opened their espionage shop in the fall of 1942. While Miss Bonney
was in Helsinki, a Harvard professor of government, Bruce Hopper, had
boarded a whale cruiser at New York bound for Liverpool; he was later
flown to Sweden by the RAF from a secret air base in Scotland. The
50-year-old New Deal liberal became the first OSS chief in neutral
Stockholm.

Hopper's capable chief of operations was Wilho Tikander, a Finn-
ish-American attorney from Chicago. His aides included Dr. Taylor
Cole, a Duke University political science professor, Washington economist Richard Huber, and New York attorney Walter Surrey. This
team had one problem in common with their OSS colleagues on the
Iberian peninsula—a running battle with the State Department. The

[e] Griffis served as American ambassador to Poland, 1947–48; ambassador to Egypt, 1948–49; ambassador to Argentina, 1949–51; and ambassador to Spain, 1951–52.

American minister in Stockholm, Herschel Johnson, was a rambunctious Georgian who saw American intelligence operations as some sort of satanic practice. The British embassy had already suffered untold embarrassment when a Swedish gangster was convicted of sabotaging German shipping on behalf of SOE. Johnson would not tolerate similar OSS behavior.

Arthur Goldberg's representative in Stockholm, Vic Shaho, a veteran Minnesota railroad union official, had arranged for Swedish transport workers to launch a strike against SKF, a Swedish company known to be secretly transporting ball-bearings to Germany. When Johnson learned of this project, he threatened to have Shaho and his OSS assistants declared personna non grata unless the strike were called off.

In spite of Johnson, the OSS group did perform some notable, if politically touchy, operations. Hopper's office became a listening-post for Soviet affairs. A mild form of espionage against America's Russian ally was encouraged by the Washington SI Branch official responsible for Swedish operations, Duke University economist Calvin Hoover.[f] He had spent several years in Russia during the early Stalin era on an academic research project, and had come away from his travels with a strong dislike for the Bolshevik regime. In domestic politics, Hoover was an avid New Dealer, but he despised the Russians and as an OSS official, he promoted several spy operations against the Soviets. There was some justification for these efforts. Moscow had consistently refused to divulge information about Soviet military forces to the British or Americans. OSS was therefore happy to purchase both the Russian Army's order of battle and the register of the entire Soviet Navy from industrious Finnish military men in Stockholm.[77]

Spying on our Russian allies was only incidental to the principal task of OSS Sweden, which was assisting in operations against the Germans in occupied Norway. OSS could not claim a hand in Norwegian operations, however, until late in 1943. The British had been determined to keep American amateurs from upsetting their own difficult relations with the Norwegian resistance.

Since the Nazi occupation of June 1940, the Norwegian military underground (MILORG) had anxiously and jealously watched SOE officers developing their own independent sabotage network in the country—with the full approval of the Socialist Norwegian government

[f] When the CIA's Board of National Estimates was founded in 1950, Dr. Hoover was among its first members.

in exile at London, whose ministers suspected the political ambitions of some resistance leaders.[78]

After the summer of 1942, when SOE and MILORG agents, working at cross purposes, came to the point of open warfare (to the obvious delight of the Nazis), the British admitted that their backhanded treatment of the resistance had been in error. The following year was a period of reconciliation with MILORG, and in the British view a poor time for OSS bunglers to arrive on the scene. The British successfully resisted American "interference" in Norwegian operations until the fall of 1943, when Colonel Joseph Haskell took command of the SO Branch in London and Dr. Hopper relinquished his own position to Wilho Tikander, his second-in-command. The new leadership convinced the British to accept an American Special Operations unit in Stockholm, the Westfield Mission.[79] The SO commander was 43-year-old George Brewer, Jr., a former Yale English teacher who had become a successful Broadway playwright.[g] SOE grudgingly concluded an operational pact with Brewer's unit. OSS would work in northern Norway (near the Russian border) and would not interfere with British activities in the south.

In London, an OSS representative was added to the Anglo-Norwegian Collaboration Committee, which directed resistance activities, and Commander George Unger Vetlesen, a Norwegian-American millionaire (and good friend of the exiled King) was wisely appointed to head the Norwegian desk of SO Branch in Grosvenor Square. But the British then placed new hurdles in the OSS path. Bernt Balchen, a Norwegian-born Arctic explorer and airplane ace, was recruited to command the OSS supply operation to northern Norway in January 1944. He was promptly faced with a flat British refusal to allow his unmarked planes to fly out of British landing fields. He protested that the Norwegian exile government had approved the project. A British officer replied tartly, "As a matter of fact, isn't Norway one of our colonies?"[80]

"The general feeling," Balchen concluded, "seems to be that we have no damn business in that neck of the woods."[81] But the fiery pilot was not willing to stop there. He took his case to his old friend Trygve Lie, the Foreign Minister of the Norwegian exile government, who

[g] Brewer wrote a Broadway hit starring Talullah Bankhead; it also became a movie with Bette Davis as the heroine, Humphrey Bogart as a horse trainer, and Ronald Reagan as a wealthy drunk. In his later years, Brewer became a champion of the cause of conservation.

then carried the issue to No. 10 Downing Street. In March 1944, by the personal order of Churchill, Balchen finally received permission to proceed with his operations. In April he began an airlift between Britain and Stockholm, evacuating Norwegian and other anti-Nazi refugees to London. Two months later, his team of sixty planes began its first supply mission to Norway. Hundreds of tons of weapons, ammunition, explosives, food, and medicine were dropped to the guerrillas.

Still another dispute with the British came at the end of 1944 when OSS decided to send an Operational Group to Norway to impede German railway movements. Most of the men were Norwegian-Americans, all trained paratroopers and skiers. In December, the Group command was given to 24-year-old William Colby, a short, wiry Minnesotan and pre-law graduate of Princeton who had distinguished himself as a Jedburgh in France.[h] But the Colby team's departure was delayed by "political considerations."[82] The British would not allow the thirty men to be dropped from RAF planes piloted by Norwegian fliers. The drop was finally made from American aircraft staffed by inexperienced crews in late March 1945. Two of the planes crashed and ten OSS men were killed. Colby and those OSS men who did reach their destination were forced to operate with a minimum of supplies; the American planes had dropped their equipment a bit off target—in Sweden.

Besides helping the Norwegians (and occasionally sparring with the British), OSS Stockholm had another more difficult responsibility: to provide Allied entree to the major espionage target of Europe, Nazi Germany.

The joint British-OSS operation which sent Swedish businessman (and secret Allied agent) Eric Ericson on a guided tour of Nazi oil facilities in Germany has been well-publicized [i] by Hollywood.[83] But other German operations of OSS Sweden, those of greater diplomatic sensitivity, remain obscured. In December 1942, Carl Langbehn, a Nazi lawyer from Berlin and an intimate of SS chief Heinrich Himmler, contacted Bruce Hopper in Stockholm. With the acquiescence of Himmler's foreign intelligence service, Langbehn told OSS that Himmler might be willing to stage a coup against the Fuehrer as a prelude to peace negotiations with Britain and the United States. Hopper politely showed Langbehn to the door.[84]

[h] Colby was CIA station chief in South Vietnam in the late 1950s; he became head of the CIA's Far Eastern operations division and in 1969 was named chief of American "pacification" programs in Vietnam.

[i] "The Counterfeit Traitor," starring William Holden as the OSS hero.

Ten months later, in October 1943, the Kersten affair began. Dr. Felix Kersten, a Baltic German who held Finnish citizenship, was a physical therapist who had become Himmler's personal physician and confidant. He commuted frequently between Stockholm and Berlin to treat the Gestapo chief. One day Kersten was introduced to an American in his early forties who identified himself as Abrams Stevens Hewitt, President Roosevelt's "special representative for European affairs."

In fluent German, Hewitt told Kersten he was willing to act as an intermediary with the Finnish government to arrange Finland's desertion of the Axis. More important, Hewitt spoke of American interest in signing a "separate" (anti-Soviet) peace treaty with Berlin in the wake of a coup by Himmler against the Fuehrer. Thus Germany and the Western powers could end the "terrible war" while blocking the "danger from the East." [85]

The negotiations proceeded, with neither Kersten nor his Gestapo friends aware that Hewitt was not a diplomat at all but a clever agent of the Donovan organization. What game was OSS playing? The answer was to be found hundreds of miles from Stockholm at an OSS base in another neutral capital.

7
Herrengasse 23

The same day Allied troops landed in North Africa, a kindly, grey-haired man with wire-rimmed glasses and a neatly-trimmed moustache sat puffing on a pipe as his train rumbled along through Vichy France on its way to Switzerland. This American traveler managed to slip across the Swiss frontier only minutes before German officers closed the border, blocking the gateway into Switzerland's neutral haven. The local newspapers in Berne, the Swiss capital, soon noted the arrival of a "personal representative of President Roosevelt." Unperturbed by this gratuitous publicity, the newcomer rented a flat at 23 Herrengasse in the picturesque, medieval section of Berne, and placed an inconspicuous sign outside his door: "Allen W. Dulles, Special Assistant to the American Minister." OSS had acquired a spy-master in the center of Hitler's Fortress Europe.

Dulles was no stranger to Berne. Twenty-five years before, he had come to the Swiss capital as a neophyte Foreign Service officer to practice diplomacy (and espionage) in the midst of an earlier world war. "That's where I learned what a valuable place Switzerland was for information," he later recalled, "and when I became interested in intelligence work." [1]

Together with a senior State Department colleague, Hugh Wilson, Dulles' task in the Switzerland of 1918 had been to collect political information from Germany and the Austro-Hungarian Empire. Early in his career, he had learned his first lesson in espionage when he inadvertently passed up an opportunity to meet with an obscure Russian visitor to Berne, who later turned out to be the revolutionary Nikolai

Lenin. Never again, Dulles resolved, would he disregard *any* source of intelligence.

The young diplomats Wilson and Dulles built up a network of European refugees and American expatriates who functioned, informally, as intelligence agents for the American embassy. One of their most important contacts was an American biologist residing in Zurich, Dr. Henry Haviland Field. He was, Wilson recalls, "a Quaker, a burly man, with bushy gray hair and beard, heavy gray eyebrows behind which lay the gentlest, bluest, most candid pair of eyes that I ever saw on an adult man. They were the eyes of an unsophisticated and lovable child." Field was the graduate of a German university and spoke the language flawlessly. He had "unique relationships" with academic and "liberal elements" in Germany, and became a "mine of information" for Wilson and Dulles.[2]

After the German defeat in 1918, Dulles joined his elder brother, John Foster, on the staff of the American delegation to the Versailles Peace Conference, then was transferred to the office of the American Commissioner in Berlin. In post-Kaiser Germany, Dulles made the acquaintance of industrialists and generals who were already concerned about the new "Bolshevik menace" in Moscow. But he also met more progressive leaders of the Weimar Republic. One was Dr. Gerhart von Schulze-Gaevernitz, an aging, bearded professor of economics with an expertise in British economic history, then serving as a deputy of the Weimar National Assembly. Gaevernitz was a member of the German Democratic Party, which, in the confused multi-party system of that decade, constituted the right wing of the political left. Gaevernitz, noted Dulles, was an eloquent advocate of an "American-British-German rapprochement as the surest way to secure world peace."[3]

From Berlin, Dulles went to Constantinople, then returned to the State Department in Washington. By 29 he had been named chief of State's Near Eastern Division. He married the daughter of a Columbia University professor and found time for the social whirl of the Coolidge administration. One of his new Washington friends was a vibrant Assistant Attorney General, William J. Donovan.

Dulles was on his way to a brilliant diplomatic career. But he was dissatisfied with his paltry government salary, and rather than accept a proffered post at the American embassy in China, he resigned from the State Department in 1927 and joined his brother's international law firm, Sullivan and Cromwell, in New York.

While practicing his legal trade, Dulles continued to keep a hand in public affairs. He became legal advisor of the American delegation to the Geneva Disarmament Conference of 1927. At a second disarmament parley in 1933, Dulles and his old friend Hugh Wilson, then serving as American Minister to Switzerland, were first confronted by the National Socialist madness that had swept Germany. At Geneva, emissaries of the new German Chancellor, Adolf Hitler, defiantly announced a program of rearmament for the Third Reich, then stomped out of the meeting. Dulles concluded unhappily, "If no arrangement between France and Germany is possible, the future for European peace is dark. There is no immediate danger of war being started by Germany as she is in no position to wage a war, but the same might not be true a couple of years hence." [4]

In conjunction with his legal work at Sullivan and Cromwell, Dulles met the elite of German industry—the same men who financed and actively supported the Nazi dictatorship. He and a future OSS aide, Russian émigré Valerian Lada-Mocarski, also sat on the board of directors of the American branch of the powerful Schroeder banking house. The German parent firm was headed by a scar-faced Prussian baron who served as a general in the SS, Hitler's elite guard.

But Dulles had no sympathy for the Nazis. Several of his law partners were Jewish; so were many of his German clients. By 1934, the law firm had already found it impossible to work within the framework of Nazi "legality." The Berlin office of Sullivan and Cromwell was shut down. [5]

Dulles continued to receive a perspective on German affairs from Hugh Wilson. In 1938, the career diplomat left his Swiss post to accept an unenviable appointment as Roosevelt's ambassador to Nazi Germany. He remained in Berlin only eight months. In November 1938, Wilson was recalled to Washington as a formal protest against the anti-Jewish pogrom at Nuremberg.

When he returned to the United States, Wilson saw a good deal of Charles Lindbergh, whom he had met in Berlin when the famed aviator was unexpectedly decorated by the Nazi government. In 1939, Wilson introduced Dulles to Lindbergh. The future leader of "America First" noted in his diary, "Dulles was interesting to talk to, and we have somewhat similar views in a number of instances." [6]

Did Dulles share Lindbergh's isolationist sentiments? If at first he doubted the wisdom of American involvement in an impending European War, he soon had other thoughts. In 1938, when he ran (un-

Allen Welsh Dulles, controversial OSS "master spy" in neutral Switzerland, later director of the CIA. His wartime network stretched throughout Europe and into the heart of Hitler's Third Reich.

successfully) for a Republican congressional nomination in New York, Dulles was hailed by the *Times* as a "liberal candidate who represents the younger and more progressive wing of the party." [7]

Dulles accepted that political label and embraced interventionism. In early 1940, he called for repeal of the arms embargo that prevented the sale of American munitions to beleaguered Britain. In January 1941, he supported the Lend-Lease Bill and urged Republican leaders to sympathize with England's plight. He told a G.O.P. audience in May 1941 that the United States should send troops to North Africa to establish a base for further supply shipments to the British. "The thing is simply too big to be met by half-way efforts." he declared. "We are faced today with the alternative of going to war or seeing a defeated England. We may yet be too late." [8]

America entered the war six months later. Both Dulles and Hugh

Wilson [a] were quickly snapped up by Donovan for his new intelligence organization. In January 1942, Dulles opened the New York office of COI in Room 3663 of the International Building at Rockefeller Plaza.

His New York staff launched intelligence projects in every part of the world, but Dulles took a personal interest in German operations. First, an encyclopedic collection of personal data about leading Nazis of the Third Reich was assembled by Baron Wolfgang zu Putlitz, a former German consul at the Hague who had "defected" to the British.[b] Then Arthur Goldberg, Donald Downes, and other officers of Dulles' Special Activities desk proposed the creation of a committee of anti-Hitler German émigrés who would act as a front for American support of a German resistance organization. The committee would be headed by émigré Heinrich Bruening, former leader of the German Catholic Center Party and one of the last Weimar Chancellors before Hitler's rise to power.[9]

The right wing of the émigré committee would be represented by Gottfried Treviranus, a former minister of the Bruening cabinet and mogul of the Prussian ultra-nationalists during Weimar days. With the aid of MI-6, he had barely escaped a Gestapo assassination squad in 1934. Transported to Canada for safekeeping by the British, Treviranus was then brought to New York to work with the Dulles staff.

The German left was not to be neglected. As a third member of their front organization, the OSS men chose a German psychologist, Dr. Karl Frank (alias "Paul Hagen" and "Willi Mueller"). Frank was a leader of the New Beginning group, a faction of young, militant émigrés who had split from the German Socialist Party in exile in 1935. Unlike the older Socialist leadership, Frank's group supported a Popular Front with the Communists in fighting Naziism. After the fall of France, Frank emigrated to New York, where he met Arthur Goldberg through mutual friends in the Jewish Labor Committee and the Emergency Rescue Committee. With the encouragement of Eleanor Roosevelt, a friend and admirer of the German psychologist, Goldberg proposed that Frank complete the Bruening triumvirate.[10]

Then the problems began. Hugh Wilson (a "monumental pain

[a] When Wilson left OSS in 1945 he became director of the Foreign Affairs Section of the Republican National Committee.

[b] In 1954, zu Putlitz appeared as an East German agent in the mysterious "defection" to the Communists of Otto John, head of the West German equivalent of the FBI. Both men had worked for the British SOE during the war.

in the ass," according to one Dulles aid) joined the FBI in denouncing Frank's left-wing past. Another OSS ex-diplomat, former Minister to Lithuania John Wiley,[c] had one of his unsuspecting assistants, Harvard English instructor Philip Horton,[d] prepare a derogatory dossier on Frank. Goldberg was furious, but he was unable to salvage the Bruening project. The Frank furor had just been quieted when another crisis arose over the OSS contact with Treviranus. Dulles' aides had hoped to use this Prussian nationalist to foment a series of assassinations of top Nazi leaders. When someone happened to ask Treviranus how he proposed to encourage an anti-Hitler rebellion, the German suggested that OSS transport his signet ring to the peasants in the area in which he had been born and raised. He believed that upon receipt of his personal jewelry, the peasants would spontaneously rise in rebellion against the Nazis.[11] Washington was not impressed. The death blow to the entire project was soon dealt by State Department objection to American support of both "dangerous Communists" and "hopelessly reactionary generals and Junkers."[12] The Bruening committee was shelved indefinitely.

The ill-fated proposal did have one beneficial side-effect. It provided Allen Dulles with a clear conception of the political sensitivity of German operations. Although he refused to abandon his principle of working with "the devil himself" to further the war effort, he learned that he must tread lightly in planning future OSS subversive warfare.

In the fall of 1942, David Bruce began preparations for his trip to England to assume command of OSS London. Donovan asked Dulles to join Bruce in cementing American friendship with the British secret services. Dulles suggested instead that he should be sent to "a less glamorous post, but one where I felt my past experience would serve me in good stead."[13] At the beginning of November 1942, he left New York for his old diplomatic stomping ground at Berne.

For the next two years, Allen Dulles remained at his OSS post in Switzerland, a neutral enclave surrounded entirely by Axis troops in France, Germany, Austria, and Italy. Sitting before the fireplace in

[c] Wiley served as ambassador to Colombia, 1944–47; ambassador to Portugal, 1947–48; ambassador to Iran, 1948–51; and ambassador to Panama, 1951–54. He was also president of the Council for Islamic Studies until his death in 1967.

[d] Horton became the first CIA station chief in Paris in 1947. From 1949 until 1968, he was executive editor of the *Reporter* magazine.

the spacious club room of his Herrengasse flat, he discreetly received Guillain de Benouville, Ferruccio Parri, and other resistance leaders, and built up an intelligence network that stretched from Algiers to Prague. But the spy-master's "first and most important task" was to penetrate Germany, the enemy heartland. Washington instructed Dulles to lift the veil of Nazi secrecy and to search out disillusioned citizens of the Third Reich who were "actively at work" to overthrow Hitler.[14]

Where to begin? Knowing that an embryonic "Opposition" to Hitler had been in contact with London since 1938, Dulles first visited his secret service counterparts at the British Legation. He found them disheartened by past dealings with alleged German dissidents. Ever since the famed "Venlo incident" of 1939, when two MI-6 officers in Holland had been kidnapped by German intelligence men posing as anti-Nazis, the British had remained cool to German overtures. The latest peace offering, sent to Stewart Menzies, head of MI-6, by the enigmatic Admiral Wilhelm Canaris, chief of the Abwehr (German Military Intelligence), had just been rebuffed by London.[15] Although some bitterly anti-Soviet officers of the British secret service favored a "separate peace" with Berlin after the elimination of Hitler by Canaris and other Opposition leaders, most MI-6 officials were wary.

In intelligence circles, a controversy continued to rage around the figure of Canaris. He was a former U-boat commander, a veteran German espionage operative, rumored to have been the employer and lover of Mata Hari, and mastermind of the murder of the German Communist Rosa Luxemburg. Canaris' proponents in Allied circles claimed that he had allowed the Abwehr to become a haven for Opposition plotters, that he had personally squelched Nazi plots to murder General Giraud and Prime Minister Churchill, that he had convinced his good friend Franco to remain aloof from an alliance with Berlin. The Abwehr organization, they noted, was a professional rival of the intelligence apparatus of the Nazi Party, Heinrich Himmler's Reich Security Office, which controlled the SD, the SS, and the dreaded Gestapo.[16]

Other intelligence reports described Canaris as an evil genius of the Third Reich, the organizer of Nazi fifth columns throughout Europe, and the scourge of Allied agents and their resistance friends. Some British officers argued that there was little practical purpose in maintaining contact with Canaris' men. MI-6 had secretly broken the Abwehr codes, and all of that organization's intelligence was already available to them.[17] The British Foreign Office had also instructed MI-6 to reject all peace feelers from military or civilian cliques of the anti-Hitler Opposition. London was unwilling to desert its Soviet allies, an essential condition of the German plotters. Whitehall deprecated the entire Berlin Opposition as the self-seeking conspiracy of a cabal of disenchanted Prussian generals. The British in Berne passed this view on to Dulles with an additional warning to beware of German agent provocateurs sent by the Gestapo in the guise of anti-Nazi agents.

While some British officers in the Swiss capital—Edge Leslie of MI-6 and John McCaffery of SOE—offered to assist the OSS effort, Dulles decided to fend for himself. But he had no OSS staff and none could be imported across the enemy territories which surrounded Switzerland. He first convinced representatives of the Board of Economic Warfare and the Office of War Information to devote their idle time to OSS pursuits. Next to be co-opted for secret service were American businessmen stranded in Berne by the sudden closing of the French border. A Standard Oil man began acquiring intelligence about petroleum; a National City Bank representative secretly purchased foreign currency for Dulles' espionage operations. Dulles eventually approached every American citizen living in Switzerland. Some were former officials of the League of Nations at Geneva, others permanent expatriates with business interests or family in Europe. Most agreed to help OSS.

One of Dulles' recruits was Gero von Schulze-Gaevernitz, a tall, handsome man of 40 and son of the liberal Weimar legislator whom Dulles had known two decades before. The elder Gaevernitz had emigrated to Switzerland after Hitler's rise to power; his wife was Jewish. The son, a naturalized American citizen, had first come to the United States in 1924 with a doctorate in economics to begin an international banking career. Despite young Gaevernitz's non-Aryan parentage, he was well-connected in German elite circles. He was an in-law of the Stinnes family, once prominent owners of a huge industrial combine in the Ruhr valley.

Gaevernitz had joined his father in Switzerland at the outbreak of war, determined to make contact with Germans who were "ready to support any workable undertaking that would get rid of Hitler and the Nazis and put an end to the war." [18] When Dulles arrived, Gaevernitz was already prepared to introduce him to anti-Nazi émigrés in Berne. Among those who became informal advisors to the OSS spy-master was Dr. Wilhelm Hoegner, former Social Democratic deputy in the Weimar Reichstag and the Munich public prosecutor who had once brought Hitler to trial for sedition. Hoegner was a fount of information on

field parallel Quaker / unitarian

political affairs in his native Bavaria, but the value of his comments was lessened by an anti-Communist fanaticism that consistently colored his views.

Dulles could not ignore the German Communist exiles. Gaevernitz did not travel in such leftist circles, but Noel Field, the son of Dulles' Quaker friend from World War I, had the necessary political entree and was willing to act as courier between OSS and the Communists. The 38-year-old Field, a lanky man who inherited his father's innocent and disarming manner, had entered the State Department in 1926 after a Harvard education. In the course of his Foreign Service career, he became enamored of left-wing causes and friendly with Comintern agents in Washington. (Dulles called him a "romantic idealist.") Field left the State Department in 1936 to join the League of Nations staff at Geneva. Three years later, he became secretary to an international commission sent to Spain to repatriate foreign volunteers who had fought for the Loyalist cause in the Spanish Civil War. This led to his appointment in 1941 as director of the Unitarian Service Committee in Vichy France, charged with assisting refugees from fascism who had fled to unoccupied French territory—a valuable opportunity for Field to meet and befriend Communist émigrés of all nationalities. After the German invasion of Vichy France, Field, like Dulles, managed to slip across the border into Switzerland just before the closing of the frontier. Officially, he then became European Director of the Unitarian Service Committee in Geneva. Unofficially, he took on extracurricular duties as Dulles' contact with the German Communist exile community in Switzerland.[19]

Dulles' German friends would have been shocked to learn of his dealings with the Communists. Gaevernitz had already introduced Dulles to agents of the anti-Hitler (and anti-Communist) Opposition in Germany—a small group of generals, politicians, and government officials of the political right and moderate left who agreed only on their resolve that Naziism must go. Dulles' view of "The Breakers" (as he code-named the Opposition) came from dissident German intelligence officers of Admiral Canaris' Abwehr, who served as couriers between the Berlin plotters and the OSS staff in Berne.

The first of these intermediaries was Hans Bernd Gisevius, a huge six-foot-four, myopic Abwehr agent with a stiff Prussian manner, assigned to the German consulate at Zurich. The descendant of an old family of German civil servants, Gisevius was an attorney who despised the Nazis but blamed Hitler's rise on the liberals and Communists of the Weimar Republic. He was a former youth leader of the right-wing People's Party and had joined the Gestapo in 1933, only to be ousted in an internal purge five months later. He then enlisted in the Berlin police, but was again dismissed for criticism of the SS. By 1938, he was a fullfledged member of the conspiratorial Opposition.

The following year, Gisevius began meeting with skeptical British officials in Switzerland. They considered him untrustworthy and MI-6 eventually dropped him as an intelligence sub-source for being too opportunistic and self-seeking.[20] Gisevius had his own complaint about the British. "There had been only occasional meetings," he wrote, "because the Allies restricted themselves largely to pure espionage. The British above all stuck to the old-fashioned scheme in which the 'enemy' was considered solely as an object of espionage. . . . Dulles was the first intelligence officer who had the courage to extend his activities to the political aspects of the war. . . . Everyone breathed easier; at last a man had been found with whom it was possible to discuss the contradictory complex of problems emerging from Hitler's war." [21]

Meeting with Dulles late in the evening under cover of the Swiss blackout, Gisevius gained the OSS man's confidence by supplying useful intelligence. The tall Abwehr man then turned the conversation to an unlikely diplomatic proposal. His anti-Nazi clique hoped to overthrow Hitler, then sign a "separate" peace treaty with Britain and the United States that would prevent the Red Army from occupying German territory in the East.

This plan was propounded to OSS by a second important German contact, the quixotic Adam von Trott zu Solz, an official of the German Foreign Office and former Rhodes scholar with important American and British connections. (On a trip to the United States in 1937, von Trott had accepted the hospitality of Bill Donovan in Washington; they "got on very well together.") [22] Trott represented a young intellectual faction within the German Opposition, the Kreisau Circle, which had formulated a reform program of Christian Socialism for postwar Germany. In January 1943, Dr. William Rappard, the American-born Rector of the University of Geneva, a labor economist of international repute, introduced von Trott to Gaevernitz, Dulles' aide.[23] Von Trott immediately set forth his recurrent theme: if OSS did not aid the Opposition, the German conspirators would inevitably "turn to the East" and be forced into the arms of Moscow.

As if in response to Trott, Gisevius, and the Opposition in Berlin, the British and American chiefs of state at their meeting in Casablanca proclaimed the policy of unconditional surrender. For the Opposition this meant that any German government, even a regime led by anti-Hitler insurgents, could bring an end to the war only by submitting to the unquestioned authority of the Allies. The same "harsh" peace terms would therefore be imposed "whether the surrender came early by action of the Germans who dared to defy Hitler or at a later date by one of Hitler's henchmen." [24] From Dulles' vantage point in Switzerland and, given his limited objective—encouragement of the anti-Nazi forces —the unconditional surrender policy was an unmitigated propaganda disaster. He believed the Opposition would be severely demoralized by the Casablanca statement.

In the light of the Roosevelt-Churchill declaration, the political sensitivity of Dulles' German contacts was heightened. This was especially true of his mysterious meetings with agents of Gestapo chief Heinrich Himmler, the bitter rival of Admiral Canaris in the German bureaucracy. Dulles knew that Himmler's representatives had approached OSS in Stockholm, proposing that Britain and the United States sanction a coup against Hitler and then sign a "separate peace" with the Gestapo chief. This was a modification of the Opposition's proposal, with Himmler appended as the Fuehrer's successor. To explore this possibility, Walter Schellenberg, one of Himmler's brightest proteges, sent Prince Max Egon von Hohenlohe-Langenburg-Rothenhaus to seek out Dulles, the "most influential White House man in Europe." [25]

Von Hohenlohe was a descendant of a prominent Sudeten German aristocratic clan. He lived in Spain with his wife, a Spanish marquise, and traveled on a passport from Liechtenstein. As a "social favorite in most of the capitals of Europe," he was in a good position to act as unofficial diplomatic emissary. He had already made peace overtures to the British in Madrid and Berne and was friendly with a whole host of international figures from the Aga Khan to the Spanish minister at the Vatican.[26]

Von Hohenlohe had known Dulles in Berlin and New York during the 1920s and their reunion in February 1943 was a pleasant one. According to Soviet-captured German documents (whose authenticity has been called into question),[e] the OSS master-spy told von Hohenlohe he

---

[e] One American intelligence official suggested to the author that the original German documents were significantly "altered" by the Soviets before release as part of their "disinformation" campaign.

was "fed up with listening all the time to outdated politicians, émigrés and prejudiced Jews."

Dulles believed, according to the alleged Gestapo memorandum, that the German state would fulfill an important role after the war as a "factor of order and progress" and the base of a "cordon sanitaire against Bolshevism." The OSS man did not "reject National Socialism in its basic ideas and deeds," but warned that the American people would never accept Hitler as "unchallenged master of Greater Germany." Dulles purportedly peppered his conversation with anti-semitic and anglophobic remarks.[27]

Even if the German documents are spurious, Dulles might justifiably have made similar comments to Himmler's messenger as part of a strategy for anti-Nazi political subversion. During the same month as his meeting with von Hohenlohe, Dulles learned from Gisevius, his Abwehr contact, that the German Opposition had at last opted for an assassination of Hitler as the prelude to an anti-Nazi putsch. The date was set for March 13, 1943.

Dulles had no way of predicting the Opposition's chances for success, but he believed he could aid their plot by fomenting dissension at the highest levels of the Nazi leadership. If Himmler were encouraged in his megalomania by reports of American sympathy, the Gestapo chief might be pressed into action against his Fuehrer. Unfortunately, Himmler could not overcome his timidity. And the first putsch attempt was unsuccessful. A bomb placed in Hitler's plane failed to explode. A second attempt in late March also ended in failure.

It appears that Dulles' ploy to provoke a Himmler coup d'etat was only one part of an anti-Nazi operation planned by OSS Washington. For in the fall of 1943, an almost identical incident occurred in Stockholm—the Kersten affair, mentioned earlier. Dr. Felix Kersten, Himmler's Finnish physician and personal confidant, had met an American named Abram Stevens Hewitt, who misrepresented himself in the Swedish capital (like Dulles in Berne), as President Roosevelt's "special representative for European affairs." Hewitt had assured Kersten of his interest in a Himmler putsch followed by an Anglo-American alliance with Berlin against the Russians.

Abram Hewitt was in reality a wealthy New York attorney, an Oxford and Harvard graduate, the grandson of his namesake, the Mayor of New York in the 1880s, and a large contributor to the Democratic Party. He had held various posts in New Deal domestic agencies and

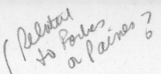

was working for the War Production Board in 1942 when OSS lured him into secret service. Through his father-in-law, a Boston banker, Hewitt had been peripherally involved in the legal muddle that followed the Ivar Kreuger Swedish Match scandal of 1932, and OSS, hoping to put Hewitt's Swedish contacts to good use, had sent him to join Dr. Bruce Hopper's team in Stockholm.

Calvin Hoover, the bitterly anti-Soviet economist who directed OSS Scandinavian espionage from Washington, remembers the aftermath of the Kersten-Hewitt meetings: "We did not for an instant really intend to deal with a Himmler government as the successor to Hitler, and certainly the United States government would not have done so. Our agent was, of course, *not* a special envoy of President Roosevelt. As far as Himmler was concerned, if the plot had been carried out, we would have been acting in complete bad faith. I felt sure that if Himmler tried to arrest Hitler, even though he would almost certainly fail, the effect upon the morale of the Nazi party and upon the German army would be shattering." [28]

Kersten sounded out Himmler on October 24, suggesting that his intelligence aide, Walter Schellenberg, should come to Stockholm to pursue the contact with Hewitt. Schellenberg flew to Sweden in strictest secrecy on November 9 and learned from "well-informed Swedish friends" that Hewitt had a "decisive influence on Roosevelt in all matters concerning Europe." He then met with the American "diplomat" and was assured that negotiations for a "compromise peace" could begin as soon as Himmler agreed to move. Schellenberg returned to Berlin and worked all night on a report to Himmler. The next afternoon, he found the Gestapo chief "confused and quite aghast at my independent actions." [29] Despite long arguments from Kersten, Himmler said he would not "betray my Fuehrer." [30] He would only agree to speak personally with Hewitt if the American were willing to fly to Berlin. But Donovan's headquarters was not willing to let the dangerous ruse be carried that far. Besides, the highest American officials were "very much concerned" that the Russians might learn of the OSS "indirect contact with Himmler and would conclude that we were planning to make a secret deal with Himmler and perhaps with reactionary circles in Germany." [31] The project was cancelled; Kersten was informed that Hewitt had suddenly "left for Washington."

The Kersten affair taught OSS an important lesson. Moscow could no longer be ignored in planning German operations. The Soviets had already staked a claim to an active role in determining the future fate of the Third Reich. Following the Nazi defeat at Stalingrad in February 1943, the Russians convinced several captured German generals to lend their names to a "Free Germany Committee," then to broadcast propaganda appeals to the Fatherland, calling upon the citizenry to rise against Hitler. The Committee was actually designed as a future vehicle for German Communist exiles waiting out the war in Moscow under the chairmanship of Walter Ulbricht.

The formation of the Free Germany Committee created a stir in Washington. Dewitt Poole, chief of the Foreign Nationalities Branch of OSS, proposed the creation of a similar exile committee in the United States, a revival of Dulles' earlier Bruening project.[32] The State Department still opposed the idea, believing that any official sanction of a German exile group would run counter to the "hard line" laid down in the unconditional surrender declaration. OSS had even run into opposition to its employment of German exiles for research work. Only through Donovan's determination had this skirmish over "personnel security" been won. The general had been greatly moved by Arthur Koestler's *Scum of the Earth*, a narrative of the plight of anti-Nazi Germans and other refugees placed, at the beginning of the war, in French internment camps. "I will never make that mistake," said Donovan. "Every man or woman who can hurt the Hun is okay with me." [33]

OSS then hired a score of German refugees, all skilled academicians, such as political philosopher Herbert Marcuse, sociologist Morris Janowitz, economist Otto Kirchheimer, historians Rudolph Winnacker and Richard Krautheimer. They were an invaluable addition to Donovan's Research Branch. Some of these men were affiliated with the Institute of Social Research, once a leading intellectual center for socialist thought in Weimar Germany. The Nazi regime closed the Institute and seized its facilities in 1933 for exhibiting "tendencies hostile to the state." Moving to Geneva, then Paris and London, and finally to New York, the Institute became an international haven for anti-Nazi German intellectuals. Since their studies concentrated on the growth and nature of German fascism, the Institute's leading lights had been natural recruits for the OSS research program. This same group of émigrés had informal ties to the liberal "American Friends of German Freedom." Arthur Goldberg's friend, Dr. Karl Frank, was research director of this group; OSS counter-intelligence official David

Seiferheld, a New York textile executive, was its secretary. Unofficial links to the Frank group and the Institute were the closest OSS could come to duplicating Moscow's plans for German political subversion.

The creation of the Moscow Committee had an electrifying effect on the German Opposition group with which Dulles was in contact. Some dissident Wehrmacht officers had already begun to consider the possibilities of a rapprochement with the Soviet Union. Other conspirators, like Adam von Trott zu Solz of the intellectual Kreisau Circle, hoped the Russian action had strengthened the Opposition's hand in dealing with OSS. Von Trott returned to Switzerland in January and April 1944 to present Gaevernitz with long memoranda for Dulles. The documents warned of Russian assistance to the German Communist underground, suggested that many leaders of the Opposition were beginning to look toward the East for support, but insisted that Washington could still outmaneuver the Russians by publicly encouraging the socialist and trade union resistance to Hitler.[34]

Dulles had private doubts about the political picture painted by von Trott of a growing German Communist movement secretly subsidized by the Russians. He knew that there were several small (and effective) Soviet espionage networks functioning in Germany and Switzerland.[35] But these were formed by professional spies, not political agitators. The few genuine Communists who escaped the Gestapo dragnet in Germany, and those who fled to Switzerland, had been deserted by their comrades in Moscow. Dulles remained in touch with these impoverished and hunted refugees through Noel Field, who transmitted some $10,000 in OSS funds to the leftists in exchange for useful intelligence.

Dulles received an even more valuable view of conditions in Germany from his greatest espionage discovery, an official of the German Foreign Office named Fritz Kolbe. A short, wiry man of forty with a few blond hairs still rimming his bald head, Kolbe had worked in the German bureaucracy for years, first as an official of the State Railways in Berlin and later as a junior diplomat at the German embassies in South Africa and Spain. He had been an early opponent of Hitler and had publicly refused to join the Nazi Party. At one point, he contemplated emigration but a sympathetic Catholic priest urged him to remain in the country and to do what he could to fight the Nazis from his official vantage point.[36]

Kolbe made contact with members of the Opposition in Berlin, but he lacked confidence in their methods and felt that Hitler's downfall could only be achieved by an Allied defeat of the Third Reich. In early 1941, he made an attempt to contact American officials in Berlin through a Catholic Church intermediary. This failed and the American embassy was soon closed. Next he went to the British in Switzerland. He offered to supply MI-6 with bundles of documents from Ribbentrop's Foreign Office. For example, he warned that a German agent was working "close to Churchill" and was sending information to Berlin by way of Stockholm.[37] The British officers in Berne were taken aback by the sudden appearance of this purported anti-Nazi. Still suspicious of double agents, they refused to listen to Kolbe.

The Americans were Kolbe's last resort. On August 23, 1943, Kolbe sent a friend, a German-born émigré doctor, to visit the American legation in Berne. The emissary was met by Gerald Mayer, an OWI propagandist of German-Jewish extraction who had been co-opted by Dulles for his OSS staff. The doctor said he represented an official of the Wehrmacht liaison section in the Nazi Foreign Office who was willing to pass information to the Allies. Mayer was skeptical, but arranged a direct meeting with Kolbe that evening. At their first rendezvous, Kolbe presented an astounded Dulles with 186 pages of microfilmed documents directly from the German diplomatic files. Under the official protection given him by his job, Kolbe (OSS code-name, "George Wood") was then able to make one trip every three months to Berne or Stockholm. He turned over to OSS some 1600 documents, mostly cables from German military attachés in twenty countries. The information on Nazi espionage and military affairs was superb.

Kolbe's documents were naturally greeted with some excitement in Washington and London, although the first reaction was one of suspicion. The leading skeptic was none other than Claude Marjoribank Dansey, the anti-American Assistant Chief of MI-6 who had so vigorously opposed a British partnership with OSS in European espionage. Dansey had been instrumental in organizing the Secret Intelligence Service's own Swiss network and had developed a "fierce proprietary obsession" about Swiss intelligence. "It was clearly impossible that Dulles should have pulled off this spectacular scoop under his nose. Therefore, he had not. The stuff was obviously a plant, and Dulles had fallen for it like a ton of bricks." When comparison of Kolbe's documents with British intercepts of Abwehr messages suggested that the material might be genuine, Dansey refused to retreat. He would not encourage OSS "to run riot all over Switzerland, fouling up the whole intelligence field. Heaven knew what damage they wouldn't do. Such matters had to be handled only by officers with experience of the pitfalls that beset the unwary. For all he knew, OSS, if egged on in this way, could blow the whole of his network in a matter of days." [38]

Washington received the Kolbe papers with greater gaiety. Donovan personally presented some of the material to President Roosevelt. Based on the information received by the beginning of 1944, OSS assembled an intelligence portrait of the "gradually weakening fabric of the whole Nazi regime." Dulles suggested that Kolbe's official documents presented a "picture of imminent doom and final downfall." [39]

The Third Reich may have been sliding toward defeat, but the German Opposition had itself been weakened by Gestapo persecution. The core of the Opposition—composed of dissident officers of Admiral Canaris' Abwehr—had been seriously damaged by the arrest of one of its top leaders in April 1943. The subsequent investigation forced Hans Gisevius, Dulles' Abwehr contact, to establish "permanent residence" in Switzerland. He remained in Berne despite Gestapo demands that he return to Germany. Gisevius' role as intermediary between OSS and the Opposition was assumed by two other Abwehr men—Eduard Waetjen, a Berlin attorney with relatives in the United States, and Theodor Struenck, director of a large insurance firm in Frankfurt.

The movements of these and other anti-Hitler Abwehr officers were further circumscribed by another victory for their Gestapo rivals. In Istanbul, two Abwehr agents defected to the British. The Gestapo pointed out that their superior, a German banker who had lived in Washington and New York before the war, was an old acquaintance of General Donovan's.[40] Weeks later, Abwehr agents in France were accused of treasonous dealings with Paul Dungler, the Giraudist agent sent to Vichy by Henry Hyde's OSS unit in Algiers. Himmler took occasion of these scandals to press for "unification" of German intelligence. On February 18, 1944, Hitler finally signed a decree relieving Admiral Canaris of his command. The military intelligence men of the Abwehr were then subordinated to Himmler's Reich Security Office, home of the SS and the Gestapo.

Dulles received this unfortunate news at the same time that the Opposition presented him with its last plea for American support of a coup d'etat, a "negotiated peace," and an alliance against the Soviets. As in the past, Dulles replied that Washington refused to discuss anything but unconditional surrender. Allied unity could not be broken.

The next message Dulles received from Berlin relayed the Opposition's new plan for a putsch. Early in July 1944, Eduard Waetjen brought word that another attempt on Hitler's life would be made before the end of the month. Gisevius, despite the threat of immediate Gestapo arrest, returned to Germany with Theodor Struenck to be in Berlin at the moment that "Operation Valkyrie," the Opposition's plan for seizure of power, went into effect. Dulles immediately flashed the news to Washington. A revolt was in the offing.

At 4 P.M. on the afternoon of July 20, Dulles was sitting in his office at the American Legation, chatting with Elizabeth Wiskemann, an official of the British Political Warfare Executive in Berne. "After we had talked a few things over," she recalled, "his telephone rang. He answered it very briefly, as if accepting a piece of news he had rather expected. He put back the receiver and said to me, 'There has been an attack on Hitler's life at his headquarters.' I was not surprised either, but rather excited: we neither of us knew whether it had succeeded." [41] Not until midnight, when he heard Hitler's voice on the radio, did Dulles learn that the plot had failed.

The day after the ill-fated assassination attempt at Rastenberg, Wilhelm Hoegner, the Socialist exile who served as an advisor to OSS Switzerland, met Dulles and Gaevernitz in Berne. "I never saw them so completely downtrodden," Hoegner later wrote. "They had always hoped that through a sudden downfall of Hitler, the war would be ended before the Soviet Russians entered Berlin. A quick peace agreement with a democratic German regime would have prevented that. But now all was lost; the continuation of the war would provide the Russians with a pathway to the Elbe in the heart of Europe. American policy had suffered a terrible defeat." [42]

The German Opposition had also been dealt a devastating blow. Himmler's Gestapo arrested all the major military and civilian leaders involved in the July 20 plot. Thousands of other suspected anti-Nazis were also jailed. Death sentences were freely meted out after trial before a "people's court." Among those executed were Admiral Canaris, former chief of the Abwehr, OSS-Abwehr courier Theodor Struenck, and Adam von Trott zu Solz of the Kreisau Circle. One of the lucky few to escape the Gestapo dragnet was Hans Gisevius. He went into hiding in Berlin and managed to send word to Dulles. Gaevernitz prepared for a personal trip to London to obtain forged papers for the Abwehr fugitive.

The journey became possible after the Allied landings on the Riviera, when the U.S. Seventh Army, pushing north from southern France, broke through the German defenses to the Swiss border near

Geneva. As soon as the frontier was reopened, Dulles crossed into France and joined a Maquis group in a secret retreat in the Rhone Valley, awaiting a plane for London. He was unexpectedly met by General Donovan, who had been combing the area for his old friend. After their first reunion in almost two years, Donovan and Dulles flew together from Lyon to London. They reached the British capital on September 8, the day the first V-2 rockets hit London.[43] Then they were off to Washington for top-level conferences.

Dulles found Donovan's headquarters a far cry from the small staff of conscientious conspirators whom he had left behind in November 1942. Hundreds of youthful Army officers flashed their security badges as they hurried into well-guarded OSS buildings scattered throughout the District of Columbia. Scores of operational committees were at work planning subversive projects in German territory, which had first been invaded by American troops on September 12, and by Soviet troops in the East a month later. Some of this activity proved useful. Under the direction of Carl Schorske, a 29-year-old Harvard history instructor, the German section of Research and Analysis had already begun production of political and administrative handbooks for the use of military government authorities in occupied Germany. An independent series of studies was directed by Dr. Robert Kempner, a German émigré who had once been chief legal advisor to the Weimar Police. He began assembling a list of anti-Nazis who might be selected for administrative posts by the American Military Government.

Less fruitful work was under way in the operational branches. British intelligence had opened the door to harebrained German projects in 1941 when they sent to still-neutral America a Hungarian astrologer who had once analyzed the stars for Hitler; his mission was "to shake American public confidence" in the "invincibility" of the Nazi dictator by reading signs of imminent doom into the Fuehrer's horoscope.[44] Not to be outdone by London, a group of OSS psychoanalysts proposed an incredible operation based on the premise that the Nazi totalitarian state would disintegrate if only its leader could be demoralized. After conducting a long-range psychological profile of Hitler's personality, this group decided the Fuehrer could be undone by exposing him to vast quantities of pornography. The OSS men collected the finest library of German smut ever assembled in the United States. The material was to be dropped by plane in the area surrounding Hitler's headquarters on the assumption that the Fuehrer would step outside, pick up some bit of it and immediately be thrown into paroxysms of madness. But the effort was in vain. The Army Air Corps Colonel sent as liaison to the pornography-collectors stormed out of his first meeting with them. He cursed Donovan's maniacs and swore he would not risk the life of a single airman for such an insane boondoggle.[45]

Still another OSS section, in cooperation with the British, printed propaganda stickers that were to be placed in chilly German lavatories by Allied agents. They read: "Make the Fuehrer cold, and this room will be warm again!" [46] At both OSS and SOE headquarters proposals were also under consideration to send a suicide commando mission to Berlin to assassinate Hitler. Both plans were rejected.[47]

Dozens of similar schemes were being hatched in OSS corridors. Dulles came upon few ideas that merited close consideration, but one suggestion caught his interest. Mrs. Emmy Rado, an attractive Swiss-born OSS analyst, the wife of an émigré Hungarian psychiatrist, proposed that the Catholic and Protestant churches could be used as a base for German political reconstruction.[f] She felt OSS could work effectively through the World Council of Churches to aid anti-Nazi German clergymen of the "Christian Socialist" variety. Dulles was impressed. He also believed that Mrs. Rado, who retained her Swiss citizenship, might prove useful in his future intelligence operations. He invited her to join his Berne team at the beginning of the new year.[48]

Dulles returned to Switzerland at the end of October to find an entirely new OSS staff awaiting him. Russell D'Oench, scion of the Grace shipping line family, left his SI Branch assignment in London to become Dulles' man in Zurich. At Basle, OSS was represented by Robert Shea, an attorney with degrees from Harvard, Oxford, Paris, and Vienna.[g] William Larimer Mellon, grandnephew of the financier and son of the president of Gulf Oil, was transferred to Geneva from his SI Branch post in Madrid.[h] At the Italian border, the OSS liaison officers to the Italian resistance, Donald Jones and Emilio Daddario, were joined by Russian émigré Valerian Lada-Mocarski, who sat with Dulles on the board of directors of the German-affiliated Schroeder

[f] No relation to Alexander Rado, the Hungarian cartographer who directed the Russian military intelligence network in Switzerland during the war.

[g] Shea was later a CIA official in Romania, 1947–49, and Switzerland, 1949–50.

[h] Mellon has since sacrificed his wealth and social position to found and direct a hospital clinic for the poor in Haiti.

bank. He had left his OSS post in Cairo to assist Dulles in contacting dissident Italian fascist officials.[i]

There were new faces in Berne as well. Mrs. Rado soon arrived from New York, Gisevius miraculously returned from Berlin in January using Gaevernitz's forged passport, and an OSS doctor appeared with plans to interrogate German scientists who might be captured by the advancing American Army. From Arthur Goldberg's Labor unit in London (then being disbanded and absorbed by the Secret Intelligence Branch), Dulles acquired the services of Washington labor attorney Gerhard Van Arkel, who had worked closely with Arthur Roseborough and Donald Downes in Algiers. Van Arkel was assisted by John Clark, an ex-union official and former correspondent for the *Washington Post*.

Though Dulles' staff worked closely with resistance forces in Italy and Austria, German espionage remained the principal mission of OSS Switzerland. But the Berne team was no longer unaided in its penetration of the Third Reich. In Italy, the SI Branch had a special Germany-Austria section under Alfred Ulmer, Jr.,[j] a 28-year-old Florida newspaper correspondent and advertising executive.[49] The advancing American armies in the west also had OSS detachments which were desperately launching dozens of missions into the enemy fatherland.

In October 1944, as the Jedburgh, SUSSEX, and other OSS teams were "overrun" by Allied troops, OSS attention turned to Germany. There had been no preparation. Following the directives of Eisenhower's headquarters, David Bruce's officers had concentrated their efforts exclusively on French operations. When the Allied armies stalled at the Nazi "Siegfried line," just inside the German border, the generals began to demand the kind of strategic intelligence which OSS had provided during the French invasions. The disappointed brass "didn't seem to realize that clandestine intelligence networks have to be set up *before* they are needed and cannot be established by push-button methods."[50] In December 1944, when the Battle of the Bulge

---

[i] Lada-Mocarski was involved in smuggling out of Italy the diaries of Count Ciano, Mussolini's former Foreign Minister, executed for treason in 1944.

[j] As CIA station chief in Athens, 1953–55, Ulmer became a good friend of Greek shipping magnate Stavros Niarchos. After several years as Agency station chief in Paris, Ulmer left the Agency in 1962 to direct Niarchos' company in London.

began, OSS had only four men inside Germany. They had no communications with London or Paris and were producing no intelligence.

The OSS command fell back in desperation upon the small German operations section formed by the Labor Branch. As early as the fall of 1943, Goldberg's aides had been recruiting anti-Nazis for future German infiltration. A handful were found in prisoner-of-war camps; some were exile German socialists or Communists. But the work had proceeded slowly; David Bruce and other OSS executives believed that no German should be trusted for American espionage work. As an alternative, Goldberg received permission for a project code-named BACH. Under the guidance of Dr. Lazare Teper, a Russian-born economist who directed the research department of the International Ladies Garment Workers Union, OSS enlisted a host of German-speaking agents—Scandinavians, Belgians, Frenchmen, Poles, and a few German exiles—who would be dropped into Western Europe to gather information on the German Army. Many came from the ranks of the International Transport Workers Federation headed by the Belgian unionist Omer Becu. The first missions to France and the Low Countries were dispatched in early 1944. By the end of the year, the entire project had been co-opted by the other OSS branches to assist in German operations.

As an emergency measure, the new SI Branch chief, a wealthy 32-year-old New York tax lawyer, William Casey, was given over-all operational control of German projects.[k] He coordinated the effort to send Polish, Belgian, and French agents to the major crossroad cities of Germany. The tactical missions were launched by Army units at the front. The deep penetrations of agents parachuted far behind the lines were flown from Namur in Belgium, or from the OSS detachment commanded by Henry Hyde (the irrepressible Algiers Giraudist) at Dijon in eastern France.

By the spring of 1945, OSS had sent over 150 men into Germany to such rail centers as Leipzig, Breslau, and Munich. A Danish resistance leader, Hennings Jessen-Schmidt, was recruited by OSS officers in Stockholm for a special German mission. He was smuggled across

[k] In 1969, Casey was chairman of a national "citizens committee" which bought large newspaper ads throughout the country supporting the Nixon administration's Vietnam policy. In March 1971, the President nominated Casey to be chairman of the U.S. Securities and Exchange Commission.

the Danish border into Germany in a fish truck on February 1, 1945, made his way to Berlin several days later, and teamed with a Swedish businessman, Carl Wiberg, became the first OSS plant inside Hitler's capital city. A second team composed of Czech Communists recruited by Labor Branch operatives was successfully parachuted to Berlin in March.[51] Other agents converged on major German cities from France, Holland, and Switzerland.[1]

While the infiltration campaigns were under way. Dulles and Gaevernitz met frequently with General Edwin Sibert[m] and Colonel William Quinn,[n] the intelligence chiefs of the advancing American armies, at points in France just over the Swiss border. At one of these meetings in December 1944, Gaevernitz suggested that "there were still some German generals who did not believe in Hitler's promises and who would be glad to surrender if it was possible for them to do so with reasonable security for themselves." He proposed that OSS should secretly make contact with such wavering Wehrmacht officers and "create the circumstances under which their surrenders could be carried out, swiftly and silently, before the long arm of Hitler and the SS could descend on them and their staffs."[52] The intelligence men of Omar Bradley's Twelfth Army Group, then headquartered at Luxembourg, were intrigued by this proposal for bloodless victories. OSS received army approval to assemble a committee of high-ranking German prisoners to help pinpoint Nazis commanders on the western front who might be willing to surrender.

Gaevernitz traveled to several Allied POW camps, and with the assistance of MI-6 collected an advisory group of German generals willing to aid the surrender plan. The group was similar to Moscow's Free Germany Committee, except that Gaevernitz did not intend to use his Wehrmacht men for political propaganda or subversion.

Before the plan could go into effect, it was referred to Washington. After a delay of several weeks, the disappointing reply arrived. The project had been rejected at a high official level. Washington "did

---

[1] In 1952, Congressman Douglas Stringfellow, a Utah Republican, began touring the country giving "inspiration talks" about his wartime "OSS mission" behind the lines in Germany. The story was exposed as a fraud during the 1954 election campaign. In a television speech, the weeping congressman admitted he had never served in OSS.

[m] Sibert was Assistant Director of CIA, 1947–48.

[n] Quinn was director of the War Department's Strategic Services Unit, which absorbed the operational branches of OSS until the creation of CIA in 1947; and deputy director of the Defense Intelligence Agency, 1961–63.

not propose using German militarists to defeat German militarism." Besides, the Soviets would have to be consulted and "they were so suspicious of any efforts of this nature that they would undoubtedly refuse to agree to any attempt to get even a partial surrender of the German forces to the United States alone." [53]

The Gaevernitz committee had just been shelved when Fritz Kolbe, Dulles' best espionage agent in Berlin, appeared unexpectedly in the Swiss capital for the first time in months. Dulles had last seen Kolbe in June 1944. No word had been received from him after the July 20 plot, and Dulles had regretfully assumed that Kolbe had been seized in the Gestapo mass arrests. Kolbe explained that he had carefully avoided contact with the Opposition plotters. When the Rastenburg assassination failed, he had agreed to aid the escape of the top civilian leader of the Opposition, former Leipzig Mayor Karl Goerdeler, but that unfortunate man had been captured before Kolbe could come to his aid.

Kolbe now appeared in Berne on behalf of a small group of socialists who had once been members of the "Reichsbanner," the uniformed military cadre of the Social Democratic Party during the Weimar era. These men, under Kolbe's leadership, now proposed to stage their own putsch in Berlin. They asked that a unit of American paratroops be dropped to the German capital to aid their revolt. This was yet another thinly disguised attempt to get Berlin into American hands before the Red Army could enter the city. Without any doubt of the result, Dulles transmitted the proposal to Washington. It was, of course, rebuffed.[54]

Another old friend then appeared with a very different idea. Noel Field had remained Dulles' link to the Communists throughout 1944. When OSS infiltration of Germany became of supreme importance in the fall of that year, Field's left-wing comrades had proved most useful to Dulles' labor union operatives, Gerhard Van Arkel and John Clark. Field's foster-daughter, 24-year-old Erika Glaser, a German-Jewish refugee whom the Fields had met in Spain, became secretary-interpreter to Van Arkel while still a member of the Swiss Communist underground youth movement.[o]

Because of Field's past assistance, Dulles was willing to listen when the American Communist came to him with a unique proposal in December 1944. The Soviet-sponsored Free Germany Committee, formed in Moscow the previous year, had since expanded to garner sup-

[o] After five years in a Communist prison, Miss Glaser "defected" to the United States in 1957.

port from German exiles in the west. After the liberation of Paris, a branch was established in France and Switzerland under the name CALPO (Comité de l'Allemagne Libre Pour l'Ouest). The front was dominated by German Communists, although some Socialists were also involved. Field proposed that OSS establish a formal working relationship with CALPO in France. The Americans could thus secure a badly needed supply of anti-Nazi German agents who would be sent behind the lines to gather intelligence and to build up a left-wing underground.[55]

Dulles, who knew the difficulties OSS London had experienced in its German operations, thought the idea had some merit. He gave Field a letter of introduction to the OSS headquarters in Paris. Reaching the French capital in January 1945, Field went to OSS headquarters and, for no particular reason, was referred to the Reports Section of the combined SI and Research Branches. The division was headed by Philip Horton, the Harvard English instructor who had become inadvertently involved in the Karl Frank case two years before. The officer who chanced to receive Field was Horton's political analyst, 27-year-old Arthur Schlesinger, Jr.

"What struck me most was his self-righteous stupidity," Schlesinger remembers. "He was a Quaker Communist, filled with smugness and sacrifice, and not a very intelligent man." [56] Schlesinger recommended that Field's CALPO plan be rejected. In this he was supported by the assistant chief of the SI Branch, Albert Jolis, an international jeweler and ex-journalist of Belgian descent, who had close ties to the Bevin faction of the British Labour Party.[p] Schlesinger and Jolis convinced the OSS command in Paris that the Field project would prove untenable on purely technical grounds. The proposed alliance with the German Communists was rejected.

The war against Germany went on. Dulles had virtually run the gamut of the political spectrum in grasping for operational projects— Gaevernitz' militarists, Kolbe's Socialists, Field's Communists. It only remained for him to establish contact with the strongest political force that remained intact within Hitler's crumbling Reich—the Gestapo entourage of Heinrich Himmler.

The Himmler clique had remained quiescent since the von Hohenlohe and Kersten affairs of 1943. The failure of the July 20 plot, however, and the subsequent purge of the Wehrmacht high command left

[p] Jolis is now Paris representative of Diamond Distributors, Inc.

the Gestapo leadership as undisputed masters of what they knew to be a disintegrating Nazi political edifice. Himmler and his top aides— Walter Schellenberg and Ernst Kaltenbrunner—felt that the time had come for renewed peace feelers to the west.

The last months of 1944 saw a rash of Himmler-backed diplomatic overtures to London and Washington. In November the Chinese Military Attaché in Paris informed the British that a high-ranking German intelligence officer was prepared to "defect" to MI-6.[57] As soon as the Nazi was taken into custody, he revealed the real reason for his desertion. He had come bearing a Himmler "peace plan"—an immediate attack on Russia by Germany, in league with Britain and the United States, to prevent "Communist encroachment" in Western Europe. That same month, a well-known Italian industrialist presented a similar proposal to the British in Switzerland.

Also in November 1944, Allen Dulles received renewed peace offerings from Himmler agents; they felt the OSS representative was "not only a man of high intelligence, but also an implacable enemy of Bolshevism, whose opposition was based on knowledge, reasoned argument, and clear-sighted vision."[58] Dulles was approached, in short order, by an Italian cleric, an Austrian industrial magnate, and the German air attaché at Berne. The theme of all three intermediaries was the hackneyed offer of a holy alliance against eastern communism. A fourth emissary from the Gestapo produced an artful modification. The Nazis, he threatened, might be forced to "open" Germany to the Red Army and form a new Hitler-Stalin Pact against the west, unless Dulles and the Americans showed an interest in "talking things over."[59]

Dulles dismissed the Gestapo overtures as an attempt to "get some good marks with the Allies to offset what was otherwise an unmitigated record of black criminality."[60] But Himmler and company believed that their plan for a "separate peace" had actually been foiled by the far more palatable surrender offer of the renegade SS General Karl Wolff and his SUNRISE negotiations.

Wolff, it will be recalled, began extending peace feelers to Dulles through Italian industrialist Luigi Parilli at the beginning of March 1945. The general, a former personal assistant to Himmler, had fallen into disfavor and was already on cool terms with other ranking officials of the Gestapo hierarchy when he initiated the offer of German surrender in northern Italy. In Berlin, Himmler aides Schellenberg and Kaltenbrunner found that Dulles had lost interest in their machinations

In the club room of his Herrengasse flat in the Swiss capital, Allen Dulles (right) discussed the SUNRISE surrender plans with Gero von Schulze Gaevernitz, his principal link to the anti-Nazi Opposition in Germany.

as he began talks with Wolff. As they sought to block the SS General's independent maneuvers, more threatening opposition came from another quarter.

The SUNRISE negotiations in the spring of 1945 absorbed the energies of Dulles, Gero Gaevernitz, and two OSS staff officers— C. Tracy Barnes,[q] a young attorney for the War Production Board, educated at Harvard and Yale, who had completed two SO missions behind the lines in France; and Paul Blum, an American businessman who had lived in Japan for many years before the war.

Dulles sent Blum, who doubled as his counter-intelligence aide and Far Eastern specialist, to open the surrender talks with Wolff's emissaries on March 3. (Dulles' choice of Blum to begin the negotiations with the SS men was an inadvertent act of poetic justice; Blum was

[q] Barnes was CIA base chief in Frankfurt, 1954–56, and station chief in London, 1957–59. He was CIA liaison with the State Department during the Bay of Pigs operation, then became chief of the agency's so-called Domestic Operations Division. He resigned from the government in 1968 to become special assistant to the President of Yale University.

Jewish.) Within a week, the Italian resistance leader Ferruccio Parri
was released by the Gestapo, and General Wolff crossed the border
into Switzerland for his first meeting with Dulles. A few days later,
Averell Harriman, the American ambassador in Moscow, notified the
Soviet government of the German peace feelers. Dulles was "relieved'"
that Moscow had been told. The Germans would thus be unable, he
reasoned, to use the SUNRISE talks to "drive a wedge between the
Russians and us." [61]

Stalin's Foreign Minister Molotov raised no objections to the
Swiss talks, but asked that the Soviets be represented at the meetings.
Neither Dulles nor the Anglo-American negotiating team in Switzerland
opposed the presence of a Russian observer. But other American officials
were less accommodating. From Moscow, Harriman recommended
that the Soviets, who had recently begun to show a "domineering attitude" toward their American allies, should not be allowed to send a
delegate to Berne. Roosevelt's top advisors agreed. And Churchill soon
added his opinion that Washington should take a "firm and blunt
stand" with the Kremlin and refuse to be "bullied into submission."
Moscow's request for representation in the Swiss talks was denied.[62]

While Dulles and the Allied negotiators, Generals Airey and Lemnitzer, met with Wolff's party near the Swiss-Italian border, a bitter
diplomatic exchange between Moscow and Washington had reached the
highest political level. Molotov condemned the western Allies for conducting negotiations "behind the back of the Soviet government, which
has been carrying on the main burden of the war against Germany."
He demanded that the talks be halted immediately. Roosevelt responded with a polite rejection of the Soviet ultimatum and deplored
the "atmosphere of regrettable apprehension and mistrust." Stalin then
entered the act with allegedly definitive evidence from his intelligence
services that the British and Americans in Switzerland were concluding
a "separate peace" with the Nazis to halt the Red Army's advance in
the east.[63]

"It would be one of the great tragedies of history," replied Roosevelt on April 4, "if, at the very moment of the victory now within our
grasp, such distrust, such lack of faith should prejudice the entire undertaking after the colossal losses of life, materiel, and treasure involved.
Frankly, I cannot avoid a feeling of bitter resentment toward your informers, whoever they are, for such vile misrepresentations of my actions
or those of my trusted subordinates." [64]

Stalin backed down a bit. In his next dispatch to Washington, the

Kremlin dictator defended the "accuracy and knowledge" of Soviet Intelligence. But he also came close to an apology, insisting that his comments were not intended to offend the Americans. On the morning
of April 12, Roosevelt, hoping to end the unfortunate affair, sent Stalin
a note referring to the "Berne misunderstanding" as a "minor incident."
The President concluded, "I feel sure that when our armies make contact in Germany and join in a fully coordinate offensive, the Nazi
armies will disintegrate." [65] That afternoon, Franklin Roosevelt was
dead.

Two days later, at a meeting in Paris, General Donovan first informed Dulles of the high-level contretemps over the SUNRISE negotiations. Dulles returned to Berne uncertain as to the future of his
peace talks. The answer soon came. In a cable of April 20, the State
Department, on the advice of the British Foreign Office, ordered the
negotiations with Wolff broken off. President Truman was unwilling
to offend the Kremlin. Dulles was bitterly disappointed. He believed
Moscow's attempt to kill the SUNRISE talks was part of a sinister
Communist plot to seize control of the Italian port of Trieste, the key
to the Adriatic, and possibly portions of north Italy itself. Wolff's surrender, he thought, might prevent such Russian inroads.

What was Moscow really thinking? Dulles never stopped to consider the situation from the point of view of his Soviet intelligence
counterparts. Switzerland had no diplomatic relations with the Soviet
Union. There was no legal Russian representation in the country. Soviet
intelligence was forced to rely upon illegal agent networks that were
constantly under threat of arrest by the Swiss Security Police. The most
effective Red Army espionage group in the neutral country, the "Lucy"
ring, had in fact been broken up by the Swiss in late 1943.

The Americans claimed that the Berne talks were proceeding on
the basis of the Casablanca formula of unconditional surrender. But
they refused to allow Soviet observers to be present. Stalin wanted to
know—what were Wolff and Dulles *really* plotting? All the intelligence
indications pointed to the "separate peace" Moscow so feared. The
NKVD knew that Gestapo officers had been making overtures to OSS
ever since the von Hohenlohe and Kersten affairs of 1943. They knew
that the tempo of these political approaches from the Himmler clique
had increased as Berlin's defeat appeared imminent.

Perhaps the NKVD also knew that during the second week of
April, while Dulles discussed SUNRISE with Donovan in Paris, one of
his OSS aides was meeting in Zurich with Wilhelm Hoettl, a top Aus-

trian Gestapo official. Hoettl offered, on behalf of Himmler's deputy, Kaltenbrunner, to prevent the Fuehrer and his fellow fanatics from retreating to an "alpine redoubt" where they might continue a guerrilla war against the Allies. In return, the Germans asked that the Red Army be prevented from participation in the occupation of Austria. (The threat of the redoubt, which later proved to be a German myth, was a major headache for military men in Washington; thirty OSS agents recruited by the French and Belgian sections of SO had parachuted into Southern Bavaria and the Austrian Tyrol to await a possible Nazi retreat to the Alps.) [66]

Also in April, Gestapo officers in occupied Holland decided to release Anton Poelhof, a Dutch university student born in the East Indies, who had been arrested by the Germans in February while on the first intelligence mission OSS had sent to Holland. Poelhof was returned to the Allied lines with a new Gestapo offer. Himmler's men would turn over to OSS their voluminous and valuable intelligence on Japan if only the Allied command would agree to stall the war on the western front while the Nazis battled the Soviets in the east.[67]

Himmler's people, the Russians knew, were tramping all over Europe floating such "separate peace" balloons. And the Soviets failed to make any distinction between SS General Wolff and his Gestapo superiors. Even President Roosevelt, in one of his early cables of reassurance to Moscow, had identified Wolff as "a German officer reputed to be close to Himmler." It was the President who had first raised the possibility that Wolff's "sole purpose is to create suspicion and distrust between the Allies." [68] Had the Russians also intercepted Wolff's own message to Himmler in which he justified his talks with Dulles as "important negotiations with the Allies with a view to separating the Anglo-Americans from the Soviets"? [69]

When the Berne talks continued, it was not entirely surprising that the Russian espionage analysts began to suspect a western conspiracy with the worst element in the Third Reich. The British had understood the Soviet suspicions when they urged Washington to halt the SUNRISE discussions, leading to the cable to Dulles on April 20. Only Wolff's sudden and unexpected offer to sign an unconditional surrender on April 22 convinced the State Department to reverse its earlier order and to allow SUNRISE to proceed.

While Dulles and the few members of his staff in Switzerland were involved in the last stages of the Italian surrender, OSS officers at other European outposts had also begun to sense that Germany's defeat was at hand. At the end of April, a captured official of the Nazi Foreign Ministry told OSS interrogators that he believed Hitler would soon commit suicide.[70]

Hitler took his own life on May 1. A week later the war in Europe was over. Allen Dulles and his OSS staff prepared to move north into a defeated Germany.

After V-E Day, J. Russell Forgan, the New York financier who had succeeded David Bruce as OSS commander in the European Theater, submitted his own resignation to General Donovan and suggested that his good friend Allen Dulles be named in his stead.

Donovan refused, declaring Dulles a "poor administrator." The general preferred to divide OSS Europe into autonomous country detachments, each reporting directly to Washington. When Forgan and his aides continued to press for Dulles' appointment, Donovan countered by threatening to name Colonel Edward Glavin, the incompetent administrator of OSS Italy, to fill the European post. The Dulles protagonists retreated in a bureaucratic rout and OSS Europe was split into separate country missions. Dulles became chief of OSS in occupied Germany only. It proved to be a difficult, full-time job.

Washington had failed to integrate Dulles' secret service organization into plans for a postwar German occupation. The British were more astute. The chief of SOE's German section, a Lieutenant General, became Director of Military Government for the entire British zone of occupation. OSS received no similar mark of recognition. A few Donovan assistants—Ohio historian Walter Dorn, Chicago journalist Wallace Deuel, Yale historian Hajo Holborn—were appointed high-level advisors to the American military government, but OSS failed to become the principal intelligence arm of the American representatives to the four-power Allied Control Council for Germany.

Dulles' detachment faced stiff competition from a score of American intelligence teams representing a dozen military and civilian agencies, all working at cross purposes and all searching for the same "strategic" information. Dulles' trained field operatives were meanwhile being siphoned off to the Far East or were taking their first opportunity to return to the United States for demobilization.[71]

Some of the remaining personnel were of questionable integrity. In the fall of 1945, Army investigators exposed an incredible black-market operation in Berlin, organized by an OSS major and captain, the top administrative officers of Dulles' detachment in the city. The success of their illegal combine rivaled the fictional "M&M Enterprises" of Heller's *Catch-22*. Every conceivable commodity, from oil stock to porcelain china, was sold by their black-market company.

None of Dulles' operational officers were involved in the scandal; they were generally conscientious and overworked, trying desperately to meet the demands of the military government authorities. The Counter-Intelligence Branch interrogated Gestapo and Abwehr officers and helped track down Nazi intelligence agents still at large. Heading the effort was Andrew Berding, an Oxford-educated journalist who had directed the Associated Press Bureau in Mussolini's Rome.[r] He was assisted by another Oxford graduate, 32-year-old John Oakes, a brilliant Rhodes scholar of Jewish descent and a former political correspondent for the *Washington Post*.[s]

OSS was also burdened by responsibility for "denazification." The military government authorities wanted lists of Nazi officials who should be arrested or barred from office. The Allied Control Council also required OSS aid in finding Germans with "respectable" records of opposition to Nazism who might be employed in administrative positions during the occupation.

OSS officer Sterling Hayden, the actor turned arms smuggler, found "denazification" a difficult task. After completing his work with the Communist Partisans in Yugoslavia, Hayden had been assigned to the OSS First Army Detachment as it moved into Germany. He had immediately clashed with the detachment commander, 24-year-old Stuyvesant Wainwright II, a wealthy, conservative Republican who had recommended that Hayden be court-martialed for giving the Communist clenched-fist salute.[t]

Having eluded young Wainwright's authority (in typical OSS fashion), Hayden began searching for Germans untainted by complicity in the Nazi movement. As his unit moved along the road from Cologne to Marburg, "there came squirming into the light millions of anti-Nazis. It was tough, they said, waving their handkerchiefs and wringing their hands with joy, to have lived under Hitler. But, only the night

[r] Berding was Deputy Director of the United States Information Agency, 1953–57; Assistant Secretary of State for Public Affairs and John Foster Dulles' personal press aide, 1957–60.

[s] Oakes is now chief editorial writer for the *New York Times*.

[t] Wainwright was a Republican congressman from New York, 1952–60. President Eisenhower sometimes called upon him as an unofficial congressional advisor on CIA and military affairs.

before, they had heated the water that would quickly yield this demo-cratic douche. The real anti-Nazis," he wrote, "were dead, or in exile, or in Belsen, Auschwitz, Buchenwald. Names, we thought, at the time, that would teach us a lesson we'd never forget." [72]

The incessant demands of military government officers for German anti-Nazis continued unabated. Dulles and Gaevernitz seized the op-portunity to promote the political futures of German exiles and a few survivors of the Opposition with whom they had worked during the war. On June 6, Wilhelm Hoegner, Dulles' Bavarian Socialist advisor at Berne (and fervent anti-Communist) was driven from Switzerland to Germany in an OSS jeep. His chauffeur was Mrs. Emmy Rado, the Swiss-born intelligence analyst who assisted Dulles in working with the German clergy. With Dulles' active support, Hoegner soon became the first Minister-President of Bavaria. He remained adamant in his refusal to have any dealings with the resurgent German Communist Party, often to the dismay of American officials who supported the idea of a German coalition government.

To continue the German church project Mrs. Rado had begun in Switzerland, Dulles also bestowed OSS favors on Dr. Stewart Herman, a Lutheran pastor who had been minister of the American Church in Berlin before the war.[u] In the fall of 1943, Herman had joined OSS in London as an advisor on German propaganda. After the surrender, he left Donovan's organization to join the staff of the World Council of Churches in Geneva. Herman was given responsibility for helping re-build the Protestant church in Germany. Dulles, who believed that strong religious institutions would be a counter-force to the growth of German Communism, provided Herman with travel orders, transporta-tion, and accommodations which enabled the pastor, despite his un-official status, to move freely through the country during the first months of the occupation.

Mrs. Rado continued to work with the clergy, but she expanded her activities into the project code-named CROWN JEWELS. The Russians had returned Walter Ulbricht's German Communist exiles to their homeland in record time after the surrender. Mrs. Rado's object was to balance the Soviet activity by expediting the return to Germany of other anti-Nazi political leaders who were dedicated opponents of the Comintern (including veteran socialist Erich Ollenhauer, who later became chairman of the West German Social Democratic Party).

Some of Dulles' subordinates were critical of his efforts to support

[u] In 1970, Dr. Herman was President of the Lutheran School of The-ology in Chicago.

"politically marginal" Germans whose chief recommendation seemed to be their hatred of Moscow. In the Donovan tradition, Dulles, though he continued to pursue his anti-Russian policy, made no attempt to silence the dissenters in his organization. In the Secret Intelligence and Research Branches, a nucleus of unrestrained liberals sought closer contact with anti-Nazis of Socialist and Communist persuasion.

Labor attorney Gerhard Van Arkel moved from Switzerland to Dulles' headquarters at Wiesbaden near Frankfurt, accompanied by his secretary-interpreter, Noel Field's foster-daughter Erika Glaser. Van Arkel worked with all factions of the reconstructed socialist trade unions and also sought to establish communication with the Communist labor movement. But the Communist response was hostile.[v] Miss Glaser, a "comrade" of long-standing, secretly made her own approach to the German Communists, offering to spy on her American employers. Amazingly, the doctrinaire Marxists were so suspicious that they refused to allow her to join the party until she severed all connections with the American secret service! [73]

OSS academicians from the Research and Analysis unit of Dulles' detachment were more successful in overcoming the wariness of some German leftists, perhaps because the professors were themselves ideologically suspect by their superiors. The FBI had frequently demanded the dismissal of several German émigrés in the OSS Research Branch, notably a former Socialist police official, Horst Baerensprung, whom the Bureau condemned as a Soviet spy.[w] The House Un-American Activities Committee then found a "red herring" in Russian-born Paul Baran, a Marxist economist and OSS analyst who had once belonged to the German Communist Party. Only weeks before the end of the war in Europe, a Washington newspaper had carried the headline, "House Unit Probe Reveals Red Link of OSS Official." [74]

Undaunted by these attacks, the German Branch of R&A sent some

---

[v] The German Communists did accept one inadvertent American favor. During the invasion of the Third Reich, OSS published and distributed a clandestine newspaper purportedly produced by a revolutionary leftist underground in Germany. The newspaper format and title, "Neues Deutschland," were later adopted as the official journal of the East German government.

[w] Baerensprung and Hans Hirschfeld, both German émigrés employed by OSS, were named in a 1961 U.S. espionage case as alleged wartime Soviet spies. Baerensprung, a postwar East German police official, had already died. Hirschfeld, a press aide to Willy Brandt, claimed the accusation was only an effort to embarrass Brandt's political party, the West German Social Democrats.

of its finest analysts to occupied Germany. The most important figure in this group was Dr. Franz Neumann, a former Berlin labor lawyer who had once been legal advisor to the Social Democratic Party of the Weimar era. Arrested by the Nazis in 1933, he escaped to England and began study at the London School of Economics. He then came to the United States to join the staff of the Institute of Social Research, the intellectual exile center from which several OSS German analysts were recruited.

Neumann and many of his fellow academicians had long been disillusioned with the old German political left. They hoped to find a revitalized left-wing in a subjugated Germany: Socialists who refused to trade "social freedom for higher wages," Communists who were unwilling to accept political prostitution to Moscow, and both factions ready to unite to destroy the economic cartels which had financed Hitler's totalitarianism.[75]

Neumann's group also hoped that an east-west Cold War could be avoided. German democracy, they believed, could only grow out of American cooperation with the young German Communists who had been stranded in France and Switzerland during the war. These Marxists were more open-minded than their comrades who had fled to Moscow; many had indirectly passed information to Dulles in earlier years through their intermediary, Noel Field.[x] The OSS analysts now befriended these Communist "westerners." And as OSS liaison with the Free University of Berlin and the Free German Trade Union League, Neumann advised the wary occupation authorities that they could "do business" with the young Communists in these new institutions of German reconstruction.[76]

The hopes of the Research men faded rapidly. Both the American and Russian elements of the Allied Control Council showed little inclination to cooperate, and the Ulbricht group soon overwhelmed the "westerners" in the German Communist Party. The OSS academicians then turned their efforts toward bringing Nazi criminals to justice. The preparatory staff of the International War Crimes Tribunal at Nurem-

[x] Field mysteriously disappeared in Prague in 1949. In the early 1950s, while he remained in a Soviet jail, he became the Stalinist scapegoat in the purge trials of Rudolf Slansky and other East European Communist leaders. Despite his mistreatment, Field chose to remain in Hungary upon his release in 1954 until his death 14 years later. It was recently suggested that Field's arrest was actually part of a British plot to split the East European Communists, as outlined in John Le Carre's *The Spy Who Came in from the Cold*.

berg was packed with OSS men. General Donovan was himself U.S. Deputy Prosecutor until he resigned in a dispute over policy with the Chief Prosecutor, Supreme Court Justice Robert Jackson. The prosecution team also included OSS General Counsel James B. Donovan [y] (no relation to "Wild Bill") and OSS Assistant Director Ralph Albrecht, a prominent New York international lawyer who had previously headed the prisoner interrogation branch of Naval Intelligence.[77]

Almost all the OSS Research Branch analysts in Germany helped interrogate the Nazi defendants and prepare the brief against Hitler's henchmen. Franz Neumann was the first Chief of Research at Nuremberg. He was succeeded by OSS colleague Henry Kellermann, also a former Berlin lawyer-in-exile.[z]

Ironically, while dozens of these OSS professors and officials helped prosecute the Nazi leadership, a contingent of German intelligence officers, once loyal Hitlerites, were living a relatively charmed existence in an enclosed compound near Frankfurt at the expense of Dulles' Secret Intelligence Branch.

In April 1945 Dulles had first learned from his key agent, Fritz Kolbe, of an entire unit of Wehrmacht intelligence men from the Eastern Front who had salvaged their espionage records and were prepared to offer their services to the United States. Since 1942, this group had been sending agents into Russia independently of Himmler's SS and SD operations. The team commander was 40-year-old General Reinhard Gehlen, a career Army officer with a mild dislike for Hitler but a stronger respect for the Prussian tradition of loyalty to the Fatherland; he had not joined the Opposition.[a]

At the beginning of 1945, foreseeing a future Soviet-American conflict, Gehlen secured a complete set of microfilms of his unit's records and files and then led his team to the Alps to surrender to the American Army. He frequently repeated an offer to put his espionage network in Russian territory at the service of the United States. But he found little interest among American military officials until his proposal came to the attention of Dulles and General Donovan. They were im-

[y] Donovan was court-appointed defense counsel for Soviet agent Rudolf Abel in 1957, the intermediary in the "spy exchange" of Abel and U-2 pilot Gary Powers in 1962, and go-between in the repatriation of the CIA's ill-fated Bay of Pigs invaders from Cuba in 1963.

[z] Kellermann was the U.S. representative to UNESCO in Paris, 1956–61.

[a] Gehlen remained chief of the West German Intelligence Service until his retirement in 1968.

pressed by his enormous practical knowledge of the techniques of anti-Soviet espionage. They accepted his prediction of an imminent Cold War, and they were receptive when the Nazi general suggested that his staff should begin work for OSS pending the reestablishment of a German government. At that time, the "Gehlen organization" might acquire official status as an instrument of the new Reich.[78]

After considerable discussion in Washington, Gehlen's proposal was accepted. His offer was too tempting to reject, even though it had come from a German prisoner of war. To develop an OSS intelligence service targeted at Russia similar to Gehlen's network might have taken the Americans years of labor and millions of dollars. Even for those policy-makers who did not welcome a European confrontation with Moscow, it seemed vital to gather intelligence about Soviet political intentions. A developing Cold War mentality, together with Gehlen's own powerful personality, persuaded the Americans to establish the Gehlen organization in an OSS compound near Frankfurt. There the Germans pursued their Russian operations as they had under the Nazi regime, but now fed and clothed by Donovan's officers.

Responsibility for American dealings with the Gehlen organization was given to Dulles' Secret Intelligence Branch, under the direction of Frank Wisner, the vibrant Wall Street attorney from Mississippi who had commanded the OSS detachments in Istanbul and Bucharest. More than any other group of American officials in the Europe of 1945, Wisner's staff lived in the ugly interregnum between World War and Cold War. They were forced to look beyond debates over German reconstruction to a new underworld of espionage in which fascism had ceased to be the target. In the minds of those men in Wisner's office, the idea of an anti-Communist Central Intelligence Agency took seed.

They were not evil or sinister figures. They were not men with vast business interests or enormous stakes in an exploitive capitalist society. They were intelligent men like Harry Rositzke, 33, a Harvard alumnus with a Ph.D. in English Literature who had sat across the room from Arthur Schlesinger, Jr., in the OSS Reports Section in Paris.[b] They were talented, able administrators like Richard Helms, 32, a tall, athletic Navy lieutenant.[c] He had spent his youth at prep schools in Switzerland and Germany, received a degree from Williams College,

---

[b] Rositzke was CIA station chief in India, 1961–63, during the ambassadorship of John Kenneth Galbraith.

[c] Helms was CIA Deputy Director for Plans from 1962 until 1965. He became Director of Central Intelligence in 1966.

then joined the United Press staff in Berlin in 1935. He gained journalistic distinction by securing an exclusive interview with Hitler which
he later published as a vignette of the Nazi corporate-military state
and the megalomaniac who directed it. In 1938, Helms returned to the
United States to become advertising manager of a Scripps-Howard newspaper in Indianapolis. He joined the Navy in the summer of 1942 and
was assigned to two successively dull posts—first as fund-raiser for the
Naval Relief Society in New York, then as staff officer of an anti-sub-
marine operations headquarters. In August of 1943 he escaped to OSS.
He served in England and France and joined the Wisner unit in Wiesbaden after V-E Day.

What view of the Soviets did Wisner, Helms, and other future
Cold Warriors form in that all-important spring of 1945? The reports
of OSS Germany suggest an unhappy answer. One told of a Socialist
leader in the Russian zone who "expressed in rather strong terms his
opposition to the Communist Party." Three days later he was "taken
in charge by several Russian officers" and was never heard from again.
Another document details rumors circulating in Berlin which accused
American soldiers of robbing elderly, well-dressed German women.
These "slandering remarks" had been spread "on higher order" by Russian propaganda specialists sent to Germany to foment "whispering
campaigns" against the United States with the aid of local Communists.[79]

Yet there was a lingering hope that Roosevelt's dream of a grand
coalition might survive. One of Dulles' Counter-Intelligence men who
pursued uncaptured Nazi agents in Berlin in late 1945 remembered:
"We didn't have any help from the Russians since they were trying
to find the same people and records, but no work of ours was directed
against them. Those were still days when we thought four-power cooperation might work, first in Germany and then in a wider sphere, the
United Nations. Berlin is perhaps where that hope was first shattered;
it is also where it originally flourished most strongly, and where we
tried to make it work in a real situation." [80]

It was a depressing moment, that instant when the Cold War
mentality first struck the unsuspecting intelligence amateur. Peter
Tompkins, having at last recovered from his harrowing experiences in
Rome, was sent to Germany to work with Socialist union groups. He
found himself "with the advance guard of the OSS in Berlin, where,
well inside the Soviet Zone, with a Russian major and a bottle of vodka,
I realized, sadly, that our enemies had changed." [81]

8

The Chinese Puzzle

Many OSS officers in Europe and the Balkans had only a brief moment to share the frantic joy of liberation with their friends of the resistance. In the fall of 1944, with the grim reminder that another war was in progress in the Far East, scores of combat-hardened OSS men were transported to new Asian battlegrounds.

In a strange, war-weary land of 400 million people that had suffered through seven years of partial Japanese occupation and military stalemate, Donovan's officers met with sudden and bitter disappointment. China was a different war in an alien world. OSS Captain Walter Mansfield, the young attorney who had parachuted to Mihailovic's Chetniks, was one officer given the task of training Chinese guerrilla forces. He and most of his American colleagues found the new assignment disheartening. "By ordinary standards of guerrilla warfare," he wrote, "these Chinese were a pretty poor lot. I could not help contrasting them with Serbian guerrillas with whom I had fought. . . . In Serbia there had been a strong sense of patriotism and duty which permeated all and gave rise to a fervent esprit de corps. Here in China, individual bravery was the exception rather than the rule." [1]

American soldiers who hoped to escape Balkan political intrigue were also discouraged by the Chinese scene. Like Yugoslavia and Greece, the mammoth oriental nation was torn by internal political strife. The Yenan Communists in the north were openly hostile to the official government at Chungking in central China, where Generalissimo Chiang Kai-shek and his nationalist Kuomintang Party held sway. American propaganda perpetuated the myth that the Chiang government represented one of the Great Powers of the wartime world, and Washington accorded no official recognition to the Generalissimo's Communist rivals.[2]

These political dilemmas were unknown to the small group of Special Operations officers of the newly named OSS who disembarked in India in July 1942. They had come to launch an experiment in Asian guerrilla warfare. Known as Detachment 101, the team was commanded by Major Carl Eifler, a hulking middle-aged master of the arts of combat and war.[a] A former chief inspector of the Mexican Border Patrol and the Hawaiian Customs Service, Eifler had one special qualification of interest to OSS Headquarters: he was an old acquaintance of General Joseph Stilwell, the commander of American forces in China, Burma, and India, as well as Chief of Staff to Chiang Kai-shek. The OSS planners hoped Eifler's friendship with the cantankerous Stilwell might help their organization gain a foothold in Asia for its unorthodox special operations. From a China base, reasoned Donovan's aides, OSS officers could launch missions to Korea, Thailand, the Philippines, Indochina, Burma, and Japan itself. But this reckoning was shattered when Eifler and his men reached New Delhi to find themselves impatiently idling for weeks in the sweltering Indian sun; for very different reasons, neither Stilwell nor the Chinese government wanted their secret services.

Stilwell was engrossed in his own problems of command. His Washington superiors regarded the military effort on the Asian mainland as secondary in importance to the projected campaigns in Europe. The general was also having difficulties with the only existing American force in China—a group of volunteer airmen popularly dubbed the "Flying Tigers." They had been recruited, supplied, and financed before Pearl Harbor with unofficial Washington support. Their commander was hawk-faced General Claire Chennault, who had resigned from the American Army in 1937 to become Chiang Kai-shek's air force advisor.[b] Chennault unwittingly supported the contentions of the Europe-first strategists by assuring the War Department that the China war could be won exclusively by his volunteer air force.

[a] Eifler is now a Protestant minister and Doctor of Divinity in California.

[b] In 1946 Chennault formed a private, China-based commercial airline, Civil Air Transport, which later became interlocked with Air America, an arm of CIA paramilitary operations in Southeast Asia.

"Vinegar Joe" Stilwell did not agree. His strategic plan was to reopen a land supply route from India to China through Japanese-occupied Burma. Stilwell, whose acid temperament masked a basic social humanitarianism, insisted that the ill-fed, underpaid, and badly trained peasant conscripts of the Chinese Army had unrealized military potential and could ably perform his strategic task. What was needed, he argued, were basic reforms in the Chinese military structure, an unpalatable prospect for Chennault's intimate friend and protector, the Generalissimo. Chiang's very political existence rested upon a shaky warlord coalition; the Chinese generals who ruled the country's provinces were not about to relinquish their power in the interests of military reform. Chiang and Chennault stood united against Stilwell, and Vinegar Joe developed personal distaste for a regime "based on fear and favor, in the hands of an ignorant, arbitrary, stubborn man," a "peanut dictator." [3]

A passionate admirer of the infantry soldier, Stilwell was just as fervently prejudiced against the "irregular" military activity proposed by OSS. He welcomed Major Eifler and Detachment 101 as combat troops, but disparaged guerrilla tactics as "illegal action" and "shadow boxing." Convinced that any "commando operations" in China were doomed to failure, he left the OSS detachment stalled in India.[4]

General Donovan's representatives at Chungking were in no position to alter Stilwell's decision. Esson Gale, an aging American professor, had spent much of his life as an official of the Chiang government's salt revenue administration, the principal tax-collecting agency of China, dominated by occidentals for over fifty years. Gale came to Chungking in March of 1942 as a member of Stilwell's entourage, with Donovan's instructions to "improvise an underground apparatus." [5] But the professor's idea of "espionage" was lunching with his old friend H. H. Kung, the Yale-educated Chinese Minister of Finance, Madame Chiang's brother-in-law, and one of the least enlightened men within the Kuomintang ruling clique. For several months, Gale supplied Washington with "intelligence" furnished by his friends in the Chinese government which, not surprisingly, heralded the glorious military "victories" of Chiang's army commanders.

Alghan Lusey, a former United Press correspondent in Shanghai, was a second Donovan agent at the Chinese capital; he had first been hired as a propaganda specialist by the Sherwood branch of COI. Lusey had little contact with Gale, having been assured by "some very influential and powerful Chinese" that the professor was "not in the best of repute." [6] Beside hatching a futile plot to smuggle submachine guns to the "Formosan independence movement," Lusey devoted his energies to cultivating the friendship of Captain Milton "Mary" Miles, a naval officer who flew to China in May 1942 with vague orders to "find out what is going on out there" and to "do whatever you can to help the Navy and to heckle the Japanese." [7] What most interested Lusey was that Miles, an experienced veteran of the U.S. Asiatic Squadron, had developed close ties to a mysterious Chinese general named Tai Li.

Operating under the innocuous title of "Director, Bureau of Investigation and Statistics," Tai Li was actually the chief of a combined secret police and intelligence organization said to control over 300,000 agents throughout China and in every foreign nation where Chinese communities existed—from Bangkok to Saigon to San Francisco.

The short, stocky Chinese was a shadowy figure who had achieved legendary stature.[8] There were whispered tales of his miraculous escapes from countless Japanese assassination attempts. It was rumored that he had acquired great wealth through his control of the opium trade; that he supervised concentration camps for critics of the Chiang government; that he had no qualms about insuring thought control through political executions. General Tai, according to one OSS report, was "not the Admiral Canaris of China, but the Heinrich Himmler." [9]

Tai Li was also the "completely trusted subordinate, and guardian, of the Generalissimo, subject only to the Generalissimo's orders." [10] His loyalty to Chiang was a unique trait among the "merry nest of gangsters" (General Stilwell's term) who comprised the Kuomintang administration.[11] Their friendship went back to the 1920s when Tai Li had joined the Chinese Communist Party to spy for Chiang, his military mentor. The Generalissimo then turned against his Communist allies, and Tai Li was assigned the task of persecuting his former comrades. The general acquired the services of an underworld group of Shanghai hoodlums, the "Green Gang," who specialized in kidnapping and extortion, and gave them official respectability as the foundation for his secret police organization.

General Tai also had a long-standing reputation as a xenophobe who rarely met with foreigners.[c] This was why Captain Miles' friend-

[c] One of the few exceptions was Herbert Yardley, director of the War Department's code-breaking "Black Chamber" during the 1920s. When his cryptographic unit was dissolved at the insistence of Secretary of State Stimson, Yardley went to China to establish a code-breaking operation for

ship with the enigmatic general was of such great interest to Lusey.
With the agreement of Chiang Kai-shek, Tai Li had already suggested
to Miles that they cooperate in a Sino-American "friendship plan" for
the training of thousands of Chinese guerrillas and espionage agents.

Miles had at first been suspicious of Tai Li. When he learned that
General Tai's men had developed poisons in the form of Bayer aspirin
tablets and Carter's Little Liver Pills, he rushed home to collect all his
household medicines and lock them away in a four-combination safe.[12]
But his wariness faded, and he soon refused to believe that Tai Li was
"the head of a Chinese OGPU with which anyone from the United
States would be embarrassed to associate." [13] Without consulting Washington, Miles agreed to the "friendship plan."

Lusey had mixed feelings about the project. He informed Washington that Tai Li's organization was "very efficient and we can use it
to great advantage—it is also considered utterly ruthless, and the inner
circle impress me as being a bunch of cut-throats." Nevertheless, to keep
in Miles' good graces, Lusey asked OSS headquarters to help procure
a shipment of short-barrelled shotguns for the use of Tai Li's "swell
bunch of hard-hitting, honest men, good gunmen, in the occupied territories." [14]

In July of 1942 Lusey was called back to Washington and offered
to transmit the "friendship plan" to the Navy Department. As Lusey
began his journey to the United States, Major Eifler and his guerrilla
band had just begun to grow impatient in India and professor Gale was
still operating his worthless "paper mill" in Chungking. General Donovan, in typical OSS fashion, sought to remedy the confusion by sending
yet another special representative to China. The new emissary reached
the Chinese capital in September, his mission cloaked in secrecy. Other
American officials in Chunking could learn only that he suffered from
an acute case of hemorrhoids, acquired while "squatting on a cold stone
floor at Stilwell's headquarters, 'looking at secret maps.' " [15]

The mystery man was another aging professor, Dr. Joseph Hayden,
chairman of the Political Science Department at the University of Michigan. Once a Far East correspondent for the *Christian Science Monitor*,

Tai Li. The outbreak of World War II found him in a similar post in
Canada. In 1942, New York Governor Thomas E. Dewey suggested to
Eleanor Roosevelt that Yardley be hired by OSS, but Donovan refused to
meet with him. (Army Intelligence had advised that Yardley was a security
risk.) Shortly after, Yardley was also dismissed by the Canadian government, reportedly at the personal insistence of Churchill.

Hayden had served as Vice-Governor of the Philippines during the first years of the Roosevelt administration. Arriving at Chungking in the company of OSS research officer and Harvard professor John King Fairbank, Hayden found himself without a mission.[d] Donovan had sent him to China to convince General Stilwell to accept the Eifler team as an autonomous guerrilla and intelligence unit. While en route, however, Hayden received a cable from Washington instructing him to disregard his original instructions and await further orders in Chungking.

In the interim, Hayden renewed old acquaintances with Chinese officials and discussed political and military problems with Chiang's bureaucrats. His most striking observation was the intensity of anti-British sentiment within the Chinese government—a prejudice that had worked to the disadvantage of Eifler's Detachment 101.

Traditional anglophobia was rooted in the suspicion that the British wanted to keep China weak and divided in order to maintain their own imperial strength in Asia. For one particular member of Chiang Kai-shek's entourage, however, hatred of the British was more personal: General Tai Li had been arrested during a trip to Hong Kong in early 1941 by British authorities who identified him as the "head of an intelligence organization modelled on the German Gestapo" with "strong German sympathies." [16] It took the Generalissimo's personal intervention to secure his release.

Tai Li did not forget the affront. He took his revenge later that year when a British-directed commando unit (similar to Eifler's 101) came to China to help organize a guerrilla force. The group had been covertly organized by the Special Operations Executive before Pearl Harbor (Britain was not yet at war with Japan) and was composed primarily of Danish nationals hired as undercover mercenaries. The commando effort was directed from Chungking by SOE officer John Keswick, a partner in the Hong Kong import-export firm of Jardine, Matheson, one of the largest British corporations in the Far East. Chiang Kai-shek soon demanded that one of his generals be given complete control of the operation. Keswick refused. The Generalissimo then ordered that the entire team be withdrawn. When the British ambassador sought to protest, Chiang refused to see him.

As the Keswick group prepared to depart, an official British military mission appeared in China in the spring of 1942. Composed entirely

[d] Fairbank was director of the U.S. Information Service in China, 1945–46, and later a target of McCarthy era witch-hunters. He is now Director of the East Asia Research Center at Harvard.

of British officers (who had also come to work with Chiang's guerrillas), this group found itself blocked at every turn by suspicious and
unfriendly Chinese. Many officers died of disease and starvation, and
the few remaining British soldiers complained bitterly of Chinese jealousy, corruption, and greed.[17]

Tai Li was quick to note that Keswick, after leaving Chungking
in disgust, assumed a new post as SOE advisor to OSS Headquarters
on Far Eastern operations. During the planning of the Eifler mission,
Keswick had warned General Donovan that the Chinese were "not at
all interested in the advice or help of foreigners, but only in the acquiring of equipment." The British officer asserted that there was a "virtually undeclared peace" between the Chinese government and the
Japanese invaders and "our experience is that the Chinese do not welcome foreign prodding to harass the Japanese and disturb the orientally
adjusted calm." Keswick's aide in Washington, a White Russian émigré
who held French citizenship, was more emphatic in publicly voicing
anti-Chiang sentiments. The Chinese embassy finally demanded his
departure.[18]

Since Detachment 101 reached India shortly after the British commando debacle, Tai Li concluded that Eifler was "tied in with the British."[19] The Chinese Himmler had thus become a strange bedfellow
of General Stilwell's in opposing Eifler's operations in China. But Stilwell did not leave the Detachment stranded for long. Pressed by strategic requirements in Burma, he was willing to temporarily forget his
critique of commando tactics. He gave Eifler a "free hand" in directing
sabotage and guerrilla operations in Burma and warned laconically that
"all he wanted was to hear 'Booms' " from the Burmese jungle. Stilwell,
concluded Eifler, "is expecting me to fail. As far as he is concerned, my
failure will be the end of operations and the verification of his belief.
He is testing me by assigning me Burma as a starting point and giving
me the green light."[20] After irately besieging OSS Washington with
requests for operational funds and equipment (which never arrived),
Eifler finally secured $50,000 from Stilwell's own military intelligence
budget and led his team into the Burmese hinterland in mid-September.
Detachment 101 would later perform the most successful OSS guerrilla
operations of the war.

Eifler's departure left the question of the OSS presence in China
undecided until Lusey returned to Chungking in October with new
instructions for Dr. Hayden. General Donovan, at Lusey's suggestion,
had convinced the Navy that Captain Miles and his "friendship plan"

Having dropped his objections to OSS guerrilla tactics, the cantankerous military idealist, Gen. "Vinegar Joe" Stilwell (left), plotted the course of his 1944 Burma campaign with Col. William R. Peers, Carl Eifler's successor as commander of OSS Detachment 101.

should be given official OSS status. To his own amazement, Miles had been named chief of OSS for the Far East.

Stilwell was piqued by the arrangement. He "did not like it a bit," recalled Miles, "that I was out there but not directly under his command." Confidentially the general gave Hayden his sour evaluation of the Tai Li–Miles partnership. "I don't think that the project is worth a damn," he commented tartly. "I don't think that it will advance the war any. But they want it and I'll play along with them." Stilwell, who had undertaken some espionage of his own as military attaché in China before the war, believed that intelligence acquired with the "aid" of the Chinese would be unreliable or deliberately faked. As for the naval captain's personal friendship with Tai Li, Stilwell remarked that "the Chinese had a great nose for money and that to them Miles probably looked like he had lots of it." [21]

Miles seemed equally unhappy with his OSS appointment. The captain, wrote Hayden, was "100 percent Navy and 00 per cent OSS." Miles told the professor in no uncertain terms that "he would tolerate

no 'interference' from OSS. He stated that he could accept no personnel not selected by himself and act upon no directive which he did
not deem wise. If this position were not accepted he would at once
sever all connection with OSS." Nor would Miles tolerate dictation
from Stilwell. The captain believed that "in any difficulty with General Stilwell, he and not the General would be backed by the Generalissimo and that the General dare not 'interfere' with anything he may
do." [22]

If Miles' comments were not sufficient to raise serious doubts
about the "friendship plan," Washington should have been alerted by
Dr. Hayden's own prophetic comment. The Chinese, he observed, who
"envy, hate, or fear Tai Li (and there are many of them) may not
understand this intimate participation of an official foreign group in
the activities of what is almost universally regarded as the Chinese
'Gestapo.' If, in general, American-Chinese relations are on the up-
grade during the next two years, and the 'Friendship Plan' is a success,
it probably will make some contribution toward further improving
those relations. If the relations between the two peoples are deteriorating," concluded Hayden, "it may be seized upon by anti-Americans to
make them even worse." [23]

Why was OSS so determined to ally itself with Miles and Tai Li?
American Army headquarters in Australia provided the answer. While
the COI was still in its infancy in the fall of 1941, General Douglas
MacArthur (who had served with "Wild Bill" Donovan in World
War I) made it abundantly clear that he "saw no reason for the creation of a new intelligence service under Donovan." [24] Some months
later Colonel Warren Clear, a veteran Army intelligence officer and
Japanese specialist, was sent to the South Pacific to investigate the
establishment of a COI espionage network. Clear ran afoul of Mac-
Arthur, and according to the general's aides gave Donovan's organization
a "bad name throughout the Far East." [25]

When Professor Hayden completed his China assignment in December 1942, Donovan dispatched him to MacArthur's headquarters
to make amends. (He was a peculiar choice for this mission, since he
had recently published a book sharply critical of MacArthur's prewar
defense plan for the Philippines.) Hayden reached Australia in January
1943. He extended Donovan's greetings to MacArthur and assured the
general that OSS did not wish "to intrude upon him." Donovan, noted
the professor, was perfectly willing to have any OSS personnel in the
Pacific Theater placed under MacArthur's command. [26]

The haughty general was at first receptive. Though he rejected an OSS plan for guerrilla operations in the Philippines, MacArthur suggested that Donovan's service could perform a valuable function by gathering information in the Netherlands East Indies. Hayden was referred to the general's intelligence aides for further discussion. But these men, to Hayden's amazement, were totally uncooperative; they had already established their own espionage networks in the Pacific and wanted no OSS interference in their area. In late February Hayden was abruptly informed that MacArthur had changed his mind—OSS would not be welcome in the Pacific Theater. The general, according to his belligerent assistants, did not care to discuss the matter further.[e]

This decision stood throughout the war, despite several OSS attempts to breach the Pacific Theater wall. A group of light-hearted OSS officers in Washington even launched a "Penetrate MacArthur" project. "We did get one OSS naval officer to the Philippines," wrote one of the plotters. "To do that required a fantastically complicated conspiracy with Naval Intelligence officers on MacArthur's staff. Our man was captured—not by the enemy—by MacArthur, and sent home." [27] Later in the war gentlemanly antagonism flared when the chief of MacArthur's Psychological Warfare section submitted a plan for secret operations against Japan. The proposal was sent to the War Department and referred to OSS for comment. The Far Eastern experts in Donovan's organization returned it with lengthy criticism. MacArthur's headquarters responded in turn with the acid remark, "Our experts state that your experts are obviously mere superficial observers." [28]

The complete exclusion of OSS from the South Pacific had one important organizational side-effect—Donovan was forced to maintain a Chinese base for Asian operations. At the moment, that meant an unhappy alliance with Miles and Tai Li. When Chiang Kai-shek personally insisted in early 1943 that the "friendship plan" be formalized by a written accord, OSS was in no position to object.

After several months of negotiations, and with Roosevelt's verbal approval, Donovan and Secretary of the Navy Knox put their signatures to a secret technical agreement with the Chinese government. This pact created a joint secret service, the Sino-American Cooperative Organization (SACO), under the directorship of Tai Li. Miles was Deputy Director, as well as Far Eastern chief of OSS and commander of Navy Group/China. SACO was to engage in guerrilla training,

[e] When MacArthur became commander of United Nations troops in Korea in 1951, he similarly refused to allow the CIA to operate in his area of command.

espionage, sabotage, and radio interception. The Chinese agreed to supply manpower and facilities, while arms and equipment would come from the United States.

The agreement came in for immediate criticism from Stilwell's State Department political advisors, John Paton Davies, Jr., and John Service. Both men had been born in China of missionary parents, spoke Chinese fluently, and had long experience in Asian affairs. They considered the SACO arrangement "hopeless and unsound." [29] An official American association with Tai Li's Gestapo, they objected, would have disastrous consequences.

The American military command in China took little note of these protestations although a distaste for Tai Li was one of the few issues on which Generals Stilwell and Chennault might have agreed. Stilwell had discovered Tai Li's agents working as servants in his own home and actually "caught them going through my papers." Recalled Stilwell, "rubber heels and a quick, unexpected return did the trick." [30] And Chennault had already refused a "proffered alliance" between his Fourteenth Air Force and "Tai Li's notorious Kuomintang secret police," [f] who were "engaged in a ruthless manhunt for Communists." [31] Neither general, however, had an adequate opportunity to consider the SACO accord. During the months of negotiation they were locked in a verbal battle to convince Washington of the value of their conflicting military strategies. And while the SACO agreement received final approval in April 1943, both Stilwell and Chennault were en route to Washington to present their military positions to the Joint Chiefs.

No sooner was SACO created than the OSS role in the organization began to disintegrate. Captain Miles flew to Washington in April, and from the moment he ventured into OSS headquarters he displayed a marked hostility toward Donovan's aides. The captain described the OSS Far East planners as starry-eyed reformers and "white supremacists." OSS Deputy Director for Intelligence, General John Magruder (who had commanded an American military mission to China before joining OSS) came in for special criticism because he had once questioned the military capabilities of Chiang Kai-shek's army.[32] Miles was also concerned about the number of "old China hands" in OSS. Before the war, this term had often carried the pejorative meaning of a West-

[f] Yet in 1958 Chennault wrote Miles, "I had worked with your good friend Dai Li at the Generalissimo's request long before you came to China. Dai Li furnished me practically all of the worthwhile intelligence I got for several years."

ern businessman who exploited the Chinese for financial gain. (Later, it would acquire the equally unhappy McCarthy-era reference to alleged subversives in the State Department.)

With an extreme phobia about old China hands who were "gunning for me," Miles insisted that Americans with previous experience in the Far East should be barred from OSS and SACO service in China. Such men, the captain argued, could not work with the Chinese on an equal basis. Many had a "positive dislike of Chiang Kai-shek's government" (to say nothing of Tai Li). These OSS critics of the Chungking regime, complained Miles, were also adhering to the "British imperial line." [33] That comment would have amazed many SOE officials in Washington, who found it impossible to shake the "apparently unlimited faith" of their OSS colleagues "in the fighting capacity of the Chinese nationalists." The SOE men returned to London convinced that "it was something like the sin against the Holy Ghost to express doubt about the value to the allies of Chiang Kai-shek." [34]

Both Miles and the British sought to stereotype an OSS staff which in fact defied generalization. The entire spectrum of American opinion on Chinese politics was represented in Donovan's organization. Even Miles admitted that "some old China hands gave SACO good backing," and he named Norwood Allman as one of his OSS Washington supporters. This Virginia-born attorney had amassed a small fortune practicing international law at Shanghai before the war. He had first achieved some notoriety for his 1927 legal defense of the Russian advisors to the Chinese government, who had been jailed by Chiang Kai-shek after a sudden ideological break with Moscow. Perhaps as a defensive reaction against a lingering suspicion of his "Bolshevik sympathies," Allman had become an unabashed devotee of the Chiang regime (and counsel for some of the more right-wing members of the Kuomintang). After his repatriation from a Japanese prison camp, he joined OSS as chief of a Secret Intelligence section. He spent much of his time briefing OSS officers on the "Chinese personality," [g] and the rest of it in vocally defending the SACO arrangement.[35]

Allman notwithstanding, Miles believed that the OSS China experts and Stilwell's State Department advisors were in league against

[g] Another China expert who briefed OSS men, but with an entirely different point of view, was Professor Owen Lattimore (later accused of Communist sympathies by Joseph McCarthy). Donovan was so impressed with one of Lattimore's books on China that he made it required reading for all OSS men on their way to Chungking.

him. Both State and OSS objected to one of SACO's pet projects—the organization of an "FBI school" for the training of Tai Li's secret police agents. The faculty was headed by a former FBI agent in naval uniform and eventually grew into a unit of fifty men that included Narcotics Bureau agents and police officers from the New York Bomb Squad, with a Mississippi district attorney thrown in for good measure. Chinese secret police agents were instructed in the use of lie detectors and shown the value of police dogs. To OSS this seemed a blatant attempt on the part of Tai Li to secure American sanction of the Kuomintang's internal political repression.[36]

Miles interpreted Washington's objections as further evidence of an OSS plot to destroy the SACO agreement. He continued to complain that old China hands were being sent into the country without his approval. He criticized Washington's plan to train SACO officers at OSS installations. He engaged in heated debate with R. Davis Halliwell, the New York textile executive who then headed the Special Operations Branch in Washington, and he objected when OSS launched operations in Thailand and Tibet which were not under his direct supervision.

Washington's decision to send American representatives to the remote theocratic government of Tibet had been made long before Miles assumed his OSS post. The State Department wished to assure the young Dalai Lama of American friendship; the War Department was interested in a possible military supply route between India and China through the Tibetan mountains. Because of the dangers of land travel to Lhasa, capital of Tibet, OSS was given responsibility for the military-diplomatic mission. Chosen for the assignment were Ilia Tolstoy,[h] émigré grandson of the famous Russian novelist, and Brooke Dolan, an accomplished adventurer and Far Eastern explorer.

The two officers left New Delhi in September 1942, and after a gruelling three-month journey reached Lhasa in December. The ten-year-old Dalai Lama received them as formal ambassadors of President Roosevelt, official gifts were exchanged (including a $2800 timepiece from FDR), and all went well. But then the subject of a radio transmitter was broached. The Tibetan government had no long-range broadcasting device with which to communicate with the remote regions of the country. Could the Americans supply one? The request

[h] Tolstoy later became general manager of a Marineland in Florida, worked on motion picture productions, and cultivated sponge beds in the Bahamas.

seemed simple enough and was relayed to OSS headquarters in Washington. While preparations were made for the dispatch of the equipment, flustered State Department officials learned of the request. The gift, they objected, would be "politically embarrassing and cause irritation and offense to the Chinese," who had territorial claims on Tibet. Chiang Kai-shek's government "would not welcome the introduction into Tibet of such a potent facility as a radio transmitter," since the Chinese would not "have any control over the transmitter or the material broadcasted." Fearful of offending "Chinese susceptibilities," the State Department urged OSS to drop the proposal immediately.[37]

Before leaving the Tibetan capital in March 1943, Tolstoy wrote Donovan, "I hope that the 'wireless question' will be settled in favor of the people that have asked for it." (It was. The radio reached Tibet in November.) "We were treated by everyone very well and I hope that we have laid a good foundation here. I know that they like the U.S.A. better now and know more about it." As the OSS men left Lhasa to begin a five-month trek to the Chinese border, they felt a "moment of sadness at leaving our friends behind." [38]

On the journey to China, Tolstoy frequently heard rumors of an impending Chinese invasion of Tibet. He and Dolan became increasingly sympathetic to the Tibetan fear of China's intentions. The American officers were themselves concerned that they might meet with a Chinese "taxi accident" before reaching Chungking.

They arrived safely, however, in July 1943. Their reports stressed the pro-Allied feeling in Lhasa and the belief of Tibetan officials that "the U.S. has no axe to grind in middle Asia." [39] The OSS men also "strongly intimated" to the American embassy that "the United States should support the Tibetans vis-à-vis the Chinese government." The Chinese Foreign Office complained that the OSS officers had already promised the Tibetans American support "in their desire to remain independent of China." [40] There was talk of a new OSS mission for Tolstoy and Dolan, to outer Mongolia. Washington, nevertheless, cited the men for an "ingenious employment of diplomacy, tact, and adaptability" and they were flown back to the United States. Months later, to the further consternation of Tai Li, Brooke Dolan reappeared—as an OSS representative to the Chinese Communists.

Miles and Tai Li condemned OSS for undertaking such missions without SACO's consent and they sought to block further expansion of Donovan's agency in China. In the fall of 1943, the Morale Operations Branch of OSS (which disbursed "black propaganda") planned to send

On their sensitive diplomatic mission to the "Forbidden City" of Lhasa, the Tibetan capital, OSS Captains Brooke Dolan (center) and Ilia Tolstoy (left), grandson of the Russian novelist, paused with their Sepoy guide at an imposing Buddhist shrine.

a team of officers to Chungking, but Tai Li withheld his approval. The MO Branch chief for the Far East, Major Herbert Little, then flew to Chungking for a confrontation with the Chinese master spy.

Little, a British-born Seattle attorney who had traveled extensively in the Far East,[i] remembered his meeting with Tai Li: "Upon arrival at Tai Li's headquarters, after meeting with the navy personnel, we and Mary Miles and his subordinate officers were invited to a dinner, hosted by Tai Li himself. For some time prior to eating, during dinner, and afterward, we were continually being served a strong Chinese wine. Waiters were constantly refilling our glasses as all of us proposed toasts, each in his turn, and with each of us finishing our toasts with Gam-Pei (meaning 'bottoms up'). . . . I suspected that the 'orange blossom' wine had been spiked with knockout drops, a trick of Tai Li's of which I had been forewarned. . . . Knowing that after dinner I would be having a serious talk with Tai Li I limited my wine drinks to two or three. During the dinner, several, in fact most of the officers, American and Chinese, either passed out or got sleepy or sick."

Following their sumptuous meal, Little and Tai Li retired to another house for a private discussion. "After the first two hours of our conversation, we made no progress at all," writes Little. "Tai Li was adamant and evasive although superbly gracious. He was a great actor with talent which I could not fail to recognize. He could have been a first-rate Hamlet. . . . Now was the time, I thought, to become firm in my demands. I told him that I had the full support and backing of General Donovan, the chief of OSS, and that, furthermore, if necessary, I would go to the President of the United States himself and suggest to him that the whole question of U.S. aid to China be reviewed in view of Tai Li's stand. . . . This seemed to break the ice. After about another hour of conversation, he agreed. And so, at about 3 o'clock in the morning, I wrote out a very informal understanding that our MO personnel could operate in China and we stamped our name chops on this. Mission accomplished." [41]

Many of Little's OSS colleagues were less fortunate in their dealings with SACO. Miles refused to allow the small OSS research office at Chungking to handle intelligence information from any source but Tai Li's espionage bureau, and he brought naval personnel to China who were not under OSS jurisdiction. Miles never thought of himself as an OSS officer and felt no responsibility to defend the agency or its operations. He continually demanded his right to control an organization to which he felt no loyalty, while he remained dedicated to a Chinese general hated by his own countrymen.

[i] Not to be confused with OSS veteran Lester Little, who was Inspector General of Chiang Kai-shek's Customs Service, 1944–50; New York representative of the CIA-funded Committee for Free Asia, 1951–53; and Personnel Director of the U.S. Information Agency, 1955–60.

By August 1943, Miles had outlived his usefulness to OSS. That month a new Anglo-American South East Asia Command was established in India. General Donovan quickly concluded an operating agreement with the commander of the Delhi-based headquarters, Lord Louis Mountbatten, which enabled OSS to expand its activities on the Asian mainland. This arrangement gave OSS greater freedom in dealing with Miles and Tai Li; an upset in the China organization would no longer force the complete exclusion of OSS from the Far East.

The stage was set for imminent confrontation between OSS and SACO in November, when Roosevelt asked Chiang Kai-shek to meet with him in Cairo before the Big Three Conference at Teheran. The Generalissimo accepted the invitation and led an official exodus to Egypt later that month. Chennault and Stilwell went along to continue their still unresolved strategic debate. After lengthy discussions with the President, Chiang and his American friend Chennault returned together to Chungking, leaving Stilwell in Cairo to await the outcome of the Teheran talks. General Donovan, who had also come to Cairo to advise Roosevelt on the thorny Yugoslav question, picked this moment to make his move. He flew from Egypt to India in the company of Lord Louis Mountbatten, then on to the Chinese capital, arriving on December 2.

At his first meeting with Tai Li, Donovan found the Chinese general to be a "mediocre policeman with medieval ideas of intelligence work." He reportedly pointed his finger at Tai Li and declared, "I'm going to have the OSS here run the way I want it, with no interference from you or anybody else!" Then he added solemnly, "General, I want you to know that I am going to send my men into China whether you like it or not. I know that you can have them murdered one by one, but I want you to know that will not deter me." [42]

Miles was next on Donovan's list. The captain repeated his charges that OSS had repeatedly violated the SACO agreement. "I don't agree with writing one thing and doing another. I quit," roared Miles. "You can't quit," Donovan answered. "You're fired." [43] On December 5, Miles was officially removed from his OSS post (though he retained his position as Deputy Director of SACO). He was replaced as OSS chief in China by 36-year-old Colonel John Coughlin, a six-foot-five West Pointer from Arizona who had served as Carl Eifler's Executive Officer since the first days of Detachment 101's Burma operations.

OSS now required a new guardian angel in China. Donovan's first choice was Air Force General Chennault. There was no doubt that

Chennault stood in Chiang's good graces and that he retained the confidence of the Generalissimo; OSS needed such political support to overcome the hostility of Tai Li, Chiang's loyal henchman.

Would Chennault accept a role as patron of Donovan's secret service? The OSS chief was optimistic, knowing that he had several warm supporters in the Flying Tiger camp. Chennault's close friend and advisor, journalist Joseph Alsop, had two brothers—Stewart and John—serving with OSS in Europe. Another OSS enthusiast was Colonel Merian Cooper, a conservative adventurer and film director ("King Kong" was his masterpiece) who had left the Visual Presentation Branch of Donovan's COI to become Chennault's Chief of Staff in mid-1942. Later that year, Cooper sent a personal letter to his friend Donovan, bitterly criticizing Stilwell's strategic doctrines. Donovan obliged by circulating the letter around official Washington (prompting Cooper's recall by an irate War Department).[44] Chennault had taken notice of Donovan's Washington influence. When Dr. Hayden came to Chungking that fall, the Flying Tiger chief assured the professor that unlike his rival Stilwell he had a "keen interest" in the development of an OSS intelligence network.[45]

Pursuing Chennault's hint before leaving Chungking, Donovan offered the Air Force general a new bureaucratic alliance which, the OSS chief hoped, would protect his organization from the wrath of its SACO antagonists.

The battle of the secret services was overshadowed in early 1944 by the return of the Chinese Communists to the political limelight. Since 1927, when Chiang Kai-shek abruptly severed his union with the Communists and instituted a reign of terror against his former political allies, there had been intermittent periods of civil war in China. Chiang's armies finally forced the leftists to flee their base in south China in the famous "Long March" to the north. They established a new headquarters at Yenan, out of the reach of Chiang and Tai Li, and found leadership in the brilliant revolutionary, Mao Tse-tung.

The Japanese invasion of north China in 1937 brought the Communists and the Kuomintang together in a short-lived "united front." When the shaky alliance disintegrated (despite renewed Japanese aggression), Chiang instituted a rigid military blockade of the Communist stronghold using twenty divisions of his best troops. OSS estimated that the bulk of Chungking's military effort was directed against the Communists rather than the Japanese.

Even before Pearl Harbor, General Donovan had received information that Chinese Communist soldiers were "the best guerrilla troops in the world, trained under veteran leaders of long experience in such tactics, and fired by a bitter hatred of the Japanese." [46] In November 1941, Donovan first proposed that an American undercover mission be sent to north China to work with the Communist partisans. Roosevelt felt the plan had "some merit" and asked his cabinet advisors for comment. Conservatives in the State Department warned of opposition from both Chiang Kai-shek and the suspicious Soviets. The War Department noted critically that the Communist guerrillas were "too short of arms, ammunition, and equipment to carry on as they once did. One of the primary reasons for this shortage has been the Central Government's blockade of their area. If Chiang Kai-shek is unwilling to equip or supply these troops for a task they are admirably fitted to perform, it appears too much to expect that the presence of a few Americans in that region would alter his policy." [47] Donovan's proposal was tabled.

For the next three years, rumors of increasing Communist strength in the north remained a matter for frustrated speculation at the American embassy in Chungking. When Miles first reached China in May 1942, he was already "convinced" that the Communist army "is not on my side of this war." But, the captain quickly added, "despite this, I am wondering if I can't get their fleet of twenty-five hundred junks which are reportedly operating on the Yellow and Yangtze Rivers to do some work for the United States." [48]

In the spring of 1944, Stilwell's headquarters, under the pressure of a new Japanese offensive against central China, began to take an interest in the Communist military. OSS again turned an eye toward Yenan. Donovan's officers at Chungking could no longer ignore reports that the Communists controlled a force of one million partisans and intelligence agents in an area of major Japanese troop concentration which was then a blind-spot for American intelligence. John King Fairbank, the Harvard China expert and chief of the OSS Research office in Chungking, repeatedly told his superiors that the Communists, "anxious both to defeat Japan and help the Americans," were also "in a very strategic position for getting information on North China." [49]

While American officials discussed the possibilities of direct communication with Yenan, OSS had at last established its new intelligence organization. In April 1944, Donovan christened a cover group with the unlikely title of the 5329th Air and Ground Forces Resources Technical Staff (Provisional), popularly known to OSS cynics as "Ag-farts." For OSS, the new group, which assumed all the intelligence duties of Chennault's Fourteenth Air Force, meant genuine independence from SACO and Tai Li.

For pro forma purposes, a small group of several dozen OSS men remained under nominal SACO control. This unfortunate contingent was commanded by a 29-year-old OSS major from Detachment 101, and his SI chief, a Hong Kong representative of the First National City Bank. Colonel Coughlin, Donovan's new commander in China, was even named a second Deputy Director of Tai Li's organization. But the locus of OSS activity had, in reality, shifted to AGFRTS. Coughlin soon moved his own headquarters from SACO's Chungking base to the city of Kunming, the site of Chennault's command, located several hundred miles to the southwest of the Chinese capital.

The AGFRTS alliance with Chennault was of little consequence to Stilwell, who spent the first half of 1944 with his combat troops in Burma. But the new group did serve as a direct affront to SACO. Miles, now a Commodore, complained that AGFRTS was "empire building, duplicating our entire service." [50] Even more stinging was AGFRTS' absorption of Chennault's own intelligence officers, most of whom "had lived in China before the war, spoke the language, knew the customs, and could live in the field on Chinese food." [51] The commander of the new unit, Lieutenant Colonel Wilfred Smith, was a nervous China-born missionary's son in his early thirties; he had learned to speak Chinese before English, and held a Ph.D. in Oriental History from the University of Michigan. Smith and his first AGFRTS recruits were, in other words, old China hands, the Asian specialists Miles found so objectionable.

Another irony of the AGFRTS alliance with Chennault was that it also opened the ranks of OSS China to some of the most ardent critics of the general's good friend and supporter, Chiang Kai-shek. Major Paul Frillmann, a 32-year-old AGFRTS pioneer, had first come to China in 1936 as a Lutheran missionary.ʲ He remained, after America's entry into the war, as chaplain to the Flying Tigers and an adept Fourteenth Air Force intelligence officer. Frillmann's love for the Chinese people was equalled only by his antagonism toward their governmental overlords. He detested Tai Li, who had "an unsavory name as a

ʲ Frillmann served as chief of the U.S. Information Service in Shanghai and Hong Kong, 1947–52. He resigned from the State Department during the McCarthy era witch-hunt.

persecutor of all critics of Chiang," and he had no greater respect for
the Generalissimo. Chiang and his cohorts, Frillmann believed, regarded the Chinese peasants as "nothing but an endlessly exploitable
source of money, food, and conscripts. They made no special effort to
help the front-line villagers against the enemy. They exorbitantly increased taxes, and had done nothing to curb the growing land monopo-
lies of the rich, including their own officials." Throughout provincial
China, Frillmann had seen "the growth of genuine popular feeling
against Chiang's monopoly of power." [52]

Frillmann's views were shared by another early AGFRTS recruit,
Captain Charles Stelle, 34, a Harvard professor of oriental studies,
born and educated in Peking.[k] He had first headed the China section of
the OSS Research Branch in Washington, but sought a more active role
in the war. In early 1944, he was dispatched to Chungking as an intelligence officer. He soon became an important OSS link to the Chinese
Communists.

Stilwell's State Department advisors had long urged the United
States to establish formal contact with the Yenan Communists, a proposal that acquired military urgency in the spring of 1944. Roosevelt
put the question to the Generalissimo, but, not surprisingly, Chiang
opposed American dealings with his political enemies. The issue remained in limbo until June, when Vice-President Henry Wallace came
to China for strategic talks with Chiang. Anxious to strengthen his
political hand against Stilwell by demonstrating a continuing spirit of
"cooperation" with the Americans, the Generalissimo abruptly waived
his previous objections to an American mission to the Communists. He
assured Wallace that an observer group could leave for Yenan as soon
as possible.

That was very soon indeed, for the mission had been planned
months earlier. Colonel David Barrett, a China specialist for Army
intelligence and a close friend of Stilwell's, was selected as commander.
Accompanying him were State Department advisor John Service and
fifteen other American military personnel, five of them from OSS. The
senior OSS officer was 25-year-old China-born Captain John Colling,
the son of an American officer who had served for some twenty years
in the U.S. Army unit at Tientsin.[l] Colling, who had just left a demoli-

[k] Stelle was Deputy Director of State Department Intelligence, 1951;
a member of the State Department's Policy Planning Staff, 1951–56; and
acting American delegate to the Nuclear Test Ban Conference in 1960.
[l] Colling was security chief of the Marshall mission to China, 1948–
49. He now operates a manufacturing company in Hong Kong.

tions post with Detachment 101 in Burma, was joined at the Communist stronghold by OSS Captains Charles Stelle, the AGFRTS Harvard professor, Brooke Dolan of the earlier OSS mission to Tibet, and two sergeants.

Barrett's group, dubbed the Dixie Mission, was given a wide range of hurriedly concocted intelligence assignments. They were to report on the military capabilities of the Japanese in north China and to assess as well the military potential of the Communists. These tasks became the prime responsibility of Colling's OSS group.

The first Dixie contingent flew to Yenan on July 24, 1944. They were cheerfully greeted by Chou En-lai and other Communist dignitaries and taken to the famous Yenan caves which housed Mao's headquarters. Even before their briefings by the Communist commanders were over, the OSS men became convinced "that as sources of information about the Japanese, the Communists were all we had hoped they would be, and even more." [53] Colling and his fellow officers were given free access to 150 Japanese prisoners of war, and to the Japanese Communists in exile who had fled to Yenan. Within a month, the OSS executive officer at Kunming, Colonel Robert Hall, a geography professor and Japanese specialist from the University of Michigan, had devised an operational plan to send Japanese Communist intelligence agents to Manchuria, Korea, and the Japanese homeland. Formerly chief of the OSS office in San Francisco, Colonel Hall had already recruited a small unit of Japanese-American leftists for OSS service. He felt the Yenan Japanese had even greater potential for espionage activities.

The delight of OSS headquarters with its new intelligence cornucopia at Yenan was lost in the hubbub of an official purge of the American military bureaucracy in China. For over a year, Chiang Kai-shek had become increasingly critical of General Stilwell, that bothersome military reformer. Hoping to salvage Chinese-American unity from this personal battle, Roosevelt sent a special emissary to Chungking in August to pacify the Generalissimo. The President's representative was Patrick Hurley, a right-wing Republican and millionaire attorney from Oklahoma who had served as Secretary of War under Hoover and frequently acted as international trouble-shooter for FDR. Hurley was ill-equipped to deal with the complexities of Chinese political intrigue, but even a latter-day Machiavelli would have been hard put to achieve Washington's dual objectives—to secure for Stilwell the command of all Chinese armies and to convince Chiang of the need for a military alliance with the Communists.

With the famous Yenan caves in the distance, Mao Tse-tung (seated, far left) joined his American friends of the Dixie Mission in reviewing Communist military exercises during the summer of 1944. The group included OSS Captains John Colling (third from right) and Charles Stelle (second from right).

That was the emergency formula approved by the Joint Chiefs of Staff in the hope of blocking the Japanese offensive that threatened to engulf central China. In September, Hurley and Stilwell began their talks with Chiang and seemed to be making some progress. Washington, however, was restive and, on September 19, Roosevelt sent the Generalissimo a harsh and intemperate personal message which demanded military action and reform. "The harpoon," Stilwell recalled, "hit the little bugger right in the solar plexus." [54] Chiang's response was tempestuous. He blamed the insult on Stilwell and demanded his immediate recall. Roosevelt was forced to comply. On October 18, Stilwell was relieved of his command. He was replaced by General Albert Wedemeyer, then serving as chief of staff to British Admiral Mountbatten at the South East Asia Command in Ceylon.

How did the "Stilwell affair" affect OSS? In October 1944, the organization's political fortunes in China were not especially high. AGFRTS commander Wilfred Smith lodged frequent complaints that OSS headquarters had promised far more support than he had received. To balance the AGFRTS command with an officer "thoroughly loyal to OSS," Philip Crowe, an advertising executive of *Fortune* magazine who had spent several years in the Orient as a "big game hunter," was transferred from his post as chief of the SI Branch in India to become Smith's executive officer.[m] In the months that followed, AGFRTS operations did expand (by late 1944 there were one hundred AGFRTS men working in the field), but Chennault's own dedication to the project seemed to wane after SACO's naval officers established "effective liaison" with the Fourteenth Air Force. Chennault "liked any help we could give," wrote Miles, "and he helped us in return." [55]

While OSS participation in the Dixie Mission provided American officers with access to valuable Communist intelligence, it was also a potential source of embarrassment. SACO took every opportunity to villify Donovan's officers for "working with the Communists." The Chungking regime had already received word of the reports that State Department officer John Service sent from Yenan, advocating more extensive American dealings with the Communists. And while Captains Colling and Stelle left political reporting to Service, their proposals for increased OSS cooperation with Yenan provided potent ammunition for the Miles–Tai Li propaganda mill.

The OSS reputation in Chungking was already at a low ebb in the summer of 1944 when a battalion of Kachin guerrillas from the Burma hills crossed the border into China under the command of OSS Detachment 101 officers. They came to retaliate against Chinese soldiers of the local Kuomintang warlord who had looted and destroyed nine Burmese villages. The Kachins and their OSS leaders attacked the garrisons of these Chinese soldier-bandits and then withdrew into Burma. Rumor had it that the OSS men found evidence that the "bandits" were actually operating under carte blanche orders personally signed by Chiang Kai-shek and approved by Tai Li. The Kachin raid created a stir in Chungking. Chiang Kai-shek sent a personal memorandum to the new Detachment 101 commander, Colonel Ray Peers.[n] (Carl Eifler had been relieved of his command at the same time as "Mary" Miles.) The Generalissimo demanded the payment of 25 million

[m] Crowe served as ambassador to Ceylon, 1953–56, and ambassador to the Union of South Africa, 1959–61. In 1969, he was appointed ambassador to Norway, succeeding another OSS veteran, Margaret Tibbets, who had held that post since 1964.

[n] Peers was chief of CIA training in 1949. In 1951, as CIA station chief on Formosa, he began training Chiang Kai-shek's commandos for covert raids against the Communist mainland. Now a Lieutenant General, Peers recently directed the Army's investigation of the My Lai massacre in Vietnam.

American dollars for damages inflicted on Chinese property. This request was dropped when an official Sino-American Army investigation diplomatically concluded that all parties to the dispute had been at fault. But the incident did not bolster the OSS popularity in Chiang's official family.[56]

OSS therefore took the occasion of Stilwell's recall to improve the outlook of its political prospectus on the Asian mainland. Major Quentin Roosevelt, a 24-year-old grandson of Theodore Roosevelt, was recruited by OSS in Europe and flown to Chungking as General Donovan's personal representative to the Chiang government.[o] It was a shrewd selection; Roosevelt's father, an old and intimate friend of the Generalissimo and Madame Chiang's, had been President of United China Relief in the United States.

Donovan then sent a new OSS commander to Kunming. Colonel Richard Heppner, 35, a graduate of Princeton and Columbia Law School (and an attorney from Donovan's law firm) had also been carefully selected for his post.[p] He and the new Theater commander, General Wedemeyer, were the best of friends. They had lived in the same barracks in Ceylon while Heppner was OSS commander at the South East Asia Command. Stilwell's replacement was already known to take a "friendly and close interest" in OSS activities. Two years before, Wedemeyer, as an Army staff officer in Washington, had helped prepare the first Joint Chiefs operational directive for Donovan's organization. Commodore Miles was justified in his fear that Wedemeyer reached Chungking determined to "transfer much of SACO's work" to OSS.[57]

Heppner's unit was swelled by the arrival of OSS veterans from the European Theater. By the end of 1944, Athens, Belgrade, Rome, Paris, and Brussels had been liberated, and battle-tested intelligence officers and saboteurs were flown by the dozens to the Far East for new assignments. The sudden influx only intensified the divisions of opinion on Chinese politics that had always existed within OSS. At one end of the spectrum, the voices of Chiang Kai-shek's admirers (who had proved so irritating to the British) were still to be heard. In Washington, OSS acquired the services of Freda Utley, a former British Com-

---

[o] Roosevelt returned to China after the war as Shanghai manager of the China National Aviation Corporation, a Pan Am subsidiary. He was killed in a plane crash near Hong Kong in 1948.

[p] Heppner was Deputy Assistant Secretary of Defense for International Security Affairs during the Eisenhower administration.

munist who had once lived in China as an advisor on Asian affairs. She was brought into the Donovan organization by C. V. Starr, an American businessman who had operated a very successful Asian insurance company in Shanghai before the war. Starr committed the unforgivable sin of helping OSS to establish a Chinese intelligence network that was independent of SACO; he was definitely on Tai Li's blacklist.[q] Miss Utley, however, had better relations with the Kuomintang. Having left the Communist Party with bitterly anti-Soviet sentiments (her Russian husband had been arrested in the Stalin purges), she became a fervent devotee of the Generalissimo. While working as a consultant for OSS, Miss Utley privately received a salary from the Chinese government for writing pro-Chiang propaganda in the United States. "I saw no conflict of interest," she wrote, "since it was all to the good of both China and America that a convinced and knowledgeable anti-Communist such as I should be sending reports analyzing Chinese developments and attitudes for the U.S. government while helping the Chinese embassy combat the Chinese Communist lobby in America." [58]

Freda Utley's enthusiasm for the Chungking regime was shared by Catholic Bishop Thomas Megan. A long-time China resident, Megan worked in Japanese occupied territory, well-armed and dressed in an unpriestly khaki uniform, as a leader of a Chinese guerrilla brigade. The bishop served both OSS and SACO in partisan operations, but he had a particular liking for Tai Li. In fact, he believed the Chinese spy chief to be "one of the most capable and businesslike Chinese he had ever come into contact with." [59]

If Megan and Utley were vocal in their beliefs, so were OSS critics of the Chunking government. Many of the research analysts of the China section at OSS Headquarters had informal ties to the Institute of Pacific Relations, created in 1924 by YMCA officials from a dozen nations who believed that the Asian area was being overlooked in the study of world affairs. The YMCA affiliation soon disappeared, and professors and businessmen with an interest in the Far East came together to form a permanent Institute with a considerable international membership. The American Council of IPR brought top executives of American corporations with Asian interests into contact with academic specialists. But its business link was no hindrance

[q] After the war, C. V. Starr organized one of the largest international insurance groups in the world; the Starr group allegedly has close financial ties to some Nationalist Chinese on Formosa.

to the IPR's political liberalism. The Institute (later a prime target of McCarthy era demagogues) helped the OSS Research Branch recruit old China hands and Far Eastern experts who were forthright in their criticism of the Chiang regime.

There were also Chiang critics in the field. One of the most informed and outspoken was Lieutenant Colonel Harley Stevens, commander of the OSS detachment at Chungking and General Wedemeyer's personal selection as director of the China Command War Room.[r] Stevens seemed a typical OSS executive—44 years old, Republican, and a corporate attorney from the most prestigious law firm in San Francisco. But he was far more imaginative and politically adept than many of his high-ranking OSS colleagues. From the moment of his arrival in China in August 1944, Stevens was disillusioned with the "reactionary, or better, moribund leadership" of the Kuomintang, "from the Gissimo on down."

"We thought originally," he wrote, "and still think we are here to beat the Japanese and establish the foundations of a lasting peace in Asia. That is the inflexible goal; but the means should be flexible. . . . It appears to some we are not only limiting ourselves unduly in choosing Chiang Kai-shek as the sole instrument of beating the Japanese —which certainly will take us longer and be more expensive in 'men and treasure'—but indeed we are mistaking one of the means for the end." [60]

Stevens found support from OSS old China hands, many of them ex-missionaries or officials of the numerous Christian colleges in China. These people had no love for Communist atheism; some were friendly with the handful of liberals in the Chungking government. But, unlike Bishop Megan, their religious beliefs served only to strengthen their opposition to the Kuomintang's corrupt and callous disregard for the welfare of the Chinese people. China hands were especially appalled by the extent of high-level Chinese collaboration with the Japanese, which they interpreted as a further reflection of personal greed in the government.

One OSS team of three old China hands, all bilingual in Mandarin, was sent to New Delhi for a special (and politically sensitive) investigation. OSS Major Oliver Caldwell, a former professor of English at Nanking University, was assigned the task of probing a Japanese

[r] As vice-president of the American Independent Oil Company, 1952–59, Stevens negotiated oil agreements with the governments of Kuwait, Saudi Arabia, and Iran.

infiltration of the Chinese embassy in India.[s] (Tai Li's men were often too busy hunting Communists to worry about enemy agents.) With the aid of Rosamond Frame, the vivacious daughter of a Chinese Christian university dean, and Joy Homer, a young liberal writer who had worked on flood relief committees in north China, Caldwell exposed two officials at the Chinese embassy who were transmitting information to the Japanese in Singapore. Miss Frame's recompense from the Chinese government was a file in Tai Li's secret police records listing her as a "dangerous thinker." [61] Miss Homer was brutally attacked by unknown assailants on the streets of Chungking and injured so severely that she died a year later at the age of thirty-one.

Other American officers who "had to check up on known or suspected Japanese agents found trails leading into the highest circles. Then the investigation would have to be dropped, to avoid embarrassing an ally." OSS was forced to subsidize its own band of smugglers at the Sino-Burmese border, since the only existing route of contraband was "operated by wealthy and politically influential Chinese" who were "utilizing present war conditions to enrich themselves." [62]

OSS intelligence files at Chungking (conscientiously maintained by a jolly amateur chef named Julia McWilliams Child) bulged with reports about the incompetence of the Chinese military command.[t] In November 1944, when Japanese troops began an offensive that threatened Chennault's air bases, groups of OSS demolition teams were sent to destroy equipment that might be captured by the enemy. A fifteen-man team commanded by a 25-year-old veteran of Detachment 101 discovered three huge ammunition dumps which held tons of arms and supplies. They were told the equipment had been collected and hoarded for years against a crisis in east China. With the Japanese only twenty miles away, the bungling Chinese Army commanders were still zealously hoarding the materiel. The Americans were forced to destroy the entire stores only hours before the Japanese entered the town.[63]

Other OSS officers were sickened by the treatment the Chinese government afforded its own troops. An OSS doctor who helped select Chinese soldiers for guerrilla training described the conditions in their army as a "crime against humanity." [64] Another OSS man wrote, "These amazing Chinese soldiers and coolies possessed nothing—absolutely

[s] Caldwell served as Assistant Commissioner of the U.S. Office of Education during the Kennedy Administration. He is now Dean of International Services at Southern Illinois University.

[t] Mrs. Child is now known as television's "French Chef."

nothing—in the way of bedding equipment, and very little clothing. They ate two meals a day, consisting of several bowls of rice with a few greens and, if they were lucky, a little pork. Upon camping for the night, they would gather around charcoal fires in cold rooms of the village mud huts and would huddle together under a few borrowed dirty, thin blankets." [65]

OSS convoys were frequently attacked by Chinese government troops posing as "bandits." In April 1945, a convoy led by AGFRTS Captain Robert North, a Hollywood writer, was "held up by a gang of wild-eyed, shouting, blood-thirsty bandits. . . . I fully expected to be casually knocked off in cold blood so they could get on with the looting. . . . I was picked clean; my pockets, my wrists, my .32 and holster, my two green jackets, and even my vest pocket notebook. . . . I expected to lose my shirt, pants, and shoes, but about that time they moved on to loot the car, and the goodies they found there distracted them so completely from bedeviling me with cocked rifles that it probably saved my life." North made his way to the office of the local Chinese magistrate and police chief and "really ate their asses out for allowing American allies to be harmed and robbed not by Japs, because we are on guard against them, but by their own countrymen, who they certainly ought to be able to control. Here we lost our young men's lives flying this scarce equipment over the Hump, struggling and worrying to get it behind the Jap lines . . . and then this little is stolen in broad daylight and murder is openly attempted on China's friends. They visibly sagged as I poured it on." But, explained the Chinese officials, the scene of the robbery was out of their geographical jurisdiction. The OSS captain then "rose to my fullest stature in rare Ciceronian style" and demanded that troops be dispatched to retrieve the equipment. Only after he noted that the stolen materiel included a bottle of heart pills from General Chennault to the local warlord were soldiers sent to search for the "bandits." [66]

All these operational hazards were crowned by a virtual "range war" between OSS and SACO in the provinces. OSS headquarters suspected, but could not definitively prove, that Tai Li's operatives were murdering Chinese agents who worked for OSS.[67] Even Chiang Kai-shek's admirers within Donovan's organization were hard put to justify the actions of Tai Li, the Generalissimo's most loyal aide. By the end of 1944, SACO was at war with OSS and it was a rare American officer who could view General Tai and the Chungking government in entirely different lights.

Less than a month after Wedemeyer assumed command in Chung-king, Patrick Hurley, the President's special representative to the Generalissimo, was named American ambassador to China, replacing a veteran diplomat whose critical view of the Kuomintang was more attuned to Stilwell's line of thinking. Though Hurley had failed miserably on his first mission to create harmony between Chiang and Stilwell, he was now faced with an even more perplexing assignment—to unify the Communist and Kuomintang armies against the Japanese. The State Department, Wedemeyer, Chennault, and the members of the Dixie Mission at Yenan all agreed on the need for such tactical unity. The real question was the extent of Washington's commitment to the Chiang government. Some State Department and OSS officials believed that American policy should have greater political flexibility in dealing with the Generalissimo. Colonel Harley Stevens, the San Francisco corporation attorney, then serving as OSS liaison to Ambassador Hurley, complained, "All you hear now is affirmations from everybody of our

General Tai Li (right), the ruthless "Chinese Himmler," and U.S. Navy Commodore Milton Miles (left), were the rivals of OSS China. Here the SACO chiefs posed with one of the many warlords who formed the political foundation of Chiang Kai-shek's regime.

support for the Kuomintang party and its leader. Everybody is shouting that so loudly, that it has become the goal. . . . Blind to our
avowed aims and ends, we talk about all-out support of Chiang which
denies support to others, and many feel [this] makes certain that a
bloody civil war will follow." [68]

Hurley was a poor choice to deal with such a delicate and complex
situation. The ambassador was a believer in "personal diplomacy"; as
he remarked to one OSS officer, "When I think I can risk telling the
Generalissimo a dirty joke, I'll feel I'm really getting somewhere." [69]
Hurley was atrociously uninformed about Chinese affairs. His favorite
stunt of yelling Oklahoma Indian war whoops branded him as a buffoon.
He reinforced that impression by referring to Chiang as "Mr. Shek"
and to the leader of the Yenan Communists as "Moose Dung." OSS
men responded by assigning Hurley a special code-name—"The Al-
batross."

Soon after Hurley's arrival in China, the Communists had invited
him to visit Yenan. He flew to their stronghold for the first time on
November 7 and was given a warm greeting. Hurley's meetings with
Mao led to the Communist acceptance of five principles of "coalition
government." Returning to Chungking in the company of Chou En-lai,
the ambassador presented the proposal to the Generalissimo. He rejected it and suggested a counter-offer which was refused by the Communists. The Yenan leaders also declined participation in any further
negotiations.

While this political jockeying was in progress, the military situation
had deteriorated so badly that Army strategists were secretly discussing
contingency plans for the evacuation of Chungking. Wedemeyer's headquarters also framed new proposals for military cooperation with the
Communist armies. These were dutifully discussed with central government officials who just as dutifully rejected them out of hand.

At the end of November, Colonel Heppner's headquarters received
word that General Donovan would soon visit China. Wedemeyer
planned to take the occasion to present the OSS chief with some comprehensive ideas for assistance to Communist guerrilla forces. Two
separate proposals emerged. The Army recommended that five thousand American paratroopers be sent to north China to work with the
Communist partisans. OSS set forth its own plan to dispatch Special
Operations officers to the north on sabotage missions against the Japanese. In return for the complete cooperation and support of the Communist forces, OSS was prepared to train and outfit 25,000 Yenan guer-

rillas and to furnish Mao's Army with an additional 100,000 pistols. This proposal was strongly endorsed by Captain Colling at Yenan. He had already requested the immediate dispatch of two plane-loads of medical and demolitions equipment for the Communist troops.

Rather than follow past practice and discuss these plans with the Chinese government, both the Army and OSS decided to first broach their plans to the Communists. State Department advisor John Davies sounded a note of caution. "They'll crucify you the way they crucified Stilwell," he warned Wedemeyer. "I don't care," replied the general.[70] Wedemeyer's Chief of Staff subsequently instructed Colonel David Barrett of the Dixie Mission, then acting as an intermediary between Hurley and the recalcitrant Communists, to present the Army's proposal to Mao.

Colonel Heppner assigned his deputy, Lieutenant Colonel Willis Bird, to carry the OSS plan to Yenan. A 36-year-old graduate of the Wharton School of Finance, Bird had been a top executive of Sears, Roebuck in Pennsylvania and New York when he was recruited for intelligence service by his friend Bill Donovan. His fellow officers remember him as a "con-man," an "operator," and a rather vain man (he reportedly carried a set of pearl-handled revolvers). One thing is certain—he could not be accused by Tai Li of liberal idealism.[u]

On December 15, 1944, Colonels Barrett and Bird flew together to Yenan with their military proposals in hand. The Communists received both propositions suspiciously, but gave their tentative approval. Days later, Tai Li's agents got wind of the discussions. It was just the opportunity SACO had been waiting for. The Communists had repeatedly warned their American contacts that "Tai's agents planned to carry out some plot in Yenan" against the Dixie Mission, "possibly involving the use of explosives." [71] In January 1945, the SACO men struck, but the explosives were verbal.

Miles had for some time carefully cultivated the friendship (and vanity) of Ambassador Hurley. Greeted by a full-dress parade at SACO headquarters complete with "flags, ruffles, and flourishes," Hurley was then wined and dined by Tai Li. The ambassador was soon convinced to use Navy radio facilities to communicate with Washington, bypassing the anti-Chiang State Department officers in his own embassy. The

---

[u] Bird established permanent residence in postwar Bangkok as an exporter and investment broker. In 1959, he was named in congressional testimony as having given a $25,000 bribe to a foreign aid official in order to secure a government construction contract in Laos.

gullible diplomat had been properly conditioned in his acceptance of SACO when Miles "revealed" that a massive conspiracy was afoot to send American troops and arms to the Communists. For greater effect, Tai Li's agents also concocted rumors that Mao Tse-tung was to be flown to Washington to meet personally with Roosevelt.

Hurley quickly shot off a letter to the President denouncing this insidious plot, which, he claimed, had emboldened the intransigent Communists in their negotiations with the Chungking regime. Wedemeyer returned from a brief trip to Burma to find Hurley—and his War Department superiors—in a huff over the SACO allegations. "I am extremely sorry," he wrote Washington, "that my people became involved in such a delicate situation." The general then directed all American officers in China to sign a statement that they would not "assist, negotiate, or collaborate in any way with Chinese political parties," unless "specifically authorized by the Commanding General." The crowning comment on the ridiculous affair was made by Chiang Kai-shek. The Generalissimo congratulated Hurley on having "purged the United States headquarters of the conspirators." [72]

And a purge did follow. Colonel Barrett was denied a promotion to Brigadier General. State Department officers John Davies and John Service were soon "Hurleyed" out of China. Only OSS emerged unscathed, perhaps because General Donovan reached the Chinese capital in time to mollify the angry Hurley. The OSS chief also received a warm greeting from Wedemeyer and was invited to attend a joint intelligence conference with British and SACO representatives.

Wedemeyer announced to the assembled group that he would no longer tolerate the chaotic state of the Allied secret services in China. He had received information that the British MI-6 had recruited several thousand agents in China whose primary mission was to spy, not on the enemy, but on the Chinese government. Wedemeyer was just as critical of Miles and Tai Li and declared his intention to have Washington abrogate the 1943 SACO agreement. OSS emerged victorious. Wedemeyer assigned responsibility to Heppner's unit for the training of twenty Chinese commando-guerrilla groups, a function greatly coveted by Miles and company.

In April 1945, the SACO agreement was altered to bring the Miles organization directly under Wedemeyer's command. One of the general's first acts was to order Miles to withdraw SACO guerrillas from certain provinces where they would be replaced by OSS-trained commandos. Donovan's officers were then given "the complete approval of the powers that be for full steam ahead" [v] and began "pouring people into the Theater." [73]

But Wedemeyer had a further proviso for clandestine operations. He centralized all planning for secret services at his headquarters and insisted that future covert activities be "cleared" by both the American Army and the Chinese government. To represent the Generalissimo in the "clearance" machinery, the Chinese government appointed a general who was actually one of Tai Li's closest aides. OSS thus met with official Chinese objections whenever an operation requiring Communist cooperation was proposed. In February 1945 a contingent of Jedburghs was flown to China for commando operations. Upon their departure from the United States, they were told that they would be working with Communist guerrillas, as many of them had done in France. But the Jeds never reached north China. Neither did an OSS team organized to direct and actually operate an entire military communications network for the Communists. The unit, commanded by Frank Farrell, a New York newspaper editor in Marine uniform, waited impatiently at OSS headquarters in Kunming throughout the spring of 1945. The central government refused to sanction the mission.

Tai Li and Miles continued to charge that OSS was collaborating with Yenan. In July, Miles claimed that OSS had dropped submachine guns to "Communist plainclothesmen" at Shanghai. Further aid to Yenan, he said, would be sent under the guise of a "Red SACO" plan. Did such OSS assistance materialize? The chief of the State Department's China Division was uncertain. "There never was to my knowledge any arms or ammunition supplied to the Communists by us," he recalled, though "there may have been some supplied in a manner by OSS or something." [74]

And what if OSS arms and supplies had actually reached the Yenan armies? Their postwar oratory notwithstanding, Hurley, Wedemeyer, and Chennault all had words of praise for the Communists during that harried spring of 1945. Even that great political conservative Curtis LeMay, then commander of the Twentieth Bomber Group in the Far East, exchanged gifts with Mao Tse-tung and remembers that "everything was smooth as silk in our mutual relations." Wedemeyer's headquarters was so sensitive to maintaining friendly relations with Ye-

[v] Intensified recruiting of Chinese-Americans for OSS service netted Dong Kingman, now a well-known San Francisco artist. He was slated for a position as OSS cartographer in Chungking, but in typical OSS fashion, he never left Washington.

nan that a special investigative board was convened to determine whether or not the American officers in SACO were assisting Tai Li's guerrillas in attacks on Communist forces.[75] [w]

OSS certainly had the best justification of all the agencies in China for establishing closer operational contacts with Yenan. Donovan's men were charged with gathering intelligence, from any and all sources. Ironically, the refusal of the Chungking government to allow OSS operatives to collect information in Communist territory may well have assisted the diplomatic position of Moscow. At the Yalta Conference of February 1945, Roosevelt's willingness to compromise on Stalin's political demands was partially based on the premise that the Russians would have to assume the major strategic role in fighting a massive Japanese Army in Manchuria. Had OSS officers been able to infiltrate the Manchurian region (through the willing cooperation of Yenan), they would have found that this highly touted enemy force had been steadily depleted to meet Japan's strategic needs in the Pacific. The result might have been a considerably lower estimate of the need for Russian assistance in the Asian war.[76]

The prospects for OSS dealings with Yenan became increasingly dim as a growing atmosphere of fear began to pervade the American bureaucracy in Chungking during the first months of 1945. On the day the Yalta Conference began, Colonel Harley Stevens wrote, "The major fault lies in the Kuomintang party and the leadership itself. This everyone who is informed knows; but too many people are afraid of saying so; and others fear mere labels." [77] OSS watched with dismay as outspoken critics of Chiang in the State Department came under attack.

In April 1945, Hurley had forced Washington to recall State Department officer John Service to the United States. Service had worked closely with OSS in China, first as a Stilwell political advisor in opposing the SACO agreement, and later as a member of the Dixie Mission and proponent of direct American military aid to Yenan. On several occasions, the Assistant General Counsel of OSS, China-born and Oxford-educated Duncan Lee, another member of the Donovan law firm, had attempted to enlist Service for OSS.[x] The young State Department

[w] Two months later, after the Japanese surrender, Miles suffered a nervous breakdown and was flown to the United States for medical care. He later became an admiral and U.S. Naval representative in Latin America. Tai Li was killed in a plane crash in March 1946, possibly as a result of Communist sabotage.

[x] In 1948, FBI informant Elizabeth Bentley made the absurd charge

officer declined the offer, preferring to remain in his diplomatic post. Ironically, OSS came close to destroying Service's career and reputation.

In early 1945, Kenneth Wells, chief of the South Asia section of the OSS Research Branch was reading the January issue of a periodical called *Amerasia*. He noticed an article on American-British rivalry in Thailand that seemed to quote verbatim from a classified OSS report. He notified the OSS security chief, wealthy publisher Archbold Van Beuren, who handed the case over to a group of special investigators. The magazine's offices in New York were placed under surveillance. On the night of March 11, 1945, OSS security officers, acting illegally without a search warrant, broke into the *Amerasia* offices and found them "literally strewn with confidential government documents" from OSS and other official agencies.[78]

Informed of this discovery, General Donovan notified Secretary of State Stettinius, who then referred the breach of security to the Attorney General. For three months, 75 FBI agents kept a close watch on the editors of *Amerasia*, collecting evidence in strictest secrecy. In June, under orders from President Truman, FBI agents armed with search warrants entered the *Amerasia* offices and seized 600 classified government documents. Six persons were arrested—the two editors of the magazine, a naval intelligence officer, a journalist, and two State Department officers, one of whom was John Service. The charge was violation of the Espionage Act.

In Chungking, Service's OSS friends refused to believe the charges which had been brought against him. Colonel Stevens wrote on June 9 that "we are all furious about the Jack S. business and are convinced it is a put-up job." Wedemeyer was also "much interested and concerned." [79] Their faith was vindicated when the Grand Jury voted unanimously not to indict Service.[y]

Drew Pearson attributed the whole affair to the work of Tai Li's

---

that Lee was a Soviet spy who had passed OSS information to the Russians. He denied the accusations under oath and no legal charges were ever brought against him. Lee later became counsel to C. V. Starr's insurance group.

[y] After the *Amerasia* uproar died down, Service returned to State Department duty. In 1950, Joseph McCarthy revived the issue, charging Service with disloyalty. After several prolonged loyalty hearings, Service was dismissed from State in 1951. He took his case to the courts and was finally reinstated in the Foreign Service in 1957. He is now on the staff of the Center for Chinese Studies at the University of California.

agents, "operating under cover in the USA against anyone opposed to Chiang Kai-shek." [80] For many American officials in China, the "Amerasia affair" also signified that critics of Chiang had become fair game for denunciation.

By the summer of 1945, the universal attention of OSS was focused on Japan. Allen Dulles was even diverted from his efforts in Germany to pursue Japanese peace feelers. A number of Japanese officials working in neutral Switzerland hoped that their country would negotiate for peace through the good offices of the OSS organization in Europe. They felt that peace feelers relayed through Dulles would receive serious consideration in Washington. Their hopes had been encouraged by the successful OSS contact with the Germans in Italy. While exploratory talks continued, Dulles attended the Potsdam Conference in late July to brief top Allied officials of the Japanese overtures. Unfortunately, the enemy representatives failed to convince Washington that they spoke for the Tokyo government and their efforts ended in futility.[81]

It had long been assumed that the American invasion of the Japanese islands would be a long and costly affair. In April 1945, an OSS "black propaganda" radio station on Saipan, staffed by American Nisei under the direction of 27-year-old Stanford graduate John Zuckerman, began beaming long broadcasts to the Japanese islands in an attempt to "soften" the enemy's morale prior to the invasion.[z] A much larger operation had been planned since mid-1944 by John Shaheen, the OSS Naval Commander (and former Republican publicity man) who had commanded the ill-fated McGregor team at the Salerno landing. As head of an OSS Special Projects Office that reported directly to General Donovan, Shaheen conceived an operational plan that was even more incredible than his earlier plot to effect the surrender of the Italian navy: he hoped to destroy two concrete tubes which provided transportation and communication between the Japanese mainland and the islands of Honshu and Kyushu. The project required some 250 OSS personnel training at a secret base in Florida and equipped with a fleet of PT boats. This phantom armada was to be directed from the air by remote control, equipped with television cameras and 50,000 pounds of explosives. Nothing whatever came of this boondoggle: men,

[z] Zuckerman was Deputy Director of the Bureau of International Business Operations, Department of Commerce, during the Kennedy administration. He now teaches at the University of Houston.

boats, cameras, and explosives had not yet left for the Pacific when the atomic bomb destroyed Hiroshima on August 6, 1945.

The bomb also abruptly interrupted the great debate over American policy in China. On August 8, Russia declared war on Japan and sent its troops into Manchuria. Two days later, Japan accepted the Allied demand for unconditional surrender. This sudden turn of events left the Chinese landscape dotted with millions of Russian, Japanese, Chinese Nationalist, and Chinese Communist troops, mixed together in confusion. The United States blundered into the middle of this chaos without any comprehensive postwar policy in China. Washington hoped to maintain "neutrality" in the internal Chinese conflict while at the same time helping Chiang Kai-shek's government establish its authority throughout the country.

OSS suffered the first pangs of bitterness caused by this internal contradiction in the American position. Months of OSS planning for cooperation with the Communists had come to nothing because of the Chiang government's recalcitrance. But now American officers were suddenly thrust into Communist territory as agents of a confused and uncertain national policy. The results were unpleasant and sometimes tragic.

OSS viewed the situation from three vantage points—Chungking, north China, and Manchuria. At the Chinese capital, diplomatic issues were still a major preoccupation. Hurley had persuaded Chiang Kai-shek to invite his Communist rival, Mao Tse-tung, to the capital for personal discussions. With victory assured, the Generalissimo finally extended this invitation on August 16. The American ambassador personally guaranteed Mao's protection and flew to Yenan to bring the Communist leader to Chungking.

On August 28, the Chungking airport was mobbed by officials awaiting Mao's arrival. Colonel Harley Stevens was there and later recalled the scene: "The place was crowded with American and Chinese military, with the representatives of many nations, with Chinese dignitaries, with the inevitable reporters and photographers. But in spite of all that was going on—the preparation for policing the field, the arrival of Lieutenant General Wedemeyer and other dignitaries—the crowd kept its collective eye on the sky. . . . We knew that for the Chinese, Mao's coming signified the renewal of an infinitely harder task than we or the Chinese—with all their bitter years of struggle—had yet known. That task was the binding up of China's wounds and the building of a great nation. . . . The plane from Yenan circled the field and came in. Out stepped Ambassador Hurley with Mao, solemn and calm. . . . Mao is a large man, unusually youthful for a person of 52, with a kindly face and firm handclasp. Severely dressed in a dark blue uniform and wearing a round-brimmed gray sun helmet, Mao said he was happy to be in Chungking and that he looked forward to seeing the Generalissimo, whom he had not seen for almost twenty years. There were no flowers and no band, but it was clear that Mao's arrival brought new hope that civil war might be averted." [82]

In the north that hope was being shattered. On August 10, Yenan announced that Communist troops claimed the right to occupy and administer any city or town held by Japanese troops or their Chinese puppet forces. Chiang immediately denounced this claim as "illegal action." The Generalissimo was in turn branded a "fascist chieftain" by Yenan.[83]

The American position in this dispute was a model of ambiguity. Wedemeyer ordered American forces to aid the central government armies in the reoccupation of enemy areas. They were to provide transport to Chiang's troops and were authorized to accept Japanese surrenders on behalf of the Chiang government. But, added Wedemeyer, none of these actions should violate the basic principle that American forces were not to be used to aid the Chinese government in a civil war with the Communists!

OSS officers were the first to see the absurdity of this dream of "neutrality." In April 1945, forty-six OSS men had set up headquarters at an old Seventh Day Adventist mission at Sian in north China, some 150 miles south of Yenan. In early August, the German-American colonel who commanded the group (he was selected for the post because the local Chinese warlord had been educated in Berlin) began dispatching his OSS teams into the field. These units encountered difficulties with Japanese and Chinese troops of all descriptions. There was a thin line, for example, between Kuomintang loyalists and Chinese puppet soldiers who had fought for the Japanese. One team commanded by a 24-year-old Jedburgh parachuted to their "drop zone" to find their "reception committee" composed of a "group of Chinese who were paid by the Japs—got their arms from the Japs and might easily be loyal to them." The local warlord "had commanded a division for the Chinese Nationalist government; when he was captured by the Japs, he commanded a division for them with the same aplomb and good nature. It was our information that he was still in correspondence with Chiang Kai-shek, and would help if he didn't risk his own neck." [84]

These puppet troops were only a temporary problem. When the war ended, the warlord generals who had been traitors to their country abruptly realigned themselves with the Chiang government. The Chungking regime accepted their support as allies against the Communists with open arms.

OSS had also become inadvertently concerned about growing Communist strength. In the last month of the war, two OSS teams dispatched from Sian to the guerrilla zones were arrested by Communist troops. In both cases, the Dixie Mission at Yenan secured their release. It appeared that local Communist zealots had acted without approval of Communist headquarters.

Then in August dozens of OSS intelligence officers were sent into the northern hinterland from Sian to report on local military conditions. Communist troops, who saw these teams as tools of the Kuomintang, deliberately harassed the Americans. In mid-August, the OSS commander at Sian anxiously wired Kunming: "Now appears all field teams face conflict with Communists in trying to carry out orders to occupy cities on Jap surrender and seize records. . . . Request instructions on what action teams should take. Suggest that if teams must fight Reds to carry out orders they be withdrawn to Sian. Sincerely feel teams should not risk their lives in conflict with Reds. Feeling in North China is civil war will start immediately after Jap capitulation." [85]

There was one comic scene in which OSS Captain George Wuchinich, the Abraham Lincoln Brigader who had fought with Tito's Partisans, decided, without consulting his headquarters, to make contact with the Chinese Communists, for whom he had some ideological affection. He led his team a considerable distance to reach Communist territory. But when he and his men arrived and camped at a Buddhist temple, they found themselves under detention by Wuchinich's supposed political friends. He later explained, "When I was getting my radio set ready to send a message to headquarters, we were surrounded in a battle between the Communists, the Nationalists, the Puppets, the Ming-Bins, the Militia, who the devil knows. All the devil knows I had four guys, the war was over by August 15, and here we were in the midst of the battle. The Communists won the battle and, in the process, discovered that we were in the temple and took us along with them. . . . I say if the other side had won, I probably would have been a dead Joe by then." [86]

There was also senseless tragedy. One OSS intelligence team was commanded by Captain John Birch, 27, a fundamentalist Baptist missionary who had joined Chennault's Fourteenth Air Force intelligence. Birch's fellow officers in China remember him as a pleasant, emotional, and ardently evangelistic young man with an extreme hatred of the Japanese. If he held any strong opinions about the Chinese Communists, Birch kept them to himself. In fact, he frequently cooperated with Yenan troops fighting the Japanese.

Birch was transferred to OSS in May 1945 and in August was selected to head one of the missions launched from Sian. On August 25, his group ran into a Communist roadblock. According to one questionable account, Birch became irate when the Communists refused to allow his team to pass and told a Chinese officer who accompanied him, "I want to find out how they intend to treat Americans. I don't mind if they kill me, for if they do, their movement will be finished. The United States will use the atomic bomb to stop their banditry." [87] Whatever his motive, Birch challenged the team of teen-aged Chinese peasants who were uneasily toying with their rifles. The captain was killed. For OSS, it was a meaningless calamity. American right-wingers later made Birch's death a symbolic Cold War sacrifice.

Still farther north, at the ancient Chinese capital of Peking, an OSS team led by Major James Kellis,[a] a Cairo-educated Greek-American and a veteran of OSS Balkan operations, crept into the city with the aid of Chinese puppet troops on August 12.[88] Some days later, they surfaced and nervously accepted the surrender of the entire Japanese General Staff for north China. At the end of August, Major Paul Frillmann, the Flying Tigers chaplain and AGFRTS officer, arrived in Peking to take command of the OSS detachment. He remained in the city for five months. Peking, during this period, was surrounded by Communist troops who had been prevented from taking control when the United States, quite literally, sent in the Marines: American Marines landed on the coast and came up to Peking by railroad, peacefully occupying the Japanese garrison. "By the time I got there," writes Frillmann, "tens of thousands of Nationalist troops were arriving in American planes, and puppet forces were being legitimized as Nationalists with a speed which suggested wartime deals. No Japanese were to be repatriated until enough Nationalists were on hand to keep the Communists out."

"I'm afraid," added Frillmann, "this isolated little patch of the free world was not much of a showcase for us. Its masters were Nation-

a Kellis worked for the CIA in the Far East until 1954. He is now a Political Science professor in Connecticut.

alists . . . grasping and venal. . . . Puppets and collaborators were bribing their way out of trial as war criminals. . . . Blackmail of lowly people who had betrayed their neighbors, or merely offended them, was a sport in corner police stations." [89]

A different source of disillusionment faced OSS officers in Manchuria. Since late July, at Wedemeyer's directive, OSS had been planning the dispatch of "mercy missions" to rescue Allied prisoners of war held by the Japanese. It was feared that the enraged enemy might slaughter these prisoners as the war came to an end. On August 11, OSS headquarters at Kunming began organizing commando groups to be sent to prison camps at Shanghai, Seoul, Hanoi, and Mukden in Manchuria, where General Jonathan Wainwright was being held. In late August, a group of OSS men reached Mukden and found the general in the midst of thousands of ill-tempered Soviet troops.

The Yalta agreement had given the Russians the right to occupy Manchuria, but only until it could be turned over to Chiang Kai-shek's government. Moscow began sending hundreds of thousands of soldiers into the area in August, and the Soviets were well in control of northern Manchuria by August 14 (the day they reaffirmed their promise to respect the sovereignty of the Chungking government).

The first OSS men to reach Russian-occupied territory found the Russians terribly belligerent for "allies." There was one tale of an OSS man who had learned the Russian language at a training school in the United States, acquiring, in the process, a theoretical admiration for the U.S.S.R. He had joined various Soviet-American friendship groups and contributed a fine timepiece of his father's to a campaign called "Watches for the Red Army." Most Americans donated cheap watches, but this young man gave his best. As the war ended, he was delighted to be assigned to the OSS "mercy mission" to Soviet-held Manchuria.

His first meeting with the Russians was disastrous. As he approached the Soviet vanguard, he flung out his arms impulsively and cried "Tovarischi! Comrades!" The Russians eyed him suspiciously and then swung their submachine guns up to a firing position. Their leader advanced, noticed an expensive wrist watch on the OSS man's arm and stretched out his hand with the gruff command, "Give me your watch." One man's theories of international friendship met a quick death.[90]

Another member of the OSS team in Manchuria was 26-year-old West Point Captain Roger Hilsman, a veteran of Detachment 101 in

Burma.[b] He came to Mukden in the hope of finding his father, an Army general captured by the Japanese. He was happily reunited with the senior Hilsman at one of the prison camps, but not before he and his teammates discovered Russian soldiers loading the entire Japanese industrial machinery of Manchuria on trains bound for the USSR. When the OSS men began to photograph the brick-by-brick dismemberment of Manchuria's industry (supposedly belonging to China) they were arrested by the Russians and finally expelled from the area under pain of death. By the end of September, Colonel Stevens in Chungking wrote unhappily that "the Soviet entry was received here with profound discouragement." [91]

OSS became accustomed to profound discouragement in its four years in China. Beyond the organizational rivalry with Miles and Tai Li, the OSS officer in China "saw a number of things that he frankly did not like. And he said so—often bluntly." Major William Lockwood, a Shanghai-born professor and China specialist who joined the OSS Research and Analysis unit at Chennault's headquarters in 1944, later reflected: "All around them in China our soldiers observed such poverty, ignorance, and disease as they had hardly imagined. Most of the people had never known, nor could they hope for, anything much better. The Chinese armies consisted in good part of ragged, illiterate peasants, miserably equipped and frequently half-starved. . . . Their leaders in many areas seemed less interested in using them to kill Japanese than to jockey for postwar political advantage. Running the country was a self-appointed bureaucracy of politicians and officials. All too often they were giving their hard-pressed people neither honest nor efficient government. . . . On every hand were merchants, landlords, and politicos sitting out the war, leaving it to their allies to finish off the Japanese. Meanwhile, they themselves waxed fat with wartime graft and profiteering, frequently at the expense of the Americans. In economic and political organization, in wartime patriotism and technical know-how, these Americans drew constantly unfavorable comparisons with their own country. As humanitarians they were shocked by the cheapness and squalor of human life. As democrats they found little to praise in Kuomintang rule and didn't

[b] Dr. Hilsman was Special Assistant to the Executive Officer of CIA, 1947. He became Director of State Department Intelligence and Assistant Secretary of State for Far Eastern Affairs during the Kennedy administration, and now teaches at Columbia University.

know whether the Communists up north were any better. As civilian soldiers they were exasperated by the disunity, the incompetence, the half-hearted spirit of the Chinese war effort."

But Lockwood saw a ray of hope. For some American officers, "long months of hardship and, in some instances, danger behind the Japanese lines increased affection for the Chinese people." Some Americans "sympathized with the sweating, blue-clad peasant trying to wring a living out of his tiny plot of land." Perhaps, Lockwood concluded, this was the "beginning of international education." [92]

9

Save England's Asiatic Colonies

"The undercurrent of distrust distressed me more than any good healthy sub-rosa political maneuvering," quipped a female OSS recruit in India. "We had been warned in Delhi," she remembered, "that the British were past masters at intrigue and had planted spies in all American agencies to piece together information." [1] It was an appropriate welcome to southern Asia.

At the Quebec Conference of August 1943, Roosevelt and Churchill agreed on the creation of a joint South East Asia Command (SEAC). This new Anglo-American headquarters was designed to solve the problems of divided authority that had arisen in the Indian rear echelon while General Stilwell remained preoccupied with his duties in China and Burma. Admiral Louis Mountbatten, chief of the British Commandos and a dapper, wealthy cousin of the King's, was chosen SEAC's "supreme commander." Stilwell was named deputy commander, while serving simultaneously (and confusingly) as Chiang Kai-shek's chief of staff, and as commander of American forces in China, Burma, and India.

Underlying the birth of SEAC was also the frail hope that Mountbatten's new command would diminish the incessant squabbling between British and American officers in India. But it soon became apparent that SEAC was a failure as a healer of Allied wounds. At American parties in New Delhi and later at Mountbatten's headquarters in Ceylon, one would often hear such jibes as "Lord Louis, our million-dollar admiral in a five-and-ten-cent war." Or "SEAC, that means Save England's Asiatic Colonies." On occasion, an irate American officer might suggest, "Why don't we fight the British instead of the Japanese? That would be a popular war." [2] One group of Army pundits even composed a SEAC theme song: "Oh, we're planning combined operations/How we treasure combined operations/The Limey's make policy, Yanks fight the Japs/And one gets its Empire, and one takes the rap." [3] These caustic remarks were more than simple diversions from boredom in an inactive and forgotten theater of war. Mutual antagonism reflected genuine differences in personalities and ideologies.

At the top of the command pyramid, it would have been difficult to find two more contrasting individuals than Mountbatten and Stilwell. The patrician manner of the dashing Lord Louis stood in sharp contrast to Vinegar Joe's incomparable (and often tactless) sarcasm. Military strategy seemed their principal point of contention, but not far below the strategic surface lay the basic issue of imperialism. Stilwell, a traditional American anti-colonialist, resented Mountbatten's "playing the 'Empah' game." [4] This emotional reaction came to be shared by virtually every American officer in the Far East.

OSS was at first spared a confrontation with its British colleagues over the colonial issue. When Carl Eifler and his Detachment 101 guerrillas appeared in India in 1942, there were some high-level flutterings in London and Washington. Donovan feared that Eifler's bid to begin operations in the jungles of Burma, one of London's colonial possessions, might "give rise to complications and friction" with the British. Instead, Eifler and his men received a note of greeting from the Scottish thread manufacturer who commanded SOE at Calcutta. "I welcome your active collaboration," wrote the British official. "You can count on all possible cooperation from me and my organization." [5]

The British were true to their word. They provided Detachment 101 with "maps and reports from their own agents in Burma. There was no report or file they considered too secret for our eyes," recalled one of Eifler's officers. "They did not propose that they had a prior claim on irregular warfare. It was their view that the more of us involved in it, the merrier would be the espionage accounts to be filed away in the top-secret files." The Eifler group, in turn, treated their British counterparts "with courtesy and with the idea that this was an Allied show." [6] A British major with long service in Asia was even appointed recruiting officer for Detachment 101 at Calcutta. (This led an anglophobic Republican congressman to charge that OSS was "dominated and directed" in the Far East by a British agent.) [7] Aided by nine thousand Kachin natives of the Burma hills who joined 101's guerrilla forces, OSS and SOE cooperated in Burma in some of the most successful irregular military operations of the war.[a]

For over a year, Detachment 101 remained the only major OSS unit in southern Asia and provided a model for Allied harmony in clandestine services. Then SEAC was created; the OSS men who arrived in India to join Mountbatten's new headquarters were unceremoniously rebuffed by the established secret services of the British military. These parochial agents of British Army intelligence feared that the American amateurs would "rummage among the cupboards where the family skeletons of Empire were concealed." Worse yet, the OSS novices might "give undue encouragement to the aspirations to freedom of the subject peoples in Asia." [8] No less dubious about the OSS presence in Asia were aides of General Stilwell who suspected that Donovan's officers, through contact with the British, would be "exposed to some subtle political contamination." [9]

Lord Louis knew of these pressures when he met with General Donovan in late 1943 to work out an agreement for OSS operations in SEAC. The British admiral and the OSS chief had become personal friends in the earlier days of the war. Donovan had long been impressed by his English colleague. "If that man had been born Mr. Mountbatten," Donovan remarked, "he might be the next Prime Minister of England." [10]

The two men happily concluded an agreement allowing OSS to expand its operations in southern Asia. A "P Division" was created at SEAC headquarters, under the command of a British officer and an OSS deputy, to coordinate clandestine activities. To fill the American position, Donovan chose Lieutenant Commander Edmond Taylor, the 35-year-old journalist who had led his Psychological Warfare Branch into verbal battle against the Vichyites in North Africa some months earlier.[11]

Taylor reached India with a case of anglophilia so acute that it seemed to justify the worst fears of Stilwell's advisors. "In principle," wrote the OSS officer, "I adhered to the Wilsonian and Rooseveltian doctrine of self-determination for all peoples, including those under

[a] One OSS Kachin leader, Naw Seng, is now chief of a Communist insurgent movement in northeast Burma, supplied and supported by Peking.

colonial rule, but I was prepared to leave the timing of its application to the liberal conscience of our allies." Taylor came to SEAC with the hope of "promoting a durable partnership between Britain and America." Neither the hope nor the partnership proved durable.[12]

Within weeks of the original Donovan-Mountbatten accord, OSS India was reorganized. In November 1943, General Donovan (then on his way to China to confront Tai Li and Captain Miles) strengthened the independence of OSS within SEAC by creating a new unit, Detachment 404, to organize all Southeast Asia operations. Taylor remained as OSS representative to Mountbatten's headquarters. But Donovan named a separate commander for the new detachment—Colonel Richard Heppner, the young attorney from the general's law firm who later became the commander of OSS China. The British were quick to remember Heppner as an aide to William Phillips, a former ambassador and London chief of OSS, on a special Presidential mission to India earlier that year. Roosevelt had felt that the conflict between the British and the Indian nationalists was threatening the war effort in the Far East, and he sent Phillips to investigate. Traveling through India with Heppner at his side, Phillips became increasingly sympathetic to the nationalist cause. He later reported to FDR that the colonial peoples should have "something better to look forward to than simply a return to their old masters." [13] The Phillips mission had no official tie to OSS, but the British had some unpleasant recollections when Colonel Heppner reappeared in India in the fall of 1943 as chief of American secret operations in the countries of Britain's Asian empire.

In the months that followed, "the relatively cordial relations that the Donovan-Mountbatten agreement had instituted between OSS and its British counterparts soon reverted to their original, and in a sense normal, state of rivalry and suspicion." Taylor recalls: "On occasion, my resources of ingenuity were severely taxed to produce for my SEAC superiors an innocent explanation for the presence of some accidentally discovered OSS intelligence team or guerrilla base in an area where no such operation had yet been authorized; fortunately, the same occasion was generally exploited by one of its British rivals to 'surface' some equally unsanctified activity of its own, so SEAC could give its retrospective blessings to both. . . . Each side cheated to about the same degree . . . and usually with a certain gentlemanly restraint." [14] When no major controversies were outstanding, the spirit of intrigue was kept alive by minor irritants. A good many British officers blushed the day OSS monitored a British native-language propaganda broadcast to

Thailand and Indochina that was announcing the invasion of Normandy; France, according to the broadcast, was being liberated by
British and colonial troops, with some "Allied" assistance. Then there
was the group of Nepalese being trained as sabotage agents. They refused to work under the command of their colonial masters in SOE and
insisted they would serve only the Americans of OSS. The British were
incensed.[15]

"The longer we stayed in the Theater," comments Taylor, "the
more OSS became permeated with the suspicion and disapproval of
Western Imperialism." [16] The British were not the only objects of
American anti-colonial sentiment. From SEAC Headquarters in Ceylon,
an OSS Maritime Unit under 30-year-old prep school instructor Fisher
Howe launched espionage infiltrations of Japanese-occupied Sumatra,
part of the Dutch East Indies.[b] The Japanese were actively encouraging
an anti-Dutch nationalist movement under Sukarno which had such
popular native support that the few OSS agents who reached Sumatra
(most of them Indonesian Communists in exile) were quickly betrayed
to the enemy by the local populace. The collaboration of the nationalists
with the Japanese provided American anti-colonialists with a slight emotional conflict, but they found a solution to their dilemma.[c] Summarizing intelligence reports from the Indies, an OSS research paper of March
1945 suggested that Sukarno was actually "anti-Japanese at heart," that
he was "forced to collaborate with the Japanese," and was "actually
powerless to act independently." [17] Following the Japanese surrender,
one of the first Americans to reach the Indies was an OSS Indonesian
specialist, 33-year-old Jane Foster, a San Franciscan educated at Mills
College who had spent several years in Java before the war.[d] After meeting with Sukarno, she happily reported that the Indonesian nationalist

[b] Howe was deputy director of State Department Intelligence, 1948–56
and executive secretary of the State Department, 1956–58. He is now assistant dean of the School for Advanced International Studies, Johns Hopkins University.

[c] Notable among the OSS Indonesian analysts was Belgian-born Paul
Kattenburg. As a State Department official and head of the Interdepart-
mental Working Group on Vietnam in 1963, he was the only high-level
official of the Kennedy administration to recommend total U.S. disengage-
ment from the Vietnam war.

[d] In 1957 a federal grand jury indicted Jane Foster Zlatovski and her
Russian-born husband, a former Army intelligence officer, on a charge of
espionage. Mrs. Zlatovski was accused of passing her OSS Indonesian reports to the Soviet NKVD in 1945.

movement was "no master plan by Russians or defeated Japs to overthrow Western imperialism, but was rather a natural eruption of the
volcanic discontent which had been rumbling for decades." The Indo-
nesians, she insisted, "were not planning a revolution. They wanted to
talk peace." [18]

In another part of Southeast Asia, OSS found more comfortable
objects for its affection. Edmond Taylor recalls the "direct emotional
reward of working with Asian leaders, as I did in Thailand, to recover
the freedom and dignity of their peoples." [19] The long-independent
nation known to the Western world as Siam seemed to have the greatest
need for OSS protection. Two of America's allies expressed an inordinate
interest in the country's future.

In late 1943, Mountbatten and Chiang Kai-shek reached a "gentle-
man's agreement" on military responsibility for the liberation of Indochina and Thailand. It provided, in Lord Louis' words, that "both of us
would . . . have the right to operate in both countries; and any areas
conquered from the Japanese would automatically become part of the
Command that reconquered them." [20] For OSS this meant that Donovan's officers would have to deal with both the Chinese and British in its
Thai operations. But OSS men had become aware of that gruesome
reality long before Mountbatten and Chiang began to carve up the
Asian mainland.

In February 1934 in the city of Bangkok, a teeming oriental metro-
polis that bore the unmistakable signs of European influence, but not
the harsh imprint of colonial servitude, a "stocky, self-reliant Siamese of
middle height, calm and slow of speech, friendly, but with great natural
dignity," sat before a Thai board of inquiry to defend himself against a
political libel.[21] His name was Pridi Phanomyong. He testified:

"I entertain no idea of setting up a government by soviets. . . . I
am only aiming at providing occupation and work for the people. . . .
With regard to class warfare, I have endeavoured to point out to various
people how improper it was, because it would only lead to bloodshed.
I utterly dislike dictatorship in any form, not only the dictatorship of the
proletariat but also the dictatorship of any class whatever. . . . I am
not a member of the Communist International, nor am I connected with
it in any way." [22]

To an America deep in the throes of economic crisis, these proceedings could hardly have seemed more distant. But for one young Presby-
terian minister the affair held special significance. Ordained at the

Princeton Theological Seminary, Kenneth Landon had chosen to spend the next ten years as a missionary in Thailand. That same decade saw Pridi Phanomyong's rise to political prominence, and when Landon returned to the United States in 1937 to pursue a doctoral degree, he began writing a book on the modernization of Thailand which emphasized Pridi's dynamic leadership. The book was completed as war in the Far East appeared imminent. To provide needed expertise in Thai affairs, Donovan's Coordinator of Information recruited Dr. Landon.

America, Landon reported, had a potential ally in Pridi, whose contacts with the West spanned some twenty years. Pridi had developed a socialist idealism as a student of law and economics at the University of Paris in the 1920s; upon returning to his homeland he found a growing number of foreign-educated professionals, bureaucrats, and military officers who had also become disaffected from Thailand's absolute monarchy and nepotistic bureaucracy. Pridi, in Landon's words, "constituted the catalytic agent which fused their purposes and urged them to boil over in revolution." [23]

On June 27, 1932, Franklin Roosevelt was nominated for the Presidency of the United States at a Chicago convention. That same week across the Pacific, tanks and machine gun emplacements appeared before the royal palace in Bangkok. A clique of influential commoners forced the king to accept a "constitutional monarchy."

As ideologist of the coup d'etat, Pridi had no illusions about the selfish political aims of his fellow conspirators, but he hoped to use his official position to promote economic reforms that would "end poverty" in Thailand. In March 1933, as FDR announced his New Deal for the American people, Pridi presented an economic plan to the new state council. This brave attempt to adapt socialist concepts to the Thai economy met with bitter opposition. When his antagonists raised the Communist specter, Pridi dejectedly resigned his official post and sailed for Europe. As if in rebuke, the government enacted legislation to "outlaw Communism."

A young Thai Army officer, Lieutenant Colonel Pibul Songgram, took advantage of Pridi's absence to strengthen his own political position. Pibul had received French military training during the same years that Pridi had spent in Paris. He had also returned to Thailand fascinated by a European political philosophy—the fascism of Mussolini and Hitler. Alarmed by Pibul's growing popularity, Pridi's friends urged him to return. At the end of September, he quietly reentered the capital.

Exonerated of a charge of Communist sympathies, Pridi returned to public service the following year as a member of the cabinet. Pibul was then Minister of Defense. Soon he would also become Commander of the Army and, finally, Premier of the government. Against the opposition of Pridi and his supporters, the country underwent a rapid course in militarization. The army budget was doubled, armaments were purchased from Japan and Italy, and Pibul founded a Nazi-style, quasi-military youth movement.

Pibul then attempted to create a political and social atmosphere on the Japanese model. His Minister of Fine Arts ominously suggested that the Chinese minority in Thailand (which held an important and resented role in the nation's commerce) should be given the same brutal treatment as the Jews of Germany. Pibul personally announced an anti-Western "cultural campaign" and his cronies began to refer to him as "the leader." Thailand had acquired all the trappings of Asian fascism.

In 1940, after the fall of France, Pibul prostituted himself to the Japanese and was rewarded with a gift of areas of French Indochina to which the Thais had long laid claim. British financiers with important interests in Thailand were alarmed by these events, but His Majesty's Government responded with caution. London still held 70 per cent of Thai trade and majority control of Thailand's chief export industries, and Whitehall's influence was great in this area, which was of strategic importance to the defense of Britain's Asian colonies. As late as the summer of 1941, the British ambassador at Bangkok was so certain that the Thai government would be "willing and able to withstand the increasing Japanese pressure" that he refused to allow SOE to make any clandestine contacts in the country. "Such preparations," he declared, would be "unnecessary and would merely upset the people." [24]

Washington took a different view. The State Department saw only Pibul's wooing of Tokyo's Greater East Asia Co-Prosperity Sphere, and when the British Foreign Office suggested that some joint effort should be made to lure the Thais away from their Japanese flirtation, Cordell Hull replied that "Thailand was already in the clutches of Japan." [25]

At the end of 1941, the question ceased to be hypothetical. Within hours of the attack on Pearl Harbor, Japanese troops invaded Thailand. Over the fervent opposition of Pridi and his friends, Pibul immediately ordered the Thai Army to offer no resistance. He then agreed to form a military defensive alliance with Japan—this was only one step short of declaring war on the Allies. Again the Thai liberals voiced strong dissent. Piqued by opposition to his decisions within the cabinet, Pibul removed Pridi from his ministerial post, "elevating" him to the figure-head position of regent of the child king who had assumed the throne in 1935. Pibul now stood unchallenged.

London still hoped for the best. The Foreign Office insisted, at the beginning of 1942, that the "majority of Thai opinion is anti-Japanese if not pro-Ally," and Whitehall counseled against an Allied declaration of war on Thailand.[26] The British arguments began to gain some credence as new voices were heard in Washington. At Donovan's COI headquarters, Kenneth Landon predicted that Thailand would develop an underground equal in importance to the anti-Nazi resistance forces of Europe. Landon found persuasive support for his argument when the Thai minister to the United States, Oxford-educated attorney Seni Pramoj, denounced the Thai-Japanese alliance. "The Thai people," he declared, "are not pro-Japanese and they are not the kind to be subservient, and I am working to carry on the struggle." [27] His sentiments were shared by the Thai military attaché, Colonel Kharb Kunjara.[e] This ambitious young officer, a product of British military training, was already in close contact with General Donovan's representatives.

Seni's Free Thai Legation in Washington also became the rallying point for pro-Allied Thai students then studying in the United States. Since Pridi's days in Paris, hundreds of young Thai scholars educated at Western universities had joined the progressive political minority within the nation's elite. After Pearl Harbor, most Thai students in America pledged their support to Seni and joined in the establishment of a Free Thai Council. The group denounced the Japanese army as "the enemy of the Thais" and repudiated Pibul's regime as a "puppet government which had collaborated with the enemy against the will of the people." [28]

In late January, Seni arrived (reportedly teary-eyed) at Cordell Hull's office. He had just received word that the Pibul government had officially declared war on the United States and Britain. He begged Cordell Hull to ignore the action. "I am keeping the declaration in my pocket," he said, "because I am convinced it does not represent the will of the Thai people. With American help, I propose to prove it." [29] He then publicly renounced the declaration of war in a statement broadcast to Bangkok by the propaganda branch of COI.

[e] Kunjara was a clever political manipulator. In 1948, when Pibul staged a coup to regain power, overthrowing a government dominated by Pridi, Kunjara supported the dictator and then became his personal military advisor.

Seni's pleas for American support found favor at the State Department. With COI encouragement, State had lost its earlier doubts about potential Thai resistance to the Japanese; Thailand was now officially considered an occupied nation rather than a willful collaborator with the Axis. The war declaration, the diplomats concluded, was not the act of a legitimate government and should not be reciprocated by the United States.

This important decision was, in a sense, the apex of a long historical record of Thai-American amity.[30] On the basis of past contacts with the West, many Thais regarded all Europeans as greedy commercial entrepreneurs and all Americans as humanitarian missionaries. For more sophisticated members of the Thai elite, this distinction had found concrete political expression in the so-called foreign advisor system. Since the turn of the century, Thailand had been politely coerced into accepting Western advisors to its government in order to prevent more serious occidental incursions upon the nation's sovereignty. The "financial advisor" had traditionally been British. While his ostensible purpose was to help maintain the Thai economy on a sound basis, he was never averse to protecting the interests of British corporations in Thailand. At the same time, the Thai government had eagerly accepted the services of "foreign affairs advisors" from the United States. At the urging of these diplomats, America became the first Western power to renounce its extra-territorial rights in Thailand in the 1920s. Rather symbolically, Francis Dolbeare, the last American to hold this post before the war (and an old friend of Allen Dulles's from Versailles days), joined Landon in OSS.[f]

In June 1942, these two men formulated the first major OSS recommendation on Thai policy. It suggested that American dealings with the Thais should stress the "cordial relations that have existed between the U.S. and Thailand in the past . . . as evidence of good will in the future." [31] As OSS recruited other "old Thai hands," especially former missionaries, to aid in its clandestine plans for Thailand, their spirit of evangelical humanitarianism came to leave its mark on official policy. Within a year, Kenneth Landon personally brought the OSS position into the diplomatic echelons when he joined the State Department as chief of its Thailand desk.[g]

The Thais in Washington also helped promote the American self-

[f] Until his death in 1962, Dolbeare served on the board of directors of the CIA-funded Free Europe Committee.

[g] Dr. Landon is now a professor at American University in Washington. His wife achieved fame as the author of *Anna and the King of Siam*.

image as protector of Bangkok's independence from the imperial greed
of other powers. One Thai student told his OSS mentor, "We have been
free for over seven hundred years. . . . It's unthinkable that our people
will tolerate the Japs for long. They've got sense enough to know that
they cannot be their own masters so long as the country is controlled by
aliens. Why do you think we fear France, Great Britain, and China?
Because they are all around us, and pressing uncomfortably close. We
Siamese resent any nation that imperils our freedom. We are for the
United States," he concluded, "because she has no territorial ambitions
in Asia." [32]

OSS required no Thai encouragement to be suspicious of the intentions of America's allies. Donovan's representatives feared that the
British SOE might infiltrate the first agents into Thailand and then
"shut off OSS from any high-level contacts in Bangkok by claiming
that any new Allied activity there would risk compromising the security
of the clandestine link already established with the Thais." [33] The
ensuing operations of OSS and SOE inevitably took on the appearance
of a spirited race to reach the Thai underground.

This rivalry was abetted by a diplomatic dispute. London had been
astounded by the Thai declaration of war. British confidence in unswerving Thai anglophilia was rudely shattered. London reacted like a
jilted lover, and rejecting American protestations declared war on
Thailand in February 1942. This was more than a technicality of international law; it branded the Thai people, in the eyes of Whitehall, as
"the enemy" (a label the State Department had unequivocally rejected).

The war declaration only whetted the SOE's interest in Thailand.
Like their counterparts in the United States, many Thai students living
in England repudiated the Pibul government after Pearl Harbor and
offered their services to the British military. There was no Free Thai
Legation in London to which the students could turn. Instead, SOE
persuaded Subha Svasti, a Thai prince living in Britain, to head an anti-
Pibul movement under the name "Major Arun." An SOE officer wrote,
"Arun was the only Siamese the British recognized as being 'good,' presumably because he was politically unacceptable to nearly all his
countrymen." A confirmed royalist, he had fled to permanent residence
in Britain after Pridi's coup against the monarchy. "Exile in London
with Siamese royalty had opened many doors to him in good society
and when he knocked on the door of No. 10 Downing Street he was
allowed in." [34] Svasti provided little assistance, however, in the SOE

recruitment of anti-royalist Thai students for military and intelligence training. Twenty-two young men were at last selected. They left London by boat for India at the beginning of 1943. Arriving in March, they were placed under Force 136, the SOE cover-name in the Far East.

OSS had, at first, a running start on the British. In April 1942, Kenneth Landon and other COI officials began to work with Seni Pramoj's Thai students in the preparation of a political warfare campaign against the Pibul government. Some were welcomed by Robert Sherwood's propaganda division and later transferred to the Office of War Information. Colonel Kharb Kunjara chose another group of twenty students to be trained as intelligence agents. They were given officer rank in a Free Thai military corps and sent, under Kunjara's command, to training camps of the newly named OSS.

In mid-year, an impetus for OSS action arrived in the person of a repatriated State Department officer from the American embassy at Bangkok. Before his internment by the Japanese, he had learned of the formation of a Free Thai movement organized by university students in the Thai capital. Their object was "to create an underground revolutionary group which at a propitious moment would seize power and free the country from the Japanese yoke and the control of its present leaders." [35] This was a small but important bit of encouragement for the OSS belief in the existence of an embryonic Thai resistance.

A bureaucratic snag prevented the immediate progress of OSS Thai operations—Donovan's officers had not yet established an official position on the Asian mainland. By late 1942, though Kunjara's students were already prepared for action, Detachment 101 was still a fledgling unit in the Burmese jungles, and Captain Miles was just receiving Donovan's short-lived blessing as OSS chief in Chungking.

After further delays, OSS at last decided to use Chinese territory as a base for the overland infiltration of the Free Thais. Colonel Kunjara would head the operation. Chosen as OSS liaison upon his return from a brief undercover assignment in Vichy France was Lieutenant Colonel Nicol Smith, the author of Burma Road and a witty lecturer who had traveled extensively through remote regions of Asia. Smith and Kunjara had just begun to outfit their Free Thais corps in January 1943 when the British-trained Thais sailed for India.

Smith quickly became aware of the delicacy of the SACO agreement which OSS was then negotiating with the "Chinese Himmler." Tai Li's representative in Washington was so pessimistic about the prospects for OSS success that Smith began to wonder if the Chinese "might not want an intelligence mission to enter Siam. . . . General Tai Li and his secret service were certainly a power that could make or break our mission. I hoped he was definitely on our side." [36]

Faced with a diplomatic labyrinth before he had even left Washington, the OSS colonel was consoled by his delightful Thai charges. The young men (known to OSS by nicknames such as "Sam" or "Ben" to avoid occidental difficulties in pronouncing such proper names as Chamroon Tishyanandana and Nithipatna Jalichandra) worked together with admirable esprit de corps, considering their diverse social backgrounds. Many of the students were of very "humble" birth, sent abroad on government scholarships, but one was a prince of royal blood and another a relative of Pridi's. All were intelligent and gregarious.

With Captain Miles established as OSS commander at Chungking, Colonel Kunjara flew to China to make preparations for the group. Smith and his Free Thai officers finally embarked by boat for India in March 1943, reaching Bombay in June and arriving in China in the summer of 1943. The British, meanwhile had not been idle. Following the arrival of the SOE Thais in India, a Siam Country Section of Force 136 was formed at Calcutta in June, commanded by an executive of the Bombay-Burma Trading Corporation, a company which held important shipping interests and teak forest leases in prewar Thailand.[37]

Following the model of SOE operations in France, the British created two independent pools of agents for Thai operations. The first teams were drawn from the Thai students recruited in Britain. They would be sent to their homeland to work with the underground, if one truly existed. London refused to believe that the Thais had organized any indigenous opposition to the Japanese and predicted that SOE's Thai agents were doomed to failure. A second set of agents was therefore chosen (with the "aid" of Tai Li) from among Bangkok-born, Thai-speaking Chinese. The Siam Country Section discovered, however, that these men were "no more than hostile Chinese agents infiltrated into the British forces." [38] SOE learned from its error. But OSS had already staked its entire Thai operation on the good will of the Chinese secret service. The SACO agreement specifically placed clandestine operations in Thailand under the jurisdiction of Captain Miles and Tai Li, and the Free Thais were soon to become another casualty of the battle between OSS and the "Chinese Himmler."

Miles greeted the young students-turned-agents who appeared at his headquarters, but later wondered "why these attractive but effer-

Author, lecturer, and explorer Nicol Smith with four of his young charges from the OSS Free Thai Army, all graduates of American universities.

vescent officers were sent to me. . . . Certainly we never asked for them. Still, there they were, and the problem was not exactly simplified when we remembered that Siam had declared war on us but we had not on them. This, as anyone can see, put the diplomatic proceedings in some doubt, especially as the Siamese, about this time, changed their name to Thais." Miles naturally turned, in his confusion, to his friend Tai Li. Repeating to Nicol Smith the official SACO litany ("To get anything done in China, you have to work with Tai Li") the captain came up with a plan. "Luckily," wrote Miles, "General Tai was in touch with a group of ten thousand well-trained Chinese at Puerh . . . near the border of Indo-China at the point nearest Thailand. We flew down to look them over and were amazed and delighted to learn that these troops, Chinese though they were, looked Thai even to the Thais themselves." Miles' plan was to send these troops through Indochina to Thailand under the command of the OSS Free Thai officers and mounted on ten thousand Tibetan horses to be "herded all the way down to the southern border of China by Chinese cowboys." [39] In December 1943, Miles was still planning his incredible "Puerh invasion" and Smith's contingent had only begun to establish an operational base in south China. SOE, meanwhile, had already made its first attempt to infiltrate a team of Thai agents by submarine.

Both American and British efforts were spurred by rumors that representatives of a Thai underground force had appeared in China. In August, Seni Pramoj's legation in Washington received a mysterious cablegram sent from Chunking by a purported representative of Pridi named Chamkad Balankura. An investigation by Colonel Kunjara led to Tai Li's reluctant admission that Balankura had indeed arrived as Pridi's envoy. But before Smith and Kunjara could fly Balankura to Washington for diplomatic discussions, he mysteriously "fell ill" and "died of cancer." [40] Tai Li had struck again.

Further inquiries in September revealed that two other Thai representatives were also in Chinese custody. One was Sanguan Tularak, former governor of a Thai penal colony who had assisted Pridi in his 1932 coup against the king.[h] The other, Dengh Tilakh, was a British-educated official of the Thai Foreign Ministry (with a well-deserved reputation as a playboy). These men assured Kunjara that a strong resistance network existed in Thailand under Pridi's command. In 1942 the underground had heard COI's short-wave broadcasts announcing Seni Pramoj's repudiation of the Pibul government. Balankura was dispatched to China to contact the Allies. He arrived in April 1943, only to be arrested by Tai Li's secret police. Tularak and Tilakh then followed him to Chungking. They had come to transmit a request from Pridi that he and other anti-Japanese politicians be smuggled out of Bangkok by the Allies to organize an exile movement. This thought terrified the British, who refused to talk to the two envoys, but OSS was interested. "By the exercise of great pressure on Chiang Kai-shek," the Americans "obtained Chinese permission to remove the Siamese party to Washington before even the slightest symptoms of carcinoma became apparent." [41]

Word of the underground contact soon reached Admiral Mountbatten, who had just arrived in India to assume command of the newly formed SEAC. While in China in October 1943 to discuss Asian strategy with Chiang, Lord Louis told Captain Miles of his own interest in Thai operations. He said that SOE had prepared a group of agents to infil-

[h] Tularak was Thailand's first postwar ambassador to China in 1946. He was dismissed from his post following Pibul's return to power in 1947. In 1951 Kunjara publicly accused Tularak, then in exile, of attending an international Communist conference in East Berlin.

trate the country under the leadership of Subha Svasti (the unpopular royalist prince), who "might succeed the King at some indefinite future date." [42]

"Later," wrote Miles, "the admiral even sent a man to see us in the hope of convincing us of the value of the plan. This person was the son of an ex-Dane and had previously been the head of the street railway company in Bangkok. But our whole Thai group took a hearty dislike to him, and they did not see eye to eye with the prince he was supporting either." [43] At a later meeting with Mountbatten, Miles was asked to combine the OSS Free Thais with the SOE group. Kunjara's young officers refused. "Knowing what they thought of the leader the British favored, as well as what General Tai's attitude would be, I knew that we could not put them under the Danish streetcar man, and in the end, the admiral and I agreed that there was room in Thailand for both groups to work separately." [44]

While SOE then proceeded to make its first attempts at infiltrating Thailand, Smith and Kunjara were stymied—the Donovan-Miles confrontation had plunged the entire OSS organization in China into total disarray. Flying to Chungking in December 1943 to relieve Miles of his OSS post, Donovan saw the projected "Puerh invasion" as another of Tai Li's ploys to gain control of OSS operations. Washington therefore cancelled the plan, leaving the Free Thais still impatiently encamped in south China. But despite Miles's dismissal, OSS was still tied to the SACO arrangement at the beginning of 1944 and Smith and Kunjara were still, unfortunately, dependent upon Tai Li for assistance.

The Chinese now proposed that the Free Thais be infiltrated as individual agents through Indochina to the Thai border. As a guide, Tai Li offered the services of a Laotian tribal prince (who was also a colonel in the Chinese army). The Laotian "spoke convincingly, saying that his agents went back and forth so often that there should be no delay." This remark led Smith to wonder why, "if there was so much traffic into Siam, Tai Li had given the Allies absolutely no military or other information about the internal affairs of the country." [45] Tai Li, who had sent his own intelligence operatives to Bangkok as early as 1942, simply had no desire to aid OSS, the Free Thais, or any other intelligence group not under his direct control.

In late February 1944, Kunjara selected five Thai officers to make the first attempt at overland infiltration under the guidance of the Laotian, but by the middle of April, all of the agents were still being stalled by their "guide." The Free Thais began to lose all hope of assistance from the Chinese. Smith and Kunjara were in despair, and Washington headquarters sent "impatient proddings."

There was good reason for official anxiety. In March and April 1944, two teams of British-trained Thais parachuted "blind" into northern Thailand. A third team of SOE's Chinese agents was dropped in May. None of these groups had yet established radio contact with Force 136 in India, but the creation of a link between the British and the Thai underground appeared to be close at hand. The State Department, involved in an acrid dispute with London over Thai policy, took a dim view of the prospect of British victory in the secret service steeplechase to Bangkok.

Wary of becoming mired down in disputes between Thai exiles, State had warned OSS some months before to avoid entangling political commitments in its Thai operations. "Mutual dislike and suspicion" between Seni Pramoj and Colonel Kunjara had already led to bitter divisions among the handful of Thais in the United States.[46] More distressing were the international complications. Thai exiles in Chungking and New Delhi accused the Chinese and British of manipulating them for "political advantage." [47] And America's allies were themselves wary of a Washington plot to boost Seni Pramoj as Thailand's postwar leader.

London brought the question of Thailand's future to the fore in February (as the SOE Thais made their first parachute infiltration). Whitehall sent the State Department a proposed public declaration of British policy which condemned the Pibul government for betraying the "long traditional friendship" between Britain and Thailand. Only if the Thai people made an effort to "save themselves from the worst consequences of their betrayal" would the British government "support the emergence of a free and independent Thailand after the war is over." The Foreign Office explained confidentially that the ambiguity of this statement would allow SOE to make the "best use" of its "Free Siamese material" without hamstringing Britain's postwar diplomacy in the Far East.[48] Dr. Landon and his State Department colleagues were not impressed with this Foreign Office ploy. They told Whitehall that a more appropriate declaration might include an "unequivocal commitment that Great Britain has no territorial ambitions in Thailand." [49]

The American diplomats were not arguing semantics. They had taken keen note of a recent speech by the prewar British ambassador to Bangkok. This seasoned diplomat (with important Foreign Office connections) ominously suggested that Southeast Asia was "not yet ready" for independence, and he singled out Thailand in arguing his case. Deploring in a single breath the "eclipse of the liberal elements" in the Thai government, the rise of Thai militarism, and Pibul's "unseemly dispute" with Anglo-American oil interests, the former ambassador concluded: "The attainment by Siam of complete autonomy . . . cannot be held to have justified itself in practice." He felt that Thailand should be placed under "some sort of tutelage" for "a period following upon the termination of the war." [50] The State Department was shocked by this suggestion of postwar imperialism, and the diplomatic debate dragged on.

Washington and London remained in heated argument while Smith and Kunjara were still bickering with Tai Li's agents. The Laotian colonel had been officially "reprimanded" for his failure to assist the Free Thais, but OSS headquarters wanted results, not protocol. The OSS Free Thais then had their first stroke of good fortune. Nicol Smith became acquainted with a Swiss-educated Chinese Catholic priest named Jean Tong, then serving as political advisor to a Chinese warlord. Smith found that Tong was thoroughly familiar with the Indochinese region and offered him one thousand dollars for the building of a church in his south China province if he would lead four of Kunjara's officers to the Thai border. Tong agreed, and he and the young Thais began their journey southward with a dire admonition from Kunjara: "Whatever happens—don't come back." [51] Two other groups began independent attempts at infiltration. Smith was hopeful that at least one of these eleven officers would successfully reach Bangkok.

The first radio message which they received in July was tragically disappointing. Two of the agents had been killed by the suspicious Japanese in Indochina. The enemy was now alerted and would probably increase the size of the patrols at the Indochina frontier.

As the remaining Free Thais in China waited nervously at their radio receiver, the OSS contingent at SEAC headquarters prepared their own plan for a Thai infiltration. Edmond Taylor, the OSS representative at Mountbatten's command, told General Stilwell that "our British rivals had already slipped an agent of their own into the country without official sanction—or so we feared—and could be expected shortly to 'surface' the operation. . . . That, it was pointed out to Stilwell, would isolate the leaders of the Thai resistance from any liberalizing U.S. influences and make them little more than native mercenaries of British imperialism; the proposed OSS operation aimed, on the contrary, at ultimately bringing Thailand into the war as a kind of secret member of

the United Nations, thus assuring its national independence and dignity
after our common victory. The argument—in which I firmly believed
myself—proved irresistible to Uncle Joe." [52]

But the British had already won the first round. On August 18,
1944, SOE headquarters at Calcutta gleefully received a first radio
message from its Thai agents in Bangkok who had made contact with
the underground. Yet neither Smith in China nor the OSS in Ceylon
could report a successful contact to Donovan. Smith was told that
Washington had angrily given up on the entire Free Thai operation and
was preparing to send Chinese army agents to "reach the Thai army
and buy them off." [53] OSS SEAC even swallowed its pride and asked
its British rivals for assistance in arranging a parachute drop to remote
northeastern Thailand. SOE's Siam Country Section seemed perfectly
willing to help, but felt that the northeast was a poor geographical area
for infiltration. A British staff officer at a higher echelon passed along
the Country Section's comment but phrased it as a reply from Pridi.
Only later did the Americans learn that the Free Thais had never been
consulted. "This unnecessary misunderstanding," recalled an SOE
officer, "did not make OSS love us in the least." [54]

Overtures to the Chinese and the British were signs of desperation.
Intelligence from Thailand was still nonexistent. Chennault's Fourteenth Air Force was clamoring for information on strategic bombing
targets. SOE was already in touch with Bangkok. And the State Department was frustrated by interminable discussions with the British over
Thai policy.

Fruitless diplomatic debate had provoked Cordell Hull's acid comment to Whitehall that it would be unfortunate if Britain and the
United States were unable to agree on the "long term objectives for
which this war is being fought." Whitehall responded in September
1944 by calling for a "much-needed clearing of the air" over Thai policy
differences. The Foreign Office suggested that discussion of Thailand's
future be postponed until the "outline of the postwar settlement in the
Far East is clear." The immediate goal, London insisted, should be to
drive the Japanese from the country and to encourage the Thai underground to "make the maximum contribution" toward the country's
liberation. The British, however, deprecated the "practical value" of
Pridi's movement. "If the resistance," declared Whitehall, "is to be
encouraged, it may need a spur rather than a sugar-plum." [55]

One day in October, the OSS Free Thais were maintaining their
normal vigil at the radio receiver in China when a transmission was

received—from Bangkok. The group of officers guided south by Father Tong had succeeded in contacting the Thai resistance and were secretly installed within the Bangkok headquarters of the national police, whose chief was a member of the underground. Within days, meteorological and military intelligence was flowing in to China. Soon other Free Thais were sent into the country on British Catalina seaplanes that landed secretly in the Gulf of Siam. An almost routine procedure was thus established for agents and Thai underground representatives journeying to and from Bangkok. Under the direction of OSS Lieutenants John Calhoun [i] and William Horrigan,[j] both New York attorneys, a secret American outpost was also established on Davis Island, 20 miles off the coast of Thailand, as a radio relay station and future supply base for the underground.[56]

The race to Bangkok had ended in a draw. The Anglo-American diplomatic dialogue was now intensified, but with little effect; the British refused to state their postwar plans in precise terms. The Thai underground could not wait. In July, the moderate elements of the Thai government joined Pridi's cohorts in a remarkable coup—they ousted Pibul from the Premiership by a parliamentary vote without provoking a Japanese reaction. As dissatisfaction with his dictatorial inclinations and costly government boondoggles had grown, Pibul's political strength had been steadily eroded. The opposition was finally able, under the suspicious eyes of the Japanese, to replace Pibul with a more temperate politician. In reality, the executive power of the government now shifted into the hands of Pridi.[57]

Having demonstrated its strength, the underground sought to assure the Allies of its willingness to assist the military effort against the Japanese. With the establishment of radio communications, daily intelligence was sent from Bangkok to SEAC headquarters in Ceylon on weather conditions, bombing targets, and Japanese troops movements. Valuable intelligence was obtained directly from the Thai embassy in Tokyo. Even hawk-faced General Chennault ventured a smile when one of his pilots, shot down over Thailand and interned by the Japanese, was rescued by the underground and returned to China.

To give the fullest international recognition to their pro-Allied sympathies, the Thai underground leaders wanted to establish a govern-

[i] Calhoun became Deputy Attorney General of the United States during the Eisenhower administration.

[j] Horrigan is now president of the Panama-based World Commerce Corporation, an international business concern founded by General Donovan that was once allegedly tied to CIA operations.

ment in exile. The State Department, however, objected to this plan, foreseeing the inter-Allied tensions that might result. Washington believed that the Chinese already controlled a Thai exile group at Chungking. And Tai Li's agents had virtually kidnapped one of Pridi's emissaries to establish direct communication with the Bangkok underground.

The British, conversely, were still resolved to downgrade the importance of the Thai resistance. Officers of SOE's Siam Country Section waged a lonely struggle against the "disinterested, frigid, and negative attitude" of skeptical London diplomats. The Foreign Office continued to deprecate Pridi's Free Thais as "nothing more than a band of intriguing politicians, without military support, more trouble than they were worth, with no prospect of developing into an effective resistance movement." To the disgust of many SOE men in India, London even contended that the messages being received from Bangkok were not authentic—that they were being sent back by agents who had been "doubled" under Japanese coercion.[58]

Washington rejected this British assessment of Pridi's movement. OSS accorded such importance to close relations with the underground that it installed Sanguan Tularak, Pridi's first representative to Washington, as an official advisor at OSS headquarters in Ceylon (where he was popularly known as "Sam"). And when, at the end of 1944, Pridi requested Allied assistance in organizing anti-Japanese guerrilla groups, Donovan was delighted. He felt the idea should be immediately explored by American officers in direct conversations with the Thai regent.

SOE had similar plans. After a long search for a knowledgeable officer to send to the Thai capital, the British settled on Brigadier Victor Jaques, a six-foot-four-inch attorney who had practiced law in Bangkok for over a decade as counsel to the British-owned Siam Electric Company.[k] But Jaques's arrival in India was inexplicably delayed and, lamented one SOE officer, "the Americans were gratuitously provided with an opportunity to put an officer into Bangkok before we did, an opportunity they proceeded to grasp." [59]

In late January 1945, two OSS majors landed by seaplane in the Gulf of Siam. They were taken by motor launch up the coast and whisked by automobile through the busy streets of Japanese-occupied Bangkok. The senior officer was Richard Greenlee, a 33-year-old Harvard graduate who had worked in Washington for the Board of Tax

---

[k] Jaques returned to Thailand after the war to become director of the International Rice Company and legal advisor to the Thai Electric Company.

Appeals before joining General Donovan's law firm.[1] For the past year, he had been serving at SEAC's headquarters as chief of the Special Operations Branch. Greenlee had no first-hand knowledge of Thailand; he was chosen to impress the British as "an outsider who would not be prejudiced in favor of the Siamese." [60] Accompanying him on the mission was an "old Thai hand," John Wester, an engineer who had lived in Thailand for over fifteen years.

Five days after his arrival, Greenlee was spirited out of the country and flown to Washington. He brought with him two gold cigarette cases, sent by Pridi to President Roosevelt and General Donovan. The "unprejudiced" major also relayed his personal endorsement of Pridi's proposal for a Thai uprising against the Japanese. To the relief of OSS headquarters and the exasperated Colonel Smith, the plan would be coordinated through SEAC rather than the China Theater. By the end of February Kunjara and the remaining Free Thais had moved their base from southern China to Ceylon, where they began training young Thai students in the "tradecraft" of clandestine operations. Before joining them, Smith was flown to Washington for direct conferences with State Department officials embroiled in the political complexities of Allied planning for Thai guerrilla warfare.

Earlier disagreement between Washington and London had created a reservoir of mutual distrust that permeated Anglo-American relations in Asia. Even in distant Chungking, Ambassador Hurley diverted his attention from an impending Chinese civil war to warn that the British might "succeed in out-maneuvering us and the Chinese and in gaining some measure of control over Thailand." [61] Washington required no caveat. In a document prepared for Roosevelt's use at the Yalta Conference, the State Department noted: "The history of European pressure on Thailand and of acquisition of territory in Southeast Asia is vivid in Asiatic memories. This government cannot afford to share responsibility in any way for a continuance toward Thailand of prewar imperialism in any guise." [62] This forthright statement was a response to diplomatic hints that the British planned to impose harsh postwar restraints on the freedom of the Thai nation. At SEAC headquarters, the British Foreign Office representative casually told an OSS official that "one of the aspirations of the British government policy, postwar, was to get Thailand to cede her two southernmost provinces to

[1] In 1962, Greenlee appeared as secretary of the Vanguard Service Corporation, a Miami-based CIA front group for a covert anti-Castro radio station which broadcast from a small island off the coast of Honduras.

Malaya." With "righteous indignation at the time," the OSS man
scurried off to inform Washington of "the implied perfidy of British
long-range planning and their inability to learn from the past." [63]

Political problems were suddenly eclipsed by alarming events in
Indochina. On March 9, the Japanese staged a coup d'etat against the
Vichy French administration which they had tolerated in Saigon.
Pridi and OSS feared that the Japanese might launch a similar coup
at Bangkok. The Thais called for emergency assistance to their secret
guerrilla forces.

But the British would not agree. Despite OSS and SOE reports
from the field, praising the growing strength and military potential of
the Thai underground, the Foreign Office still insisted that no "great
results" should be expected from the resistance. British agents, however, told a different story. "There was a reception committee for every
drop," recalled an SOE-trained Thai who joined an infiltration mission. "Transport, food, shelter, and cover-stories were provided. . . .
As practically all the government officials and the civilian population
were with us there was no hide-and-seek with the Japanese counter-
espionage. . . . Once established in our respective areas, all we had to
do was to state what we required: the categories of men for the different
types of work and the number of recruits we wanted. The underground
responded promptly. . . . Guerrilla and subversive activities would have
been well-nigh impossible had it not been for the organization inside
Siam. . . . Without local help we would not have lasted long." [64]

OSS was more receptive to the equally glowing accounts of its
Free Thai officers. Donovan and his SO Branch chief, New York
attorney Carl Hoffmann,[m] were determined to supply and train the
Thai guerrilla force whatever the political consequences. Somewhat
to its surprise, the State Department discovered that a "high OSS
officer" had promised the Thais American military assistance long
before Washington even began to consider the matter. "This promise
may well have been unauthorized," admitted the diplomats sheepishly.
Nonetheless, State believed it was of the "highest political importance"
to honor the commitment.[65]

What if the British objected to aiding Pridi's guerrillas? OSS was
prepared to carry out its operations without British consent—and, if

m Hoffmann served as Consul General for the Thai government in
New York, 1945–50. Donovan became a registered foreign agent for the
Thai government after the war and in 1953 was appointed U.S. ambassador
to Thailand.

necessary, in contravention of Mountbatten's directives. Luckily, Donovan's men avoided a direct confrontation. At the end of April, SOE Brigadier Victor Jaques finally reached Bangkok in the company of Prince Subha Svasti. The unpopular royalist had been included in the mission at London's insistence, against the advice of Force 136, and to the perplexity of the Free Thais. The prince was swiftly shunted off to a "liaison" post at the Burmese border and Jaques then received a warm welcome from Pridi. Within a week the brigadier was flown back to Ceylon to lend his vigorous support to Pridi's requests for military aid. Mountbatten agreed in principle. Thailand, the admiral noted, "already contained the nucleus of a well-organized resistance movement. This movement, when armed, supplied, and controlled by a Mission from SEAC headquarters, would be able to give us valuable assistance; at the moment, however, it was very short of equipment, and largely untrained, and therefore incapable of initiating a coordinated revolt. And it was important that its rising should not be premature; for this might provoke strong Japanese counter-measures which would make the eventual task of our own forces more difficult." [66] Whitehall accepted Mountbatten's recommendations for aid to the underground, but retreated to a new position that the guerrillas should be restrained from "premature" action before the launching of an Allied "invasion." OSS cynics observed that this restraint served British diplomatic objectives by preventing indefinitely any overt Thai contribution to the country's liberation, for Mountbatten's "invasion" would be long in coming.[67]

At least OSS was now free to pursue its operational plans. Major Greenlee returned to Bangkok in April accompanied by OSS Captain Howard Palmer, a 27-year-old Harvard Law School graduate.[n] Palmer's father had been Dean of Bangkok Christian College before the war and was a close friend of Pridi's.[68] The young Palmer, who had lived in Thailand until the age of nine, shared Kenneth Landon's missionary background and emotional sympathy for the Thai people. He had spent the preceding months working with Sanguan Tularak at SEAC headquarters in OSS planning for Thai operations. Now Palmer had come to Bangkok to replace John Wester. After two months as the only OSS officer in the Thai capital, Wester was in a state of deteriorating health under the psychological strains of his clandestine existence. He was secretly flown out of the country in a state of delirium.

[n] Palmer is now legal counsel for the Arabian-American Oil Company.

At the beginning of May, as Germany's surrender appeared imminent, both OSS and SOE expanded their missions in Thailand. Allied officers who had seen service with European guerrilla forces received fresh assignments in the Thai hinterland. Many of these new OSS arrivals were fascinated by the Thai nation and its exotic culture. The Thais were equally taken with these easy-going Americans. One of the most popular OSS men sent into the country was a young officer who attempted to deliver a short after-dinner speech in halting Thai to an informal conference of guerrilla leaders. "American officers," he said in words gleaned from a hasty language-training course, "hate Japanese, love Thai people. Otherwise [they are] no good, all the time drink whisky, shoot crap, fornicate, masturbate." This result of the officer's confused syntax "spread spontaneously throughout the entire kingdom in a remarkably short space of time and enormously enhanced American prestige." OSS SEAC representative Edmond Taylor explained. "The cultural and political implications of the anecdote—to all Siamese who heard it—were that Americans were really different from other Westerners because they did not stand on their dignity and try to appear superior, therefore they must have some sincere affection and respect for the Siamese people and were possibly truthful in proclaiming that they had no motive except to help the Siamese drive out the Japanese." [69]

Through OSS channels, Pridi (who had become known in all official diplomatic papers by the OSS code-name "Ruth") thanked Washington for its offer of assistance. American aid, he noted, would be "invaluable to the Thai in their struggle against the Japanese if it can be rendered soon enough." [70] Pridi's messages frequently emphasized the urgency of the situation. He spoke of Japanese suspicion and an impending crisis. "The Jap desire to fight," stressed Pridi, "can be weakened if the resistance movement no longer tries to remain under cover." [71]

Echoing Mountbatten's warning against premature rebellion, Washington responded with pleas for Thai restraint. State Department officials expressed private doubts that the Japanese planned any action against the Thai government. After all, in early May, after the German surrender, the Thais had taken the Nazi diplomatic officials into "protective custody" and had seized German property—all without Japanese objection.

Why, then, the worried cables from Bangkok? There was certainly some genuine fear in Pridi's camp of a sudden Japanese coup. But Washington suspected that continued requests for American assistance to open revolt also contained some hint of concern with the attitude of British diplomats. The Thais could understand the inability of the Allied command to deliver the 900 tons of equipment requested for the guerrilla camps. Aircraft for supply drops had simply been pre-empted by immediate strategic requirements in Burma and Malaya. (By the end of the war, only 175 tons of equipment actually reached the 10,000 guerrillas of the Thai underground.) It was more difficult, however, to accept British frigidity in conferences with Thai envoys at SEAC headquarters.

At first opportunity in the fall of 1944, Pridi had asked that a small party of Free Thai leaders be exfiltrated to Ceylon for discussions with Mountbatten. SOE's Siam Country Section welcomed the idea, only to be reprimanded by higher echelons. An SOE officer recalls the irate reaction of his superiors: "Damn it, it practically amounted to making peace with Siam! How dare we!" [72]

The proposal was revived at the beginning of 1945. Three Thai representatives were at last brought to SEAC headquarters in late January. Mountbatten declined to see them. The Thais nevertheless requested a public Allied declaration guaranteeing the country's post-war independence. Such a statement, they said, would greatly strengthen Pridi's hand inside the country. They were handed a written reply from His Majesty's government. Whitehall favored Thailand's independence, according to the statement, but "the road to be trodden before this goal is reached is not a smooth one. Much will depend on measures which Thailand makes to contribute towards expulsion of the Japanese from Thai territory." [73] While British diplomats told the Thais their postwar freedom hinged upon open resistance to the enemy, a British admiral paradoxically refused to sanction such military action.

The Thais had no doubts about British official duplicity. On one occasion, a senior Thai officer was sent to SEAC headquarters at Kandy in Ceylon with a special message from Pridi to Mountbatten. He also carried a pair of gold cufflinks bearing the emblem of the Thai King as a present for the admiral. Similar gifts had been gratefully accepted as symbols of Thai friendship by General Donovan and other OSS officials, and even by President Roosevelt. When the Thai officer reached Ceylon, however, he was met by an SOE colonel who "had the unpleasant task of telling him that it was the view of Lord Mountbatten's political advisor that he should not accept the links," since they came from an "enemy" nation. The envoy "seemed puzzled by the mysterious ways of the occident." [74]

The Thai guerrilla forces, meanwhile, grew stronger. The capture

of Rangoon freed Burmese airfields for flights to Thailand. Supply shipments to the guerrilla camps increased. So did the number of OSS
and SOE men who slipped into the country, all confident that their
own service's activities in Thailand were paramount. One British officer
who dropped into the Thai countryside in the summer of 1945 recalled
with assurance that there were "very few OSS officers in Siam, this
theater of operations being the agreed responsibility of the British."
Another British official noted that OSS operations were "less organized
than ours, and established for the most part in less vital areas." Nicol
Smith and his fellow Americans had a different view. SOE officers in
Thailand, wrote Smith, were "engaged in the same kind of operations
as ours, except on a smaller scale." [75] Security measures explain the
contradiction only in part. Purposeful lack of coordination was the real
key. SEAC headquarters reasoned that the "rival firms" would not cooperate in Thailand and should therefore be kept "reasonably well
apart." [76] OSS and SOE men were, therefore, rarely in contact with
one another in the Thai rural areas. American and British camps were
always in different parts of the country and field officers were not told
the location of the other guerrilla bases.

OSS officers who downplayed the SOE effort spoke as much out
of pride as ignorance, a pride that grew out of passionate admiration
for the Free Thais. Far to the north of the Thai capital, OSS Major
John Holliday, an ex-missionary who spoke fluent Thai, worked as
an espionage agent and director of a rural medical clinic. Holliday was
a "stocky, well-built man in the early fifties, with a bronzed square face,
a strong jaw, and a quiet, friendly manner." Even the British admitted
that the major was "held in great affection and respect by the Siamese
people." [77]

Such "old Thai hands" comprised only a minority of the OSS
mission. Most American officers in Thailand were on their first "trip"
to the strange Asian nation, but they too developed an emotional rapport with the Thais and a special admiration for Pridi. Howard
Palmer's successor as OSS Bangkok commander was Major James
Thompson, a Princeton graduate and New York architect recruited
earlier in the war by OSS officer Edwin Black to serve with the underground in Italy and France.° Both Thompson and his top aide, Lieutenant Commander Alexander MacDonald, adopted Thailand as their

° In 1967 Black was a brigadier general commanding U.S. forces in
Thailand.

new home after the Japanese surrender.[p] MacDonald had already traveled extensively in the Far East as a journalist, but this Asian experience was only a prelude to his love affair with the Thai people. He held a particular fondness for Pridi. "I had always admired him," Thompson remembered, "since first reading of his career back in OSS days, then knowing him personally. For me he had always been a romantic figure. Pridi, more than any other man in my time, had shaped the course of Siam's modern history. . . . Despite any differences of opinion, his leadership had become for me something of a cause. . . . Wherever he was affected I probably should never be fully objective in my thinking or writing. I thought of the young student in Paris, fired by the impact of new ideas. . . . I thought of the resistance leader, working dangerously and hard for the cause of his kingdom. . . . Without being asked, I had hitched my wagon to those starry promises of the 1932 revolution. The things their little revolution stood for—the passing of power from king to people, the chance for men of any breed to win honors by their own efforts and talent—were the things for me. . . . Such freedoms are born only when the spirit of the people is aroused by the unselfish leadership of men such as Pridi must have been in 1932, and, I believed, still was in 1945." [78]

The State Department officials under Dr. Landon's direction conjured up their own image of America as the guarantor of Thai independence. "The Thai authorities," read a State policy paper in late June, are "afraid of British ambitions" and "Chinese intentions"; the Thais "regard the United States as their refuge in a turbulent postwar period and will look to the United States to protect them from undue extension of British and Chinese influence over Thailand." [79]

This was the political mentality of American officialdom as V-J Day approached. If diplomacy became a preeminent concern, however, it was because military developments were anticlimactic. In mid-year, Mountbatten had decided that SEAC would be unable to undertake an invasion of Thailand until December; he informed the Thais that their uprising would have to wait.

This was not an easy decision for the well-organized underground to accept. OSS and SOE officers, together with arms and supplies, were

[p] MacDonald became editor of Bangkok's largest English-language newspaper in the late 1940s. Thompson founded a multi-million-dollar silk export business in Bangkok. He was frequently reported to have CIA connections and he disappeared in Malaya under mysterious circumstances in 1967.

already landing at secret resistance airfields in the very heart of the country. At the capital, OSS was covertly housed in the exquisite Palace of Roses, which had been used by the dictator Pibul Songgram until his ouster from power. Inside the building, powerful radio transmitters beamed hourly transmissions to OSS teams in the rural areas and to SEAC headquarters. Since SOE Brigadier Jaques was quartered in another part of the city, OSS officers were escorted across town to conferences with the British by Thai military police under the very noses of the Japanese.

Both Thais and Americans found the days of inaction almost unbearable, as Nicol Smith discovered when he made his first clandestine trip to Bangkok in July. The OSS colonel was rushed to a conference with Pridi. "Dressed elegantly in white pongee trousers and coat and a delicately embroidered white silk scarf about his neck that set off his full features and ruddy coloring," the Thai Regent, noted Smith, "was a handsome, vigorous man. He dominated the room from the moment he entered." Pridi came directly to the point. "I am having difficulty holding my people back," he told Smith. "I cannot do so indefinitely." [80] As instructed by his superiors, Smith could only repeat the empty formula for restraint.

As August arrived, the Japanese threatened to force the Thais into action. Having discovered three secret SOE airfields in the north, the Japanese command at Bangkok summoned Thai leaders to an official meeting to discuss what should be done about the "traitors" of the underground who had built the fields. Pridi told Howard Palmer that he feared assassination. Then news came that a company of Japanese were on their way to one of the OSS airfields to investigate. OSS men and Thai guerrillas prepared to do battle at long last.

But Tokyo surrendered before the shooting began and the Japanese command in southeast Asia sued for peace. The termination of hostilities finally brought into the open the submerged diplomatic conflict of the previous three years. The war was over, but a different sort of battle was yet to be fought.

OSS formed the front rank of the American forces on the new diplomatic battlefield. On August 19, several weeks before the formal surrender of Japan, two OSS men hurriedly left SEAC headquarters en route to the Thai capital, where Japanese troops still remained under arms: they were Dr. S. Dillon Ripley,[q] a noted ornithologist and chief

[q] Dr. Ripley is now Secretary of the Smithsonian Institution in Washington.

of the OSS counter-intelligence branch for southeast Asia, and Edmond Taylor, then SI Branch chief for SEAC. (Taylor had relegated his unenviable liaison post at Mountbatten's headquarters to Harry Berno, the unsuspecting president of a Cleveland cement company who had been lured into an OSS colonel's uniform.)[r]

Taylor, recalled Ripley, "wanted to be in Bangkok at the earliest moment when something could be done to help the Allied, and particularly the American, prisoners of war who had been serving as slave labor for the Japs in Burma, Siam, and Malaya for three years. . . . My particular interest lay in finding out about the state of mind of the Jap commander and his forces and their potentialities." [81] Taylor adds a revealing note about the purpose of his trip: "I was sent on a clandestine mission to Bangkok, ostensibly to make arrangements for the rapid evacuation of American prisoners held by the Japanese in Thailand, but no less, I gathered, to stiffen Thai resistance to any British encroachments on the nation's sovereignty." [82]

They were met in Bangkok by Howard Palmer, then OSS commander in the city, and taken to meet Pridi, "the most impressive man in Siam and one of the real statesmen of Asia." The Regent, added Ripley, was "a gracious man and expressed his gratitude frankly and wholeheartedly for the help of our organization in maintaining radio communications for him with the outside world as well as for the training and supplying that we had done." [83]

The OSS men busied themselves with the evacuation of Allied prisoners. While this task was under way, during the last week of August, SEAC headquarters requested that a Thai military mission come to Ceylon as soon as possible. Mountbatten had provided a plane which would fly directly out to Rangoon and then south to Ceylon. Since Dr. Ripley's own mission in Bangkok was coming to an end, he arranged to join the group in its flight on September 1. They reached Ceylon on September 2, the same day the Japanese signed the formal terms of surrender in Tokyo Bay. The British were already prepared for a repetition of that ceremony with their Thai "enemies."

In early August, the British had sent the State Department their proposed peace terms for Thailand. Whitehall asked that the specifics be kept "strictly confidential" and not be divulged to the Thais. State

[r] In 1946 Berno transferred to Germany and became chief of the heavy industries division of the American military government, a post that brought him into contact with many wealthy right-wing German industrialists. Five years later, he died of a heart attack in a New York hotel. An ex-FBI agent later charged that Berno was "silenced" by Soviet agents.

officials promptly raised ardent objections to many clauses of the treaty. More fundamentally, Washington argued that British political negotiations with Thai representatives should not take place under the auspices of an Anglo-American headquarters like SEAC. While these problems were still being shunted through diplomatic channels, the Thai delegation reached Ceylon. Lord Mountbatten insisted that the Thais sign the proposed treaty within forty-eight hours. Neither the State Department nor the American military command at SEAC were informed of the British ultimatum.

Then, according to one journalistic account, the OSS chief in Bangkok, Howard Palmer, "learned that the Siamese were about to submit to some severe British demands." Palmer sent a priority message to Colonel John Coughlin, the tall West Pointer who commanded OSS SEAC. "Coughlin managed to see a copy of the little paper. It was the list of twenty-one demands that 'would have made Siam a slave state for years to come,' in the words of Seni Pramoj. Shocked, Coughlin coded a cable to Washington and on his own responsibility persuaded the Siamese to sign nothing till the United States government was heard from. Owing to Coughlin's initiative, the luncheon failed to conclude exactly as planned. The Siamese picked out five demands to which they felt they could honorably agree—the rest they referred to Bangkok." [84]

This version gives a bit too much credit to OSS. Colonel Coughlin and his aides first notified State Department officials in India. Then the commanding general of American forces in the South East Asia Command convinced the Thais to withhold their agreement until Washington could be informed. A message was dispatched through OSS channels and received at the State Department by Kenneth Landon. He and his associates on the Thai desk "hustled our Under-secretary, Joseph Grew, to the scrambled telephone to get him to talk with his opposite number in the Foreign Office." [85] The ultimatum was thus set aside and the negotiations delayed. When an Anglo-Thai peace treaty was at last signed under the watchful eyes of American diplomats, in January 1946, the Thai nation emerged with its sovereignty unimpaired.

Why all the diplomatic sound and fury? One SOE official in Ceylon later pooh-poohed the significance of the incident. He accused the Thais of adeptly "playing off Britain and America against each other." The Thai government, he added, "became convinced that, when the moment to conclude a treaty arrived, it would be able to avoid any terms it disliked by appealing for American intervention." The proposed Anglo-Thai treaty, this British officer concluded, contained "nothing like the dictatorial terms which rumor had spread abroad." [86]

The Thais had indeed used the anti-colonial predilections of their American friends to good advantage. But the SOE protagonist glossed too easily over the terms of the original treaty. That document would have given British occupational authorities in Thailand complete supervision of Thai banks, commercial enterprises, foreign exchange, shipping, ports, and communications. The Thais, in addition, would have been prevented from placing any restrictions on the operations of British companies in their country without the approval of His Majesty's government.

Several years earlier, Winston Churchill had startled the American public with his virtual disavowal of the principles of the Atlantic Charter. "We mean to hold our own," he proclaimed. "I did not become His Majesty's first minister in order to preside over the liquidation of the British Empire." [87]

With the encouragement of his OSS friends, Seni Pramoj, Thailand's first postwar premier, had an apt reply to London's imperial determination.[s] "I told the British," said Seni, "that I did not become the King's first minister in order to sell my country into bondage for two generations." [88]

Seni saved a final barb for the world's second great colonial power. "As for France," he said, "she is the last nation entitled to play the role of injured innocence toward us." [89] The French government was vocally demanding the return of all Indochinese territory that Pibul's government had forcibly seized with Japanese aid in 1941. When the Thais suggested that control of these areas of Laos and Cambodia be decided by a United Nations plebiscite, Paris suspected "OSS agents" of fomenting a Thai plot against the French colonies.[90]

What irked the French even more than the territorial dispute was the overt support both the Thais and their OSS friends were giving to Indochinese nationalists in their struggle for independence.

---

[s] Seni soon broke with Pridi and resigned his post. Pibul overthrew Pridi's Free Thai government in 1948. Pridi went into exile, and after an unsuccessful attempt to depose Pibul in 1949 he settled in Red China to head a Thai "liberation committee." Pibul was himself overthrown in 1957 and died a Buddhist monk in Tokyo nine years later.

In western Indochina, just across the Mekong River from Thailand, the Laotian inhabitants had close bonds of race and language with the Thais. This area was also populated by sizable minority communities of ethnic Annamites or Vietnamese. The Japanese surrender found two nationalist groups organizing in this territory to prevent the return of the French.

A Free Lao movement was directed from Vientiane by the royal Laotian family, while the Annamites looked for political leadership to the Viet Minh organization, based some three hundred miles to the north in Hanoi. Across the Mekong on Thai territory, OSS and SOE teams were preparing to begin the disarmament of the Japaneese troops in Laos. Inevitably, these Americans and British became entangled in the impending Indochinese war against colonialism.

At the beginning of August, French officers parachuted into Laos for the ostensible purpose of rescuing French civilians interned by the Japanese. Their real objective, however, was to reestablish French sovereignty in the colony. These officers promptly found themselves faced with armed resistance from the Free Lao and the Viet Minh; they appealed for aid to their allies in Thailand. The British SOE teams answered the call by smuggling arms and supplies across the river to the French. But the OSS men in Thailand had other ideas.

One OSS team under the command of Major Aaron Banks, an ex-Jedburgh, set up camp at the Thai border across the river from the Laotian capital of Vientiane where the Free Lao forces were already in direct conflict with the French.[t] Banks and his men crossed the Mekong River and confronted the startled French with the demand that they immediately "cease their aggression" against the Laotians.[91] The American team then moved farther south and established its base in the Thai province which faced the Laotian towns of Thakhek and Savannakhet. Here the Viet Minh was the principal nationalist group.

When the OSS men found SOE officers in Thailand actively aiding the French against the Vietnamese, they began their own forays into Laos in support of the Viet Minh. In mid-September, according to the account of SOE officer Peter Kemp (who had fought for Franco during the Spanish Civil War), Major Banks met with Viet Minh leaders and "assured them that he was determined to put

[t] Ironically, it was Aaron Banks who first proposed to the Defense Department and CIA in the early 1950s that Special Forces units be formed to work as guerrillas in Communist territory. Banks was thus the "father" of the Green Berets.

an end to what he called French aggression," and to support "the establishment of a 'national and democratic government' in Indochina, free from the rule of France." [92] Soon the entire OSS team moved its headquarters into Laos and settled in a house provided by the Viet Minh.

Disregarding Viet Minh warnings to stay out of the area, a French officer, accompanied by Kemp, crossed the Mekong into Laos on September 27. As soon as they reached the other side of the river they were halted by Viet Minh troops who announced, "The Frenchman is under arrest and will come with us. The French declared war on us yesterday in Saigon." While OSS "neutral" observers stood by watching, Kemp and the Frenchman tried to escape to their boat, but the Vietnamese shot the French officer in the back. Turning to the embarrassed Americans, Kemp shouted angrily, "I hope you're proud of your Annamite friends." Pointing to his colleague's body on the ground he cried, "That is the direct result of your work!" [93]

Within a week, the American team made an involuntary departure. The French government had lodged a formal protest with Washington against the pro-nationalist activities of American officers in Laos. Paris asked that "instructions be sent to these officers, who are presumably cut off from their bases and acting on their own authority." [94] The diplomatic note was couched in sarcasm. By the end of September, the French had received persuasive proof that the OSS action in Laos was no isolated incident of American anti-colonialism.

10

Mission to Indochina

Three months after the government of Marshal Pétain capitulated to the Nazi conquerors, a second stunnning blow was dealt to the helpless French empire. In September 1940, Japanese troops swept into Tonkin, the northern division of France's Asian colony. Brief resistance was easily overcome and the Japanese took full military control of the whole of Indochina. For reasons of political convenience, the invaders chose to preserve intact the Saigon administration of Admiral Jean Decoux, the former commander of the French Navy in the Far East. As the personal choice of Admiral Darlan for the colonial governorship, Decoux swore loyalty to the Pétainist regime at Vichy. With the acquiescence of his collaborationist superiors in the metropole and, in return for the continuance of nominal French authority in the colony, Decoux promised his complete cooperation to the Japanese. The French colonials (only 40,000 of Indochina's 23 million inhabitants) were permitted to maintain control of their own army, so long as the vanquished troops did not interfere with Japanese military operations against the Allies.[1]

For the Vietnamese people (or Annamites, as they were then known), Asian imperialism was little better than European domination. Most native nationalists were resolved to win the independence of their country from both Tokyo militarists and their Vichyite collaborators. The defeat of the French by an oriental power only gave the Vietnamese new faith in the vulnerability of the colonial system. The nationalist movement included groups of every political and religious stripe. But the Communists, already experienced in the tactics of conspiracy, stood in the forefront of the battle for independence.

In May 1941, as the Decoux administration became firmly established in Saigon under Japanese auspices, a cabal of Vietnamese revolutionaries met in southern China to reorganize their scattered ranks into a unified political organization. The leader of this new Viet Minh movement was Nguyen Ai Quoc, a frail, bearded Communist agitator who had devoted his life to the cause of Vietnamese independence.

The Viet Minh had just begun to expand its nationalist front when Nguyen Ai Quoc was suddenly arrested in August 1942 by Tai Li's omniscient police agents. Wary of Quoc's Communist background, the Chinese had laid their own plans to build a Vietnamese nationalist movement subject to Kuomintang domination.

While Quoc languished in a Chinese jail, his lieutenants diligently constructed an effective military intelligence network throughout Tonkin. The success of Viet Minh espionage was not lost on Chiang Kai-shek's generals. In September 1943, after a year of confinement, Nguyen Ai Quoc agreed, in return for his freedom, to enlist the Viet Minh organization on behalf of one important Chinese warlord. Without the knowledge of Tai Li's minions, the warlord secured Quoc's release. The Viet Minh leader then assumed a new name to cloak his identity from General Tai's agents; he now called himself Ho Chi Minh.

Although he directed a large umbrella organization of Vietnamese nationalist groups, most of the hundred thousand Chinese dollars Ho received every month for espionage operations in Indochina was carefully funneled to the Communist-dominated Viet Minh network. Slowly and methodically, this intelligence organization was transformed into a small guerrilla army under the brilliant military command of Vo Nguyen Giap, a former Hanoi schoolteacher whose wife had died at the hands of the French police.

As Viet Minh strength increased, Ho's relations with his Chinese financial patrons became strained. By 1944, the Communists and their supporters were no longer in need of Kuomintang assistance. Late that year, the Viet Minh leaders sought new Allied sponsorship—at OSS headquarters in Kunming. At first with reluctance, OSS grasped the Viet Minh offer of cooperation. After months of impatience with internecine conflict among the French secret services in China, American officers welcomed any relief from the transplanted intrigue of North African resistance politics.

MISSION TO INDOCHINA

When Captain "Mary" Miles left Washington en route for China after the signing of the SACO agreement, he stopped briefly in Algiers to confer with French officials about future intelligence operations in Indochina. He reached North Africa in May 1943, days before de Gaulle arrived in Algiers to begin his climb to political dominance. Still intent, however, on sailing against the prevailing political winds, the OSS command at Algiers hustled Miles off to an audience with Washington's diplomatic creation, the hapless General Giraud, who agreed to assign a French officer to aid Miles in the creation of an Indochinese espionage network. Giraud's choice for this post was Robert Meynier, a 27-year-old naval commander.[2]

Meynier had distinguished himself as captain of a French submarine engaged in attacking Axis shipping. He held British and French decorations for gallantry, and although he was aligned politically with the Giraudist camp, he had received equal praise from the Gaullists. Meynier also had unique Indochinese ties. His beautiful Eurasian wife, "princess" Katiou Do Hun Thinh, was a member of the Vietnamese royal family. When Meynier escaped from France after the German occupation of Vichy in November 1942, his wife had been left behind. Miles learned that she was being held in a German prison camp. Stressing her value to OSS operations in Indochina, the captain left it to the SO Branch at Algiers to arrange her rescue. OSS requested British assistance and, soon after, a successful commando rescue mission was mounted. Several French and British officers died aiding Madame Meynier's escape.

While the "princess" was being smuggled out of occupied France, the Anglo-American conflict over French politics was coming to a head. With London's reluctant support, de Gaulle had already begun to dominate the French Committee of National Liberation at the expense of his Giraudist rivals. OSS thus foresaw British opposition to the appointment of the pro-Giraudist Meynier as coordinator of French-American intelligence operations in China. The result was a laborious American subterfuge to hide the Meynier plan from London. The deception was no simple task, for when the French commander left Algiers for India in the summer of 1943, he brought with him a team of Vietnamese, recently liberated from Vichy concentration camps. To disguise their nationality, the Vietnamese traveled incognito on a British vessel as agents of a mysterious "Philippine Army of Liberation." After their arrival in India in late 1943, Meynier's "Filipinos" received cordial British hospitality while OSS officers nervously arranged for their flight to Chungking.

Madame Meynier followed an equally devious route. Brought to London after her daring escape, OSS provided her with a cover as an American WAC. Until her departure for India, she remained ensconced in a London hotel, pretending to have a sore throat that made it impossible for her to speak. She soon joined her husband at SACO headquarters.

This complex conspiracy proved to be an enormous waste of American energy. To their dismay, the Meyniers found a Gaullist military mission already established at Chungking under the command of General Zinovi Pechkov of the French Foreign Legion, a one-armed Russian émigré (and bastard son of novelist Maxim Gorki). The fact that Meynier, a Giraudist, was working with Miles and SACO only compounded his difficulties with the French military mission, which was itself at odds with Tai Li. General Tai had accused the Gaullists of importing spies; Pechkov counter-charged that Chinese agents had killed French officers at the Tonkinese border to prevent them from reaching Indochina.[3]

Despite these problems, and with characteristic bravado, Captain Miles assured General Donovan that "within a few months we can have 200,000 to 300,000 agents working for us in Indochina if we want them." [4] The Meyniers planned to organize an intelligence and sabotage group and to smuggle rubber and tin contraband over the border into China. They hoped to work through Madame Meynier's uncle, Hoang Trong Phu, once titular governor of Tonkin. Phu's close association with the French colonial administration had made him the wealthiest Vietnamese in Hanoi.

These great expectations were short-lived. Meynier did succeed in sending one of his agents, a priest from North Africa, to aid in the rescue of Allied fliers from Tonkin. And he was able to establish contact with officials of the Decoux regime through anti-Gaullist French businessmen in Kunming. But the French military mission then intervened to prevent further operations. Miles complained to OSS headquarters in North Africa about the obstructive Gaullists; from Algiers came the sad response that high-level diplomacy had already altered the political balance of power in favor of de Gaulle.

The French mission at Chungking soon demanded that it be given a greater voice in the control of the Meynier group. The issue was swiftly resolved after Miles' dismissal as chief of OSS China in December 1943. By the middle of 1944, Meynier was also relieved of his position.[a] Miles believed that OSS was simply unwilling to further antagonize the Gaullists, who were then working closely with American officers in France. General Donovan, Miles complained, had "aligned himself firmly with those who wished to preserve the prewar Asian status quo."[5]

In one sense, the captain was correct. While Gaullist predominance in North Africa had been a victory over the reactionary forces of Vichy, Gaullist supremacy in the Far East was no triumph for French liberalism. In a speech at Algiers in December 1943, de Gaulle spoke of a "new political order" for Indochina within the "French community," a thinly veiled euphemism for the restoration of the old Empire. The following month, the French Committee of National Liberation held a conference at Brazzaville in French Equatorial Africa to consider the question of future relations between metropolitan France and its colonies. The delegates concluded that "the aims of the work of civilization which France is accomplishing in her possessions exclude any idea of autonomy and any possibility of development outside the French Empire bloc. The attainment of 'self-government' in the colonies, even in the most distant future, must be excluded."[6] Gaullist intentions were perfectly clear—Indochina would not be granted independence, not even in the "most distant future."

French imperial policy drew sustenance from British diplomats concerned over the fate of London's own colonial possessions in Asia. When the South East Asia Command came into existence in November 1943, the SOE's Force 136 established an Indochina Section at Calcutta under the command of a Gaullist colonel to direct clandestine operations in Vietnam, Laos, and Cambodia. The French colonel received his political directives from François de Langlade, director of a rubber plantation in prewar Malaya and de Gaulle's representative in India.

SOE coordinated its plans for the creation of an armed resistance group in Vietnam with the espionage operations of the Gaullist military mission at Chungking, which had already made contact with several separate intelligence networks in Indochina. One group of pro-Gaullist

[a] Meynier is now an admiral of the French Navy. In 1947 he and his wife appeared in Saigon with a new intelligence mission—to form a Vietnam Democratic Socialist Party as an opposition front to the Viet Minh. This effort was no more successful than Meynier's earlier SACO operations.

French landholders and businessmen, most of them owners of rubber plantations, had established an extensive espionage organization in the Saigon area. Intelligence was also received from a source of less ideological purity—"reformed" colonial army officers of the Vichyite Decoux administration. As an Allied victory in Europe appeared on the horizon, these French collaborators, who had maintained their official positions in Indochina through Japanese benevolence, developed sudden fits of patriotism and came into increasingly close contact with Gaullist agents.

Shortly after the Normandy invasion, the Free French envoy in India, de Langlade, parachuted into Indochina to meet with generals of the French colonial army who had agreed to aid the Gaullists in creating an anti-Japanese resistance organization. Three months later, the French commander at Saigon was secretly named de Gaulle's "delegate general" in Indochina. The British then began to parachute arms, ammunition, and agents to the newly formed underground.

Meanwhile, still another intelligence net in Tonkin was providing information to both the French and OSS. It was organized by Laurence Gordon, a Canadian businessman who had owned a coffee plantation in Kenya before beginning a career in international oil.[b] Gordon had supervised oil-drilling operations for Cal-Texaco in Africa, China, Egypt, and Madagascar, and at the outbreak of war he was directing the Cal-Texaco operation at Haiphong in North Indochina. Joining with Paul Bernard, an official of the British-owned Asian tobacco monopoly, and a Chinese businessman named Tau, Gordon organized the "G-B-T" espionage group in Indochina to provide information to the Allies. Unlike the French spy networks, Gordon's group was willing to work closely with any useful clandestine source, including the Viet Minh nationalist movement.

By late 1944, Ho Chi Minh and Vo Nguyen Giap had created a well-organized underground organization in the northern provinces of Tonkin. Having gained complete independence of its Chinese financial angels, the Viet Minh moved its headquarters to Vietnamese territory, began to supply Gordon and other Allied sources with invaluable intelligence, and aided in the rescue of downed pilots from Chennault's Fourteenth Air Force. The French, Gaullists and Vichyites alike, viewed this Viet Minh activity with alarm and refused to have anything to do with the Vietnamese underground.

[b] In 1957 Gordon was director of the overseas division of Cal-Texaco in Paris.

The Americans in China did not share the French reserve. At the beginning of 1945, Ho Chi Minh made several direct contacts in Kunming with OSS Colonel Paul Helliwell,[c] a Florida attorney who headed the SI Branch, and his deputy for Indochinese operations, Major Austin Glass, once an official of Socony Oil. Helliwell later denied that he had given significant assistance to the Viet Minh. "OSS China," he protested, "was at all times consistent in its policy of giving no help to individuals such as Ho, who were known Communists and therefore obvious sources of trouble." [7] The colonel admitted that he had sent Ho six revolvers and twenty thousand rounds of ammunition, but only as a token of appreciation for the rescue of American fliers. He had refused, he said, to send other arms shipments to the Viet Minh unless they agreed not to use them against the French, a condition that Ho would not accept.[8] Helliwell, however, did not speak for all divisions of OSS. The course of events in Indochina soon forced other officers of Donovan's organization to take a more intense interest in the Viet Minh movement.

Since the former Vichyite loyalists at Saigon first turned their eyes toward the Gaullist horizon, the underground in Indochina had grown by geometric proportions, as if to erase the memory of French defeat and collaboration with the Japanese. By January 1945, four months after the liberation of Paris, the French colonial population openly expressed support for the resistance. Soldiers went into the countryside to gather military supplies dropped by SOE; these arms were collected and then stupidly placed in the regular regimental arsenals in full view of the Japanese. French troops drilled and dreamed of liberation and a picture of de Gaulle hung openly in the offices of the French high command at Saigon.

The Japanese were not blind. On March 9, 1945, they presented Admiral Decoux with an ultimatum. The French armed forces, police, and administration were to be placed under Japanese command. The colonial governor-general was given two hours to reply; he asked for more time to study the demand. The Japanese responded by arresting Decoux, seizing administrative buildings, public utilities, radio stations, telegraph centers, banks, and industries. They attacked police and military garrisons and interned all French troops. The Free French underground of Indochina was squelched before it lifted a finger of resistance. Only one major underground force then remained in Indochinese territory—the Viet Minh.

[c] Helliwell is now consul-general for the Thai government in Miami.

The American response to the events in Saigon was formulated in an atmosphere of confused diplomacy. Two years earlier, at a Quebec conference of the Institute of Pacific Relations, Ralph Bunche and other officials of the OSS Research and Analysis Branch had first suggested postwar international trusteeships for the colonial areas of Southeast Asia. The idea was viewed with favor at the State Department and even more warmly received by the White House. Roosevelt had often told his close advisors that Indochina "should never be simply handed back to the French to be milked by their imperialists as had been the case for decades." [9] At the Cairo and Teheran Conferences in December 1943, he suggested to Stalin, Churchill, and Chiang Kai-shek that Indochina be placed under a trusteeship leading to eventual independence. The Chinese and Soviets were receptive; the British raised vigorous objections.

Whitehall was still adamant in its opposition to the trusteeship proposal when Roosevelt raised the question again the following year. In October 1944, when the ex-Vichyites at Saigon began to organize their underground organization in the colony, the President cautioned Cordell Hull that "we should do nothing in regard to resistance groups or in any other way in relation to Indochina," until the Anglo-American disagreement was resolved.[10]

The problem arose again at the Yalta talks in February 1945, weeks before the Japanese coup against the Decoux regime. Again the physically ailing President, requiring Churchill's support on other diplomatic issues, temporarily abandoned the trusteeship proposal. On the return journey to Washington he told a group of reporters that Stalin and Chiang "would go along" with the idea. But "as for the British, it would only make the British mad. Better to keep quiet just now." [11]

Having failed to win Allied agreement on the future decolonization of Indochina, Roosevelt was determined that the French would receive no American aid in returning to their colony. He clearly expressed this resolve after the March coup. Although the Japanese had succeeded in arresting most of the senior commanders of the French colonial army, some officers in Tonkin got wind of the Japanese plans and placed their forces on alert. After Decoux's arrest, these army units, commanded by Generals Allesandri and Sabattier, succeeded in escaping from Hanoi. They made their way north to the airfield at Dien Bien Phu and there radioed the American forces in China for supplies and air support. The messages were received by General Chennault at Kunming; he promptly expressed his willingness to help. But then, despite frantic French cables asking "Where are the Americans?" both supply drops and air support against the Japanese failed to materialize. Chennault had received instructions from Wedemeyer's headquarters that "no arms and ammunition would be provided to French troops under any circumstances." Wedemeyer, in turn, traced his orders directly to the President.[12]

While several thousand French and Vietnamese soldiers waited impatiently at Dien Bien Phu, their fate became a muddled international affair. On March 14, de Gaulle issued a statement in Paris criticizing the Allies for their delay in coming to the aid of the colonial army. Two weeks later, François de Langlade, then the official French envoy at SEAC, and André Dewavrin (Colonel "Passy" of the BCRA), flew into Dien Bien Phu on a British plane, their brief visit designed to dramatize the plight of the stranded colonial troops.

On the following day, OSS Lieutenant Robert Ettinger, a French-American of Jewish descent, arrived at the airfield as liaison to Sabattier's forces. He joined the French and Vietnamese troops as they began their fight through Tonkin to China, confronted by Japanese attacks, hunger, disease, and the anti-French Vietnamese populace. The American authorities had meanwhile relented, and in response to Ettinger's requests, Chennault's Fourteenth Air Force was allowed to strafe hostile Japanese columns along the line of retreat.

Weeks passed before Sabattier's troops reached the Chinese border. Hundreds died in the course of the march. But the victims had become pawns in an international political contest; not even the French government seemed genuinely concerned with their survival. De Gaulle was looking toward the forthcoming United Nations Conference at San Francisco, where the question of an Indochina trusteeship might arise. The general had callously concluded that "French blood shed on the soil of Indochina would constitute an impressive claim" to continued French sovereignty in the colony.[13] While official spokesmen at the Quai d'Orsay publicly grumbled that lack of American assistance was hindering Sabattier's withdrawal, de Gaulle privately urged his commanders in Tonkin to "prolong resistance on Indochinese soil whatever the difficulties." [14]

After fifty-seven days of struggle Sabattier's decimated corps finally trudged into Kunming in May 1945. Some 5500 troops, 3000 of them Vietnamese, survived the gruelling retreat. Many of the soldiers were flown to Burma for medical attention. The remaining forces were at first disarmed by the Chinese, then reorganized with the apparent objective of integration into the Chinese army, a plan which the French bitterly resisted. French officers told OSS men who met them at the Chinese border that they simply wanted "a chance to redeem their honor and go back and fight Japs as soon as they were reequipped." [15]

Many OSS men in China sympathized with the French predicament. There were notable French-Americans in the OSS ranks at Kunming, including AGFRTS Lieutenant Thibaut de Saint Phalle,[d] the nephew of an important Parisian banker, and Colonel Jacques di Sibour, a famous airplane pioneer. These men felt a personal sense of empathy for Sabattier's men. So did Lieutenant Ettinger, the OSS officer who had accompanied the Sabattier group from Dien Bien Phu. He quickly organized a new French-American operation to launch maritime infiltrations of Tonkin from the Chinese coast. Other American officers who had worked behind the lines with the Maquis in occupied France struck up rapid friendships with the displaced colonials who swelled the ranks of Kunming's French population.

Sabattier's tale of woe also received a sympathetic hearing from Colonel John Whitaker, the former foreign correspondent who had accompanied General Donovan to his meeting with Benedetto Croce on Capri two years earlier. As OSS Deputy Director for Intelligence in China, he worked closely with an old friend, the French chargé d'affaires at Kunming, to save many of Sabattier's troops from being placed under Chinese command.

Whitaker proposed to transfer some of these soldiers directly into OSS for clandestine training under the direction of Captain Archimedes L. A. Patti, chief of the Indochina desk of the SI Branch in Kunming (and later commander of the OSS mission to Hanoi). A former aide to Whitaker at the Psychological Warfare Branch in Italy, Patti was the son of an Italian-American New York attorney, a political associate of General Donovan's. The captain had met General Sabattier at the Chinese border and accompanied him to Kunming. From there, Sabattier was flown to Chungking for a meeting with Wedemeyer. In early June, an agreement was finally reached to transfer 100 Vietnamese soldiers and 25 French officers to OSS operational control for Tonkinese missions.

Some of these projected operations were actually launched before

[d] Saint Phalle is now Treasurer of the National Committee for an Effective Congress, a bipartisan group that supports liberal congressional candidates.

the end of the war, but internal French bickering again obstructed genuine progress. The Sabattier troops destined for secret service came under the command of an independent French intelligence group at Kunming known as Mission 5. This was an operating arm of André Dewavrin's secret service and was entirely free from French military control (to the constant irritation of General Sabattier).[16] Mission 5, which traced its origins to the Gaullist group that routed Meynier in 1943, was commanded by Jean Sainteny, a French resistance leader, former Hanoi banker, and son-in-law of a former governor-general of Indochina. Sainteny came into personal conflict with Sabattier and showed little enthusiasm for the integration of the general's men into OSS. "The French," deduced SI Branch chief Paul Helliwell, "were infinitely more concerned with keeping the Americans out of Indo-china than they were in defeating the Japanese or in doing anything to bring the war to a successful conclusion in that area." [17]

OSS men were forced to look elsewhere for assistance in their Indochinese operations. Even those who felt a strong emotional bond with the French were unable to deny that the Gaullists were no longer adequate sources of intelligence. One of the first OSS sabotage teams to infiltrate Tonkin, commanded by an ex-Jedburgh major, received faulty information from the French and was ambushed by a Japanese patrol.

The March coup had indeed eradicated the French underground and its intelligence network. But the guerrilla forces of Vo Nguyen Giap emerged unscathed from the political convulsion; by June, six entire Tonkinese provinces were in Viet Minh hands. The Allies were forced to accept Viet Minh strength as a military reality. The British SOE reluctantly rescued Vietnamese Communists who had been sent to political exile on Madagascar and parachuted them into the Ton-kinese hinterland.

OSS also began to send liaison officers to the Viet Minh. One OSS lieutenant, an official of the Chase Manhattan Bank, was dropped to Ho Chi Minh's headquarters in May and spent several months living and working with the Viet Minh guerrillas. He later recalled that Ho expressed a particular interest in the American Declaration of Independence. The Viet Minh leader "kept asking me if I could remember the language of our Declaration," the lieutenant recalls. "I was a normal American, I couldn't. I could have wired up to Kun-ming and had a copy dropped to me, of course, but all he really wanted was the flavor of the thing. The more we discussed it, the more he actually seemed to know more about it than I did. As a matter of fact, he knew more about almost everything than I did, but when I thought his demands were too stiff, I told him anyway. Strange thing was he listened. He was an awfully sweet guy. If I had to pick one quality about that little old man sitting on his hill in the jungle, it was his gentleness." [18] The lieutenant told his headquarters that Ho was sincere in wanting to cooperate with both France and the United States.

The bearded revolutionary and his Viet Minh guerrillas also aroused the curiosity of some perceptive Frenchmen. One of these astute observers was Jean Sainteny, chief of Mission 5 at Kunming. On a hurried trip to Paris in July, Sainteny found, to his alarm, that most French officials believed "the Indochinese await our return with impatience and prepare to greet us with open arms." [19] His warnings of an impending conflict with Vietnamese nationalists were met only with skepticism at the Quai D'Orsay.

Sainteny left Paris for China on July 27 filled with foreboding. He stopped in Athens, where his plane was disabled, and there came upon General Donovan, who was waiting to depart for SEAC headquarters. Donovan recalled Sainteny's name and offered him a seat in his plane. They flew together to India, pleasantly engaged in conversation. It was Sainteny's last cordial encounter with OSS.

Sainteny was already well aware of OSS dealings with the Viet Minh. The Americans had, in fact, become the major link between Ho and the French in China. In early summer, the OSS command at Kunming organized a Special Operations team to be sent to Viet Minh Headquarters in Tonkin. The commander was a young Michigan attorney who had served with OSS in France, Major Allison Thomas, assisted by a radio operator and an interpreter, 23-year-old Henry Prunier.[e] A recent graduate of a small Catholic university in New England, Prunier had studied the Annamese language at a University of California army training program. While at Berkeley, he was recruited for OSS, shipped to China, then tapped for the Thomas mission.

At the insistence of Sainteny's aides, the Thomas group was also to be accompanied by a French lieutenant posing as an American officer. On July 16, this joint group landed at a small village some seventy-five miles northwest of Hanoi. They were met by guerrillas who

[e] Prunier is now a building contractor in Massachusetts.

escorted them to Viet Minh headquarters and then anxiously directed
the Americans to a small bamboo hut in the center of the camp. Lying
on a mat in the darkest corner of the room was Ho Chi Minh. French
intelligence had described him as "cunning, fearless, sly, clever, powerful, deceptive, ruthless—and deadly." But the OSS officers saw only "a
pile of bones covered with yellow dry skin." He was "shaking like a
leaf and obviously running a high fever." [20] Thomas and Prunier did
what they could to keep him alive until their China base could dispatch
a medic.

Two weeks later, four new OSS arrivals joined the team. One was
Paul Hoagland, an OSS medic who had received his training aboard a
Swedish prisoner-exchange ship in the early days of the war.[f] "This
man doesn't have long for this world," exclaimed Hoagland when he
saw Ho. Diagnosing the Viet Minh leader's malady as a combination
of malaria, dysentery, and assorted tropical diseases, Hoagland quickly
injected him with quinine and sulfa drugs. The medicines proved
effective. Within days, Ho was on his feet again, ambling around camp
and chatting with the Vietnamese partisans who idolized him.

Not long after Ho's recovery, he met with the American team at
a formal military briefing. To Thomas' surprise, Ho pointed to the
French lieutenant masquerading as an OSS officer and declared, "This
man is not an American." Despite the protests of the OSS major and
his men, Ho insisted, in his colloquial English, "Look, who are you
guys trying to kid? This man is not part of the deal." He then correctly
identified the officer as Lieutenant Montfort of the French army.
Amazed by this evidence of Ho's superb intelligence network, the
Americans feared for the life of their French colleague. Again to their
surprise, Ho simply sent him, under guard, to the Chinese border. "It
will be interesting to hear the French reaction," mused Ho after Montfort's departure. "Perhaps they will not think of me as a murderous
bandit." [21]

The unhappy incident did not destroy the friendly relationship
between the Americans and the Viet Minh. The OSS men apprecia-
tively received (and, according to military custom, sadly declined)
Ho's offer of potent jungle aphrodisiacs, together with the company
of some pretty young Vietnamese girls from Hanoi who had come to
"entertain" the troops. The Americans, who adopted guerrilla garb

---

[f] Hoagland joined the CIA at its inception and remained with the
agency until his death in 1970.

Ho Chi Minh and guerrilla leader Vo Nguyen Giap (in white suit at left) with the American officers of the OSS "Deer" team who parachuted to Viet Minh headquarters in the Tonkinese jungle and later accompanied Ho on his triumphal march to Hanoi. Paul Hoagland (far left) was the medic (and later CIA official) who saved Ho's life.

and a sparing diet of rice and bamboo shoots, were pleased, in return, to respond to Viet Minh requests for arms and military training. Ho's army commander, Vo Nguyen Giap, a "wiry little man, with large calculating eyes and a perpetually angry look," frequently bemoaned the ragged state of his poorly equipped troops. To replace the antique muskets and homemade knives carried by the Viet Minh soldiers, the Thomas team was able to secure small OSS supply shipments of rifles, mortars, machineguns, grenades, and bazookas. The OSS men held training sessions for 200 troops, the elite of Giap's guerrilla force. "They had an uncanny ability to learn and adapt," recalls Prunier. "They learned to pull a rifle part and put it together again after being shown only a couple of times." [22]

The casual military training schedule left much time for idle conversation, and Ho held daily discussions with his American friends. Usually dressed in a long-sleeved white shirt and khaki shorts (which revealed his spindly legs), he would speak to the OSS men in his typically subdued voice.

"Ho was a very quiet type of man," Prunier remembers. "He listened to everything you had to say. He would ask you leading questions and draw answers out of you. He was a very intense person. . . . He seemed very genuine, very honest. He wasn't after things for himself. It was always for his people. Everything he did was for his people."

The United States was a favorite topic of conversation for the Viet Minh leader. "I learned a great deal about your country and your people," he told the Americans, recalling that he had worked as a waiter in New York and Boston during the 1920s. Prunier remembers, "He knew American history well and he would talk about American ideals and how he was sure America would be on his side. . . . He thought that the United States would help in throwing out the French and in establishing an independent country. . . . He was convinced that America was for free, popular governments all over the world, that it opposed colonialism in all its forms. . . . And he seemed sincere in his desire to have our help." [23]

In his talks with Thomas' second-in-command, René Defourneaux, a French-American from New York, Ho spoke of America's own colonial record. "I have always been impressed with your country's treatment of the Philippines," he told Defourneaux. "You kicked the Spanish out and let the Filipinos develop their own country. You were not looking for real estate, and I admire you for that." Then he would plead for American aid. "I have a government that is organized and ready to go," he would argue. "Your statesmen make eloquent speeches about helping those with self-determination. We are self-determined. Why not help us? Am I any different from Nehru, Quezon, even your George Washington? Was not Washington considered a revolutionary? I, too," he concluded, "want to set my people free." [24]

The OSS officers believed that Ho was a "true patriot" and "much more a nationalist than he was a Communist." [25] But, they explained, they were army officers, not diplomats. They could only transmit Ho's messages to OSS headquarters for consideration at higher levels. Consequently, Ho sent frequent pleas for official support to the American military command. And to Sainteny he relayed a plan for universal suffrage and gradual independence of Indochina.

Ho also expressed his eagerness to meet with official French authorities. Both the Thomas team and Laurence Gordon, the Cal-Texaco official who had first established OSS contact with the Viet Minh, became intermediaries in an attempt to arrange a meeting between Sainteny and Ho. Unfortunately, torrential rains in July and August prevented the rendezvous from taking place. The Viet Minh were disappointed. They had already prepared "tricolors and welcome pennants" for the occasion.[26] By the beginning of August, as Sainteny awaited the eventual French return to Hanoi, the Viet Minh at last proceeded to wrest control of Vietnam from the Japanese.

On August 7, the atomic bomb destroyed Hiroshima. The Indochinese Communist Party hurriedly convoked an urgent national conference in Tonkin and called for a general insurrection against the Japanese. On August 16, a National Liberation Committee came into existence. That same day, the first detachments of Viet Minh guerrillas entered Hanoi. Suddenly, Viet Minh leaflets appeared throughout the country, and mass demonstrations were organized by the Viet Minh— under the sympathetic eyes of the former Japanese enemy. Ho's forces presented themselves as the Vietnamese arm of the victorious Allies.

On August 17, during a public meeting in front of the Hanoi Municipal Theater, Viet Minh representatives appeared on the balcony and replaced the French flag with the gold star on a red background that was the Viet Minh banner. Giap's military units then occupied all important public buildings, except the Bank of Indochina, which was still guarded by the Japanese.

At this time, Ho transmitted another message in English to OSS headquarters by way of the Thomas team's radio set. It read: "National Liberation Committee of VML begs U.S. authorities to inform United Nations the following. We were fighting Japs on the side of the United Nations. Now Japs surrendered. We beg United Nations to realize their solemn promise that all nationalities will be given democracy and independence. If United Nations forget their solemn promise and don't grant Indochina full independence, we will keep fighting until we get it." [27] The Viet Minh was now prepared to greet the Allies.

At the Big Three Conference at Potsdam, Germany, in late 1945, a minor strategic decision was reached that would alter the course of Indochinese history. Months before, after the Japanese coup, General Wedemeyer had raised vigorous objections to operations in Tonkin undertaken by the British SOE from Admiral Mountbatten's SEAC headquarters. An ensuing dispute over operational boundaries was carried to the Chiefs of Staff and then still higher. When Harry Truman assumed the Presidency after Roosevelt's death, this strategic conflict was one of the first problems to reach his desk. The issue was finally resolved at Potsdam. Indochina was divided at the 16th parallel into two zones of occupation. Tonkin and northern Laos would fall within Wedemeyer's China theater and would therefore be "liberated" by Chinese troops. Cambodia and the southern division of Vietnam known as Cochin China, with its capital at Saigon, would become the responsibility of Mountbatten's SEAC, and would be occupied by the British.

While the OSS had concentrated its attentions in Indochina on the Viet Minh guerrilla organization in Tonkin, a Vietnamese nationalist movement also existed in Cochin China. Unlike Ho Chi Minh's unified organization in the north, however, the nationalists in Saigon were divided into an assortment of rival political and religious groups, all striving for independence from the French. The Viet Minh had its own representatives in Saigon, but they were forced to compete for leadership with other nationalist organizations, including the more militant Trotskyites. Confusing the situation still further were thousands of Japanese troops who had just received word of their country's surrender. An additional twenty thousand French civilians and soldiers had been living under Japanese persecution since the March coup ended their comfortable collaborationist existence.

In anticipation of the arrival of British occupation troops, the Viet Minh hurriedly organized its forces in the weeks after Hiroshima. Their first concern was to take control of the nationalist movement. By August 25, Ho Chi Minh was already in full control at Hanoi, but the Viet Minh in Saigon had only just succeeded in creating an uneasy alliance with the other nationalist groups. A unified Committee for the South was created to function as Cochin China's first native government.[28]

The Committee was immediately preoccupied with the maintenance of order. Riotous groups of armed Vietnamese roamed through the Saigon streets; in the nearby countryside, peasants were on the rampage, murdering village leaders, wealthy landlords, and unpopular officials. The Committee proceeded to take power in Saigon swiftly and peaceably. It occupied the government buildings and ran the public services, determined to make a "peaceful" showing in the eyes of the Allied representatives who might arrive at any moment. But not all members of the nationalist organization shared the Viet Minh's desire to present a conservative façade to the occidentals. The Trotskyites, in particular, continued to preach immediate and violent revolution. The Committee for the South responded with the warning that anyone who provoked the populace to violence would be treated as a saboteur.

On the eve of September 2, declared by Ho Chi Minh in Hanoi as Vietnam Independence Day, Viet Minh spokesmen drove through the Saigon streets appealing for order. They told the people that it was vital to the future of Vietnam that Allied forces, due to arrive in the city the next day, receive a favorable impression of the reign of peace and security in Saigon.

But the morning of September 2 found huge crowds milling in the streets. Someone—a Vietnamese extremist, a French fanatic, or Japanese provocateur—managed to incite a violent riot which ended in the death of several Frenchmen and Vietnamese demonstrators. The crowds then forced their way into French houses, pillaging and looting. Nearly 200 Frenchmen were arrested while their houses were being robbed. These unfortunate prisoners were soon released at the insistence of the first and only Allied force which reached the city that week— a confused team of seven OSS men under the command of 28-year-old Lieutenant Colonel A. Peter Dewey.

Like many of his OSS colleagues, Dewey was a young man of great accomplishment. His father, a conservative, anti–New Deal and isolationist Republican congressman from Chicago, was an old friend of General Donovan's from the days of the Coolidge administration. Young Dewey studied French history at Yale and then became a journalist in the Paris office of the Chicago Daily News. There he worked under another Donovan friend, Edgar Mowrer, and met fellow journalists, and later OSS officers, Edmond Taylor and Louis Huot. While reporting the German invasion of France for his paper, Dewey felt a need for more direct military action. In May 1940 he joined the Polish army fighting in France (his father had once been a financial advisor to the Polish government). When the Pétain government capitulated, Dewey escaped to Portugal and then returned to the United States. After writing a book about the French defeat, he joined Nelson Rockefeller's Coordinator of Inter-American Affairs, and became that agency's liaison to de Gaulle's Free French.

In August 1942, Dewey entered the American army as a lieutenant and served as an intelligence officer in Africa and Arabia. When General Giraud visited the United States in July 1943 during his short-lived "alliance" with de Gaulle, Dewey, who spoke fluent French, accompanied the general as his interpreter. The following year, Captain Dewey, now all of 27 years of age, joined the OSS in Algiers. In August 1944, he led a parachute team of three Americans and seven Frenchmen into southern France. Traveling through the area in captured German staff cars, Dewey's team sent back valuable intelligence on the eve of the Allied landing on the Riviera, then worked with the local resistance forces in capturing 400 Nazi prisoners and destroying three enemy tanks. His mission successfully completed, Dewey returned to the United States in October. In Washington, he worked on the OSS history project under the direction of *New Yorker* columnist Geoffrey Hellman.

In July 1945, in response to a hurried request from SEAC Headquarters, Dewey was chosen to head the OSS team that would enter Saigon after the Japanese surrender. A group of fifty OSS men had been assembled as the American contingent of the British occupation forces. But at the last moment British General Douglas Gracey, commander of the occupation troops, strongly objected to the American presence and sought to bar all OSS participation. Colonel Richard Heppner sent a special message from OSS China headquarters to his old friend Admiral Mountbatten protesting the arbitrary British action. As a result of these high-level stirrings, Dewey's team of OSS men was allowed to leave Ceylon en route to Indochina at the beginning of September. They flew first to Rangoon and Bangkok, where they refueled, then on to Saigon. The group landed at the city's municipal airport where they were met by the highest officers of the Japanese command. The Americans were also greeted by crowds of Vietnamese, who received them with "ebullient enthusiasm." Banners and placards which covered the route from the airport read, "Welcome to the Allied deliverers," and "Since 83 years we didn't cease struggle." [29]

The first objective of the team was to free the two hundred American prisoners of war in Saigon. At dawn of the following day, these ragged survivors of Japanese internment were flown out on seven DC-3s which had followed the OSS group to the city. Their mercy mission completed, the OSS men were then instructed to remain in Saigon to "represent American interests." This included a search for air crews that had disappeared in action over Indochina, a survey of American missionary property in the area, and, most important, "political surveillance" for the State Department. Inevitably, the American officers were thrust into the midst of the revolutionary drama unfolding

The unfortunate OSS Col. Peter Dewey (left) talked in the streets of riot-torn Saigon with his radio operator (right) and Sgt. George Wickes (center), who became Dewey's secret liaison with the Viet Minh government of the city.

in Cochin China. Dewey wrote his wife some weeks after his arrival that "the political situation is immensely complex, but one which our group considers but impersonally and objectively since it does not concern us." [30] But the colonel was not an "impersonal" man. He had strong feelings and prejudices—a very deep love for France (which he called "my second land"), a critical view of the British, and a traditional American anti-colonialism.

With these conflicting impulses, Dewey began his intelligence mission. He and his men first observed the great lengths to which the Committee for the South went in attempting to maintain order. On September 7, the Committee again issued an appeal to the populace. "In the interests of our country," it read, "we call on everyone to have confidence in us and not let themselves be led astray by people who betray our country. It is only in this spirit that we can facilitate our relations with the Allied representatives." Saigon radio then assured the French: "We will continue to respect your possessions. You can continue to work in our country, but on condition that you submit to our laws. Put aside your arms. We want to live in liberty." [31]

These pleas for peace were rejected by Vietnamese revolutionaries and reactionary French colonials alike. The Vietnamese were stirred by Trotskyite-prompted rumors that the British occupation troops planned to aid the French in the reimposition of colonial rule. Many nationalists therefore refused to surrender their arms to the Committee for the South.

On September 12, ten days after the arrival of the Dewey team, the first British soldiers—actually Indian Gurkhas from Rangoon—flew into Thanh Son Nhut Airport and joined forces with a company of French paratroopers newly arrived from Calcutta. The Committee for the South openly welcomed the long-expected soldiers; Trotskyites denounced this reception as treason and capitulation.

The following day, the British commander, General Douglas Gracey, flew to Saigon to observe Vietnamese, Frenchmen, Japanese, Indians, Englishmen, Chinese, and Americans mingling uneasily in the city streets. The general also found the Committee for the South functioning independently and ably as the government of Cochin China. The Vietnamese "came to see me," Gracey later recalled, "and said 'welcome' and all that sort of thing. It was an unpleasant situation and I promptly kicked them out." [32]

Gracey had been given specific instructions by Mountbatten to restrict his actions to disarming the Japanese. But the general, who had no sympathy for Asian nationalism, took it upon himself to "restore order." Ignoring the Viet Minh's request for peaceful negotiations with the French, Gracey imposed censorship on the indigenous press, proclaimed martial law, declared a strict curfew, and banned all demonstrations and public meetings.

The OSS team looked on with mixed sentiments as Gracey sought to deprive the Committee for the South of its new-found authority. Colonel Dewey was certainly too much of a francophile to be anything but the best of friends with the French officers in the city. He and OSS Captain Joseph Coolidge, 29-year-old graduate of Harvard with a degree in engineering, had frequent meetings with the French. Coolidge, a cousin of Harvard zoologist Harold Coolidge (who was then a high OSS official in Washington) had been working for OSS in Delhi as a Burmese intelligence analyst. He was selected for the Saigon mission as "one of three OSS bodies in the theater who could speak

French." Shortly after the team's arrival, Coolidge was accosted by a former French brigadier of police who "surreptitiously persuaded me to follow him into a back alley in true Georges Simenon fashion. He pressed some hand-written material into my hands and disappeared." [33] The makeshift documents contained intelligence on Viet Minh cadres, arms caches, and troop movements. This data was shared with the British MI-6 team that had also begun operations in the city.

As an intelligence officer (and an OSS American who felt some sympathy for the Vietnamese cause in spite of his francophilia), Dewey sought more direct contacts with the Vietnamese nationalists. Without the knowledge of either British or French, the OSS kept almost nightly clandestine midnight rendezvous with representatives of the Viet Minh. Dressed incognito in a prisoner-of-war uniform was the OSS envoy, 22-year-old Sergeant George Wickes, a graduate of the University of Toronto trained in the Vietnamese language in an army program at Berkeley.[g] The principal purpose of these meetings was to gather intelligence, and the OSS Research Branch even sent a special analyst, German émigré economist Konrad Bekker, to assist in the collation of information.[h] Wickes, who was as well-informed on Indochinese affairs as any member of his team (his cousin was a nun in a convent north of Saigon), told the Viet Minh representatives that the OSS had no authority to take any position toward their political movement. The Vietnamese, nevertheless, grasped the slightest indication of American interest as a sign that the United States was sympathetic to their battle for independence.

On September 17, in answer to Gracey's restrictive measures, the Committee for the South declared a boycott of all French employers—in effect, a general strike. Five days later, Gracey took further "impartial" action. He released and armed over a thousand French colonial troops who had been interned by the Japanese after the March coup. In a "pre-dawn attack on September 23," wrote one OSS official, "this force looted the arsenal and embarked on a program of massacre and brutality against the generally defenseless Annamese population, secured control over a large part of Saigon, and became the nucleus of the French forces which were later to arrive." [34] The French soldiers seized the government buildings from the Vietnamese and attempted,

[g] Wickes is now Professor of English at the University of Oregon.
[h] Bekker is presently Counselor for Economic Affairs at the U.S. embassy in Bangkok.

without success, to arrest the members of the Committee for the South, who fled the city.

Now it was the French turn for disorder. The colonial population of Saigon went wild; they insulted and attacked any Vietnamese who dared appear on the street, as French and British soldiers looked on. Vietnamese were arrested for no reason and subjected to brutal treatment. As Saigon approached a state of anarchy, the OSS team was quietly headquartered on the outskirts of the city in a spacious mansion owned by the president of the Bank of Indochina and occupied during the war by a Japanese admiral. The British already suspected these American officers of intriguing with the Viet Minh and were outraged when Dewey openly criticized Gracey's move against the nationalists. With the encouragement of the newly arrived French commander, General Leclerc (the "liberator" of Paris), Gracey soon declared the OSS colonel personna non grata. Dewey was ordered to leave Saigon as soon as possible. The return flight to Ceylon was arranged for September 26.[35]

On September 25, after the French riot had been calmed by Gurkha troops, violence erupted again. The Vietnamese called another strike, the city's power supply was cut, and sniper fire broke out. In one area which remained under Japanese supervision, a wild band of Vietnamese descended on French civilians, inflicting appalling atrocities and torturing women and children while the Japanese stood by passively.

That evening, Captain Coolidge was returning to Saigon with a mixed group of British, Canadian, French, Australian, Dutch, and Japanese officers from Dalat, 300 kilometers to the northeast. On a previous trip to Dalat to inspect an American Baptist mission, Coolidge had been confronted by a "seedy-looking Annamese in a quasi-uniform carrying a rifle-cum-bayonet, which he placed against my solar plexus in a marked manner." (He was rescued by a Japanese interpreter who turned out to be an ex-graduate student form Ohio State.) On this trip, the Vietnamese seemed more friendly. The Allied group was "greeted by a parade of joyful Annamese. It must have been a half-mile-long column and eight abreast. They were singing, and in the van were a couple of dozen Annamese beauties, bearing large bunches of gladioli and other flowers. We appeared to be the heroes of the hour." [36]

On the return trip, however, the convoy received word that "the Viet Minh had declared war on the entire world." Shortly before dusk, they came upon a crude roadblock at an intersection and were forced

The first American casualty in Vietnam—September 1945. OSS Captain Joseph Coolidge, badly wounded in a Viet Minh ambush, was placed aboard a hospital plane bound for the United States, surrounded by watchful Indian Gurkhas.

to stop to dismantle it. Later that evening, they encountered a second roadblock some ten miles outside of Saigon. When the convoy pulled to a halt, it was surrounded and attacked by a group of several hundred Vietnamese. Some of the officers were wounded before a truck of Japanese arrived to break up the action. Most seriously hit was Coolidge, who received a bad neck wound. The next morning, he was taken to a

British field hospital in Saigon, after receiving emergency treatment from a Dutch doctor.[1]

That same morning, the OSS team first received word of Coolidge's misfortune. Colonel Dewey and OSS Major Herbert Bluechel, a California businessman attached to SI Branch at SEAC headquarters, drove to the hospital to see Coolidge before Dewey's scheduled departure for Ceylon that day. Driving through the city in an open jeep, the two men heard sniper fire in the distance, but were scarcely aware of the real danger. Many of the newly arrived French troops in Saigon were wearing American-issue uniforms and it was almost impossible to distinguish them from American officers. In addition, General Gracey had angrily forbidden Dewey to fly an American flag from his jeep, insisting that only the "senior officer" in the city was entitled to that privilege of national identification.

Dewey and Bluechel drove out to the airport at 11:30 A.M. and waited for the plane, scheduled to arrive at noon. By one o'clock it had not yet come and they decided to return to OSS headquarters for lunch. Dewey chose a side road which was a shorter route to the OSS villa than the main highway through the heart of the city. As they approached within 100 yards of their headquarters along an unused golf course, they saw a Vietnamese roadblock. Driving past the logs, which blocked only a part of the road, Dewey screamed something in French at the Vietnamese standing at the roadside. Major Bluechel, who knew no French, believed that Dewey had cursed these men, still angered by the attack on Coolidge. Whatever Dewey actually said, it was most certainly in French, and the Vietnamese apparently mistook him for a French officer. They opened fire with a machine gun placed about ten yards from the jeep. Dewey was hit in the head and killed instantly; the jeep overturned and fell into a ditch. Bluechel crawled under the vehicle and then, shooting backward at his pursuers with a pistol, managed to inch his way through tall grass toward the OSS headquarters. Eluding machine gun and rifle fire, he reached the building and alerted the other American officers and two resident war correspondents who broke out the arsenal. The headquarters was not flying an American flag and could not be identified by the Vietnamese, who besieged the house for some three hours. The telephone lines were cut and Bluechel was forced to radio OSS headquarters in Ceylon, which in turn con-

[1] Coolidge miraculously survived his wounds and was released from an Army hospital eight months and thirteen operations later. He has since worked as a TV writer, film editor, and producer.

tacted the British at Saigon. At last, Gurkha troops arrived and the Vietnamese fled, taking with them Dewey's body. Several weeks later, Dewey's brother, Charles, who had just completed his own OSS intelligence and sabotage mission behind the lines in southern China, flew to Saigon to claim his brother's remains. Bluechel and Wickes sadly told him that the colonel's corpse had never been recovered.[37]

The murder of Colonel Dewey, the first American to die in Vietnam, immediately assumed diplomatic importance. Radio Hanoi reported that the killing was the work of French criminals; in Saigon, the Vietnamese nationalists offered a reward for the return of the body.[38] And Ho Chi Minh sent a personal note of condolence to Colonel Archimedes Patti, then chief of the OSS mission in Hanoi. The French simultaneously blamed the murder on the Viet Minh. The real truth probably lies in a tragic case of mistaken identity, as Arthur Krock suggested some weeks later: "Lieutenant Colonel Dewey of the Office of Strategic Services was not meant to perish in the way he did—from the gunfire of insurgents in a strange land who mistook him for a French officer, and therefore a symbol of what they consider their oppressor. . . . Peter Dewey boldly met every risk which high spirit, total absence of physical fear, and hatred of autocracy impelled him to seek. He survived these, to be shot from ambush by natives whose protest against foreign domination he had examined with the sympathy he felt for all who are thus subject. It is one of the first American casualties in the bodeful era of peace-making that has released passions as violent as those of war." [39]

The day after Dewey's death, General Gracey arrested the Japanese commander in Saigon and threatened to have him tried as a war criminal if his troops did not aid in battling the Vietnamese. The Japanese general consented; his units were then added to the British and French forces attempting to "pacify" Cochin China.

The Viet Minh and French declared a temporary truce on October 2. Three days later, the first troops arrived from metropolitan France. Then the truce agreement broke down, negotiations collapsed, and fighting resumed. The Vietnamese nationalists retreated into the countryside to continue their fight. The French launched a "pacification" campaign, and both antagonists resorted to tactics of brutality and terror. The Indochina war had begun.

Concerned over events in the area, General Donovan sent a series of utterly confused young officers to Saigon to succeed Dewey as OSS commander. The first was James Withrow, Jr., an attorney from Donovan's law firm who had directed the Morale Operations Branch in India. He was soon replaced by Major Alexander Griswold, a wealthy young investment banker from Baltimore who had participated in Thailand operations.[j]

Another OSS observer who flew in for a brief visit was Edmond Taylor, recently returned from his anti-colonialist jaunt to Bangkok. He described the chaotic scene which he found in Cochin China: "The conflict had reached its climax. By force of circumstances, the British had been drawn into the war of extermination, marked by appalling atrocities on both sides, which the French and the Annamese were waging against one another. In retaliation for the murderous Annamese guerrilla tactics, the British had deliberately burned down great sections of the native quarter of Saigon. This further inflamed the anti-British sentiments of the Annamese, whose fanatical if clumsy attacks became such a menace to the inadequate British occupation forces that for a long time they had to cease disarming the Japanese and to use their late enemies as auxiliaries in fighting the newer ones." [40]

Taylor's account continues, "Thanks to the recent arrival of some trained French forces under General Leclerc, Saigon was reasonably safe by day, but even in the bright sunlight the atmosphere was that of a town newly occupied by Franco's forces in the Spanish Civil War. At night delusion ruled the darkened streets and heavy fighting—mostly French and British patrols shooting at each other or at shadows—went on until dawn. Annamese terrorists were kidnapping French women and children, usually killing them and mutilating their bodies, while the French were torturing and shooting the rebels they captured." [41]

As senseless violence became the norm and the fighting continued into the fall of 1945, the OSS team received still another commander, OSS Captain Nicholas Deak.[k] A brilliant Hungarian-born economist with degrees from Swiss, French, and Hungarian universities, he had worked as a financial expert for the Overseas Bank of London and later for the League of Nations. Recruited for OSS, he served ably on assignments in Syria, Egypt, Italy, Malaya, and Singapore. But nothing in his vast experience had equipped him to deal with the chaotic situation which he found in Indochina at the end of 1945.

[j] Like several of his OSS colleagues, Griswold took up permanent residence in Thailand after the war and has become an expert on Thai art.

[k] Deak is now president of the largest foreign currency exchange firm in the United States, Canada, and the Far East, and holds controlling interests in Swiss and Austrian banks.

The "local population," he wrote, "was in great part anti-French."
The Vietnamese looked upon the Americans as either "supporters of
the old French colonial policy" or "representatives of a new future."
There was "general confusion and, in many respects, a lack of directives
from Washington." [42]

American policy received some clarification when the United
States government announced that France would be sold $160 million
in war equipment for use against the Viet Minh in Cochin China.
Deak's OSS group was then instructed to requisition spare parts for
British and French planes, to provide the French with transportation
and communications, and to serve as "observers to punitive missions
conducted by the French against the rebellious Annamites." [43]

Not all OSS officers were delighted with this new stance. One of
Deak's subordinates was George Sheldon, a 25-year-old OSS officer who,
like his colleagues George Wickes and Henry Prunier, had received
Vietnamese language training at the University of California.[1] Sheldon's
words expressed the bitterness of the hour. "For one who has been
there," he wrote upon his return from Saigon, "the conclusion is inevitable that the French have learned almost everything under Hitler
except compassion." [44]

Far to the north, in Tonkin, events had taken an entirely different
turn. There were no French soldiers to "pacify" Vietnamese guerrillas
in the paddy fields, no French officials to issue administrative directives
in Hanoi. Tonkin was Vietnamese territory in which Frenchmen moved
with trepidation and lived in fear. No longer a colonial metropole,
Hanoi had become the capital of the Democratic Republic of Vietnam.

At the moment of Tokyo's capitulation, these developments were
still unknown to French officials in China. When news of the Japanese
surrender reached Kunming on August 15, Jean Sainteny of the French
intelligence mission quickly decided, in the absence of specific instructions from Paris, to go to Hanoi to reestablish the official French
"presence." On August 15, he asked OSS to fly him to the Tonkinese
capital. The Americans gave their assent.

The OSS command at Kunming had already laid plans to send its
own mission to Hanoi, but General Wedemeyer had at first been reluctant to grant his approval, fearing that an American team would become "involved in politics." OSS headquarters then took a different

[1] Sheldon disappeared into the ranks of the CIA in 1950. He appeared
briefly in Saigon in 1957 as a "foreign aid" official.

tack. At this time, Colonel Heppner and his aides were dispatching "mercy missions" to rescue Allied prisoners of war in Manchuria, Korea, and China. Wedemeyer was finally convinced that a similar group should be sent to Hanoi. Code-named the Quail Mission, it was to be headed by OSS Major Archimedes L. A. Patti, the Italian-American who headed the North Indochina desk of SI Branch at Kunming.[45]

Sainteny was told that he and his officers could accompany the Patti team, but unaware of typical OSS inefficiency, he waited impatiently for his promised departure. The first plane, scheduled for August 16, never arrived. The next day he made independent arrangements to leave in a French aircraft, but at the last moment Patti appeared with a cable from General Wedemeyer—no aircraft of any nationality was to leave China for Hanoi until the Japanese command's reaction to the surrender had been ascertained. When the French attempted to circumvent this order, their plane was seized by Chinese troops. Patti assured Sainteny that the Chinese had taken this action on their own initiative, but the French officer was not convinced. He already suspected an American plot to keep him out of Hanoi.

The French continued to press for transport to Indochina; the Americans replied with new reasons for delay. The weather, they noted, was inclement; Kunming was inundated with torrential rains which made flying risky. Wedemeyer's headquarters was also genuinely concerned about a hostile Japanese reception. That very week, an American plane flying over Hanoi had been hit by anti-aircraft fire. Sainteny discounted both explanations and believed that OSS was simply inventing new pretexts to delay his flight.

Finally, a week after the surrender, on August 22, an American plane carrying five French and seven American officers under the command of Sainteny and Patti, flew out of Kunming airport bound for Tonkin. Within two hours, Hanoi came into view. "Our emotion is profound," wrote Sainteny, who had last seen the city in 1931. As they viewed Hanoi from the air, however, the French noted "strange red flowers" dotting the landscape. The plane descended and they found, to their amazement, that the city streets were draped with peculiar red flags. "The reception," Sainteny feared, "will perhaps not be as we had hoped." [46]

Several of Patti's men first parachuted to the ground to survey the scene. The plane then set down at Hanoi's Gia Lam Airport. The French and Americans were immediately met by a joyous group of

Indian POW's and a more grim-faced squad of heavily armed Japanese officers. Patti informed the Japanese that he was charged with preparations for the arrival of the Allied surrender commission. Sainteny added that he had come to examine the condition of the four thousand French prisoners interned during the March coup.

The Allied group was escorted into Hanoi by the Japanese as crowds of Vietnamese stood by, watching silently. Viet Minh flags were everywhere and huge banners were hung from tree to tree across the boulevards, written neither in French nor Vietnamese, but in English. The signs denounced French imperialism, proclaimed "Independence or Death" and "Vietnam for the Vietnamese." "The French will not have an easy task," remarked Patti to Sainteny.[47]

The small convoy soon reached the Hotel Metropole in the center of the city. The building was largely occupied by frightened French civilians who greeted Sainteny and his men elatedly and poured out tales of Vietnamese maltreatment, assault, and even murder. For the first time, Sainteny now learned that the Viet Minh had come to power in Hanoi.

This brief French reunion was abruptly interrupted. A frantic Japanese lieutenant appeared to announce that hostile crowds of Vietnamese were massed in front of the hotel, held in check only by a row of Japanese troops "armed to the teeth." The lieutenant insisted that Sainteny and his men leave the hotel for their own safety. The OSS men remained at the Metropole, while the French were moved to the palace of the Governor-General, the building from which the French colonial administrators had ruled Indochina. But the French were no longer rulers. They lived under guard, virtual prisoners of the Japanese, their movements confined to the palace grounds. That first evening of their captivity, the French radioed Kunming a message of alarm: "Political situation at Hanoi worse than we could have foreseen." [48]

While Patti's men were comfortably settled at the Metropole and the French uncomfortably interned at the palace, Ho Chi Minh and his guerrillas, accompanied by Major Thomas's OSS group, were making their triumphant march to Hanoi. On the journey, the Americans had a chance to see Ho's sensitivity, and his ruthlessness as well. As the entourage advanced, a group of Viet Minh soldiers moved ahead of the main body to make certain that all was "secure." The OSS officers later came across villages where buildings had been burned to the ground and village chiefs executed. They were told that the countryside had been ravaged by the retreating Japanese. But the Americans knew that the carnage had been carried out under orders from Ho to insure the support and "cooperation" of the villagers.

Yet the Americans observed that this same veteran revolutionary who had ordered the execution of recalcitrant officials would often halt the line of march to personally distribute rice to the starving populace, especially children. "How can I eat when so many of my people are hungry?" he would ask with undisguised emotion.[49]

The OSS group was part of Ho's triumphant army as it approached Hanoi. The troops boarded open cars and trucks and began their victory ride into the heart of the city. "The reception was fantastic," one OSS man remembered. "The people seemed to genuinely love Ho, and the feeling seemed to be mutual." The streets were lined with cheering people, many of them carrying the Viet Minh flag. Again, political banners abounded, proclaiming "Peace is Here," and "Welcome Allies." [50]

Finding Major Patti's team already settled in the city, Thomas and most of his men prepared to return to China after weeks in the jungle. Before their departure, Ho gave them a warm send-off. "I want to thank each of you for what you have done for us," he said. "We are truly grateful." And he added, with a paternal grin, "You are welcome to come back any time." [51]

One member of Patti's group took a particular interest in Ho's arrival. A 30-year-old civilian we shall call "Roberts" had joined the team some days after their arrival.[m] Like many OSS officers, Roberts was a product of Harvard, where he had received a graduate degree in psychology. In the course of his academic studies he developed an interest in propaganda, and this led to his recruitment by OSS as a psychological warfare expert. Roberts, however, was too much of an activist to tolerate the daily routine of Washington committee meetings and he persuaded OSS to send him to Cairo. Before long, he was leading an OSS sabotage team behind the German lines in Greece. He formed close friendships with Greek leftist guerrillas, who welcomed his open sympathy for their socialist and anti-monarchist political aims. His mission completed, Roberts returned to Washington headquarters for a time, then was sent on to China. At Kunming he became another stalwart member of the anti-Kuomintang faction of OSS. After the surrender, the SI Branch sent him to Hanoi to join the Patti group,

m "Roberts" is now a professor of Psychology at a New England university.

ostensibly as "political advisor" to the mission. His actual instructions were to establish friendly relations with the Vietnamese nationalists and collect intelligence about their movement.

In the days that followed, Roberts met frequently with Ho. The Viet Minh leader constantly expressed his friendship for America. He admired the United States, he told Roberts, as the first colonial nation to gain its independence through revolution. The Vietnamese, he noted, had looked to America for aid in their nationalist cause almost a century before when the Annamite emperor sent a message to Abraham Lincoln, proposing a pact of amity.

To supplement the political intelligence he received from Ho, Roberts recruited a Vietnamese named Le Xuan as his personal agent.[n] Xuan's first bit of interesting information was that Shandra Bose, an Indian nationalist leader whose hatred of the British had led him to espouse the cause of the Axis (and to fight alongside the Japanese), was then hiding in Hanoi. Not until later did Roberts learn that this rumor was false, and that Bose had died in a Japanese hospital after his plane crashed en route from Hanoi to Tokyo. But at first, Roberts failed to pass it along to the local British intelligence officers, who were eager to capture the Indian renegade. The OSS man's reasoning was simple. He knew that the betrayal of any Asian nationalist, even one with pro-Japanese sentiments, would have angered Ho Chi Minh, and Roberts was resolved to maintain the best possible relations with Ho.

While the Americans were occupied in meetings with Viet Minh leaders, the French, still prevented from leaving their "golden cage" by Japanese troops, contented themselves with dispatching radio messages to Kunming deploring their misfortune. Sainteny was now more than ever convinced that the Americans were scheming against him. One afternoon, Major Patti visited the government palace, accompanied by the Viet Minh guerrilla leader, Vo Nguyen Giap, since elevated to the post of Interior Minister of Ho's government. Patti introduced Giap to Sainteny and the Frenchman was impressed by this "extraordinarily hard, sly, and intelligent" Vietnamese, "one of the most brilliant products of our culture." Giap declared that he and his comrades would be happy to receive "counsel and direction" from the French, and the meeting ended on a cordial note.[52]

[n] Le Xuan appeared in Shanghai in 1946 as an Associated Press employee; ten years later he surfaced in Paris, a disgruntled CIA agent who tried to sell his "autobiography" to the French and Soviet intelligence services.

When Giap left the palace, Sainteny asked Patti to stay for lunch. They took a stroll in the park under the beautiful tropical trees that graced the palace grounds. The OSS major seemed cheerful and congratulated Sainteny on his masterful diplomacy in dealing with the Vietnamese. But the Frenchman was "not duped by these compliments." [53]

Sainteny and his aides were by now certain that the OSS team was lending its support to the anti-French campaign of the Viet Minh. If this came as a shock to the French, it was all the more poignant because most members of the Sainteny team, including its chief, had fought alongside more friendly OSS officers in the French resistance. One member of the group, Roland Sadoun, had even been employed by the Secret Intelligence Branch of OSS in London and France.[o]

To characterize the OSS group as manifestly anti-French, however, would be too simple. The team included several men who took issue with Patti's anti-colonial thrust. Robert Ettinger, the French-American who had joined Sabattier's forces at Dien Bien Phu, was one Patti subordinate who was violently critical of his team commander. The major tried, unsuccessfully, to have Ettinger returned to China.

Another dissenter was Captain Lucien Conein, a sour-faced but likable ex-Jedburgh from Missouri who had spent the summer months in the Tonkinese jungle as OSS liaison to a French guerrilla group.[p] One message which Conein received from his China headquarters in early August read, "The French must, under no circumstances, penetrate into Indochina." [54] Conein agreed, in essence, with this anti-colonial stance.[45] And he soon came to believe that Ho was a great statesman whose nationalism transcended his Communist background. But Conein still sympathized with the plight of the local French. He feared that the civilian population in Hanoi might soon be slaughtered by the Viet Minh, and he embarked on a one-man crusade to rescue high French officials from both Japanese and Viet Minh retribution. He also persuaded Patti to use the tremendous prestige of the OSS with Ho and his comrades to prevent any serious violence against the colonial populace. Even the most disgruntled French were later forced

---

[o] Sadoun is now director of the French equivalent of the Gallup Poll.
[p] According to the "Pentagon Papers," Conein was in charge of CIA sabotage and paramilitary operations in North Vietnam at the time of the French defeat and withdrawal in 1954. Nine years later, he was the CIA liaison with the Vietnamese generals who overthrew the Diem regime in Saigon.

to admit that the presence of the American team in Hanoi had saved the French population from probable massacre.

Those American officers who supported Patti's anti-colonialism were themselves divided by mixed motivations. Some, like Roberts, were ideologically committed. But at least one officer's position was related to two attractive Annamese girls whom he convinced to share his bungalow. To the disgust of Roberts and other OSS colleagues, this lieutenant busily rushed about town seeking a doctor who would "inspect" his female friends.[55]

Patti's own motivations were somewhat obscure. He was hardly an ideologue. Like his father, a political friend of General Donovan's, he was a committed Republican. The French, of course, accused Patti of having accepted Viet Minh gold, a charge that was manifestly untrue. Patti's own explanation to his colleagues was tinged with mystery. He spoke of having been called to the White House in the spring of 1945 before his departure for China, to receive "special instructions" about dealings with the French. And he often made quizzical references to "working for two bosses." The implication was that his antipathy toward the French was directed from a much higher level than Kunming.

It was not difficult for the Americans, even without strategic instructions, to find fault with the intense colonial chauvinism of Sainteny and his men. During another visit to the government palace, Patti again went walking with Sainteny in the park outside the building. They caught sight of three young French girls strolling down the street outside the palace gate. One was wearing a blue outfit, another a white dress, and the third was clothed in red. Sainteny was immediately stirred to emotion; the sight brought tears to his eyes. Noting the Frenchman's reaction, Patti wryly remarked, "The first French flag that I have seen in Hanoi since we arrived, isn't it?" "Yes," replied Sainteny, "but I give you my word that it will not be the last."

Later that day, after Patti had left, Sainteny wired Calcutta, "We are faced with a joint maneuver by the Allies to oust the French from Indochina." He later added, "I must go through Patti for everything. I am convinced of the fact that, at this moment, the Allied attitude is more dangerous than that of the Viet Minh." [56]

On September 1, a week after the French arrival, the Japanese guard at the government palace was withdrawn and replaced by Vietnamese sentries. Sainteny's men were now captives of the Viet Minh. The following day, September 2, 1945, the members of the French mission stood at their windows and watched a huge crowd march past the palace, assembled in celebration of the independence of Vietnam. That day, Ho Chi Minh issued a Vietnamese Declaration of Independence. Like the banners which decorated the city, the document drew its inspiration from American political ideals. It began, "All men are created equal" and echoed the first words of America's Declaration of Independence. Then Ho added his own interpretation—"All peoples on earth are equal from birth, all peoples have a right to life and freedom." [57]

A peaceful crowd of several hundred thousand including, by French admission, a notable representation of Catholic priests, assembled in the heart of Hanoi that day to hear their political leaders proclaim the nation's independence. Ho's speech impressed the French by its moderation. As for Giap, he pointedly observed the presence of an OSS delegation at the ceremonies and stated, "As regards foreign relations, our public opinion pays very much attention to the Allied missions in Hanoi, because everyone is anxious to know the result of the foreign negotiations of the government." The future victor of Dien Bien Phu spoke of "particularly intimate relations" with the Americans, "which it is a pleasant duty to dwell upon." [58] Later that afternoon, Giap stood beside Patti in reviewing the Viet Minh troop units. As the band struck up the "Star Spangled Banner," Giap raised his arm in the clenched-fist Communist salute.

The French reacted bitterly to the American friendship with the Viet Minh. "We seemed to the Americans," wrote Sainteny, "incorrigibly obstinate in reviving a colonial past to which they were opposed, in the name of an infantile anti-colonialism which blinded them to almost everything." The OSS men, he complained, were "housed and flattered by the crafty members of the new Annamite government, swollen with egotism by the importance which the French accorded them, convinced of the necessity of saving these poor Annamites squashed under the weight of French colonialism." Why, asked Sainteny, did a fine organization like OSS, "so rich in men of valor," send officers to Hanoi who were "incapable of grasping the stakes and incalculable consequences" of the Viet Minh rise to power? [59]

Were the American motives more sinister? In one of his later reports, Sainteny informed Paris of a startling bit of intelligence. Patti, he learned, had proposed to Ho that economic interests connected with General Donovan would help reconstruct Vietnamese railroads, highways, and airfields, in exchange for economic privileges in Indochina.

Ho Chi Minh proclaimed September 2, 1945 as Viet Nam Independence Day. Communist guerrillas marched in review in Hanoi and the band struck up the "Star Spangled Banner" while OSS Col. Archimedes Patti (left foreground) and Viet Minh military genius Vo Nguyen Giap (right foreground) saluted. Standing behind Patti was "Roberts," the Harvard psychologist who openly sympathized with the Viet Minh cause.

Ho, according to Sainteny's report, rejected the offer. Sainteny's source for this information was Ho Chi Minh himself.[60]

But the French had underestimated the crafty Vietnamese revolutionary. The truth of the matter was that Ho had approached the Americans to request massive economic aid in the reconstruction of Indochina. He openly welcomed American technicians and American investments. If that was imperialism, then Ho Chi Minh was the guilty party.

And it was the Americans who failed to grasp the offer. In response to Ho's recurrent economic overtures, Roberts of the OSS team finally agreed to form a Vietnamese-American Import-Export Company. This promising business concern never became more than a paper organization. By mid-September, the OSS officers were no longer free agents and their importance in the eyes of the Vietnamese had begun to dwindle.

The change in events was due to the arrival, on September 9, of the Chinese occupation forces who had been assigned the task of "liberating" Tonkin. A massive Chinese army, equipped with American arms and supplies, and manned by thousands of ragged, ill-disciplined local units, first crossed the border into Tonkin on August 28. It took two weeks for this mob to reach Hanoi. Arriving at the government palace, the Chinese unceremoniously expelled Sainteny and his group from the premises to make way for their own commander, General Lu Han. The French, who had so long complained of their imprisonment, now complained of their ouster. Sainteny wired Calcutta that immediate action should be taken to "defend our compatriots, who have been jeered at, pillaged, and expropriated by the Japanese and Annamites, and now by the Chinese, under the neutral and impassive eyes of the Americans." [61]

The Chinese proceeded to disarm the Japanese troops, the task that they had been delegated to perform by the Allies. But they soon became preoccupied with less orthodox activities. Black-marketeering and looting swelled with their arrival and the Vietnamese economy was bled dry. Chinese troops filed out of Hanoi, carrying their loot in bullock carts, captured Japanese trucks and, if need be, on their backs. They took everything—plumbing fixtures, roof tiles, furniture—even stripped pipes from buildings.

Arriving with the Chinese army was an official American military mission commanded by General Phillip Gallagher, a member of Wedemeyer's staff. Gallagher obligingly adopted the Patti team as his intelligence arm. One of his first requests was for detailed information about Ho Chi Minh.

Even after the Chinese arrival, Roberts had continued his discussions with Ho, marveling at the Viet Minh leader's command of both the French and English languages. At Gallagher's request, Roberts made a special effort to gather intelligence about Ho's political background. Through his agent, Le Xuan, Roberts bribed an old Vietnamese nationalist politician with a pouch of opium and thus secured a full dossier on Ho's revolutionary background, including the record of his years in Moscow. When Roberts frankly questioned Ho about his Communist past, the veteran agitator laughed and replied, with a twinkle in his eye, "I have difficulty remembering some parts of my long life. That is the problem of being an old revolutionary."

Roberts had long since concluded that Ho was a great and charismatic leader, a nationalist who was "above Communism." The Viet Minh also appeared to have the confidence of the entire populace and the active support of many non-Communist nationalists. Roberts developed a personal friendship with two young Vietnamese of aristocratic descent. They were hardly sympathetic to the tenets of Marxist doctrine, but, they declared, they would give their support to Ho without hesitation in a battle against the French.

These two young men were also active in an OSS-sponsored group called the Vietnamese-American Friendship Association. The VAFA was created at the beginning of October, shortly after Patti was relieved of his post and recalled to China. Colonels Heppner and Helliwell had made a brief trip to Hanoi from OSS headquarters in Kunming, just before the formal Japanese surrender in Hanoi on September 27. They quickly reached the conclusion that Patti [q] was too closely identified with the past days of ill-feeling and should be replaced. In his stead they named OSS Lieutenant Commander Carleton Swift, Jr., who arrived in Hanoi resplendent in a shining white naval uniform that was a constant source of amusement to the Vietnamese.[r] The 26-year-old Harvard graduate, scion of the Swift meat family, was no less critical of French colonialism than his other OSS colleagues. He and Roberts formed a rapid friendship and worked closely together in promoting their Friendship Association.

The VAFA came to include high officials of the Viet Minh, OSS officers, and members of General Gallagher's staff. The inaugural meeting was held on October 17, and Gallagher was persuaded to sing a rendition of the Vietnamese national anthem over the Viet Minh radio. The general then delivered a speech in which he welcomed Vietnamese students to study at American universities. According to a jaundiced French report, Gallagher declared that the students would be warmly welcomed by "American coeds." [62]

But the OSS days of influence in Hanoi were already drawing to a close. The American military command in China was becoming in-

[q] After his retirement from the Army in 1957, Patti became an official of the U.S. Office of Emergency Planning.

[r] Swift was First Secretary of the American embassy in Iraq in 1958 when leftists seized control of the government during the Lebanon crisis.

creasingly leery of the intelligence team's political associations. A special
group of OSS counter-intelligence officers (including a number of ex-
FBI agents) appeared in Hanoi. Roberts suspected that they had come
to spy on the remaining OSS personnel. Finally, in late October, OSS
was ordered to withdraw its entire mission from the Tonkinese capital.

Roberts sadly wrote a final report, strongly recommending American support for Ho and his nationalist movement. But it was too late.
By October 25, the State Department had already informed OSS in no
uncertain terms that the United States would "respect French sovereignty" in Indochina.

After a month without intelligence reports from Hanoi, Wedemeyer's headquarters decided to send new observers to make a fresh assessment of the political situation in northern Indochina. The responsibility devolved upon two members of Peter Dewey's original OSS
team in Saigon, Sergeant George Wickes (who had been Dewey's
liaison with the Viet Minh), and Major Frank White.[s] In October
1945 they were ordered to proceed to Hanoi.

White was a Stanford graduate, a journalist by profession who had
worked for the United Press in Mexico. Recruited into OSS in 1944, he
handled rescue operations in Burma until his selection for the Dewey
team. Together with Wickes and a radio operator, he reached Hanoi at
the end of 1945 and found "a strange and stricken town, restive,
covered with a film of red dust, raised, more often than not, by crowds
of tense demonstrators moving in the streets." [63] A profusion of anti-
Viet Minh splinter parties had just begun to reassert themselves with
French encouragement. Sainteny was still there, now as official French
commissioner for Tonkin, and was negotiating with Ho over Vietnamese "independence within the French union." The first French
troops had just arrived at the port of Haiphong in a show of force that
only heightened tensions. And the Chinese army still swarmed like
locusts over the countryside, crippling the Tonkinese economy.

White and Wickes established themselves in the Hotel Metropole, recently abandoned by Patti's contingent, and sent a message of
introduction to Ho at his government palace. Shortly after, White received an invitation to meet with the Viet Minh leader. "Ho," recalls
White, "wore the traditional high buttoned tunic and floppy pants of
the same khaki material. His beard was then wispy and his manner
curiously detached. I was unprepared for a person so slight." [64]

[s] White is now Director of Time-Life Films in New York.

Ho began the conversation by emphasizing the desire of the Vietnamese people for independence. He touched upon the history of the early Chinese invasions, the more recent French and Japanese occupation, and the postwar hardship and destruction caused by the Chinese Army. No matter who the invading power might be from century to century, he noted, the Vietnamese people had always maintained the will to resist.

As for the future, Ho felt that some Frenchmen, like Sainteny, accepted the demise of traditional colonial rule and were prepared to grant real independence to Vietnam over a period of years, but he was not certain that the French government would sanction this position. Nor was he confident that many of his own people would be willing to trust the French or abide the delays. "Patience," he said, "has come to an end."

Ho then discussed the Soviet Union. He referred to his young days as an "idealist" and his resulting troubles with the French police. He admitted that he had gone to Moscow to study the teachings of Marx and Lenin and had personally come to accept the Communist doctrine. But Ho did not feel that Russia could or would make any real contribution to the building of a new Vietnam. What his country needed, he said, were large investments of money and machines. The war-torn Russian economy could not provide such capital.

The United States, said Ho, was in the best position to aid Vietnam in the postwar years. America had emerged from the war with enormous power and prestige, and particularly in the Far East. The American people, he believed, were sympathetic to the concept of self-determination and generous in making contributions to less fortunate states. Yet Ho was not optimistic about the prospects of American aid. He could not expect, he concluded, that a small country like Vietnam would ever loom large in Washington's preoccupations.

When the conversation had ended, White returned to his hotel, only to find an invitation to a reception at Ho's government palace that evening. Some of the high-ranking members of Ho's cabinet, including Giap, were already in attendance when the OSS major arrived. Then came the French, Sainteny and three army generals. They were followed, in short order, by two Chinese generals and Colonel Trevor Wilson, chief of British intelligence in Hanoi. White felt a bit uneasy in such exalted company.

"Befitting my modest rank," White remembers, "I held back until all the others had found their places and were seated at the table. If there hadn't been an empty chair, I was prepared to slink away. But there was—and it was next to Ho's. I sat down.

"The dinner was a horror. The French confined themselves to the barest minimum of conversation and scarcely spoke to the Chinese, who quickly became drunk. . . . At one point I spoke to Ho very quietly. 'I think, Mr. President, there is some resentment over the seating arrangement at this table.' I meant, of course, my place next to him." The wiry little Communist looked up at the OSS major. His subdued reply still rings with tragic irony after the events of the past twenty-five years. "Yes," he said, "I can see that, but who else could I talk to?" [65]

11

OSS and CIA:
The Espionage Gap

In the main hall of CIA headquarters at Langley, Virginia, there hangs a large oil portrait of General Donovan, a tribute to the man who founded OSS and, in so doing, laid the foundations for contemporary American espionage.

The Office of Strategic Services was the direct lineal ancestor of today's Central Intelligence Agency. Critics of CIA have often wondered how an amateur secret service that once gave hope to Ho Chi Minh's guerrillas could have evolved into an "invisible government" of the Cold War era. The answer is simple. The CIA is no aberrant mutation of "Donovan's dreamers"; it is in many ways the mirror image of OSS. Edmond Taylor, the OSS man who fought Vichyism in Africa and colonialism in Asia, reflected in a recent memoir that the wartime activities of his organization established "a precedent, or a pattern, for United States intervention in the revolutionary struggles of the postwar age. The Donovan influence on U.S. foreign and military policy has continued to be felt even since his death; for good and ill he left a lasting mark on the mind of the nation's power elite. However indirectly, many of our latter-day Cold War successes, disasters, and entrapments can ultimately be traced back to him." [1]

CIA inherited from OSS the crucial Donovan principle of merging Secret Intelligence and Special Operations in the same organization. The functional titles changed to Foreign Intelligence and Covert Action but the theory was the same: to centralize all clandestine operations in a single bureaucracy. "Few of the people," wrote Allen Dulles in 1966, "who today hotly debate the wisdom of this arrangement can recall the high auspices under which the decision was made some twenty-five years ago or the attention given the subject when the OSS and later the CIA were organized." [2] Dulles was exaggerating. The "decision" was little more than a product of Donovan's fertile imagination in 1941; it was never seriously challenged when the CIA was created six years later. Any official discussion of the issue remained hidden from the public. JFK?

Even more fundamental was the CIA's inherited justification for clandestine political operations unrelated to espionage and intelligence analysis. There had been no doubt as to the ethics of OSS foreign interventionism in the course of the battle against fascism. Yet CIA received, as a matter of unquestioned right, the same mantle of morality. The most notorious CIA-fomented coups in Latin America, Asia, and the Middle East were, technically speaking, only extensions of Donovan's mandate for political warfare. The secret service remained the same—only the world had changed. CIA officials who "had been in the OSS during World War II and had worked with the resistance in Europe and Asia" were responsible for planning the ill-fated invasion of Cuba.[3] In Southeast Asia and elsewhere, former OSS men who had once aided underground partisans became leading experts on counter-insurgency and the suppression of left-wing rebellions. In 1969 OSS veteran and CIA officer William Colby, who fought bravely behind the lines with French and Norwegian resistance forces against the Nazis, was appointed director of American anti-guerrilla "pacification" in Vietnam.

Even OSS dynamism became twisted in the Cold War period. "The CIA," writes OSS veteran Francis Miller, "inherited from Donovan his lopsided and mischievous preoccupation with action and the Bay of Pigs was one of the results of that legacy." [4] CIA men, like their OSS predecessors, have been imaginative, free-wheeling, aggressive, and often more politically knowledgeable than their State Department colleagues. And, like the men of Donovan's organization, CIA "spooks" abroad still resist headquarters "interference" in their activities. But history caught up with OSS. The chaotic administration of a dynamic, unmanageable wartime secret service proved dangerous in an era of uneasy peace. During a World War, Donovan had felt, justifiably, that the smallest success would probably outweigh the greatest blunder. In the nuclear age, the most minute blunder—a reconnaissance flight detected or an espionage operation "blown"—could lead to irreparable disaster.

But there was more to the OSS legacy. Donovan's agency had been torn by political and ideological conflict as bright young gadflies in khaki took sharp objection to the predilection of their superiors for the Darlans and Badoglios and Chiang Kai-sheks of the world. The postwar fate of that tradition of dissent within America's intelligence service is an ignored page in the history of CIA.

In the fall of 1944, at the request of President Roosevelt, General Donovan submitted a secret memorandum to the White House outlining the creation of a permanent American intelligence service. "When our enemies are defeated," wrote Donovan, "the demand will be equally pressing for information that will aid us in solving the problems of peace." He proposed prompt action to transform OSS into a "central intelligence service" that would report directly to the President. OSS had "the trained and specialized personnel needed for the task. This talent should not be dispersed." [5]

While Donovan's proposal was still under consideration in official circles, his memorandum became the center of a political storm. The conservative Chicago Tribune acquired a copy of the top-secret document and then printed a series of articles by journalist Walter Trohan denouncing Donovan's plan for a "super-spy system" in the "postwar New Deal." Trohan claimed that the organization proposed by Donovan would be an "all-powerful intelligence service to spy on the postwar world and to pry into the lives of citizens at home. . . . The unit would operate under an independent budget and presumably have secret funds for spy work along the lines of bribing and luxury living described in the novels of E. Phillips Oppenheim." [6]

The Donovan memorandum was leaked to the press in a flagrant breach of security by the perennial enemy of OSS, FBI Director J. Edgar Hoover. He was determined to see the demise of his rivals in the intelligence field, and his ploy was successful. A congressional uproar followed. One anti-Roosevelt congressman bellowed, "This is another indication that the New Deal will not halt in its quest for power. Like Simon Legree it wants to own us body and soul." [7] In the ensuing political hubbub, the White House ordered the whole matter tabled.

At the beginning of April 1945, Roosevelt decided to revive the Donovan proposal. But a week later, the President was dead. His successor, Harry Truman, wanted no part of a peacetime "Gestapo." On September 20, 1945, he issued an executive order disbanding the Office of Strategic Services.

The OSS organization was then dispersed among the other agencies of the government. The remains of the Secret Intelligence and Special Operations branches were transferred to the War Department and placed under the command of Donovan's Deputy Director for Intelligence, General John Magruder. This Strategic Services Unit was nothing more than a caretaker body formed to preside over the liquidation of the OSS espionage network. By February 1946, Magruder had already resigned in protest against the dismemberment of his intelligence unit and its "expensively trained, hand-picked personnel." [8] Only a few stalwart SSU officers remained at their former OSS posts to administer the skeleton of a secret service—Philip Horton in France, Richard Helms in Germany, Alfred Ulmer in Austria, James Angleton in Italy, Albert Seitz in the Balkans, and James Kellis in China.

The Research and Analysis Branch of OSS was meanwhile shunted off to the State Department. Alfred McCormack, a New York corporation lawyer credited with revitalizing Army intelligence during the war, was appointed at the suggestion of Under-Secretary Dean Acheson to direct the 900 men and women of the Interim Research and Intelligence Branch. Some of the finest analysts of the OSS Research office —H. Stuart Hughes, Franz Neumann, Herbert Marcuse, Charles Stelle, Allan Evans—remained in McCormack's organization in the hope of fostering the first genuine intelligence effort in the State Department's history.

But it was not to be. Congressional critics of the defunct OSS decimated McCormack's budget. No less hostile were old-line diplomats who had no understanding of intelligence work and saw no need for State Department support of these academic upstarts. Spruille Braden, then Assistant Secretary of State for Latin American affairs (and more recently a devotee of the John Birch Society) led the opposition. He later told a congressional committee, "[We] resisted this invasion of all these swarms of people . . . mostly collectivists and 'do-gooders' and what-nots." [9]

In March 1946, while McCormack and Dean Acheson struggled to secure a renewed appropriation for the Research unit, the chairman of the House Military Affairs Committee charged that persons with "strong Soviet leanings" had joined the State Department intelligence group. McCormack denied the charge and demanded a retraction. Instead, Congress cut the entire appropriation for his unit. Conservative State Department administrators had convinced influential legislators that the ex-OSS analysts were ideologically "far to the left of the views held by the President and his Secretary of State," and committed to "a socialized America in a world commonwealth of Communist and Socialist states dedicated to peace through collective security, political, economic, and social reform; and the redistribution of national wealth on a global basis." [10]

On April 23, Colonel McCormack resigned. His successor, Colonel William Eddy (of OSS North African fame) was given the task of dismantling the R&A group as an integral unit and assigning each geographic division to the regular State Department desks. The analysts who remained "floated in limbo, distrusted by the State Department professionals and seldom listened to." They took sharp issue with the Cold War mentality of their diplomatic superiors, but, as H. Stuart Hughes remembers, "We felt most of the time as though we were firing our memoranda off into a void. The atmosphere was that of Kafka's *Castle*, in which one never knew who would answer the telephone or even whether it would be answered at all." [11] A few dauntless academicians languished at State for a year or two, but they knew that the Department had already abdicated its potential role in the production of foreign intelligence.[a]

Private enterprise at first hoped to fill the void. One former OSS Deputy Director approached "Pop" Watson of IBM with a business proposition. Why not form a private intelligence organization and offer its services on contract to the government? The two men raised the initial capital for the venture, but their efforts were in vain. The White House soon approved the creation of a National Intelligence Authority and a subordinate Central Intelligence Group, the bureaucratic brainchild of the wartime ambassador to Vichy France, Admiral Leahy. These were stopgap measures that proved inadequate substitutes for OSS. The following year, Congress provided for the creation of a Central Intelligence Agency. Donovan's dream had at last come true.

The new CIA was a strange mixture of professional military officers and civilian OSS veterans (who soon became the dominant force

[a] The coup de grace for the State research group came in early 1947 when Carl Marzani, former deputy chief of the OSS Presentation Branch who had transferred to State along with the R&A academicians, was indicted and sent to prison on a charge of "disloyalty" and concealing membership in the Communist Party.

in the Agency). The two principal operating divisions were the Office of Policy Coordination (OPC), assigned the task of political subversion, and the Office of Special Operations (OSO), responsible for espionage and intelligence collection. James Angleton, chief of OSS counter-intelligence in Rome, and William K. Harvey, an ex-FBI agent who had run afoul of J. Edgar Hoover, directed OSO. Frank Wisner, OSS chief in Istanbul and Bucharest and Allen Dulles' top aide in Germany, became director of OPC. He was assisted by Franklin Lindsay, commander of the last OSS mission to Tito.

As the OSS veterans gained influence at the expense of the West Pointers in CIA, the old Donovan rivalry with the military services was revived. The Pentagon began to view the CIA leadership as a "wild-eyed bunch of intellectuals whose colleges don't want them back." [12] Organizational strife often concerned vital issues of American foreign policy. In 1948, Army intelligence predicted an imminent Soviet invasion of Western Europe. The Pentagon was irked by the CIA's dissenting and more optimistic view of Moscow's intentions. Time proved the CIA analysts correct.[13]

The FBI was also predictably unhappy with the newly created CIA. The espionage barony operated in Latin America by J. Edgar Hoover's men since 1941 was to be replaced by a CIA network. In some American embassies south of the border, FBI men destroyed their intelligence files rather than bequeath them to their CIA rivals. The first years of CIA's existence also saw Hoover busily promoting charges that a sinister Communist spy network had subverted OSS.

The accumulated enemies of CIA were given their first opportunity to strike back in 1949 while civil war raged on the Chinese mainland. A CIA colonel told a State Department committee convened to consider the Chinese situation that the Communist forces enjoyed "high morale, high combat effectiveness, and have demonstrated a particular mobility in their operation." The Nationalist troops were "characterized by professional ineffectiveness and, generally speaking, they lack the will to fight." The CIA man added, "The Communist capabilities for taking Taiwan are greatest in causing the fall of the island from within. The discipline and morale of the troops is at a low ebb. It is the result of past defeats and inadequate leadership. . . . There is another factor on Taiwan. The excesses of the Nationalist administration in Taiwan since V-J Day have earned for the Chiang Kai-shek regime the earnest hatred of the Taiwanese." [14]

A month later, two officers of Wisner's OPC—Lyle Munson and

Edward Hunter, a former OSS propagandist—were called to a meeting with John P. Davies of the State Department, the former political advisor to General Stilwell. Davies suggested to the CIA men that a number of old China hands, including former OSS analyst John Fairbank, be employed as consultants by the Agency.

Unfortunately, both Munson and Hunter were Chiang Kai-shek supporters while Davies' old China hands had all been vocal critics of the Kuomintang regime. When Munson resigned from CIA in 1950, he told the FBI that Davies had recommended "known Soviet agents" for CIA employment. This information soon came into the hands of Alfred Kohlberg, popularly known as the "China lobby man." Kohlberg and his cabal were already promoting charges of disloyalty against every competent Far Eastern expert in the State Department. He and his allies of the American right wing turned their attention toward far bigger game in America's sacrosanct intelligence service.[15]

This was a period of growth for the Agency. In 1950 General Walter Bedell Smith, former chief of staff to General Eisenhower and ambassador to Moscow, became Director of CIA. His appointment was, in itself, no liberal victory. ("I know you won't believe this," an ex-CIA man told this writer, "but Smith once warned Eisenhower that Rockefeller was a Communist.") "Beetle" Smith had one stroke of genius. To assist him as Deputy Director in charge of all operational activity, he brought OSS spy-master Allen Dulles to Washington.

The Smith regime at CIA saw an influx of personnel to the Agency and the development of ideological factions. In his 1953 memoirs, OSS veteran and CIA Balkans expert Albert Seitz noted with joy that "the ethical balance" in American politics was "swinging again to the right." [16] The CIA certainly acquired its share of determined conservatives. Charles Black, husband of former child movie star Shirley Temple, donned a Marine uniform and became one of the first CIA junior officer trainees. Writer James Burnham, later the editor of William Buckley's *National Review*, was brought into the Agency by OSS veteran Kermit Roosevelt to help plan the CIA coup against Mossadegh in Iran. Another recruit was Buckley's sister. Her brother-in-law was Senator Joseph McCarthy's administrative assistant.

These same years saw a determined effort by Allen Dulles to bring American liberals into intelligence work. One CIA newcomer was William Sloane Coffin, later Chaplain of Yale University (and recently in the public eye as a co-defendant with Dr. Benjamin Spock in the so-called "draft conspiracy" trial). Twenty years ago, this same man was a CIA officer in Eastern Europe. Why did he join the Agency? Coffin later recalled, "Stalin made Hitler look like a Boy Scout. I was very strongly anti-Soviet. In that frame of mind I watched the Korean War shape up. But I didn't follow it too closely, or question the causes. When I graduated from Yale in 1949, I was thinking of going into the CIA, but I went into the seminary instead. After a year at the Union Theological Seminary, when war with the Soviet Union seemed to be threatening, I quit to go into the CIA, hoping to be useful in the war effort." Coffin, who remained with the Agency until 1953, added, "I've a mixed set of feelings" about the CIA, "knowing that during the Joe McCarthy period liberals in the CIA won a great victory—they were able to use the non-Communist left to beat the Communist left. The CIA financed the non-Communist left; they gave with minimal strings attached. In those days, I had no quarrel with American policy—but, in retrospect, I wouldn't be so innocent and smirchless." [17]

The "great victory" of the CIA liberal faction was the operational brainchild of another Dulles recruit, 32-year-old Thomas Braden, an OSS veteran who accepted Dulles' offer to join CIA in 1951 as Assistant Director. Once a Jedburgh in France, this imaginative young man had worked in civilian life as a newspaper reporter, a Dartmouth English professor, and an art museum director before accepting the CIA post.

At Braden's suggestion and with the support of Allen Dulles and Frank Wisner, the CIA began its covert support of the non-Communist political left around the world—trade unions, political parties, and international organizations of students and journalists. The original purpose of this "covert action" was to counter the $250 million dollar annual effort of the Soviet Union in supporting a whole series of international Communist front organizations. Many of the same secret CIA programs which evolved—including financial aid to American voluntary organizations with international programs, such as the National Student Association—might have been openly undertaken by the State Department or some other public agency had it not been for the dominant political atmosphere of the time: McCarthyism.

Braden later recalled: "In the early 1950s, when the cold war was really hot, the idea that Congress would have approved many of our projects was about as likely as the John Birch Society's approving Medicare. I remember, for example, the time I tried to bring my old friend, Paul Henri-Spaak of Belgium to the U.S. to help out in one of the CIA operations.

"Paul Henri-Spaak was and is a very wise man. He had served his country as foreign minister and premier. CIA Director Allen Dulles mentioned Spaak's projected journey to the then Senate Majority Leader William F. Knowland of California. I believe that Mr. Dulles thought the senator would like to meet Mr. Spaak. I am sure he was not prepared for Knowland's reaction: 'Why,' the senator said, 'the man's a socialist.' 'Yes,' Mr. Dulles replied, 'and the head of his party. But you don't know Europe the way I do, Bill. In many European countries, a socialist is roughly equivalent to a Republican.' Knowland replied, 'I don't care. We aren't going to bring any socialists over here.' " [18]

Far more threatening to the Braden operation and to the CIA itself was the already popular demagoguery of Joseph McCarthy, the senator from Wisconsin. "Nearly every liberal in the federal government was viewed with suspicion," recalls Lyman Kirkpatrick, an OSS veteran who served as CIA Inspector General during McCarthy's meteoric rise to infamy. "It had something of the atmosphere that must have been present during the French revolution when denunciations and trials led to the guillotine. While there was no guillotine in Washington, there was perhaps an even worse fate in the destruction of an individual's career, and the wrecking of his life." [19]

Having permanently demolished the morale of the State Department, McCarthy turned an eye toward the CIA, a "major and much more important target, particularly from the point of view of getting him greater personal publicity." [20] In February 1952, ex-CIA man Lyle Munson had publicly told a congressional committee about John Davies' recommendation that old China hands be hired by CIA. Chiang Kai-shek's China lobby quickly assured McCarthy that "persons who were remnants of the China mistake occupied high positions" in CIA. McCarthy also learned that Braden's International Organization Division had "granted large subsidies to pro-Communist organizations." [21] And in the fall of 1952, McCarthy received an inadvertent boost from CIA Director "Beetle" Smith. At the height of the Stevenson-Eisenhower presidential contest, McCarthy sued one of his leading critics, Democratic Senator William Benton, for libel. Testifying on Benton's behalf, General Smith was asked his view on Communist infiltration of the government. Under cross-examination, he replied, "I believe there are Communists in my own organization. . . . I do everything I can to detect them, but I am morally certain, since you are asking the question, that there are." [22]

While McCarthy planned his assault on CIA, Eisenhower took office and named Allen Dulles as the new CIA Director. Dulles was determined to prevent McCarthyism from destroying the Agency and CIA became something of a haven for foreign policy "freethinkers." Richard Bissell, a State Department liberal who joined CIA, remembers the Agency in the early 1950s as "a place where there was still intellectual ferment and challenge and things going on" while "much of the challenge and sense of forward motion had gone out of other parts of the government." [23]

These same qualities made CIA a prime target for McCarthy. The senator's first problem was how to penetrate the CIA cloak of secrecy in order to discover those "Communist agents" who had "subverted" the country's intelligence operations. Dulles warned his employees that he would fire anyone who went to McCarthy without his personal authorization. Some CIA personnel had already received mysterious phone calls from McCarthy associates. They were told that "it was known that they drank too much, or were having an 'affair,' and the caller would make no issue of this if they would come around and tell everything that they knew about the Agency" to a McCarthy devotee.[24]

The senator had other sources of information, including a private intelligence organization in Baltimore called the International Services of Information Foundation. The director of this group was Ulius Amoss, the Greek-American businessman once relieved as OSS executive officer in Cairo for administrative mismanagement. Amoss' group claimed responsibility for the 1953 defection to the west of a Polish pilot in his Russian MIG jet, a bonus for American intelligence (and Fairchild Aircraft, which funded the operation). The organization was also involved in a mysterious plot promoted by a conservative millionaire to kidnap Stalin's son from Moscow. Meanwhile, Amoss became friendly with an ex-FBI agent on McCarthy's staff and apparently aided the senator in his private "investigation" of the CIA.

McCarthy's channels of information, however, left much to be desired. He made his first public charge against a CIA employee in July 1953 with an attack on William Bundy, a member of CIA's Board of National Estimates (and Dean Acheson's son-in-law). The senator's charges against Bundy were so patently ridiculous (Bundy had contributed $400 to the Alger Hiss Defense Fund) that Dulles was able to launch a counter-attack.

The CIA Director told the President he would resign unless McCarthy's vituperation was silenced. Eisenhower had been reluctant to stand up to the politically powerful (and politically useful) senator. But he accepted Dulles' contention that McCarthy's attacks on the

Agency were damaging to the national security. Vice-President Nixon was dispatched to pressure McCarthy into dropping his plans for a public investigation. The senator suddenly became "convinced" that "it would not be in the public interest to hold public hearings on the CIA, that that perhaps could be taken care of administratively." [25]

The "administrative" remedy McCarthy demanded as the price of his silence was a vast internal purge of the Agency. The senator privately brought his charges against CIA "security risks" to Dulles' office. He had lists of alleged "homosexuals" and "rich men" in CIA employ and provided Dulles with voluminous "allegations and denunciations, but no facts." [26] To insure, however, that his charges were taken seriously by CIA, McCarthy continued to threaten a public investigation. At his infamous hearings on alleged subversion in the Army, the senator frequently spoke of "Communist infiltration and corruption and dishonesty" in CIA. He called this a "very, very dangerous situation" which "disturbs me beyond words." [27]

The pressure took its toll. Security standards for Agency employment were tightened, often to the point of absurdity, and many able young men were kept from pursuing intelligence careers. In one case, the CIA's loss was Hollywood's gain. A young political science graduate with a classic New York accent named Peter Falk applied for entrance to CIA's training program in 1953. His application was rejected for security reasons—he had once belonged to a left-wing union, had received a B.A. degree from the "radical" New School for Social Research, and had spent six months in Yugoslavia with a "girl I loved very much." [28]

Worse yet were the expulsions of CIA employees after "re-investigation." One victim, Sylvia Press, later described her case at length in a slightly fictionalized novel, The Care of Devils. She had joined the OSS New York office (then under Allen Dulles) in 1942 and remained with CIA after the war. A Kafkaesque security investigation in 1954 led to her dismissal without any real justification. An appeal to Dulles was fruitless. One charge brought against her was that she had worked in OSS with Francis Kalnay, the Hungarian writer whose recruitment of pro-Tito Yugoslavs had so upset OSS headquarters—a full decade before.

The employees of Tom Braden's International Organization Division were subjected to special scrutiny because of their obvious political liberalism. Braden's director of trade union operations was fired because he had briefly belonged to the Young Communist League in the 1930s. The FBI happily assisted in the purge of CIA officers and produced one particularly inane "derogatory" report on a tall intense young man "with a preoccupied smile and wavy brown hair" whom Braden had recruited as his assistant.[29] His name was Cord Meyer, Jr.

On the morning of July 22, 1944, on the island of Guam in the South Pacific, a Japanese grenade rolled into a foxhole and a 23-year-old Marine lieutenant was severely wounded. The explosion cost him the vision of his left eye and he remained in a hospital for months, recovering from burns and shrapnel wounds. But out of this misery of war, Lieutenant Cord Meyer underwent a spiritual rebirth.

Months before, he had written his parents: "As we buried our dead, I swore to myself that if it was within my power I should see to it that these deaths would not be forgotten or valued lightly. I felt more strongly than ever the wrongness of so many things. Their motionless young bodies, their inarticulate lips, seemed a monumental reproach to us the living, seeming to say, 'Well, we did all you asked. We gave up everything, all we might have been and done, all love, all hope, all laughter, all tomorrows. What are you going to do now? Is it going to be any different, any better now? If you don't do what you can, at least you will never forget us. We will trouble your midnight and your noon's repose with the specter of our speechless gaze. Certainly we can do no more. The rest lies with you.' So, remembering them, I find heart for the long road and the many battles and determination for the peaceful time. If there be a God may He give us all the strength and the vision that we so badly need. . . . I really think, if possible, I should like to make a life's work of doing what little I can in the problems of international cooperation. No matter how small a contribution I should happen to make it would be in the right direction. We cannot continue to make a shambles of this world, and already a blind man can see the shortsighted decisions that point inevitably to that ultimate Armageddon." [30]

In the mud of Guam, an explosion nearly brought Meyer very real blindness. And as he returned to the United States to convalesce from his wounds, he found new grief—his twin brother had been killed in action on Okinawa. But a new inner strength and maturity developed where an emotional scar might have appeared in a lesser man. Meyer no longer thought of the horrors of war only in terms of the dead soldiers he once commanded. He now believed that armed conflict was an institutionalized hell for all mankind.

The son of a wealthy State Department officer, Meyer was not accustomed to personal crisis in his youth. He attended an exclusive prep school and went on to Yale, where he belonged to the best social clubs, played on the hockey team, and edited the literary magazine, showing a particular affinity for poetry. In September 1942, he graduated Summa Cum Laude and Phi Beta Kappa and was honored as the Yale senior who had "contributed most intellectually to the university." Two weeks after leaving New Haven, Meyer enlisted in the Marine Corps; he served as a machine gun platoon leader in the Pacific until he was wounded on Guam.

Returning to the United States to recover from his injuries, Meyer was chosen as one of two wounded veterans to assist Harold Stassen at the United Nations Conference at San Francisco in April 1945. There he met Charles Bolte, another wounded veteran who shared Meyer's hopes for world peace after the war.[b] Bolte, a former newspaper reporter who had lost his leg while fighting the Germans in North Africa, was attending the conference as a representative of the American Veterans Committee. He had founded the AVC in 1944 in the belief that the established veterans groups were far too conservative for the new breed of young soldiers who wanted a new order in America and the postwar world. Dedicated to Roosevelt's New Deal and to international peace through the United Nations, the AVC attracted the active support of many influential young men and its membership grew geometrically after the end of the war.

An early recruit to Bolte's Veterans Committee, Meyer also devoted his energies to the growing American movement for effective world government. In early 1947, several national and state organizations which supported the concept of a strengthened United Nations as the key to world peace merged to form a new group called the United World Federalists. Meyer became its articulate and dynamic president.

By then his evolving view on world politics had already been affected by his experiences within the AVC. At the second national convention of the committee in 1947, a minority supported by the American Communist Party made an all-out attempt to seize control of the convention and dominate the writing of its platform. They were resoundingly and decisively defeated. Meyer was a member of the AVC majority and the organizational battle left him with a profound hatred of Communist political tactics. He was particularly disturbed by the Communist Party "line" which denounced all proponents of world

[b] Bolte was vice-president of the Carnegie Endowment for International Peace, 1966–71.

government as "reactionary plotters." At the AVC convention, the radical faction had taken the conservative position on the one question Meyer considered most crucial—the abolition of the veto within the U.N. Security Council as an important first step toward peace. In thus following the dictates of Moscow, the American Communists had aligned themselves with right-wing southern senators who believed that strengthening the United Nations would hamper their own chauvinistic form of American nationalism.[31]

Meyer and his AVC friends, despite their battle with American Communists, were alarmed by a rapidly impending Soviet-American Cold War and consequent American support for "corrupt and oppressive" regimes in Greece, Turkey, and China. Meyer concluded unhappily that America's anti-Communist zeal was obliterating the democratic principles of American foreign policy. And, at first, he believed that the Soviets should be offered the opportunity to "cooperate in building the institutions of a durable peace."[32]

As the Cold War progressed, the Communist coup in Czechoslovakia and the Russian blockade of Berlin seemed to cast serious doubt on any theory of Moscow's peaceful intent. Nor did the Soviets alter their opposition to the world government concept. In 1949, Meyer wrote, "I have to admit that the present leadership in the Kremlin is opposed to the idea of world government. As a matter of fact Moscow radio has spent some time attacking us [the United World Federalists] and it attacked me personally not so long ago as the fig leaf of American imperialism." The following year, a Moscow newspaper described the movement for world government as an attempt to "beautify the boundless expansion of American imperialism."[33]

When he testified before the Senate Foreign Relations Committee in February 1950 on a proposal to revise the U.N. charter, Meyer, like the country at large, was preoccupied with Soviet belligerence. He warned that "we have failed in many respects to meet the ideological challenge and no quantity of bombs can make up for that failure to appeal to the hearts and minds of men."[34] Perhaps the outbreak of the Korean War in June 1950 solidified his decision to take a more active part in fighting a Cold War he had once viewed with skepticism. Months later, he left the United World Federalists in the capable hands of California liberal Alan Cranston and went into the CIA as assistant to Tom Braden.[c] "It was a great surprise to his friends," reflected one

[c] Cranston is now the senior United States Senator from California.

close associate. "He was not the CIA type. He was a world government man." [35]

Meyer soon wished he had remained in the world government movement, for he became an early target of the McCarthyites and their FBI friends. But unlike his CIA colleagues who dejectedly accepted their dismissal from the Agency, he "fought back doggedly against slurs on his loyalty. . . . Meyer was suspended from the Agency while preparing in his own defense a brief that ran into hundreds of pages. Dulles, who had recruited Meyer to the Agency, stood by his embattled aide." Meyer also secured the help of Washington attorney (later Supreme Court Justice) Abe Fortas and he eventually "won his battle against the impugners on Capitol Hill." [36] When Braden left the Agency in 1954, Meyer succeeded him as chief of CIA's Covert Action operations. Today he is one of the highest officials of the Central Intelligence Agency.

How did the ordeal affect Meyer? A friend recalls, "He was one of the most promising guys. Very sensitive, very intelligent. His whole spirit was one of great humanity." But, after years in CIA, "he got Cold Warized." [37] Many liberals who came under attack during the McCarthy era later developed a pervasive and sometimes blind anti-Communism as a defense against future criticism of their ideological integrity. And Meyer had further cause for the development of personal cynicism and a bitter outlook on the world—one of his sons was killed in an auto accident and his wife was murdered by an unknown assailant. In time, all the idealistic fervor of that young Marine lieutenant of 1945 was drained out of Cord Meyer, Jr.

Over the years, it also became increasingly difficult to remain both a liberal and a CIA officer. The Agency's covert power was consistently exercised on behalf of political repression and dictatorship. Heavy-handed interventionism in the political affairs of underdeveloped nations became the CIA norm.

Throughout the Eisenhower administration, CIA often gained the upper hand in relations with the State Department, and Agency officers frequently succeeded in establishing an immunity from diplomatic supervision. It was an inescapable fact that the Director of Central Intelligence was the brother of the Secretary of State. During periods of crisis at meetings of the National Security Council, Allen Dulles would be asked "What should we do about it?" Determined to maintain the myth that the CIA did not "make policy," Dulles would reply, "Well, that's none of my business. That's the business of the

Secretary of State." And there would often be a ripple of laughter around the table.

One measure of the CIA's Washington influence was the extent to which the Agency, like OSS before it, became a breeding-ground for statesmanship. CIA "graduates" included Robert Thayer, Agency Station Chief in Paris, who became ambassador to Romania in 1955; CIA Vietnam expert Robert Komer, appointed ambassador to Turkey during the Johnson administration; and Alexander Trowbridge, Secretary of Commerce under Johnson. William Bundy, the McCarthy era target, left CIA to become Assistant Secretary of Defense for International Security Affairs during the Kennedy administration, and successor to OSS-CIA veteran Roger Hilsman as Assistant Secretary of State for Far Eastern Affairs during the Johnson administration. G. Warren Nutter, who now holds Bundy's job at the Defense Department, was in CIA. So was Joseph Sisco, now Assistant Secretary of State for Near Eastern Affairs, and William Macomber, Jr., Assistant Secretary of State for Congressional Relations.

State Department officials have learned the power of their clandestine opposite numbers. In March 1954, a Texas attorney with long business experience in South America was named Assistant Secretary of State for Latin American Affairs. At one of his first briefings, the Texan learned that the CIA had set aside $20 million to overthrow a leftist regime in Guatemala. The Assistant Secretary raised vigorous objections to the whole plan until he was silenced by his superior, the Undersecretary of State—who happened to be ex-CIA Director Walter Bedell Smith. On several other occasions during the 1950s, John Foster Dulles felt that his own ambassadors could not be "trusted" and should not be informed of CIA operations in their countries. And those operations, as often as not, were undertaken by arrogant adventurers who had developed operational independence from a relatively enlightened staff at CIA's Washington headquarters.

How did the CIA liberals survive? Again, Allen Dulles was the key. He was a truly professional intelligence officer. Like his wartime associate William Donovan, he believed that apolitical pragmatism should dominate operational policy. And that meant subordinating personal political opinions to the goal of operational effectiveness. Dulles was certainly a political conservative and he had good cause to hate the Communists—his only son had been severely wounded while serving as an Army officer in Korea. But Dulles was also a man of terrific imagination and he was not afraid to use it, whatever the consequences. After Stalin's death in March 1953, when Eisenhower wanted to present a "peace plan" to the new Soviet leadership, it was Allen Dulles who, to the utter amazement of his brother, proposed consideration of a then startling proposal: in the very midst of the McCarthy furor, the CIA Director suggested that Washington offer to join Moscow in a program of economic assistance to Communist China.[38]

This same Allen Dulles was willing to allow the CIA liberals to give active support to the Algerian revolutionaries and to anti-Portuguese guerrillas in Angola and Mozambique. At a time when scarcely anyone in the State Department had a strong interest in African affairs, it was the CIA that maintained close and friendly contacts with such African radicals as Frantz Fanon, now a hero of the American New Left. And Dulles was at least willing to listen to the CIA minority who suggested that the new Castro regime in Cuba might adopt a "liberal" non-Communist position if not cold-shouldered by the United States. One right-wing Cuban exile complained, "The CIA men who handled the bulk of the investigative work on Castro were doctrinaire liberals. 'Progressives' was probably the word they preferred. Almost instinctively they found themselves passionately anti-Batista and therefore, quite illogically, strongly pro-Castro." [39] When the "liberal" prediction seemed to prove a disastrous error, the CIA went overboard in the other direction; the Bay of Pigs fiasco was the result.

By the advent of the Kennedy administration, the CIA had indeed become a schizophrenic organization, torn between political left and right. Yet few outside the government understood these divisions. The CIA conservatives and swashbucklers found warm support for their position in Congress; the Agency liberals were forced to fend for themselves. Arthur Schlesinger, Jr., Special Assistant to the President, explained to his friends in the academic world that the CIA's influence was not "always, or often, reactionary and sinister. In my experience its leadership was politically enlightened and sophisticated. Not seldom CIA representatives took a more liberal line in White House meetings than their counterparts from State." [40]

Schlesinger showed a personal interest in the Agency's "covert action." He believed that the liberals in the CIA and the operations they launched could best be sustained if they were to have the active support of the American liberal community at large. As a result, officials of Americans for Democratic Action, the arm of "established" American liberalism, participated in the formation of a CIA-financed International Study Group for Freedom and Democracy.

The Group came to include such vehement CIA critics as the Reuther brothers and Andreas Papandreou (then an Economics Professor at the University of California), even though it seemed to be generally known that the executive secretary of the Study Group, OSS veteran Dana Durand, Jr., was a former CIA officer, and that its ostensible purpose was to build the foundation for more effective covert support of the Third World non-Communist Left—of men like Holden Roberto and Tom Mboya in Africa, and of Figueres, Betancourt, Frei, and Bosch in Latin America. But with the death of President Kennedy, the Study Group disappeared as quickly and as silently as it had been formed.

Four years later, some of the same American liberals who had endorsed the Study Group's objectives became the most vocal critics of the CIA's covert action. In February 1967, *Ramparts* magazine revealed that the CIA, under Cord Meyer's direction, had financed the international programs of the National Student Association and a host of other groups. Leaders of the NSA had pleaded with the magazine not to expose the funding because it would damage the "enlightened, liberal, internationalist wing of the CIA" to the delight of the CIA conservatives. *Ramparts* rejected this argument as a "pathetic" indication of "how deeply the corruption of means for ends has become ingrained in our society, and how much dishonesty is tolerated in the name of the Cold War." [41]

The only half-hearted defense of the Agency's funding operations in Congress came from the Richard Russell and Mendel Rivers clique of southern legislators who sat on the appropriations subcommittees which oversee the CIA budget. The congressional liberals, paradoxically, could produce nothing but bitter condemnations.

Congresswoman Edith Green, a liberal Democrat, commented with incongruous sarcasm: "The House Committee on Un-American Activities must be chagrined that left-leaning students and labor leaders who have so aroused its ire are representatives of organizations financed and perhaps guided by a government agency it previously considered an unimpeachable ally. It would be an amusing spectacle to see the House Committee on Un-American Activities and the Central Intelligence Agency investigate each other." [42] Even the Americans for Democratic Action, in a fit of apparent hypocrisy, noted that CIA financing of the international activities of various politically progressive groups "indicated a serious perversion of the democratic process." ADA felt it necessary to add the paradoxical statement, "It matters little that the activities were in many cases positive advances over the declared foreign policy of the United States." [43]

Many American liberals saw the new exposés of CIA operations as only a continuation of their traditional criticism of America's intelligence service. But there was a difference. For years, the Agency's critics had justifiably censured the covert support of right-wing dictatorships. But where were the reactionaries in 1967? Were they in the National Student Association? Were they in the CIA-financed International Labor Research Institute, which had operated a trade-union training program in the Dominican Republic under the aegis of Juan Bosch? Norman Thomas, who headed the Institute, was slightly perplexed. "This CIA thing is the strangest thing I've ever heard," said the veteran Socialist. "When Bosch was overthrown we always thought the CIA was fighting against us." Some of the Institute's funds, Thomas added, had been used to "publish a strong attack on the American government's intervention in the Dominican Republic. The CIA didn't get much for that money." [44]

Many political conservatives saw the ideological issue in the CIA disclosures more clearly. Shortly after the exposé of the National Student Association financing was printed, two Republican congressmen called for a legislative investigation of "how much CIA money has been channeled to private organizations which was used for leftist purposes having nothing to do with the conduct of the cold war." [45] Another congressman said on the floor of the House, "I wish very strongly that the CIA would have 'subverted' some of the NSA members to work in behalf of American interests and national policy. Although the vast majority of NSA membership is not Communist nor even sympathetic to Communist positions, a significant influence by Communist-oriented students on NSA policy is beyond question." He concluded, "I believe that the CIA can serve our country well, but the use of the people's money to subsidize an organization with a record like that of the National Student Association raises serious doubts as to the competency and purposes of some of the decision makers in the Agency." [46]

An official of the right-wing Young Americans for Freedom declared, "There can be no justification for the use of American taxpayers' money to support this kind of radical left-wing group. The Congress has a duty to see that those responsible for this policy in the CIA are removed and that such subsidies are ended." [47] The state chairman of the New York Conservative Party commented, "I think the

CIA choosing NSA to further American foreign policy throws the political acuity of the CIA into grave question." [48] And even Barry Goldwater got into the act by stating on nationwide television that the dastardly CIA had used government funds to "finance socialism in America." [49]

The most extreme analysis was suggested by a right-wing Congressman, a John Bircher who represented California's Orange County. He asked this rhetorical question: "If NSA's official positions reflected the wishes of the CIA, then what is the CIA doing having the NSA annual congresses adopt resolutions in almost total opposition to U.S. foreign policy?" The congressman proposed an answer which seemed a throwback to the McCarthy era. "It raises," he said, "grave questions as to whether or not NSA in calling for the many questionable things which it has called for was speaking for the American college students or one of its principal financial sponsors—the CIA. Perhaps NSA's declarations that American college students do not support winning the war in Vietnam is not really the voice of the American college community." [50] Only a Bircher could believe that the Central Intelligence Agency had even the slightest sympathies with American critics of the Vietnam war. How ridiculous! Or was it?

One of the few liberal voices to defend the Agency was Senator Robert Kennedy (who was a close friend of ex-CIA official Tom Braden). He said that the CIA should not be made to "take the rap" for covert action programs which had been approved by high officials of three administrations. And, in a private conversation with his friend Jack Newfield of the *Village Voice*, Kennedy elaborated. "What you're not aware of," he told Agency critic Newfield, "is what role the CIA plays within the government. During the 1950s, for example, many of the liberals who were forced out of other departments found a sanctuary, an enclave, in the CIA. So some of the best people in Washington, and around the country, began to collect there. One result of that was the CIA developed a very healthy view of Communism, especially compared to State and some other departments. They were very sympathetic, for example, to nationalist, and even Socialist governments and movements. And I think now the CIA is becoming much more realistic, and critical, about the war, than other departments, or even the people in the White House. So it is not so black and white as you make it." [51]

Newfield was incredulous. So were many of the television viewers who heard a CBS national news broadcast on the evening of February

23, 1968 (only a month before Lyndon Johnson halted the bombing of North Vietnam and announced his withdrawal from the Presidential contest). Dan Rather reported: "The latest administration reports on the way say in essence that the Allies are making progress and that the Communists have suffered a major defeat in their Lunar New Year offensive. But these and other optimistic assertions are being disputed by one important Washington agency. . . . Central Intelligence Agency reports about Vietnam have been for several months much bleaker than the public assessments of the Johnson administration. As a result, there is now a running feud between some CIA men and the President's principal White House advisor, Walt Rostow. Rostow is one of the original architects of our Vietnam policy under Johnson and Kennedy. Some sources say CIA Director Richard Helms now is in direct disagreement. They quote Helms as telling the senators the Vietnam war, as it is now being run, could last 100 years. White House News Secretary George Christian says that is pure bunk, that Helms and Rostow are in agreement. But one spokesman says the CIA types are trying to get Rostow ranked below Helms. It is pointed out that Rostow and the President evaluate all intelligence agency information, not just that from the CIA. The frustrated CIA officials who feel Rostow is wrong and has been all along about Vietnam apparently have started leaking their most pessimistic recent reports to newspapers and senators. They blame Rostow for misleading public optimism and for the President's refusal to believe pessimistic assessments of what is happening now in Vietnam. There is nothing this President detests more than leaks of this sort. And several of the ranking CIA authorities involved are quoted as saying their jobs are in jeopardy. They fear a major CIA shakeup." [52]

The report was exaggerated. There was no personal animosity between OSS veterans Rostow and Helms. And no massive CIA purge followed. But at least one top CIA officer subsequently chose the Agency's "early retirement" option. Fifty-year-old Thomas McCoy had first joined CIA in 1951 and held top Agency posts at Rome and Madrid. He retired from the government in the spring of 1968 to become a top campaign aide to peace candidate Eugene McCarthy.

In May 1968, McCarthy appointed Thomas Finney, 43, a Washington lawyer, as his new West Coast campaign coordinator. Finney, a former aide to Democratic Senator Mike Monroney of Oklahoma, was a law partner of Clark Clifford's before Clifford joined the Johnson administration as Defense Secretary. Finney was also an ex-CIA officer who had served in Copenhagen in the early 1950s. When he accepted the campaign post, he asked McCoy, a prominent CIA critic of the war, to join him. Their entry into the political organization of the liberal senator (a vehement and long-standing critic of CIA) threw the entire McCarthy campaign into temporary disarray. The young intellectuals of McCarthy's "children's crusade" shrugged their shoulders in disbelief. CIA men for peace?

The Agency had in fact been a repository for anti-war sentiment in Washington throughout the Vietnam buildup of the Johnson administration. The "Pentagon Papers" reveal the following facts:

CIA reports challenged the myth that the Viet Cong movement was controlled and sustained by the North Vietnamese leadership in Hanoi.

CIA reports disputed the "domino theory" that Asia would "fall" if South Vietnam came under Hanoi's hegemony.

CIA reports questioned the economic or psychological value of U.S. bombing of North Vietnam.

CIA reports questioned the wisdom of committing American ground troops to battle in South Vietnam. The Agency warned: "We will find ourselves mired down in combat in the jungle in a military effort that we cannot win and from which we will have extreme difficulty extracting ourselves." [53]

And there was the human side. In October 1969, during the national Vietnam Moratorium, a few of the younger (and braver) CIA analysts strolled through Agency headquarters wearing black armbands, a symbol of protest against the war. Even the Central Intelligence Agency can have its generation gap.

There are still sensitive, progressive men in the CIA, but they are becoming scarcer by the moment. The Agency's career trainees no longer come from the Phi Beta Kappa ranks of Harvard, Yale, or Berkeley. The Agency is widely regarded on college campuses as the principal symbol of all that is wrong with our nation. "For the world as a whole," wrote Arnold Toynbee recently, "the CIA has now become the bogey that communism has been for America. Wherever there is trouble, violence, suffering, tragedy, the rest of us are now quick to suspect the CIA has a hand in it." Millions of college students and young professionals, the future "power elite" of the United States, would accept that judgment.

That is a tragedy for America and its foreign policy. The CIA has not yet become the reactionary monster the New Left has created as its straw man. But unless the Agency leadership makes a determined effort to renew the OSS passion for democratic dissent in yet another generation of American intelligence officers, the reality of CIA may soon coincide with its sinister image in the intellectual community. The spirit of the Office of Strategic Services would then be no more than a reminiscence of an idealistic past.

Notes

Notes

*Complete authors' names, full titles, and pub-
lication data may be found in the Bibliography*

Chapter 1

1. The Nazi propaganda broadcast is quoted by Drew Pearson in his
"Washington Merry Go-Round" for December 3, 1941; Lindbergh's re-
mark (in response to an invitation from Donovan to join COI) is in his
War Memoirs, p. 573; military opposition to COI and OSS is noted by
Phillips, *Ventures in Diplomacy*, p. 335.

2. Taylor, *Awakening from History*, p. 319.

3. Ford, *Donovan of O.S.S.*, p. 126.

4. Warburg, *The Long Road Home*, p. 190.

5. Ford, *op. cit.*, p. 337.

6. Dulles, *The Secret Surrender*, p. 9.

7. Smith and Clark, *Into Siam*, p. 56.

8. Alsop and Braden, *Sub Rosa*, p. 21.

9. U.S. Office of Strategic Services, Psychological Assessment Staff,
Assessment of Men, p. 10.

10. Arnold, *Global Mission*, p. 535.

11. From David Bruce's letter of eulogy to the *New York Times* after
Donovan's death, February 15, 1959.

12. Stevenson memo to Donovan, February 23, 1942, and Donovan's
reply, February 25, 1942. (Preston Goodfellow Papers, Hoover Institution,
Stanford University.)

388

13. Gervasi, "What's wrong with our spy system?" p. 13.

14. Hoover, *Memoirs of Capitalism*, p. 196.

15. Morgan, *The O.S.S. and I*, p. 16.

16. Alcorn, *No Bugles for Spies*, p. 36.

17. Alsop and Braden, *op. cit.*, p. 20.

18. Frillmann and Peck, *China*, p. 234.

19. Alcorn, *No Banners, No Bands*, p. 182.

20. Moore and Waller, *Cloak and Cipher*, p. 89.

21. Grell, "A Marine with OSS," p. 16; also Cooke, *A Generation on Trial*, p. 310.

22. Downes, *The Scarlet Thread*, p. 292.

23. Thayer, *Hands across the Caviar*, p. 119.

24. The team commander is now a ranking Far Eastern Intelligence analyst for the CIA.

25. As told to the author by Dr. Hughes.

26. Alsop and Braden, *op. cit.*, p. 122.

27. Lovell, *Of Spies and Stratagems*, pp. 18 and 22.

28. Alsop and Braden, *op. cit.*, p. 126.

29. Dulles, *op. cit.*, pp. 88 and 113.

30. Taylor, *op. cit.*, p. 345.

31. Bruce letter to the *Times*, *op. cit.*

32. Alcorn, *No Bugles for Spies*, p. 134.

33. Weyl, *The Battle Against Disloyalty*, p. 180.

34. Alcorn, *No Bugles for Spies*, p. 35.

35. *New York Times*, August 31, 1948, p. 3.

36. Alsop and Braden, *op. cit.*, p. 26.

37. MacDonald, *Undercover Girl*, p. 2.

38. Speech by Allen Dulles, "William J. Donovan and the National Security," to the Erie County Bar Association, Buffalo, New York, May 4, 1959.

39. Arthur Schlesinger, Jr., *A Thousand Days* (Boston, 1965), p. 171.

40. For example: "The Communists, speaking through the Communist Minister of the Interior . . . have emphatically denied any intention of imposing a Soviet system upon Bulgaria, and the on-the-spot reports confirm that they are meticulously adhering to this policy. The Red Army is receiving an enthusiastic welcome from the Bulgarian people, and its arrival is everywhere a stabilizing factor which promotes support for the new regime." (*European Political Report*, September 22, 1944.)

41. Morris, *Nelson Rockefeller*.

42. Obolensky, *One Man in His Time*, p. 388.

43. Arthur Goldberg in a review of the Braden and Alsop book in *The Nation*, March 23, 1946, pp. 349–50.

44. Drew Pearson, "Washington Merry-Go-Round," July 9, 1945.

45. Tompkins, *A Spy in Rome*, p. 274.

46. Barmine, "New Communist Conspiracy," in *Reader's Digest*, October 1944, pp. 27–33; see also Barmine's testimony in U.S. Senate, "Hearings on the Institute of Pacific Relations," pp. 182–222.

47. Letter from Mr. Du Berrier to the author, September 9, 1970.

48. Toledano, *Lament for a Generation*, pp. 78–79.

49. Morgan, *op. cit.*, p. 190.

50. OSS Psychological Assessment Staff, *op. cit.*, p. 10.

51. Bruce, "The National Intelligence Authority," p. 363.

52. Hyde, *Room 3603*, p. 165.

53. Downes, *op. cit.*, pp. 87–97.

54. Deane, *The Strange Alliance*, p. 55; Hoover's objections are noted by Whitehead, *The F.B.I. Story*, p. 228.

55. Hoover, *op. cit.*, p. 197.

56. Bruce, *op. cit.*, p. 358.

57. Israel, ed., *The War Diary of Breckinridge Long*, p. 234.

58. *Ibid.*, p. 252.

59. Miller, *Man from the Valley*.

60. Leahy, *I Was There*, p. 71.

61. The problems with Mrs. Shipley are mentioned by Hoover and MacDonald, *op. cit.*

62. Heckscher, *A Pattern of Politics*, p. 69.

63. Adamic, *Dinner at the White House*, p. 157. On the contrary, Poole felt that American support of reactionary forces was a disastrous policy which played into the hands of the Soviets. In a September 1943 memorandum he deplored the high political cost of America's Vichy policy, "then grotesquely and quite unnecessarily exacerbated by dalliance with Otto von Hapsburg (whoever was responsible for that!). We may not blink at the plain fact that all this has jeopardized our moral leadership in the Western World and, for the moment anyhow, turned the minds of innumerable good people toward Soviet Russia as offering a wiser and more courageous leadership." Dewitt Poole Papers, State Historical Society of Wisconsin, Madison.

64. George, *Surreptitious Entry*, p. 203.

65. Oliver, *Syngman Rhee*, p. 182.

66. Dulles, *op. cit.*, p. 3.

67. Solborg's memoranda, "Broad Outline of Special Activities," October 21, 1941, and January 13, 1942, and Lincoln's memo for OSS Assistant Director Charles Cheston, December 17, 1943, are in the Goodfellow Papers, Stanford.

68. Welch, *The Life of John Birch*, p. 82.

69. Dulles, *op. cit.*, p. 87.

70. Testimony of Sterling Hayden before the House Committee on

Un-American Activities, "Hearings on Communist Infiltration of the Hollywood Motion Picture Industry" (Washington, D.C., 1951), pp. 132–33.

71. OSS Psychological Assessment Staff, *op. cit.*, p. 30.

72. Sheean, *This House against This House*, p. 298.

73. Taylor, *op. cit.*, p. 345.

74. MacDonald, *op. cit.*, p. 2.

75. Bowie, *Operation Bughouse*.

76. Seitz, *Mihailovic*, p. 49.

77. Ford, *op. cit.*, p. 61.

78. Geroid Robinson, "Three Invaders of Russia," p. 79.

79. This was a message written by Stephenson for the Director of British Naval Intelligence. Hyde, *op. cit.*, p. 44.

80. Philby, *My Silent War*, p. 90.

81. Morgan, *op. cit.*, pp. 131–32.

82. Sweet-Escott, *Baker Street Irregular*, p. 149.

83. This is the Hoskins mission mentioned in Chapter Four. The motto was invented by André Pacatte, a French-American officer who served OSS in Italy.

84. Tompkins, *Italy Betrayed*, p. 253.

85. Taylor, *Richer by Asia*, p. 233.

86. Taylor, *Awakening from History*, p. 352.

87. An anonymous OSS report entitled "American Strategy and Revolutionary Movements in Asia," October 25, 1943, in U.S. Senate Committee on the Judiciary, *The Amerasia Papers* (Washington, D.C., 1971), pp. 280–81.

88. McClachlan, *Room 39*, p. 233.

89. From a 1941 Donovan memorandum to the President, in the Goodfellow Papers, Stanford.

Chapter 2

1. Donovan and Mowrer, *Fifth Column Lessons for America*, p. 8; also Mowrer's autobiography, *Triumph and Turmoil*.

2. Taylor, *Awakening from History*, p. 317.

3. David Bruce questioned this rationale in "National Intelligence Authority," p. 361.

4. De Gaulle, *War Memoirs: Unity, 1942–1944*, p. 10.

5. From an intercepted German intelligence report dated March 16, 1942, in the Goodfellow Papers, the Hoover Institution, Stanford University. The report also had this comment about Robert Murphy: "Tall, slim, good-looking, polyglot, a man of the world, cultured, fond of social life, an excellent conversationalist, easy-mannered, able to deal with any situation,

making an excellent impression. . . . He is a man of ideas far above the average from a European point of view, and certainly an extraordinary type for an American."

6. Pendar, *Adventure in Diplomacy*, p. 33.

7. Langer, *Our Vichy Gamble*, p. 230; also Murphy, *Diplomat among Warriors*.

8. Letter from Robert Solborg to the author, June 22, 1971.

9. William Eddy letter to Leland Rounds, 1954, in Leland Rounds Papers, the Hoover Institution, Stanford University.

10. Murphy, *op. cit.*, p. 92.

11. Langer, *op. cit.*, p. 239.

12. *Ibid.*, p. 240.

13. *Ibid.*, pp. 242–44; also Eddy cable to OSS headquarters, April 14, 1942, in the Goodfellow Papers, Stanford.

14. Memorandum from Franklin Canfield (later SO Branch, London) to Colonel M. P. Goodfellow, April 15, 1942, in the Goodfellow Papers, Stanford.

15. Langer, *op. cit.*, p. 244.

16. Leahy, *I Was There*, p. 71.

17. Cassady's mission is mentioned by Arthur Funk, "American Contacts with the Resistance in France." Bickham Sweet-Escott speaks of Nicol Smith's difficulties with the State Department in *Baker Street Irregular*, p. 134.

18. Nicol Smith dispatches to OSS Headquarters, August 27, 1942, and September 11, 1942 in the Goodfellow Papers, Stanford.

19. Downes, *The Scarlet Thread*, and Leahy, *op. cit.*, p. 143.

20. Langer, *op. cit.*, p. 274.

21. Letter from Robert Murphy to Colonel Goodfellow at OSS headquarters, June 1942, in the Goodfellow Papers, Stanford.

22. Cable from Robert Solborg to OSS headquarters, June 25, 1942, in the Goodfellow Papers, Stanford.

23. *Ibid.*

24. Cable from Colonel Donovan to Robert Solborg, June 15, 1942, in the Goodfellow Papers, Stanford.

25. Langer, *op. cit.*, p. 284.

26. Memorandum from William Eddy to the Joint Chiefs of Staff, June 10, 1942; also the minutes of the Joint Psychological Warfare Committee, August 3, 1942, in the Goodfellow Papers, Stanford.

27. Pendar, *op. cit.*, p. 33.

28. Langer, *op. cit.*, p. 276.

29. Alsop and Braden, *Sub Rosa*, p. 87.

30. Eddy Memorandum for the Joint Chiefs, *op. cit.*

31. There is extensive documentation of the SOE negotiations in the Goodfellow Papers, Stanford.

32. Memorandum from Robert Solborg to Colonel Donovan, July 25, 1942, in the Goodfellow Papers, Stanford.

33. Langer, *op. cit.*, p. 296.

34. Richard de Rochemont, letter to the author, March 18, 1970.

35. Langer, op. cit., pp. 212, 261, and 258. The dissension within the Gaullist ranks is also discussed by Raoul Roussy de Sales, *The Making of Yesterday*, p. 243.

36. White, *Seeds of Discord*, p. 445; also a dispatch from Nicol Smith to OSS headquarters, September 29, 1942, in the Goodfellow Papers, Stanford.

37. Phillips, *Ventures in Diplomacy*, p. 338.

38. Langer, *op. cit.*, p. 296.

39. Dewavrin, *Souvenirs, 10 Duke St. Londres*, vol. 2, p. 145.

40. *Ibid.*

41. D'Astier de la Vigerie, *Seven Times, Seven Days*, p. 78.

42. Langer, *op. cit.*, p. 297.

43. Dispatch from Nicol Smith to OSS headquarters, September 25, 1942, in the Goodfellow Papers, Stanford.

44. Official history of the SUSSEX Operation in the Francis P. Miller Papers, General George C. Marshall Library, Lexington, Virginia.

45. Leahy, *op. cit.*, p. 114.

46. Clark, *Calculated Risk*; also the 1954 letter from Eddy to Rounds in the Leland Rounds Papers, Stanford.

47. Alsop and Braden, *op. cit.*, p. 92; Langer, *op. cit.*, p. 310; and Butcher, *My Three Years with Eisenhower*, p. 128.

48. Taylor, *op. cit.*, p. 320.

49. Langer, *op. cit.*, p. 316.

50. For varying accounts of the invasion planning, see Mark Clark, Harry Butcher, Kenneth Pendar, and Robert Murphy; also Tompkins, *The Murder of Admiral Darlan*.

51. Langer, *op. cit.*, p. 365.

52. Pendar, *op. cit.*, p. 113.

53. Langer, *op. cit.*, p. 371.

54. MacVane, *Journey into War*, and Funk, *Charles de Gaulle*.

55. Letter from William Eddy to Leland Rounds, November 29, 1942, in Leland Rounds Papers, Stanford.

56. See, for example, Vice Consul Ridgeway Knight's letter to Robert Murphy, November 1942, in the Leland Rounds Papers, Stanford.

57. Taylor, *op. cit.*, p. 321.

58. *Ibid.*, p. 324.

59. *Ibid.*, p. 326.
60. *Ibid.*, p. 324.
61. *Ibid.*, p. 327.
62. Pierre-Gosset, *Conspiracy in Algiers.*
63. Carroll, *Persuade or Perish*, p. 62.
64. The most thorough account of the assassination is in Tompkins, *op. cit.*
65. Taylor, *op. cit.*, p. 333.
66. Pierre-Gosset, *op. cit.*, p. 229.
67. Taylor, *op. cit.*, p. 335.
68. *Ibid.*, p. 335.
69. *Ibid.*
70. Pierre-Gosset, *op. cit.*, p. 233.
71. Sherwood, *Roosevelt and Hopkins*, p. 665.

Chapter 3

1. Funk, *Charles de Gaulle*, p. 65.
2. Pendar, *Adventures in Diplomacy*, p. 33.
3. Letter from W. A. Roseborough to the author, December 15, 1970.
4. *Ibid.*
5. Letter from Leland Rounds to Henry Villard of the State Department, October 8, 1943, in Leland Rounds Papers, Hoover Institution, Stanford University.
6. Roseborough letter, *op. cit.*
7. Letter from Gerhard Van Arkel to the author, December 15, 1970.
8. Letter from August Heckscher to the author, December 2, 1970.
9. Downes, *The Scarlet Thread*, p. 98.
10. *Ibid.*, p. 56.
11. Roseborough letter, *op. cit.*
12. Price, *Giraud and the North African Scene*, p. 179.
13. Downes, *op. cit.*, p. 110.
14. Taylor, *Awakening from History*, p. 327.
15. Downes, *op. cit.*, p. 102.
16. Heckscher letter, *op. cit.*
17. Stilwell, *Stilwell Papers*, p. 20. Stilwell was quoting a COI man named Shapiro who had just returned from Spain in January 1942.
18. Downes, *op. cit.*, p. 109. Jerry Sage's remarkable escapes from POW camps are described in Wager, "Slippery Giant of the OSS," p. 32, and Kelly, "He Never Stopped Trying," p. 42.
19. Downes, *op. cit.*, p. 109.
20. Hoare, *Complacent Dictator*, p. 95.

21. Kemp, *No Colours or Crest*, p. 23.

22. OSS intelligence report, July 19, 1942, in the Goodfellow Papers, Stanford.

23. Memorandum from Vanderbilt to Colonel M. P. Goodfellow, June 9, 1942, in the Goodfellow Papers, Stanford.

24. Hillgarth's activities are described in McLachlan, *Room 39*, pp. 186–96, and with less admiration in Philby, *My Silent War*, p. 66.

25. Memorandum from Robert Solborg to Colonel M. P. Goodfellow, July 8, 1942, in the Goodfellow Papers, Stanford.

26. Hayes, *Wartime Mission in Spain*, p. 17.

27. *Ibid.*, p. 128.

28. Kennan, *Memoirs*, p. 150.

29. Downes, *op. cit.*, p. 122.

30. Heckscher letter, *op. cit.*

Chapter 4

1. The "flap" over this OWI broadcast is described by Warburg, *The Long Road Home*.

2. Delzell, *Mussolini's Enemies*, p. 233; this is still the definitive American study of the Italian resistance.

3. Delzell gives a full description of these events; see also Tompkins' partisan account, *Italy Betrayed*, and Kogan, *Italy and the Allies*.

4. The testimony of White and other American officials involved in the ONI-Mafia accord is found in the Kefauver Hearings: U.S. Senate Special Committee to Investigate Organized Crime, "Hearings on Organized Crime in Interstate Commerce" (Washington, D.C., 1950).

5. A quote attributed to W. W. Downey, the first SO Branch area officer for North Africa in Washington.

6. Tompkins, *op. cit.*, p. 15.

7. Obolensky, *One Man in His Time*, p. 363.

8. Romanticized versions of "McGregor" are in Lovell, *Of Spies and Stratagems*, pp. 114–21, and Ford and McBain, *Cloak and Dagger*; for a less reverent account by one of the participants, see Tompkins, *op. cit.*

9. Downes, *The Scarlet Thread*, p. 152.

10. *Ibid.*, p. 153.

11. Joyce Lussu (the sister of SOE Major Max Salvadori), *Freedom Has No Frontier*, p. 146.

12. Williams (according to the *New York Times*, July 29, 1932) gave $10,000; he was topped only by Averell Harriman's sister (Mrs. C. C. Rumsey), who contributed $18,000. The list of other larger contributors reads like the Social Register: Guggenheim, Rockefeller, Whitney, Chrysler, Thayer, Aldrich, Field, Warburg, Pratt, Vanderbilt, and so on.

13. Downes, *op. cit.*, p. 153.

14. The story of Croce's escape is told by SOE Lieutenant Adrian Gallegos, *From Capri into Oblivion.*

15. Whitaker, *We Cannot Escape History*, p. 91.

16. Croce, *Croce, the King, and the Allies*, p. 19; also see the Tompkins version, *op. cit.*

17. Tompkins, *op. cit.*, p. 260.

18. *Ibid.*, p. 277.

19. Munthe, *Sweet Is War*, p. 169. Munthe was later wounded at Anzio.

20. Salvadori, *The Labour and the Wounds*, p. 165. Salvadori was basically a conservative who favored Giraud over de Gaulle and Mihailovic over Tito.

21. Croce, *op. cit.*, p. 144.

22. Tompkins, *A Spy in Rome*, p. 77.

23. *Ibid.*, p. 25.

24. Elizabeth Wiskemann of the British Political Warfare Executive in Switzerland recalls, "The majority of the Italians with whom I came together felt bitterly against the House of Savoy for, as they felt, betraying the interests of their country. . . . I used sometimes to try to explain this to Dulles who took Churchill's view over this issue." *The Europe I Saw*, p. 182.

25. Max Corvo, "America's Intelligence Dilemma," in the Hartford *Courant*, May 28, 1961.

26. Delzell, *op. cit.*, p. 314.

27. Memorandum of a meeting between Badoglio, Colonel C. C. Carter and Major J. H. Angleton, May 10, 1944, in the Goodfellow Papers, Hoover Institution, Stanford University.

28. Icardi, *American Master Spy*, pp. 13 and 20–21.

29. Irving Fajans, "Ravage Repeat Ravage," in *Infantry Journal*, March 1947, pp. 24–33. This is a slightly fictionalized account of the Lincoln Brigaders' espionage operations.

30. Croce, *op. cit.*, p. 77.

31. Tompkins, *A Spy in Rome*, p. 140.

32. *Ibid.*, p. 215.

33. Carter-Badoglio memorandum, in the Goodfellow Papers, Stanford.

34. Tompkins, *A Spy in Rome*, p. 302.

35. The Hungarian mission, code-named "Sparrow," is described by Duke, *Name, Rank, and Serial Number*; also Kallay, *Hungarian Premier*, and Paloczi-Horvath, *The Undefeated*.

36. Letter from Mr. William Davis, Jr., to the author, January 11, 1971.

37. Hall, *You're Stepping on My Cloak and Dagger*, p. 39.

38. Romualdi, *Presidents and Peons*, pp. 21–22.

39. *Ibid.*, pp. 23–30.

40. Hughes, *The United States and Italy*, p. 127.

41. L. B. Taylor, Jr., "OSS Mission"; also MacDonald, *Undercover Girl*, pp. 258–61.

42. Dugan and Stewart, *Ploesti*, p. 290; also the slightly fictionalized version of the Bucharest mission in Bowie, *Operation Bughouse*. A year earlier, OSS had recruited several American oil company executives in a zany plot to sabotage the Ploesti oil fields. A team of thirty, including economist Nicholas Deak (later chief of OSS Saigon), was assembled to parachute to the Axis oil fields dressed, of all things, as Romanian firemen. The group never left Cairo. Another team that was to drop into the Transylvania area of Romania to disrupt German transport in the spring of 1944 was also cancelled. Russian representatives at Cairo refused to grant "clearance" for its departure.

43. Garlinski, *Poland, SOE, and the Allies*.

44. Downes, *op. cit.*, p. 184.

45. Delzell, *op. cit.*, p. 424.

46. The case against Icardi was argued in muddled fashion before the House Armed Services Committee. "Testimony and Confessions Relating to the Disappearance of Major William Holohan" (Washington, D.C., 1953). Icardi presented his defense in *American Master Spy*. As the case dragged on, Icardi acquired the famed Edward Bennett Williams as his legal counsel. Williams was assisted in his investigation by Robert Maheu, a former FBI agent with alleged CIA connections, most recently an executive of the Howard Hughes gambling empire. In his autobiography, *One Man's Freedom*, Williams blamed Holohan's death on a Communist plot to "frame" Icardi. The long legal battle ended in 1956 with Icardi's technical acquittal.

47. Icardi, *op. cit.*, p. 64.

48. Tilman, *When Men and Mountains Meet*, pp. 170–71.

49. White, "Some Affairs of Honor," pp. 136–54. Other accounts of British and American missions behind the Italian lines include Kelly, "Operation Aztec," pp. 66ff.; Kelly, "One Against a Thousand," pp. 14ff.; Kelly, "The Bionda Mission," pp. 56ff.; Farran, *Winged Dagger*; and Cooper, *Adventures of a Secret Agent*.

50. Dulles, *The Secret Surrender*, p. 21.

51. *Ibid.*, p. 66.

52. Dollmann, *Call Me Coward*, p. 176.

53. *Ibid.*, p. 43. Dollmann describes Parri as "a man of limited intelligence" and "a complete frost."

54. Dulles, *op. cit.*, p. 94.

55. Farran, *Operation Tombola*, p. 45. The Russians had no radio contact with the Soviet Army and the Communist partisans, while "flattered that the distant Red Army recognized their existence," were "more interested in a liaison mission that could summon aircraft to drop them arms."

56. Delzell, *op. cit.*, p. 482.

57. Dulles, *op. cit.*, pp. 183–84.

58. Delzell, *op. cit.*, p. 512.

59. Dulles, *op. cit.*, p. 184.

60. *Ibid., pp.* 186–92. Gaevernitz gave another account to John Toland in *The Last 100 Days*, pp. 486–87.

61. Letter to the author from Mr. Leo Frances, a member of Operational Group Roanoke, September 22, 1970.

62. Icardi, *op. cit.*, pp. 185.

63. Dulles, *op. cit.*, p. 236.

64. Kelly, "Torture Preferred."

65. Letter from Mr. John I. B. McCulloch to the author, July 21, 1970.

66. Mecklin, "Of Our Sincere Gratitude," pp. 98–99.

Chapter 5

1. Macmillan, *The Blast of War*, p. 527.

2. Sweet-Escott, *Baker Street Irregular*, p. 129.

3. *Ibid.*, pp. 73–74.

4. From a postwar conversation between Frank Wisner and David Bruce, quoted by Sulzberger, *A Long Row of Candles*, p. 777.

5. Hayden, *Wanderer*, p. 310.

6. Sweet-Escott, *op. cit.*, p. 137.

7. *Ibid.*

8. Dr. Gordon Laud was the Arab SI chief in Washington. After the war, he allegedly worked for the CIA in Cairo.

9. In late 1943, an OSS team in northeast Greece sabotaged a train bound from Istanbul to Germany. One of the passengers was a German intelligence courier. The Americans captured his document pouch and found evidence that key agents of OSS and MI-6 in Turkey had been "doubled" by the Germans.

10. Wisner's Bucharest team included George Bookbinder, now president of the Rand Development Corporation, and Columbia political scientist Henry Roberts.

11. Myers, *Greek Entanglement*.

12. Sarafis, *Greek Resistance Army*, p. 113.

13. Woodhouse, *Apple of Discord*, pp. 104–5.

14. Jordan, *Conquest without Victory*, p. 200.

15. George Vournas in the *National Herald*, June 27, 1965; also a letter from Mr. Vournas to the author, February 11, 1970.

16. *Time*, January 29, 1945, p. 36; also Kelly, "With the Greek Underground," pp. 91ff.; and Kelly, "Behind the Enemy Lines," pp. 24ff.

17. From a speech by Allen Dulles, "William J. Donovan and the National Security," to the Erie County Bar Association, Buffalo, New York, May 4, 1959.

18. The transliteration of this and other Yugoslav names in the chapter has been given a consistent spelling throughout.

19. Churchill, *The Grand Alliance*, p. 836.

20. Some of the newspaper charges are quoted by Ford, *Donovan of O.S.S.*, p. 106. The coup was actually fomented by British agents.

21. Fotic, *The War We Lost*, p. 108. Fotic was representative of the Yugoslav government in exile at Washington.

22. Peter II of Yugoslavia, *A King's Heritage*, pp. 144–45. Despite the vigorous opposition of General Donovan, 416 food cases intended for Mihailovic were diverted to Malta at the request of Richard Casey, British Minister of State for the Middle East, in August 1942.

23. For differing views of this early period see Davidson, *Partisan Picture*, and Clissold, *Whirlwind*.

24. Martin, *Ally Betrayed*, p. 284.

25. Peter II, *op. cit.*, p. 125.

26. The unreliable account of a Nazi intelligence officer alleges that the Germans had close contacts with both Partisans and Chetniks at the highest levels. Hoettl, *The Secret Front*, pp. 162–64.

27. Wiskemann, *The Europe I Saw*, p. 171. But another source states that Dulles met with Partisan representatives through his Communist intermediary, Noel Field, and that "Dulles said afterward that this meeting was a first contact which led eventually to large-scale American military support for Tito. . . . According to Dulles, it was one of Noel's major services. High-ranking Yugoslavs who spent the war with Tito were inclined to shrug off the importance of the contact in Switzerland, however, and later said that Miso Lompar, the main person involved with Noel, had no communications with Tito at the time." Lewis, *Red Pawn*, p. 161.

28. Martin, *op. cit.*, p. 215.

29. Jones, *Twelve Months with Tito's Partisans*, pp. 72 and 118.

30. Sweet-Escott, *op. cit.*, p. 164.

31. Seitz, *Mihailovic*, p. 81.

32. MacLean, *Escape to Adventure*, p. 212.

33. Dedijer, *With Tito*, p. 197.

34. Huot, *Guns for Tito*, pp. 227–29.

35. *Ibid.*; Huot later assured King Peter that Tito was more nationalist than Communist. See Sulzberger, *op. cit.*, p. 223.

36. Dedijer, *op. cit.*, p. 202.

37. Adamic, *Dinner at the White House*, pp. 150–51.

38. MacLean, *op. cit.*, p. 298.

39. U.S. Department of State, *The Conferences at Cairo and Teheran* (Washington, D.C., 1961), pp. 606–15.

40. Mansfield, "Marine with the Chetniks," p. 16.

41. Seitz, *op. cit.*, pp. 10, 13, 44–45, and 122.

42. Peter II, *op. cit.*, p. 195; also Walter Mansfield, "Is There a Case for Mihailovic?" in *American Mercury*, June 1946, pp. 716–17.

43. Churchill, *Closing the Ring*, p. 404.

44. U.S. Department of State, *Foreign Relations of the United States, 1943.* Vol. II, p. 1022. (Cited hereafter as *FRUS*.)

45. *FRUS*, 1943, II, p. 1039.

46. Peter II, *op. cit.*, p. 200.

47. Macmillan, *op. cit.*, p. 527.

48. Kemp, *No Colours or Crest.*

49. *Ibid.*

50. Seitz, *op. cit.*, pp. 104 and 122.

51. Kemp, *op. cit.*

52. Seitz, *op. cit.*, p. 81.

53. From a memorandum by the British ambassador to the Yugoslav government in exile, December 3, 1943, U.S. Department of State. *The Conferences, op. cit.*, p. 777.

54. Wolff, "Mihailovic: A Post Mortem," pp. 43–49.

55. Hayden, *op. cit.*, p. 314. The Tofte team also smuggled guns to Communist Partisans in Albania. Earlier, an SI team commanded by Thomas Stefan had established friendly liaison with the Albanian Communist guerrilla leader Enver Hoxha.

56. *Ibid.*, p. 313.

57. U.S. House of Representatives, Committee on Un-American Activities, "Hearings on Communist Infiltration of the Hollywood Motion Picture Industry" (Washington, 1951), pp. 132–33.

58. Thayer, *Hands across the Caviar*, p. 20.

59. Martin, *op. cit.*, p. 91.

60. Wilson, *Eight Years Overseas*, p. 214.

61. Kemp, *op. cit.*

62. Murphy, *Diplomat among Warriors*, p. 221.

63. *FRUS*, 1944, IV, p. 1356.

64. *FRUS*, 1944, IV, p. 1349.

65. Macmillan, *op. cit.*, p. 526.

66. Kelly, "The Halyard Mission," p. 52.

67. *FRUS*, 1944, IV, p. 1405.

68. Thayer, *op. cit.*, pp. 140–41.

69. *FRUS*, 1944, IV, pp. 1415–16.

70. *Ibid.*, p. 1422.

71. U.S. War Department, Strategic Services Unit, Intelligence report from Austria (LS-704), dated January 7, 1946. In the Hoover Institution Library, Stanford University.

72. *FRUS*, 1944, IV, pp. 1339–40.

73. *FRUS*, 1944, IV, p. 1367.

74. Peter, *op. cit.*, p. 218.

75. *Ibid.*, p. 214.

76. *FRUS*, 1944, IV, p. 1378.

77. Thayer, *op. cit.*, pp. 55–56.

78. *Ibid.*, pp. 44 and 101.

79. *FRUS*, 1944, IV, p. 1411.

80. Macmillan, *op. cit.*, p. 27.

81. Thayer, *op. cit.*, p. 27, and *FRUS*, 1945, V, p. 1209.

82. *FRUS*, 1944, IV, p. 1412.

83. Thayer, *op. cit.*, pp. 54–55.

84. As told to the author by Congressman Blatnik.

85. *FRUS*, 1945, V, p. 1209.

86. Dedijer, *op. cit.*, p. 201.

87. Thayer, *op. cit.*, p. 103.

88. *Ibid.*, p. 101.

89. *FRUS*, 1944, IV, p. 1420.

90. Macmillan, *op. cit.*, p. 535.

91. *Ibid.*, p. 591.

92. Letter from Mr. Yarrow to the author, May 26, 1970; also *FRUS*, 1944, IV, p. 1415.

93. Thayer, *op. cit.*, p. 159.

94. *Ibid.*, p. 163.

95. *FRUS*, 1945, V, p. 1228.

96. Armstrong, *Tito and Goliath*, pp. 64–65.

97. Quoted by Sulzberger, *op. cit.*, pp. 244–45.

Chapter 6

1. Muggeridge, "Book Review of a Very Limited Edition," p. 84.

2. From a speech by Ambassador Bruce to the annual dinner meeting of the veterans of OSS, Washington, D.C., May 26, 1971.

3. Kirkpatrick, *The Real CIA*, p. 24.

4. The rivalry between MI-5 and MI-6 is detailed by Deacon, *A History of the British Secret Service*, and Page et al., *The Philby Conspiracy*, Chapter 9.

5. Philby, *My Silent War*, Chapter 4.

6. Quoted in an official history of the SUSSEX operation, Secret Intelligence Branch War Diary, European Theater, in the Francis P. Miller Papers, General George Marshall Research Library, Lexington, Virginia. (Cited hereafter as SUSSEX History.)

7. The description of Passy is from Marshall, *The White Rabbit*.

8. Kenneth Pendar, one of the Murphy Vice Consuls in North Africa, repeats the anti-BCRA charges in *Adventures in Diplomacy*. Donovan's interest is mentioned by Soustelle, *Envers et Contre Tout*, Vol. 2, p. 316.

9. Letter from Dr. William Maddox to the author, January 30, 1971.

10. Philby, *op. cit.*

11. To mollify the French, a second SOE section was created to work *with* the BCRA in building a unified resistance movement in France. For a full discussion of SOE-BCRA relations see Foot, *SOE in France*, and Cookridge, *Inside SOE*.

12. Resistance unification is described by Ehrlich, *Resistance: France*.

13. The OSS was represented at these meetings by the ubiquitous Colonel Huntington; by George Brewer, Jr., a New York playwright, then senior SO officer in London, and later SO chief in Stockholm; and by Paul van der Stricht, the pro-Gaullist attorney assigned to the West European Directorate of SOE. See Dewavrin, *Souvenirs*, Vol. 3.

14. Conflicting views of the "Swiss Affair" are given by Soustelle and Dewavrin, *op. cit.*, and by de Benouville, *The Unknown Warriors*.

15. De Benouville, *op. cit.*, p. 204.

16. *Ibid.*, p. 177.

17. The conflicts between BCRA and DSR/SM are detailed by Stead, *Le Deuxième Bureau*, and Garder, *La Guerre Secrète des Services Spéciaux Français*.

18. For much of the diplomatic background of this chapter I have relied on Funk's excellent work, *Charles de Gaulle*.

19. Chester Wilmot describes the development of the invasion plans in *The Struggle for Europe*; see also Eisenhower, *Crusade in Europe*.

20. William Maddox in a dispatch to Washington, August 1, 1943. Quoted in the SUSSEX History.

21. David Bruce speech, *op. cit.*

22. The formation of SO/SOE is described in Funk, "American Contacts with the Resistance in France."

23. Wager, "The Private War of Peter Ortiz," and Wager, "They Called Him Widow-Maker."

24. For a first-hand account of the Jeds see Alsop and Braden, *Sub Rosa*, pp. 136–83.

25. SUSSEX History.

26. The DSR/SM role in the liberation of Corsica is described by Captain L'Herminier, commander of the French submarine that smuggled

guns to the island, in *Casabianca*. The political consequences of the island's liberation are considered by Soustelle and Funk, *op. cit.*

27. According to Cate, *Antoine de Saint-Exupéry*, p. 508.

28. Lambert's mission is described in some detail in the SUSSEX History.

29. Quoted by Sherwood, *Roosevelt and Hopkins*.

30. Miller, *Man from the Valley*.

31. Renault-Roulier, *Memoires*, Vol. III.

32. SUSSEX History.

33. Grell, "A Marine with OSS."

34. Brinton, "Letters from Liberated France," p. 136.

35. Letter from Mr. William Davis, Jr., to the author, January 11, 1971.

36. Cate, *op. cit.*, p. 507.

37. Soustelle, *op. cit.*, p. 382.

38. This aspect of the Dungler mission is described by one of Pétain's aides, Gabriel Jeantet in *Pétain contre Hitler.*

39. Foot, *op. cit.*, p. 359.

40. Funk discusses these organizational problems in his article in *Military Affairs*, *op. cit.*

41. Miller, *op. cit.*

42. According to Funk, neither Bruce nor Joseph Haskell recall any order for a general uprising. Robert Aron, however, describes the meeting, based on Koenig's personal account, in *De Gaulle before Paris*, p. 131.

43. Miller, *op. cit.* De Gaulle was finally informed of the date and place of the invasion when he reached London on June 4.

44. Lasky, *Arthur J. Goldberg*, p. 16.

45. David Bruce speech, *op. cit.*

46. *Ibid.*

47. SUSSEX History.

48. Kirkpatrick, *op. cit.*

49. Letter from Dr. Bernard Knox to the author, March 4, 1971.

50. Aron, *op. cit.*, pp. 251–81.

51. Lynn Case, "The Maquis Republic of Vercors," in *Infantry Journal*, April 1947, pp. 29ff.

52. Aron, *op. cit.*, p. 251.

53. Letters to the author from Mr. Paul van der Stricht, April 14, 1971, and Mr. Franklin Canfield, August 17, 1971.

54. Foot, *op. cit.*, p. 142.

55. Morgan, *The OSS and I*, pp. 175–83; also Obolensky, *One Man in His Time*, p. 386.

56. Grell, *op. cit.*, p. 18; also Stewart Alsop, "The Coming Holocaust" in *Newsweek*, March 3, 1969, p. 92.

57. Ford and McBain, *Cloak and Dagger*, p. 81; also Morgan, *op. cit.*, pp. 198 and 271; and Richard Kelly, "Jedburgh Mission Hamish," pp. 86ff.

58. Braddon, *The White Mouse*, pp. 210–11.

59. Obolensky, *op. cit.*, pp. 387–88.

60. Grell, *op. cit.*

61. Morgan, *op. cit.*, p. 202.

62. Conflicts between OSS groups and the Communists in the south are mentioned by Aron, *De Gaulle Triumphant*, p. 118.

63. Adleman and Walton, *The Champagne Campaign*, pp. 58–59.

64. *Ibid.*, p. 189.

65. Collins and Lapierre, *Is Paris Burning?* p. 25. This is a quote from an OSS report apparently compiled from BCRA sources.

66. Brinton, *op. cit.*, pp. 9, 23, and 137–38.

67. De Gaulle, *War Memoirs*, Vol. 2, p. 326.

68. Baker, *Ernest Hemingway*, p. 410.

69. *Ibid.*, p. 411.

70. Collins and Lapierre, *op. cit.*, p. 183.

71. Baker, *op. cit.*, p. 413.

72. *Ibid.*

73. Collins and Lapierre, *op. cit.*, p. 271.

74. *Ibid.*, p. 304.

75. Finnish relations with Britain and America during the early years of the war are analyzed by Langer and Gleason, *The Undeclared War*.

76. Griffis, *Lying in State*.

77. Hoover, *Memoirs of Capitalism*.

78. This analysis of the Norwegian underground is based on the paper by Kjelstadli in *European Resistance Movements*.

79. SOE officer Ewan Butler comments on Brewer's mission in *Amateur Agent*.

80. Balchen, *Come North With Me*, p. 262.

81. *Ibid.*

82. Hall, *You're Stepping on My Cloak and Dagger*, pp. 196ff.

83. Alexander Klein dramatized the mission in *The Counterfeit Traitor*; some of Klein's factual errors are corrected by Shearer, "Master Spy," pp. 6–8.

84. Ulrich von Hassel, a member of the anti-Hitler Opposition, speaks of the Hopper-Langbehn meeting in *The Von Hassel Diaries*.

85. Kersten, *The Kersten Memoirs*, pp. 190–91.

Chapter 7

1. Cook, "The CIA," p. 535.

2. Wilson, *Diplomat between Wars*, p. 20. Another member of the

embassy staff was a young code-clerk, Robert Murphy, later of North African fame. Murphy was considerably less friendly to Field, whom he felt had been responsible for the unwarranted dismissal of the American consul general in Zurich on a false charge of "consorting with the enemy." Murphy *Diplomat among Warriors*, p. 7.

3. Dulles, *The Secret Surrender*, p. 16.

4. Wilson, *Disarmament and Cold War in the Thirties*, p. 41.

5. Dulles was indirectly accused of pro-Nazi sympathies by Fred Cook, *op. cit.* Dulles vigorously denied the charge in his interview with the John Foster Dulles Oral History Project, Princeton University.

6. Lindbergh, *Wartime Journals*, p. 283.

7. *New York Times*, September 13, 1939, p. 22.

8. *New York Times*, May 1, 1941, p. 3.

9. Donald Downes touches upon the zu Putlitz and Bruening projects in *The Scarlet Thread*, pp. 67–73. Drew Pearson related an inaccurate version of the Bruening Committee in "Washington Merry-Go-Round," February 9, 1945.

10. Frank's role in the German socialist exile movement is discussed by Edinger, *German Exile Politics*; his assistance to the OSS-supported Emergency Rescue Committee, which later evolved into the CIA-supported International Rescue Committee, is detailed by Fry, *Surrender on Demand*. Former FBI agent Guenther Reinhardt in *Crime Without Punishment* depicts Frank as a notorious Communist conspirator.

11. Hoover, *Memoirs of Capitalism*, p. 201.

12. Downes, *op. cit.*, p. 71.

13. Dulles, *op. cit.*, p. 11.

14. Dulles, *Germany's Underground*, Introduction, xi.

15. The approach to Menzies in late 1942 is mentioned by F. W. Winterbotham, chief of Air Intelligence for MI-6, in *Secret and Personal*, p. 162. Winterbotham favored the German offer: "It would certainly not have pleased Stalin, but why we should fall over backwards to appease those who were, and are, pledged to destroy our way of life, I shall never understand." Another approach to Menzies by a personal meeting between Canaris and the MI-6 chief in occupied France is described by Collins and Lapierre, *Is Paris Burning?* p. 13. According to Deacon, *A History of the British Secret Service*, Menzies personally preferred to pursue the negotiations with Canaris but was blocked by Foreign Office officials "for fear of offending Russia."

16. Colvin, *Chief of Intelligence*, Manvell and Fraenkel, *The Canaris Conspiracy*.

17. Philby, *My Silent War*, p. 65.

18. Dulles, *The Secret Surrender*, p. 17.

19. Lewis, *Red Pawn*; see also Toledano, "The Noel Field Story," pp.

5ff.; and Thompson, "What Has Stalin Done with Noel Field? pp. 17ff.

20. British criticism of Gisevius is noted by Franklin Ford, a Harvard historian (later Dean of the Faculty of Arts and Sciences at Harvard) who served in the OSS R&A Branch in France and Germany: "The 20th of July," pp. 609–26; also Wiskemann, *The Europe I Saw*, p. 168.

21. Gisevius, *To the Bitter End*, p. 481.

22. Sykes, *Troubled Loyalty*, p. 188. On a later trip to a conference of the Institute of Pacific Relations in 1939, von Trott also met Whitney Shepardson, later Donovan's SI Branch chief in Washington.

23. Carolsue Holland, "Foreign Contacts Made by the German Opposition to Hitler," unpublished Ph.D. dissertation, University of Pennsylvania, 1967. Mrs. Holland had access to some original OSS documentation in the National Archives.

24. Dulles, *The Secret Surrender*, p. 30.

25. From the alleged Gestapo report on the Hohenlohe-Dulles conversation, printed in the Moscow *New Times*, July 1960.

26. Hohenlohe's earlier conversations with the British ambassador and the Aga Khan in Switzerland in July and December 1940 are outlined in U.S. Department of State, *Documents on German Foreign Policy* (Washington, 1957), Series D, Vol. X, pp. 245, 287 and 294. His overtures to the British in Madrid are mentioned by Hoare, *Complacent Dictator*, p. 92, and Crozier, *Franco*, p. 374.

27. Portions of the alleged German transcript of the conversation were first printed in a communique of the Soviet Information Bureau, Moscow, "Falsificators of History," February 1948. The full text was printed in the Moscow *New Times*, *op. cit.* and reprinted by two British Labour Party M.P.'s, Edwards and Dunne, *Study of a Master Spy*.

28. Hoover, *op. cit.*, p. 217.

29. Schellenberg, *The Labyrinth*, p. 371.

30. Kersten, *The Kersten Memoirs*, p. 194.

31. See Poole's memorandum to the OSS Planning Group, July 29, 1943. DeWitt Poole Papers, State Historical Society of Wisconsin.

32. Dulles, *Germany's Underground*, p. 138.

33. Farago, *Burn After Reading*, p. 220. German émigrés were first hired by Shortwave Research, Inc., a front organization for the COI Foreign Information Service that was interlocked with both the Emergency Rescue Committee and the American Friends of German Freedom.

34. Dulles, *Germany's Underground*, p. 138.

35. For example, the "Lucy" and "Rote Kapelle" networks. See Foote, *Handbook for Spies*; Accoce and Quet, *A Man Called Lucy*; and Perrault, *The Red Orchestra*.

36. Gallin, *Ethical and Religious Factors in the German Resistance*. This is the only previously published reference to Kolbe's real name. Ed-

ward Morgan describes "George Wood" and his activities in detail in "The Spy the Nazis Missed," pp. 21ff.

37. Gallin, *op. cit.*, pp. 128–29.

38. Philby, *My Silent War*, pp. 103–4.

39. Dulles, *The Secret Surrender*, p. 23.

40. The Abwehr officer was Paul Leverkuehn. He mentioned his friendship with Donovan to Admiral Canaris' sympathetic biographer, Ian Colvin, *op. cit.*, p. 181; see also Leverkuehn's defense of Canaris in *German Military Intelligence*.

41. Wiskemann, *op. cit.*, p. 189.

42. Hoegner, *Der Schwierige Aussenseiter*, pp. 172–73.

43. Allen Dulles, "William J. Donovan and the National Security," Speech to the Erie County Bar Association, Buffalo, New York, May 4, 1959.

44. Hyde, *Room 3603*, p. 191; also Sweet-Escott, *Baker Street Irregular*, p. 147.

45. Dr. Franz Neumann of OSS R&A later told this possibly apocryphal anecdote to students at Columbia University.

46. Delmer, *Black Boomerang*, p. 124.

47. *Ibid.*

48. MacDonald, *Undercover Girl*, pp. 248–49.

49. Ulmer describes his Austrian infiltration operations in "The Gulliver Mission," pp. 56ff.

50. Kirkpatrick, *The Real CIA*, p. 51.

51. The Jessen-Schmidt mission is discussed in Andersen, *The Dark City*, and Ryan, *The Last Battle*. The Czech team is mentioned in Ford, *Donovan of O.S.S.*, p. 280.

52. Dulles, *The Secret Surrender*, p. 36.

53. Dulles, *Ibid.*, p. 41; also Kirkpatrick, *op. cit.*, p. 62.

54. Morgan, *op. cit.*

55. Lewis, *op. cit.*, pp. 172–73.

56. Arthur Schlesinger's review of the Lewis book in *New York Review of Books*, February 11, 1965, pp. 10ff.

57. Whitwell, *British Agent*, p. 205.

58. Hoettl, *The Secret Front*, p. 285.

59. Dulles, *The Secret Surrender*, p. 50.

60. *Ibid.*

61. Dulles, *op. cit.*, p. 109.

62. U.S. Department of State, *Foreign Relations of the United States*, 1945, Vol. III, pp. 733–47. (Cited hereafter as FRUS.)

63. FRUS, 1945, III, pp. 737–40.

64. *Ibid.*, p. 746.

65. *Ibid.*, p. 756.

66. Dulles, *op. cit.*, p. 152, and Hoettl, *op. cit.*, pp. 288–90.

67. Various versions of the Poelhof mission are given by Ford, *op. cit.*, pp. 277–79; Alsop and Braden, *Sub Rosa*, pp. 47–74; and Pinto, *Friend or Foe?* pp. 67–108. According to Braden and Alsop, Poelhof felt the Dutch exile government in London had "fascist tendencies," while the exile government thought Poelhof was "left-wing, perhaps Communist." Pinto, who was counter-intelligence chief for the exile government, said Poelhof was suspect for having Nazi sympathies. And Ford assures the reader that Poelhof was "a very religious young Hollander." One wonders if the Russians were half as confused as the espionage historians, all of whom had access to "official" documents.

68. *FRUS*, 1945, III, p. 741.

69. Dulles, *The Secret Surrender*, p. 156.

70. The official, Herr Blanckenhorn, chief of protocol for the Wilhelmstrasse, was taken into custody by Henry Ringling North of OSS and brought to Paris for interrogation.

71. The OSS role in military government is discussed by Zink, *The United States in Germany*, and Neumann, "Political Intelligence," pp. 70–85.

72. Hayden, *Wanderer*, p. 331.

73. Lewis, *op. cit.*, p. 185; also U.S. House Committee on Un-American Activities, "The Erica Wallach Story."

74. Sweezy, ed., *Paul Baran*.

75. Neumann, "The Social Sciences."

76. *FRUS*, 1945, III, p. 1045.

77. Donovan, *Challenges*. Donovan also discusses some of his legal problems as OSS General Counsel.

78. Hagen, *The Secret War for Europe*, pp. 35–38.

79. U.S. War Department, Strategic Services Unit, SSU Report 1-1035, November 29, 1945, and SSU Report LB-138, January 15, 1946. In the Hoover Institution on War, Revolution, and Peace, Stanford University.

80. Letter from Mr. Lawrence de Neufville to the author, April 26, 1971.

81. Tompkins, *A Spy in Rome*, p. 317.

Chapter 8

1. Mansfield, "Ambush in China," p. 42.

2. The background material on China is taken from Feis, *The China Tangle*; White and Jacoby, *Thunder out of China*; Eldridge, *Wrath in Burma*; and Tuchman, *Stilwell*.

3. Stilwell, *The Stilwell Papers*, p. 37.

4. Miles, *A Different Kind of War*, pp. 76–78.

5. Gale, *Salt for the Dragon*, p. 215.

6. Dispatch from Lusey to Colonel Donovan, May 23, 1942, in the Goodfellow Papers, Hoover Institution, Stanford University.

7. Miles, *op. cit.*, p. 18.

8. C. Lester Walker presents an uncomplimentary vignette of Tai Li in "China's Master Spy," pp. 162–69; more sympathetic views of the general are found in Miles, *op. cit.*, and Dobbins, "China's Mystery Man," p. 19.

9. A comment attributed to State Department officer John Service by OSS official Turner McBaine in a report to General Donovan, June 1944, Goodfellow Papers, Stanford.

10. From a State Department memorandum in U.S. Department of State, *Foreign Relations of the United States: China*, 1942, p. 221; cited hereafter as FRUS China.

11. Stilwell, *op. cit.*, p. 346.

12. From an incomplete Navy history of SACO in the Milton Miles Papers, the Hoover Institution, Stanford University.

13. Miles, *op. cit.*, p. 53.

14. Dispatch from Lusey to Donovan, May 23, 1942, Goodfellow Papers, Stanford; also a Lusey report of July 1942 quoted in the Naval history of SACO, Miles Papers, Stanford.

15. Peck, *Two Kinds of Time*, p. 140.

16. A report from British Security Coordination, New York, to OSS headquarters, June 8, 1942, in the Goodfellow Papers, Stanford.

17. Adamson, *The Forgotten Men*; Miles, *op. cit.*, p. 132; and the Miles Papers, Stanford.

18. British Security Coordination memorandum, *op. cit.*; also Sweet-Escott, *Baker Street Irregular*, p. 141.

19. Miles, *op. cit.*, p. 90.

20. Eifler dispatch to Colonel M. P. Goodfellow, OSS headquarters, September 28, 1942, Goodfellow Papers, Stanford.

21. Miles, *op. cit.*, p. 76; also a memorandum from Joseph Hayden to Donovan in Joseph Hayden Papers, University of Michigan Historical Collections.

22. Hayden memorandum, *op. cit.*

23. *Ibid.*

24. Mowrer, *Triumph and Turmoil*, p. 323.

25. "Memorandum, 1943, Conferences with MacArthur and Merle Smith regarding OSS operations in the Southwest Pacific Area," in Joseph Hayden Papers, University of Michigan.

26. *Ibid.*; see also the MacArthur version in Allison Ind, *Allied Intelligence Bureau*.

27. Downes, *The Scarlet Thread*, pp. 62–63.
28. Mashbir, *I Was an American Spy*, p. 22.
29. McBaine memorandum, *op. cit.*
30. Stilwell, *op. cit.*, p. 220.
31. Chennault, *Way of a Fighter*, p. 257. The postwar letter is in the Miles Papers, Stanford.
32. Miles, *op. cit.*, p. 117. Magruder's remarks are found in FRUS, 1942, China, p. 14.
33. Miles, *op. cit.*, p. 117.
34. Sweet-Escott, *op. cit.*, p. 141.
35. Allman wrote a prewar autobiography, *Shanghai Lawyer* (New York, 1943).
36. Stratton, SACO, *The Rice Paddy Navy* (New York, 1950), pp. 338–39; and Miles, *op. cit.*, pp. 124 and 198–200.
37. FRUS, 1943, China, pp. 624–25.
38. Dispatch from Tolstoy to OSS headquarters, March 17, 1943, in the Goodfellow Papers, Stanford; also Ilia Tolstoy, "Across Tibet from India to China," in *National Geographic*, August 1946, p. 215.
39. Report from Tolstoy and Dolan to OSS headquarters, July 25, 1943, Goodfellow Papers, Stanford.
40. FRUS, 1943, China, p. 637.
41. Letters from Herbert Little to the author, January 20, January 31, and March 10, 1971.
42. Taylor, *Awakening from History*, p. 343; Miles, *op. cit.*, p. 169.
43. Miles, *op. cit.*, pp. 169–70.
44. Chennault, *op. cit.*, p. 211.
45. Hayden memorandum, *op. cit.*
46. War Department Memorandum to Donovan, December 12, 1941, in the Goodfellow Papers, Stanford.
47. *Ibid.*; there is extensive documentation of the "Larsen-Underwood" plan for Chinese guerrilla warfare, including correspondence between Roosevelt and the State Department, in the Goodfellow Papers, Stanford.
48. Quoted in the Naval history of SACO, Miles Papers, Stanford.
49. Memorandum on "Intelligence Systems" by Dr. John K. Fairbank, January 9, 1944, in U.S. Senate Committee on the Judiciary, *The Amerasia Papers*, p. 314.
50. Miles, *op. cit.*, p. 318.
51. Chennault, *op. cit.*, p. 258.
52. Frillmann and Peck, *China: The Remembered Life*, pp. 261–62, 210 and 232.
53. Barrett, *Dixie Mission*, p. 34.
54. Stilwell, *op. cit.*, p. 333.
55. Miles, *op. cit.*, p. 307.

56. Peers and Brelis, *Behind the Burma Road*, p. 178.

57. Miles, *op. cit.*, p. 434.

58. Utley, *Odyssey of a Liberal*, p. 299.

59. This was Megan's comment to a State Department officer, recorded in U.S. Senate, *Amerasia Papers*, p. 473.

60. Letters from Colonel Stevens in Chungking to his wife in Washington, D.C., November 22, 1944, and February 8, 1945. In the possession of Mrs. Stevens.

61. MacDonald, *op. cit.*, p. 211.

62. Memorandum from Carl Eifler to Stilwell's headquarters, December 9, 1942, in the Goodfellow Papers, Stanford.

63. White and Jacoby, *op. cit.*, p. 196.

64. Quoted in Stuart, *Kind-Hearted Tiger*, p. 347. Stuart was an Australian officer seconded to the OSS Operational Groups in China.

65. Mansfield, *op. cit.*, p. 15.

66. From North's report to OSS headquarters in the Goodfellow Papers, Stanford.

67. These rumors are cited by Walker, *op. cit.* One former OSS major told the author that Tai Li privately admitted that he had ordered the assassination of OSS Chinese agents.

68. Stevens Papers, *op. cit.*

69. Peck, *op. cit.*, p. 612.

70. This incident is recalled by John Colling, senior OSS officer at Yenan.

71. U.S. Senate, the *Amerasia Papers*, p. 903.

72. Romanus and Sunderland, *United States Army in World War II*, vol. 3, pp. 251–53; also Lohbeck, *Patrick J. Hurley*, p. 336.

73. Letter from Colonel Harley Stevens, April 20, 1945, Stevens Papers, *op. cit.*

74. Miles, *op. cit.*, p. 488; U.S. Senate Committee on the Judiciary, "Hearings on the Institute of Pacific Relations."

75. LeMay, *Mission with LeMay*, p. 336; Miles, *op. cit.*, p. 488.

76. General Donovan suggested the connection between Yalta and Manchurian espionage in "Intelligence: Key to Defense," p. 106.

77. Stevens Papers, *op. cit.*

78. A right-wing account of the case by Dr. Anthony Kubek is in U.S. Senate, the *Amerasia Papers*. For Service's rebuttal see *The Amerasia Papers: Some Problems in the History of U.S.–China Relations*.

79. Letter from Colonel Harley Stevens, June 9, 1945, Stevens Papers, *op. cit.*

80. Wedemeyer, *Wedemeyer Reports*, p. 317.

81. Butow, *Japan's Decision to Surrender*.

82. Stevens, "Prelude to Chinese Unity," p. 1.

83. Feis, op. cit., p. 357.

84. Cyr, "We Blew the Yellow River Bridge," p. 18.

85. Dispatch from Colonel Gustav Kraus, OSS Sian commander, quoted in Craig, The Fall of Japan, p. 178.

86. Testimony of George Wuchinich to the U.S. Senate Committee on the Judiciary, "Hearings on Interlocking Subversion in Government Departments," p. 706.

87. For various accounts of Birch's death see Craig, op. cit., and Welch, The Life of John Birch.

88. Kellis' earlier exploits in Greece are described in Kelly, "Mission to Greece," p. 76.

89. Frillmann and Peck, op. cit., pp. 257 and 261.

90. Moorad, Lost Peace in China, pp. 155–57.

91. Letter from Colonel Stevens, September 30, 1945, Stevens Papers, op. cit.

92. Lockwood, "The GI in Wartime China," pp. 9–11.

Chapter 9

1. MacDonald, Undercover Girl, p. 121.

2. Taylor, Richer by Asia, p. 33.

3. Eldridge, Wrath in Burma, p. 263.

4. Stilwell, The Stilwell Papers, p. 239.

5. Colin MacKenzie (a director of J&P Coats, the largest British sewing thread company in India) in a letter to Carl Eifler, October 10, 1942, in the Goodfellow Papers, Hoover Institution, Stanford University.

6. Peers and Brelis, Behind the Burma Road, pp. 39 and 58. Other sources dealing with OSS-SOE operations in Burma are Barrett, Chinghpaw; Beamish, Burma Drop; and Kelly, "Burma Mission," p. 74.

7. From a speech by Congressman Leon Gavin, Congressional Record, May 22, 1945, p. A2434.

8. Taylor, op. cit., p. 32.

9. Taylor, Awakening from History, p. 349.

10. Taylor, Richer by Asia, p. 37.

11. Taylor, Awakening from History, p. 349.

12. Ibid., p. 353.

13. Phillips, Ventures in Diplomacy, p. 388.

14. Taylor, Awakening from History, pp. 351–52.

15. Eldridge, op. cit., p. 238; the Nepalese affair is discussed by Alcorn, No Banners, No Bands.

16. Taylor, Awakening from History, p. 353.

17. OSS Research and Analysis Report 2512 (February 1945), "Nationalist Groups in the Netherlands East Indies," in the Hoover Institution Library, Stanford University.

18. MacDonald, *op. cit.*, pp. 297–98.

19. Taylor, *Awakening from History*, p. 354.

20. Mountbatten, *Report to the Combined Chiefs of Staff*, p. 7.

21. Gilchrist, *Bangkok Top Secret*, p. 16.

22. Landon, *Siam in Transition*, pp. 319–23.

23. Landon, *op. cit.*, p. 22; also Thompson, *Thailand*, pp. 75–101; Chandruang and Prabhu, "Our Siamese Underground," pp. 530–34.

24. Chapman, *The Jungle Is Neutral*, p. 14.

25. Hull, *Memoirs*, p. 997.

26. U.S. Department of State, *Foreign Relations of the United States*, 1942, Vol. 1, p. 913. (Cited hereafter as *FRUS*.)

27. *New York Times*, December 25, 1941, p. 9.

28. Samrej, "That Thailand May Be Free," pp. 94–95.

29. *Newsweek*, September 3, 1945, p. 26.

30. I am indebted for this analysis to an unpublished Masters thesis by Phan Wannamethee, "Thailand–United States Relations, 1941–1952," University of California, Berkeley.

31. OSS Research and Analysis Report of June 19, 1942, "Social Conditions, Attitudes and Propaganda in Thailand with Suggestions for American Orientation toward the Thai," quoted by Wannamethee, *op. cit.*

32. Smith and Clark, *Into Siam*, p. 33.

33. Taylor, *Awakening from History*, p. 352.

34. Gilchrist, *op. cit.*, p. 30.

35. *FRUS*, 1942, I, p. 920.

36. Smith and Clark, *op. cit.*, p. 20.

37. Sweet-Escott, *Baker Street Irregular*, p. 237.

38. Gilchrist, *op. cit.*, p. 33.

39. Miles, *A Different Kind of War*, p. 164.

40. Gilchrist, *op. cit.*, p. 21.

41. *Ibid.*, p. 22.

42. Miles, *op. cit.*, p. 166.

43. *Ibid.*

44. *Ibid.*

45. Smith and Clark, *op. cit.*, p. 142.

46. *FRUS*, 1943, III, p. 1121.

47. *Ibid.*

48. *FRUS*, 1944, V, pp. 1312–13.

49. *Ibid.*

50. Crosby, "Observations on a Post-War Settlement in Southeast Asia," pp. 357–68.

51. Smith and Clark, *op. cit.*, p. 155.

52. Taylor, *Awakening from History*, pp. 352–53.

53. Smith and Clark, *op. cit.*, p. 180.

54. Gilchrist, *op. cit.*, p. 190.

55. *FRUS*, 1944, V, pp. 1315–19.

56. Kelly, "Chance Island," p. 62.

57. OSS Research and Analysis Report 2608, October 1944, "The Trend Toward Democracy in Thailand," in the Hoover Institution, Stanford.

58. Gilchrist, *op. cit.*, pp. 83 and 92.

59. *Ibid.*, p. 108.

60. Kelly, "Mission to Bangkok," p. 88.

61. *FRUS*, 1945, VI, p. 1247.

62. *Ibid.*, p. 1243.

63. Letter from Dr. S. Dillon Ripley to the author, July 28, 1970.

64. Chakrabandhu, "Force 136 and the Siamese Resistance Movement," p. 169.

65. *FRUS*, 1945, VI, pp. 1261 and 1266.

66. Mountbatten, *op. cit.*, p. 180.

67. Strangely enough, the British saw their delaying tactics as "a diplomatic game which suited Pridi's book. . . . In a sense, he was establishing the position of having worked his passage home without having taken any warlike action at all." Gilchrist, *op. cit.*, pp. 195–96.

68. Kelly, "Mission to Bangkok," contains a long narrative of the mission by Palmer.

69. Taylor, *Richer by Asia*, pp. 225–27.

70. *FRUS*, 1945, VI, p. 1268.

71. *Ibid.*, pp. 1268–70.

72. Gilchrist, *op. cit.*, p. 85.

73. *FRUS*, 1945, VI, p. 1251.

74. Sweet-Escott, *op. cit.*, p. 252.

75. Kemp, *Alms for Oblivion*, p. 26; also Gilchrist, *op. cit.*, p. 195; and Smith and Clark, *op. cit.*, p. 288.

76. Gilchrist, *op. cit.*, p. 188.

77. Kemp, *op. cit.*, p. 26.

78. MacDonald, *Bangkok Editor*, pp. 82, 89, and 163; see also Jim Thompson's biography and the tale of his mysterious disappearance in Warren, *The Legendary American*.

79. *FRUS*, 1945, VI, p. 570.

80. Smith and Clark, *op. cit.*, pp. 229–31.

81. Ripley, "Incident in Siam," pp. 262–76.

82. Taylor, *Awakening from History*, p. 354.

83. Ripley, *op. cit.*

84. Snow, "Secrets from Siam," pp. 37, 39, and 41.

85. Letter from Dr. Kenneth Landon to the author, July 5, 1970.

86. Alec Peterson, "Britain and Siam," pp. 364–72.

87. Quoted by Wendell Willkie, *One World* (New York, 1943), p. 174.

88. Snow, *op. cit.*, p. 39.

89. *Ibid.*

90. Mullender, "L'évolution récente de la Thailande," pp. 213–33; also Dessinges, "La Rivalité anglo-américaine au Siam."

91. Kemp, *op. cit.*; also Michel Caply, *Guerrilla au Laos* (Paris, 1966).

92. Kemp, *op. cit.*, pp. 51–52.

93. *Ibid.*, p. 57.

94. *New York Times*, October 4, 1945, p. 3.

Chapter 10

1. Background material for this chapter is taken from Buttinger, *Viet nam*; Devillers, *Histoire du Vietnam*; and Hammer, *The Struggle for Indochina*.

2. This account of the Meynier operation is found in Miles, *A Different Kind of War*. There are also some useful notes and documents in the Miles Papers, the Hoover Institution, Stanford University.

3. The French charges are confirmed by an OSS research report dated January 24, 1944. Quoted by Cooper, *Case Studies in Insurgency*, p. 106.

4. Miles, *op. cit.*, p. 186.

5. *Ibid.*, p. 191.

6. De Gaulle's statement is quoted by Buttinger, *op. cit.*, p. 302. The Brazzaville document is in Lancaster, *The Emancipation of French Indochina*, p. 123.

7. Quoted in Shaplen, *The Lost Revolution*, p. 33.

8. From Helliwell's statement to Bernard Fall, *The Two Viet Nams*, p. 100.

9. Roosevelt, *As He Saw It*, p. 251.

10. Shaplen, *op. cit.*, p. 31.

11. Hammer, *op. cit.*, p. 44.

12. Chennault, *Way of a Fighter*, p. 342; and Wedemeyer, *Wedemeyer Reports!* p. 340.

13. De Gaulle, *War Memoirs: Salvation, 1944–1946*, p. 187.

14. Sabattier, *Le Destin de l'Indochine*, pp. 192–93.

15. MacDonald, *Undercover Girl*, p. 191.

16. The coolness between Sainteny and Sabattier had political overtones. Cooper, *op. cit.*, quotes an OSS research report of May 1945 which notes that the Gaullist intelligence men mistrusted the French colonial

army officers as Vichyite collaborators. Decoux's generals, according to this report, later charged that the Gaullists preferred losing Indochina to using colonial troops to "liberate" the colony.

17. Shaplen, *op. cit.*, p. 41.

18. As told to Shaplen, *op. cit.*, p. 29.

19. Sainteny, *Histoire d'une Paix Manquée*, p. 47.

20. Defourneaux, "Secret Encounter with Ho Chi Minh," pp. 32–33.

21. *Ibid.*

22. From an interview with Henry Prunier in the Worcester *Evening Gazette*, May 14–15, 1968.

23. Prunier interview, *op. cit.*

24. Defourneaux, *op. cit.*

25. Prunier interview, *op. cit.*

26. Sainteny, *op. cit.*, p. 59.

27. Shaplen, *op. cit.*, p. 30.

28. The best account of this period is Ellen Hammer's, *op. cit.*

29. Letter to the author from Mr. Joseph Coolidge, January 27, 1971.

30. From Geoffrey Hellman's epilogue to Dewey's book, *As They Were*, p. 232.

31. Hammer, *op. cit.*, pp. 109 and 113.

32. Buttinger, *op. cit.*, p. 327.

33. Coolidge letter, *op. cit.*

34. George Sheldon, "The Status of the Viet Nam," p. 374.

35. This account is based on information supplied by Joseph Coolidge, Herbert Bluechel, Frank White, and Dr. George Wickes.

36. Coolidge letter, *op. cit.*

37. Dewey's death was widely, and inaccurately, reported in the *New York Times*, the *Washington Post*, and the New York *Herald Tribune*. The incident is also mentioned in Hammer, *op. cit.*, pp. 118–19. But Bluechel has given a more exact version based on memory.

38. The Viet Minh charges against the French were reported by *Le Monde*, October 6, 1945.

39. *New York Times*, October 3, 1945, p. 18.

40. Taylor, *Richer by Asia*, p. 386.

41. *Ibid.*

42. From a postwar report to General Donovan by Mr. Nicholas Deak.

43. *Ibid.*

44. Sheldon, "The Case for Viet Nam," pp. 393–95.

45. MacDonald, *op. cit.*, p. 232.

46. Sainteny, *op. cit.*, p. 71.

47. *Ibid.*, p. 74.

48. *Ibid.*, p. 80.

49. Defourneaux, *op. cit.*

50. Prunier interview, *op. cit.*

51. Defourneaux, *op. cit.*

52. Sainteny, *op. cit.*, p. 86.

53. *Ibid.*, p. 87.

54. Sainteny, *op. cit.*, p. 95.

55. This and other incidents are taken from discussions with "Roberts," Archimedes Patti, Lucien Conein, Roger Bernique, Carlton Swift, Jean Sainteny, and Roland Sadoun.

56. Sainteny, *op. cit.*, p. 91.

57. *Ibid.*, p. 234.

58. Hammer, *op. cit.*, p. 131.

59. Sainteny, *op. cit.*, pp. 95 and 125.

60. The report was first suggested by René Dessinges in *Le Monde*, April 13, 1947.

61. Sainteny, *op. cit.*, p. 100.

62. Gallagher's alleged remark is quoted by Bernard Fall in an article in *Politique Etrangère*, July 1955.

63. Letter to the author from Mr. Frank White, March 9, 1971.

64. *Ibid.*

65. *Ibid.*

Chapter 11

1. Taylor, *Awakening from History*, pp. 350–51.

2. Dulles, *The Secret Surrender*, p. 9.

3. Kirkpatrick, *The Real CIA*, p. 191.

4. Miller, *Man from the Valley.*

5. Ford, *Donovan of O.S.S.*, p. 340.

6. *Ibid.*, p. 303.

7. *Ibid.*, p. 304.

8. "Have We An Intelligence Service?" in *Atlantic Monthly*, April 1948, p. 70.

9. Quoted by Dean Acheson, *Present at the Creation* (New York, 1969), p. 160.

10. *Ibid.*, p. 162.

11. H. Stuart Hughes, "The Second Year of the Cold War," in *Commentary*, August 1969, p. 27.

12. Miles Copeland, *The Game of Nations* (London, 1969), pp. 30–31.

13. Hanson Baldwin in the *New York Times*, July 23, 1948, p. 5.

14. U.S. Department of State, "Transcript of Round Table Discussion of American Policy Toward China," October 1949, pp. 112–122.

15. U.S. Senate Committee on the Judiciary, "Hearings on the Institute of Pacific Relations," pp. 2751–71; also Joseph Keeley, *The China Lobby Man* (New York, 1969), p. 130.

16. Seitz, *Mihailovic*, p. 2.

17. Quoted by Jessica Mitford, *The Trial of Dr. Spock* (New York, 1969), pp. 38–39.

18. Thomas Braden, "I'm Glad the CIA Is 'Immoral,' " in *Saturday Evening Post*, May 20, 1967, pp. 10–14.

19. Kirkpatrick, *op. cit.*, p. 136.

20. *Ibid.*

21. Roy Cohn, *McCarthy* (New York, 1968), p. 63.

22. U.S. House Committee on Un-American Activities, "Testimony of General Walter Bedell Smith" (Washington, D.C., 1952), p. 4290.

23. Remark by former CIA Deputy Director for Plans Richard Bissell, Jr., to the John Foster Dulles Oral History Project, Princeton University.

24. Kirkpatrick, *op. cit.*, p. 136.

25. Cohn, *op. cit.*; and U.S. Senate Committee on Government Operations, "The Army-McCarthy Hearings" (Washington, D.C., 1954), p. 1904.

26. Kirkpatrick, *op. cit.*, p. 138.

27. U.S. Senate, "The Army-McCarthy Hearings," p. 1944.

28. Gerald Nachman, "Peter Falk—All American Boy," in the *Oakland Tribune*, Sept. 6, 1970, p. 3-EN.

29. *Time* magazine, February 16, 1948, p. 28.

30. Cord Meyer, Jr., "On the Beaches," in *Atlantic*, October 1944, pp. 42–46.

31. Daniel James, "The Battle of A.V.C.," in *The Nation*, June 14, 1947, pp. 706–8.

32. Cord Meyer, Jr., *Peace or Anarchy* (Boston, 1947), p. 218.

33. Cord Meyer, Jr., "A Plea for World Government," in *Annals of the American Academy of Political and Social Science*, July 1949, pp. 6–13.

34. Meyer's testimony to the U.S. Senate Committee on Foreign Relations, "Hearings on Revision of the U.N. Charter" (Washington, D.C., 1950), p. 130.

35. *New York Times*, March 30, 1967, p. 30.

36. "These Men Run C.I.A.," in *Esquire*, May 1966, p. 167.

37. *New York Times*, March 30, 1967, p. 30.

38. Emmet John Hughes, *The Ordeal of Power* (New York, 1962), p. 106.

39. Mario Lazo, *Dagger in the Heart* (New York, 1968), p. 233.

40. Schlesinger, *A Thousand Days* (Boston, 1965), p. 428.

41. Sol Stern, "NSA and the CIA," in *Ramparts*, March 1967, p. 38.

42. *Congressional Record*, February 23, 1967, p. 4404.

43. Americans for Democratic Action, *ADA World*, September-October 1968, p. 23.

44. *New York Times*, February 22, 1967, p. 17.

45. *New York Times*, February 23, 1967, p. 25.

46. *Congressional Record*, February 16, 1967, p. 3594.

47. *Ibid.*, p. 3517.

48. *New York Times*, February 23, 1967, p. 25.

49. *New York Times*, February 27, 1967, p. 1.

50. *Congressional Record*, February 16, 1967, pp. 3514–17.

51. Jack Newfield, *Robert Kennedy*, p. 79.

52. Walter Cronkite news report, CBS network, February 23, 1968.

53. *The Pentagon Papers* (New York, 1971), p. 386.

Bibliography

Bibliography

I. SOURCE MATERIAL ON THE O.S.S.

Adamic, Louis. *Dinner at the White House*. New York: Harper, 1946.

Adleman, Robert, and George Walton. *The Champagne Campaign*. Boston: Little, Brown, 1969.

Alcorn, Robert. *No Banners, No Bands*. New York: D. McKay, 1965.

————. *No Bugles for Spies*. New York: D. McKay, 1962.

Alsop, Stewart, and Thomas Braden, *Sub Rosa: The OSS and American Espionage*. New York: Harcourt, Brace and World, 1964.

Andersen, Hartvig. *The Dark City*. New York: Rinehart, 1954.

Baker, Carlos. *Ernest Hemingway*. New York: Charles Scribner's Sons, 1969.

Balchen, Bernt. *Come North with Me*. New York: Dutton, 1958.

Barmine, Alexander. "New Communist Conspiracy" *Reader's Digest*, October 1944, pp. 27–33.

Barrett, David. *Dixie Mission: The United States Army Observer Group in Yenan*. Berkeley: Center for Chinese Studies, 1970.

Barrett, Neil. *Chinghpaw*. New York: Vintage, 1962.

Becker, Henry. "The Nature and Consequences of Black Propaganda," *American Sociological Review*, April 1949, pp. 221–35.

Bowie, Beverly. *Operation Bughouse*. New York: Dodd, Mead, 1947.

Braddon, Russell. *The White Mouse*. New York: W. W. Norton, 1956.

Brelis, Dean. *The Mission*. New York: Random House, 1958.

Brinton, Crane. "Letters from Liberated France," *French Historical Studies*, Spring 1961, pp. 1–27; and Fall 1961, pp. 133–56.

Bruce, David K. E. "The National Intelligence Authority," *Virginia Quarterly Review*, Summer 1946, pp. 355–69.

Calderon, Joseph. "How Can I Face Them?" *Commonweal*, May 10, 1946, pp. 87–90.

Cate, Curtis. *Antoine de Saint-Exupéry*. New York: Putnam, 1970.

Chamberlain, J. "OSS," *Life*, November 19, 1945, pp. 119–24.

Clark, Leonard. *The Marching Wind*. New York: Funk, 1954.

Cook, Fred. "The CIA," *The Nation*, June 24, 1961, pp. 529–72.

Corvo, Max. "America's Intelligence Dilemma," *Hartford Courant*, May 28, 1961.

Coster, Donald. "We Were Expecting You at Dakar," *Reader's Digest*, August 1946, pp. 103–7.

Craig, William. *The Fall of Japan*. New York: Dial Press, 1967.

Cyr, Paul. "We Blew the Yellow River Bridge," *Saturday Evening Post*, March 23, 1946.

Davis, Forrest. "The Secret Story of a Surrender," *Saturday Evening Post*, September 22, 1945, pp. 7–11ff.; September 29, 1945, pp. 17ff.

Deane, John. *The Strange Alliance*. New York: Viking, 1947.

Defourneaux, René. "Secret Encounter with Ho Chi Minh," *Look*, August 9, 1966, pp. 32–3.

Dessinges, René. "Les Intrigues Internationales en Indochine Française," *Le Monde*, April 6–13, 1947.

Donovan, James. *Challenges*. New York: Atheneum, 1967.

Donovan, William J. "Intelligence: Key to Defense," *Life*, September 30, 1946, pp. 108ff.

———, and Edgar Mowrer. *Fifth Column Lessons for America*. Washington, D.C.: American Council on Public Affairs, 1941.

Downes, Donald. *The Scarlet Thread*. London: Verschoyle, 1953.

Du Berrier, Hilaire. "How We Helped Ho Chi Minh," *The Freeman*, April 19, 1954.

Duke, Florimond. *Name, Rank, and Serial Number*. New York: Meredith Press, 1969.

Dulles, Allen W. *The Craft of Intelligence*. New York: Harper and Row, 1963.

———. *Germany's Underground*. New York: Macmillan, 1947.

———. *The Secret Surrender*. New York: Harper and Row, 1966.

———. "William J. Donovan and the National Security," Speech to the Erie County Bar Association, Buffalo, New York, May 4, 1959.

Edwards, Bob, and Kenneth Dunne. *Study of a Master Spy*. London: Housmans, 1961.

Fajans, Irving. "Ravage Repeat Ravage," *Infantry Journal*, March 1947, pp. 24–33.

Farago, Ladislas. *Burn After Reading*. New York: Walker, 1961.

Ford, Corey. *Donovan of O.S.S.* Boston: Little, Brown, 1970.

———, and Alistair McBain. *Cloak and Dagger*. New York: Random House, 1945.

Frillmann, Paul, and Graham Peck. *China: The Remembered Life*. Boston: Houghton Mifflin, 1968.

Funk, Arthur. "American Contacts with the Resistance in France," *Military Affairs*, February 1970.

Gale, Esson. *Salt for the Dragon*. East Lansing: Michigan State College Press, 1953.

George, Willis. *Surreptitious Entry*. New York: Appleton-Century, 1946.

Gervasi, Frank. "What's Wrong with Our Spy System?" *Colliers*, November 6, 1948, pp. 13ff.

Goldberg, Arthur. "Top Secret," *The Nation*, March 23, 1946, pp. 348–50.

Goodfellow, Millard Preston. Papers and Correspondence. The Hoover Institution on War, Revolution, and Peace, Stanford University.

Grell, William. "A Marine with OSS," *Marine Corps Gazette*, December 1945, pp. 14–18.

Griffis, Stanton. *Lying in State*. New York: Doubleday, 1957.

Hall, Roger. *You're Stepping on My Cloak and Dagger*. New York: W. W. Norton, 1957.

Hayden, Joseph Ralston. Papers and Correspondence. University of Michigan Historical Collections.

Hayden, Sterling. *Wanderer*. New York: Knopf, 1963.

Hellman, Geoffrey. *How to Disappear for an Hour*. New York: Dodd, Mead, 1947.

———. "That Was the War," *New Yorker*, November 18, 1947, pp. 73–85.

Hoover, Calvin. *Memoirs of Capitalism, Communism, and Nazism*. Durham: Duke University Press, 1965.

Huot, Louis. *Guns for Tito*. New York: L. B. Fischer, 1945.

Icardi, Aldo. *American Master Spy*. New York: University Books, 1956.

Ind, Allison. *Allied Intelligence Bureau*. New York: D. McKay, 1958.

Kellis, James. "The Development of U.S. National Intelligence," unpublished Ph.D. dissertation, Georgetown University, Washington, D.C., 1963.

Kelly, Richard M. "Behind the Enemy Lines," *Blue Book*, January 1946, pp. 24ff.

———. "Bionda Mission," *Blue Book*, May 1947, pp. 56ff.

———. "Burma Mission," *Blue Book*, June 1947, pp. 74ff.

———. "Chance Island," *Blue Book*, March 1946, pp. 62ff.

———. "Guarding Patton's Flank," *Blue Book*, January 1947, pp. 62ff.

———. "The Halyard Mission," *Blue Book*, August 1946, pp. 52ff.

———. "He Never Stopped Trying," *Blue Book*, September 1946, pp. 42ff.

———. "Jedburgh Mission Hamish," *Blue Book*, July 1946, pp. 86ff.

———. "Mission to Bangkok," *Blue Book*, December 1946, pp. 88ff.

———. "Mission to Greece," *Blue Book*, November 1946, pp. 76ff.

———. "One Against a Thousand," *Blue Book*, February 1946, pp. 14ff.

———. "Operation Aztec," *Blue Book*, May 1946, pp. 66ff.

Kelly, Richard M. "Secret Agent in Brussels," *Blue Book*, September 1947.
————. "Secret Agent in Munich," *Blue Book*, October 1947.
————. "Spy Work Ahead," *Blue Book*, August 1947, pp. 90ff.
————. "Torture Preferred," *Blue Book*, June 1946.
————. "With the Greek Underground," *Blue Book*, July 1947, pp. 91ff.
Kent, Sherman. *Strategic Intelligence for American World Policy*. Princeton: Princeton University Press, 1951.
Kirkpatric, Lyman. *The Real CIA*. New York: Macmillan, 1968.
Klein, Alexander. *The Counterfeit Traitor*. New York: Holt, Rinehart, 1958.
Kobler, John. "He Runs a Private OSS," *Saturday Evening Post*, May 21, 1955, pp. 31ff.
Krock, Arthur. "OSS Gets It Coming and Going," *New York Times*, July 31, 1945.
Langer, William. *Our Vichy Gamble*. New York: W. W. Norton, 1947.
————. "Scholarship and the Intelligence Problem," *American Philosophical Society Proceedings*, 1948, pp. 43–5.
————, and S. Everett Gleason. *The Undeclared War*. New York: Harper Brothers, 1953.
Lasky, Victor. *Arthur J. Goldberg, The Old and the New*. New York: Arlington House, 1970.
Lewis, Flora. *Red Pawn, The Story of Noel Field*. New York: Doubleday, 1965.
Lewis, Wilmarth. *One Man's Education*. New York: Alfred A. Knopf, 1967.
Lovell, Stanley. *Of Spies and Stratagems*. New York: Prentice-Hall, 1963.
MacDonald, Alexander. *Bangkok Editor*. New York: Macmillan, 1949.
MacDonald, Elizabeth. *Undercover Girl*. New York: Macmillan, 1947.
Mansfield, Walter. "Ambush in China," *Marine Corps Gazette*, March 1946.
————. "Is There a Case for Mihailovic?" *American Mercury*, June 1946, pp. 713–21.
————. "Marine with the Chetniks," *Marine Corps Gazette*, January 1946, pp. 3–9; February 1946, pp. 15–20.
Martin, David. *Ally Betrayed*. New York: Prentice-Hall, 1946.
Mashbir, Sidney. *I Was an American Spy*. New York: Vantage, 1953.
Mecklin, J. M. "Of Our Sincere Gratitude," *New Republic*, July 29, 1946.
Miles, Milton. *A Different Kind of War*. New York: Doubleday, 1967.
————. Papers and Correspondence, The Hoover Institution on War, Revolution, and Peace, Stanford University.
Miller, Francis P. *Man from the Valley*. Chapel Hill: University of North Carolina, 1971.
————. Papers and Correspondence. General George C. Marshall Research Library, Lexington, Virginia.

Moore, Dan, and Martha Waller. *Cloak and Cipher*. New York: Bobbs-Merrill, 1962.

Morgan, Edward. "The Spy the Nazis Missed," *True*, July 1950.

Morgan, Dr. William. *The O.S.S. and I*. New York: Norton, 1957.

Mowrer, Edgar. *Triumph and Turmoil*. New York: Weybright, 1968.

Muggeridge, Malcolm. "Book Review of a Very Limited Edition," *Esquire*, May 1966.

Neumann, Robert. "Political Intelligence and Its Relation to Military Government," in Carl Friedrich, ed., *American Experiences in Military Government in World War II*. New York: Rinehart, 1948.

Obolensky, Serge. *One Man in His Time*. New York: McDowell-Obolensky, 1958.

Pash, Boris. *The Alsos Mission*. New York: Award House, 1969.

Pendar, Kenneth. *Adventure in Diplomacy*. New York: Dodd, Mead, 1945.

Peers, William, and Dean Brelis. *Behind the Burma Road*. Boston: Little, Brown, 1963.

Phillips, William. *Ventures in Diplomacy*. Boston: Beacon, 1953.

Poole, Dewitt. Papers and Correspondence. State Historical Society of Wisconsin, Madison.

Prunier, Henry. "City Man Helped to Train Guerrillas of Ho Chi Minh," Worcester *Evening Gazette*, May 14–15, 1968.

Reinhardt, Gunther. *Crime without Punishment*. New York: Hermitage House, 1952.

Ripley, S. Dillon. "Incident in Siam," *Yale Review*, Winter 1947, pp. 242–76.

Romualdi, Serafino. *Presidents and Peons*. New York: Funk and Wagnalls, 1967.

Rounds, Leland. Papers and Correspondence, the Hoover Institution on War, Revolution, and Peace, Stanford University.

Seitz, Albert. *Mihailovic: Hoax or Hero?* Columbus: Leigh House, 1953.

Shearer, Lloyd. "Master Spy," *Parade*, August 21, 1960, pp. 6–8.

Smith, Nicol, and Blake Clark. *Into Siam, Underground Kingdom*. Indianapolis: Bobbs-Merrill, 1946.

Snow, Edgar. "Secrets from Siam," *Saturday Evening Post*, January 12, 1946, pp. 13ff.

Stevens, Harley, "Prelude to Chinese Unity," *Pacific News Letter*, April 1946, p. 1.

Stratton, Roy. *SACO, the Rice Paddy Navy*. New York: C. S. Palmer, 1950.

Stuart, Gilbert. *Kind-hearted Tiger*. London: Deutsch, 1965.

Sweezy, Paul, ed. *Paul Baran, A Collective Portrait*. New York: Monthly Review Press, 1965.

Taylor, Edmond. *Awakening from History*. Boston: Gambit, 1969.

———. *Richer by Asia*. Boston: Houghton Mifflin, 1947.

Taylor, L. B. "OSS Mission," *Man's Magazine*, April 1965.

Thayer, Charles. *Hands across the Caviar*. New York: Lippincott, 1953.

Thompson, Craig. "What Has Stalin Done with Noel Field?" *Saturday Evening Post*, December 15, 1951, pp. 17ff.

Toledano, Ralph de. *Lament for a Generation*. New York: Farrar, Straus and Giroux, 1960.

———. "The Noel Field Story," *American Mercury*, April 1954.

Tolstoy, Ilia. "Across Tibet from India to China," *National Geographic*, August 1946, pp. 169–222.

Tompkins, Peter. *Italy Betrayed*. New York: Simon and Schuster, 1966.

———. *The Murder of Admiral Darlan*. New York: Simon and Schuster, 1965.

———. *A Spy in Rome*. New York: Avon, 1962.

Tully, Andrew. *CIA: The Inside Story*. Greenwich: Fawcett Publications, 1962.

Ulmer, Alfred, Jr. "The Gulliver Mission," *Blue Book*, April 1946, pp. 56ff.

U.S. House Committee on the Armed Services. "Testimony and Confessions Relating to the Disappearance of Major William Holohan." Washington, D.C.: Government Printing Office, 1953.

U.S. House Committee on Un-American Activities. "Hearings regarding Communist espionage in the United States Government." Washington, D.C.: Government Printing Office, 1948.

———. "The Erica Wallach Story." Washington, D.C.: Government Printing Office, 1958.

U.S. Office of Strategic Services, Psychological Assessment Staff. *Assessment of Men*. New York: Rinehart, 1948.

U.S. Senate Committee on the Judiciary. *The Amerasia Papers*. Washington, D.C.: Government Printing Office, 1971.

———. "Hearings on the Institute of Pacific Relations." Washington, D.C.: Government Printing Office, 1951–52.

———. "Interlocking Subversion in Government Departments." Washington, D.C.: Government Printing Office, 1953–55.

Utley, Freda. *The Odyssey of a Liberal*. Washington, D.C.: Washington National Press, 1970.

Wager, Walter. "Slippery Giant of the OSS," *Men*, July 1961, pp. 32ff.

———. "The Private War of Peter Ortiz," *See*, November 1960.

———. "They Called Him Widow Maker," *Male*, April 1958, pp. 22ff.

Warburg, James. *The Long Road Home*. New York: Doubleday, 1964.

Warren, William. *The Legendary American*. New York: Houghton Mifflin, 1970.

Welch, Robert, Jr. *The Life of John Birch*. Boston: Western Islands, 1965.

Weyl, Nathaniel. *The Battle against Disloyalty*. New York: Crowell, 1951.

White, William L. "Some Affairs of Honor," *Reader's Digest*, December 1945, pp. 136ff.

Whitehead, Don. *The F.B.I. Story*. New York: Random House, 1956.

Wise, David, and Thomas Ross. *The Espionage Establishment*. New York: 1967.

———. *The Invisible Government*. New York: Random House, 1964.

Zacharias, Ellis. *Secret Missions*. New York: Putnam's Sons, 1946.

II. SOURCE MATERIAL ON FOREIGN SECRET SERVICES AND UNDERGROUND MOVEMENTS

Accoce, Pierre, and Pierre Quet. *A Man Called Lucy*. New York: Coward-McCann, 1967.

Adamson, Iain. *The Forgotten Men*. London: G. Bell, 1965.

Amery, Julian. *Sons of the Eagle*. London: Macmillan, 1948.

Bauer, Yehuda. *Flight and Rescue: Brichah*. New York: Random House, 1970.

Beamish, John. *Burma Drop*. London: Elek Books, 1958.

Benouville, Guillain de. *The Unknown Warriors*. New York: Simon and Schuster, 1949.

Buckmaster, Maurice. *They Fought Alone*. New York: W. W. Norton, 1958.

Bulloch, John. *M.I.5*. London: A. Barker, 1963.

Butler, Ewan. *Amateur Agent*. New York: W. W. Norton, 1963.

Caply, Michel. *Guerrilla au Laos*. Paris: Presses de la Cité, 1966.

Case, Lynn. "The Maquis Republic of Vercors," *Infantry Journal*, April 1947, pp. 29ff.

Chakrabandhu, M. C. Karawik. "Force 136 and the Siamese Resistance Movement" in *Asiatic Review*, April 1947, pp. 168–70.

Chandruang, Kumut, and C. Prabhu. "Our Siamese Underground," *Asia and the Americas*, November 1945, pp. 530–32.

Chapman, F. Spencer. *The Jungle Is Neutral*. London: Chatto and Windus, 1949.

Colvin, Ian. *Chief of Intelligence*. London: Gollancz, 1951.

Cookridge, E. H. (pseud.) *Inside SOE*. London: A. Barker, 1966.

Cooper, Bert. *Case Studies in Insurgency and Revolutionary Warfare: Vietnam, 1941–54*. Washington, D.C.: Special Operations Research Office, 1964.

Cooper, Dick. *Adventures of a Secret Agent*. London: Muller, 1957.

Croce, Benedetto. *Croce, the King, and the Allies*. London: Allen and Unwin, 1950.

D'Astier de la Vigerie, Emmanuel. *Seven Times, Seven Days*. London: MacGibbon and Kee, 1958.

Davidson, Basil. *Partisan Picture*. London: Bedford Books, 1946.

Davies, "Trotsky." *Illyrian Venture*. London: Bodley Head, 1952.

Deacon, Richard. *History of the British Secret Service*. London: Muller, 1969.

Dedijer, Vladimir. *With Tito*. London: A. Hamilton, 1951.

Delmer, Sefton. *Black Boomerang*. London: Secker and Warburg, 1962.

Delzell, C. L. *Mussolini's Enemies*. Princeton: Princeton University Press, 1961.

Dewavrin, André. *Souvenirs*. 3 vols. Monte Carlo: R. Solar, 1947–51.

Dobbins, Charles. "China's Mystery Man," *Colliers*, February 1, 1946.

Dollmann, Eugen. *Call Me Coward*. London: Kimber, 1956.

Edinger, Lewis. *German Exile Politics*. Berkeley: University of California Press, 1956.

Ehrlich, Blake. *The Resistance: France, 1940–45*. Boston: Little, Brown, 1965.

Farran, Roy. *Operation Tombola*. London: Collins, 1960.

————. *Winged Dagger*. London: Collins, 1948.

Fielding, Xan. *Hide and Seek*. London: Secker and Warburg, 1954.

Foot, Michael. *SOE in France*. London: Her Majesty's Stationery Office, 1966.

Foote, Alexander. *Handbook for Spies*. New York: Doubleday, 1949.

Ford, Franklin. "The 20th of July in the History of the German Resistance," *American Historical Review*, July 1946, pp. 609–26.

Fry, Varian. *Surrender on Demand*. New York: Random House, 1945.

Gaevernitz, Gero V. S. *They Almost Killed Hitler*. New York: Macmillan, 1947.

Gallegos, Adrian. *From Capri into Oblivion*. London: Hodder and Stoughton, 1959.

Gallin, Mother Mary Alice. *Ethical and Religious Factors in the German Resistance to Hitler*. Washington, D.C.: Catholic University of America, 1955.

Garder, Michel. *La Guerre Secrète des Services Spéciaux Français*. Paris: Plon, 1967.

Garlinski, Josef. *Poland, SOE, and the Allies*. London: Allen and Unwin, 1969.

Gilchrist, Andrew. *Bangkok Top Secret*. London: Hutchinson, 1970.

Gisevius, Hans B. *To the Bitter End*. Boston: Riverside Press, 1947.

Hagen, Louis. *The Secret War for Europe*. New York: Stein and Day, 1969.

Hassel, Ulrich von. *The Von Hassell Diaries*. New York: Doubleday, 1947.

Hoegner, Wilhelm. *Der Schwierige Aussenseiter*. Munich: Isar Verlag, 1959.

Hoettl, Wilhelm. *The Secret Front*. New York: Praeger, 1954.

Holland, Carolsue. *Foreign Contacts Made by the German Opposition to Hitler*. Unpublished Ph.D. dissertation, University of Pennsylvania, 1967.

Hyde, H. Montgomery. *Room 3603*. New York: Farrar, Straus, 1962.

International Conference on the History of the Resistance. *European Resistance Movements, 1939–1945*. London: Pergammon, 1964.

Jeantet, Gabriel. *Pétain contre Hitler*. Paris: Le Table Ronde, 1966.

Jones, William. *Twelve Months with Tito's Partisans*. London: Bedford Books, 1946.

Jordan, William. *Conquest without Victory*. London: Hodder and Stoughton, 1969.

Kemp, Peter. *Alms for Oblivion*. London: Cassell, 1961.

————. *No Colours or Crest*. London: Cassell, 1958.

Kersten, Felix. *The Kersten Memoirs*. New York: Macmillan, 1957.

Kimche, Jon. *Spying for Peace*. London: Weidenfeld and Nicholson, 1961.

Leverkuehn, Paul. *German Military Intelligence*. New York: Praeger, 1954.

L'Herminier, J. *Casabianca*. London: Muller, 1953.

Lockhart, R. H. Bruce. *Comes the Reckoning*. London: Putnam, 1947.

Lussu, Joyce. *Freedom Has No Frontier*. London: M. Joseph, 1969.

McLachlan, Donald. *Room 39*. London: Weidenfeld and Nicolson, 1968.

MacLean, Fitzroy. *Escape to Adventure*. Boston: Little, Brown, 1951.

Manvell, Roger, and Heinrich Fraenkel. *The Canaris Conspiracy*. New York: McKay, 1969.

Marshall, Bruce. *The White Rabbit*. London: Evans, 1954.

Maugeri, Franco. *From the Ashes of Disgrace*. New York: Reynal and Hitchcock, 1948.

Munthe, Malcolm. *Sweet Is War*. London: Duckworth, 1954.

Myers, E. C. W. *Greek Entanglement*. London: R. Hart-Davis, 1955.

Nogueres, Henri. *Histoire de la Résistance en France*. Paris: R. Laffont, 1969.

Page, Bruce, et al. *The Philby Conspiracy*. New York: Doubleday, 1969.

Paloczi-Horvath, George. *The Undefeated*. Boston: Little, Brown, 1959.

Perrault, Giles. *The Red Orchestra*. New York: Simon and Schuster, 1969.

Philby, Kim, *My Silent War*. New York: Grove Press, 1968.

Pinto, Oreste. *Friend or Foe?* New York: Putnam, 1953.

Renault-Roulier, Gilbert. *Mémoires d'un Agent Secret de la France Libre*. Paris: Editions France Empire, 1961.

Rootham, Jasper. *Miss-Fire*. London: Chatto and Windus, 1946.

Rothfels, Hans. *The German Opposition to Hitler*. New York: H. Regnery, 1948.

Sabattier, G. *Le Destin de l'Indochine*. Paris: Libraire Plon, 1952.

Sainteny, Jean. *Histoire d'une Paix Manquée*. Paris: Amiot Dumont, 1953.

Salvadori, Massimo. *The Labour and the Wounds*. London: Pall Mall Press, 1958.

Samrej, Nai. "That Thailand May Be Free," *Asia and the Americas*, February 1945, pp. 94–95.

Sarafis, Stefanos. *Greek Resistance Army*. London: Birch Books, 1951.

Schellenberg, Walter. *The Labyrinth*. New York: Harper, 1956.

Schlabrendorff, Fabian von. *The Secret War against Hitler*. New York: Pitman, 1965.

Soustelle, Jacques. *Envers et contre Tout*. Paris: R. Laffont, 1950.

Stead, Philip. *Le Deuxième Bureau*. Paris: Fayard, 1966.

Sweet-Escott, Bickham. *Baker Street Irregular*. London: Methuen, 1965.

Sykes, Christopher. *Troubled Loyalty*. London: Collins, 1968.

Tilman, H. W. *When Men and Mountains Meet*. Cambridge: Cambridge University Press, 1946.

Walker, C. Lester. "China's Master Spy," *Colliers*, February 1, 1946.

White, Dorothy Shipley. *Seeds of Discord*. Syracuse: Syracuse University Press, 1964.

Whitwell, John (pseud.). *British Agent*. London: Wm. Kimber, 1966.

Winterbotham, F. W. *Secret and Personal*. London: W. Kimber, 1969.

Wiskemann, Elizabeth. *The Europe I Saw*. London: Collins, 1968.

Woodhouse, C. M. *Apple of Discord*. London: Hutchinson, 1951.

III. SOURCE MATERIAL ON MILITARY AND POLITICAL BACKGROUND

Adleman, Robert, and George Walton. *Rome Fell Today*. Boston: Little, Brown, 1968.

Armstrong, Hamilton Fish. *Tito and Goliath*. New York: Macmillan, 1951.

Arnold, H. H. *Global Mission*. New York: Harper, 1949.

Aron, Robert. *France Reborn*. New York: Charles Scribner's Sons, 1964.

———. *De Gaulle before Paris*. London: Putnam, 1962.

———. *De Gaulle Triumphant*. London: Putnam, 1964.

Butcher, Harry. *My Three Years with Eisenhower*. New York: Simon and Schuster, 1946.

Butow, Robert, *Japan's Decision to Surrender*. Stanford: Stanford University Press, 1954.

Buttinger, Joseph. *Vietnam: A Dragon Embattled*. New York: Praeger, 1967.

Carroll, Wallace. *Persuade or Perish*. Boston: Houghton Mifflin, 1948.

Chennault, Claire. *Way of a Fighter*. New York: Putnam's Sons, 1949.

Churchill, Winston. *The Second World War*. New York: Houghton Mifflin. 5 vols., 1948–53.

Clark, Mark. *Calculated Risk*. New York: Harper, 1950.

Clissold, Stephen. *Whirlwind*. New York: Philosophical Library, 1949.

Collins, Larry, and Dominique Lapierre. *Is Paris Burning?* New York: Simon and Schuster, 1965.

Crosby, Josiah, "Observations on a Post-War Settlement in Southeast Asia," *International Affairs*, July 1944, pp. 357–68.

Crozier, Brian. *Franco*. Boston: Little, Brown, 1967.

Deakin, F. W. *The Last Days of Mussolini*. New York: Pelican, 1962.

De Gaulle, Charles. *War Memoirs*. 3 vols. New York: Simon and Schuster, 1955–60.

Dessinges, René. "La Rivalité anglo-américaine au Siam," *Le Monde*, April 16, 1947.

Devillers, Philippe. *Histoire du Vietnam*. Paris: Editions du Sueil, 1952.

Du Berrier, Hilaire. *Tragedy of a Betrayal*. Boston: Western Islands, 1965.

Eisenhower, Dwight D. *Crusade in Europe*. New York: Doubleday, 1948.

Eldridge, Fred. *Wrath in Burma*. New York: Doubleday, 1946.

Fall, Bernard. *The Two Vietnams*. New York: Praeger, 1964.

Feis, Herbert. *Churchill, Roosevelt, and Stalin*. Princeton: Princeton University Press, 1957.

———. *The China Tangle*. Princeton: Princeton University Press, 1953.

Fotic, Constantin. *The War We Lost*. New York: Viking, 1948.

Funk, Arthur. *Charles de Gaulle, The Crucial Years*. Norman: University of Oklahoma Press, 1959.

Gould, Randall. *China in the Sun*. New York: Doubleday, 1946.

Hammer, Ellen. *The Struggle for Indochina*. Stanford: Stanford University Press, 1959.

Hayes, Carlton. *Wartime Mission in Spain*. New York: Macmillan, 1945.

Heckscher, August. *A Pattern of Politics*. New York: Reynal, 1947.

Hoare, Samuel. *Complacent Dictator*. New York: Alfred A. Knopf, 1947.

Hughes, H. Stuart. *The United States and Italy*. Cambridge: Harvard University Press, 1953.

Hull, Cordell. *Memoirs*. New York: Macmillan, 1948.

Ingersoll, Ralph. *Top Secret*. New York: Harcourt, Brace, 1946.

Israel, Fred, ed. *The War Diary of Breckinridge Long*. Lincoln: University of Nebraska Press, 1966.

Kallay, Miklos. *Hungarian Premier*. New York: Columbia University Press, 1954.

Kennan, George. *Memoirs, 1925–50*. Boston: Little, Brown, 1967.

Kogan, Norman. *Italy and the Allies*. Cambridge: Harvard University Press, 1956.

Kolko, Gabriel. *The Politics of War*. New York: Random House, 1968.

Lancaster, Donald. *The Emancipation of French Indochina*. London: Oxford University Press, 1961.

Landon, Kenneth. *Siam in Transition*. Chicago: University of Chicago Press, 1939.

Leahy, William. *I Was There*. New York: McGraw-Hill, 1950.

LeMay, Curtis. *Mission with LeMay*. New York: Doubleday, 1965.

Lindbergh, Charles. *Wartime Journals*. New York: Harcourt, Brace, Jovano-
vich, 1970.

Lockwood, William. "The GI in Wartime China," *Far Eastern Survey*,
January 15, 1947, pp. 9–11.

Lohbeck, Don. *Patrick H. Hurley*. Chicago: H. Regnery, 1956.

Macmillan, Harold. *The Blast of War*. London: Macmillan, 1947.

MacVane, John. *Journey into War*. New York: Appleton-Century, 1943.

Moorad, George. *Lost Peace in China*. New York: Dutton, 1949.

Morris, Joe Alex. *Nelson Rockefeller*. New York: Harper and Row, 1960.

Mountbatten, Lord Louis. *Report to the Combined Chiefs of Staff from
the Supreme Commander, Southeast Asia*. New York: Philosophical
Library, 1951.

Mullender, Philippe. "L'évolution récente de la Thailande," *Politique
Etrangère*, April-May 1950, pp. 213–33.

Murphy, Robert. *Diplomat among Warriors*. New York: Doubleday, 1964.

Neumann, Franz, "The Social Sciences," in *The Cultural Migration, The
European Scholar in America*. Philadelphia: University of Pennsylvania
Press, 1953.

Oliver, Robert. *Syngman Rhee*. New York: Dodd, Mead, 1954.

Patton, George. *War as I Knew It*. Boston: Houghton Mifflin, 1947.

Peck, Graham. *Two Kinds of Time*. Boston: Houghton Mifflin, 1950.

Peterson, Alec. "Britain and Siam," *Pacific Affairs*, December 1946, pp.
364–72.

Pierre-Gosset, René. *Conspiracy in Algiers*. New York: The Nation, 1945.

Price, G. Ward. *Giraud and the North African Scene*. New York: Macmillan, 1944.

Robinson, Geroid. "Three Invaders of Russia," *New Republic*, July 21,
1941.

Romanus, Charles, and Riley Sunderland. *United States Army in World
War II: China-Burma-India Theater*. Washington, D.C.: 1959.

Roosevelt, Elliott. *As He Saw It*. New York: Duell, Sloan and Pearce, 1946.

Root, Waverly. *Secret History of the War*. New York: Charles Scribner's
Sons, 1945.

Roussy de Sales, Raoul. *The Making of Yesterday*. New York: Reynal and
Hitchcock, 1947.

Ryan, Cornelius. *The Last Battle*. New York: Simon and Schuster, 1966.

Service, John. *The Amerasia Papers: Some Problems in the History of U.S.-
China Relations*. Berkeley: Center for Chinese Studies, 1971.

Shaplen, Robert. *The Lost Revolution*. New York: Harper and Row, 1965.

Sheean, Vincent. *This House against This House*. New York: Random
House, 1946.

Sheldon, George. "The Status of the Viet Nam," *Far Eastern Survey*, December 18, 1946.

————. "The Case for Viet Nam," *Commonweal*, January 31, 1947, pp. 393–95.

Sherwood, Robert. *Roosevelt and Hopkins*. New York: Harper, 1950.

Stilwell, Joseph. *The Stilwell Papers*. New York: W. Sloane, 1948.

Stimson, Henry, and McGeorge Bundy. *On Active Service in War and Peace*. New York: Harper, 1948.

Stein, Gunther. *The Challenge of Red China*. New York: McGraw-Hill, 1945.

Sulzberger, C. L. *A Long Row of Candles*. New York: Macmillan, 1969.

Thompson, Virginia. *Thailand, the New Siam*. New York: Macmillan, 1941.

Toland, John. *The Last 100 Days*. New York: Random House, 1966.

Truman, Harry S. *Memoirs*. New York: Doubleday, 1956.

Tuchman, Barbara. *Stilwell and the American Experiences in China, 1911–1945*. New York: Macmillan, 1971.

Wedemeyer, Albert. *Wedemeyer Reports!* New York: H. Holt, 1958.

Wheeler-Bennett, John. *Nemesis of Power*. London: Macmillan, 1964.

White, Theodore, and Annalee Jacoby. *Thunder out of China*. New York: W. Sloane, 1946.

Wilmot, Chester. *The Struggle for Europe*. New York: Harper, 1952.

Wilson, Hugh. *Diplomat between Wars*. New York: Longmans, Green, 1941.

Wilson, Jr., Hugh. *Disarmament and Cold War in the Thirties*. New York: Vantage, 1963.

Wilson of Libya, Lord. *Eight Years Overseas*. London: Hutchinson, 1948.

Wolff, Robert. "Mihailovic: A Post Mortem," *Atlantic*, December 26, 1946, pp. 43–49.

Zink, Harold. *The United States in Germany*. Princeton: Van Nostrand, 1957.

IV. PERSONAL INTERVIEWS

(* signifies telephone conversation)

Alsop, Stewart
Barnes, C. Tracy
Barrett, Col. David
Berding, Andrew
Bernique, Roger
Blatnik, John
Bluechel, Herbert
Bocquet, Fournier
Boggs, William
Bonney, Therese
Braden, Thomas

Brennan, Earl
Bross, John
Bunche, Dr. Ralph
* Canfield, Franklin
Colling, John
Conein, Lucien
Constance, Dr. Lincoln
* Coon, Dr. Carleton
Davis, Thomas, Jr.
Dedijer, Dr. Stephen
Diebold, Dr. William

Doering, Otto, Jr.
Downs, Kenneth
Ekstrom, Arnold
Evans, Dr. Allan
Gaevernitz, Gero V. S.
Gisevius, Hans Bernd
Goldberg, Arthur
Goodfellow, M. Preston
Hamilton, Dr. James
Haskell, John
Haskell, Joseph
Haugland, Col. Knut
Hilsman, Dr. Roger
Hiss, Alger
Horton, Philip
Houston, Lawrence
Howe, Fisher
Hughes, Dr. H. Stuart
Kellis, Dr. James
* Kingman, Dong
Kirkpatrick, Dr. Evron
Knapp, Dr. Robert
Lambert, Robert
Langer, Dr. William
MacLeish, Dr. Archibald
McBaine, Turner

MacKinnon, Dr. Donald
Maddox, Dr. William
Morgan, Henry
Murphy, Hon. Robert
* Obolensky, Serge
Patti, Archimedes L. A.
* Petris, Nicholas
Pickus, Robert
Roper, Elmo
Sadoun, Roland
Sainteny, Jean
Schlesinger, Dr. Arthur, Jr.
* Schoonmaker, Frank
* Schorske, Dr. Carl
Service, John
Smith, Nicol
Stevens, Mrs. Harley
Surrey, Walter
Swift, Carlton, Jr.
Thomson, John
Tompkins, Peter
Wainwright, Stuyvesant II.
* Wand, Ralph
Wickes, Dr. George
Yarrow, Bernard

V. CORRESPONDENCE RECEIVED

Allinsmith, H. B.
Allman, Norwood
Alsop, John
Ashley, Ira
Bailey, Dr. Stephen
Barth, Alfred
Berding, Andrew
Bernstein, Nahum
Bross, John
Browne, Gordon
Burkhardt, Dr. Frederick
Caldwell, Dr. Oliver
Casey, William
Cater, Douglass
Child, Paul

Cline, Dr. Ray
Conein, Mrs. Lucien
Corvo, Max
Crockett, David
Crowe, Hon. Philip
Davis, William P.
Deak, Nicholas
de Neufville, Lawrence
De Rochemont, Richard
Dewey, Charles, Jr.
Downes, Donald
Drymalski, Raymond
Duff, William
Fenn, Dr. William
Forgan, J. Russell

Fragos, Chris
Frances, Leo
Frances, Philip
Freidberg, Sidney
Gengerelli, Dr. Joseph
Gigliotti, Dr. Frank
Halperin, Dr. Maurice
Halsey, Van
Haskell, John
Hays, Donald
Heckscher, August
Hellman, Geoffrey
Herman, Dr. Stewart
Hoover, Dr. Calvin
Hopper, Dr. Bruce
Houston, Lawrence
Katz, Dr. Milton
Kellermann, Dr. Henry
Kempner, Dr. Robert
Knox, Dr. Bernard
Landon, Dr. Kenneth
LeBarre, Dr. Weston
Legendre, Gertrude
Lindsay, Franklin
Little, Herbert
Lockwood, Dr. William
Lorbeer, Arnold
Lowman, Lawrence
McCulloch, John I. B.
MacDonald, Alexander
Macomber, William
Maddox, Dr. William
Mellon, Paul
Miller, Col. Francis
Moss, George, Jr.
North, Henry Ringling
Ostheimer, Fred

Palmer, Theodore
Place, Russell
Pretzat, Walter
Prunier, Henry
Ripley, Dr. S. Dillon
Rogers, James G.
Roseborough, W. Arthur
Saint Phalle, Thibaut de
Salvadori, Dr. Massimo
Scamporino, Vincent
Schlesinger, Dr. Arthur, Jr.
Scribner, Joseph
Scrivener, Samuel
Seiferheld, David
Shaplen, Robert
Smith, Dr. James
Solborg, Robert
Streeter, Thomas
Strunk, Norman
Szabad, George
Taylor, Edmond
Thomas, Allison
Van Arkel, Gerhard
van der Stricht, Paul
Vanoncini, Lesley
Vournas, George
Wainright, Stuyvesant II.
Wand, Ralph
White, Frank, Jr.
Will, Hon. Hubert
Wilson, Junius, Jr.
Winton, David
Wolff, Milton
Yarrow, Bernard
Younger, Hon. Evelle
Zuckerman, Dr. John

Index

Tai Li, General (*continued*)
284, 289, 297–301, 303, 306, 321, 323

Tangier, 41–42, 47, 49–50, 52, 56–57, 75

Tarchiani, Alberto, 92, 92n

Tatra mountains (Czechoslovakia), 107

Taylor, Edmond, 57, 57n, 58, 62–67, 70–71, 73, 86, 90, 288–89, 291, 303, 310, 315, 337, 346, 361

Teheran Conference, 139–40, 142–43, 151, 258, 327

Temple, Shirley, 367

Teper, Lazare, 225

Thailand, 15, 22, 25, 34, 243, 254, 277, 290–318, 346

Thai resistance, 305–14

Thakhek (Laos), 318

Thayer, Charles, 152, 152n, 153–58, 160–61

Thayer, Robert, 376

Thomas, Allison, 331–35, 349–50

Thomas, H. Gregory, 79, 79n

Thomas, Norman, 379

Thompson, James, 312, 313n

Thompson, Robert, 145

Tibbets, Margaret, 265n

Tibet, 25, 254–56, 263

Tientsin (China), 262

Tikander, Wilho, 199, 201

Tilakh, Dengh, 300

Time, 27, 52, 104

Tito, 6, 7, 16, 29, 32, 131–35, 135n, 136–40, 142–44, 144n, 145–48, 150–58, 160–61

Tofte, Hans, 145, 145n, 399n

Togliatti, Palmiro, 99, 100

Toledano, Ralph de, 18, 18n, 19

Tolstoy, Ilia, 16, 254, 254n, 255–56

Tompkins, Peter, 86–88, 90–91, 93–97, 100–3, 110–11, 241

Tong, Father Jean, 303

Tonkin. *See* Vietnam

TORCH, 51–66, 70–74, 78, 83, 85, 136, 153, 169, 171, 177, 180

Toscanini, Arturo, 113

Toulmin, John, 124–26, 128

Toynbee, Arnold, 382

Trans-Africa Co., 72

Transjordan, 125

Transylvania, 396n

Treviranus, Gottfried, 208–9

TRIDENT Conference, 171

Trieste (Italy), 160–61, 232

Trohan, Walter, 363

Trott zu Solz, Adam von, 213, 218, 221, 405n

Trowbridge, Alexander, 376

Truman, Harry, 10, 37n, 232, 277, 336, 364

Tularak, Sanguan, 300, 300n, 306, 309

Tunisia (French), 38–39, 42, 60–61, 64, 75, 87

Turin (Italy), 117

Turkey, 125–26, 374. *See also* Istanbul

Turkish Security Service, 126, 397n

Twelfth Army Group (U.S.), 226

Twentieth Bomber Group (U.S.), 275

Twentieth Century Fund, 71n

Tyrol, Austrian, 233

U-2 flights, 239n

Ulbricht, Walter, 217, 236, 238

Ulmer, Jr., Alfred, 224, 224n, 364

Unconditional Surrender doctrine, 214, 217, 220, 232–33

Union Theological Seminary, 368

Unitarian Service Committee, 212

United Auto Workers, 104n

United China Relief, 266

United Fruit Company, 15, 123

United Nations Conference, San Francisco, 328, 373

United Press, 103, 241, 244, 358

United States Army Intelligence, 12, 38n, 41, 47, 51, 69, 172, 193, 246n, 262, 364, 366

United States Information Agency, 18n, 235n, 247n, 261n, 257n

United States Steel Co., 5, 157

United World Federalists, 373–74

University of California, 277n, 331, 341, 378

University of Geneva, 213

University of Michigan, 150, 246, 261, 263

University of Paris, 292

University of Pennsylvania, 127n, 189

University of Pittsburgh, 109, 148

University of Toronto, 341

University of Wisconsin, 108

Uruguay, 106

Ustashi (Yugoslav fascist militia), 133

Utley, Freda, 266–67